D0926703

The Pictorial Encyclopedia of
The Evolution of Man

The Pictorial Encyclopedia of

The Evolution of Man

J. Jelínek

Hamlyn

London · New York · Sydney · Toronto

The chapter entitled 'The origin and evolution of Man'
was written with the assistance of Z. Mazáková

Translated by Helga Hanks
Designed and produced by Artia for
The Hamlyn Publishing Group Limited
Astronaut House, Feltham, Middlesex, England

© Copyright 1975 Artia, Prague
Translation © Copyright 1975
The Hamlyn Publishing Group Limited

All Rights Reserved. No part of this publication
may be reproduced or transmitted in any form or
by any means, electronic or mechanical, including
photocopy, recording, or any information storage
and retrieval system, without permission in writing
from the copyright owner.

ISBN 0 600 37030 5
Printed in Czechoslovakia by Svoboda, Prague
3/05/06/51

CONTENTS

6 List of colour plates
7 Preface
7 Time and dating in the evolutionary process of man
10 The process of man's development
12 The cultural development of man

Part I
15 The origin and evolution of man
17 The development of man — a slow and complicated process
17 The position of man and his ancestors within the zoological system
21 The development of the apes
40 The development of man and his immediate ancestors

Part II
119 Stone tools — their manufacture and use
130 Stone tools — manufacture and Palaeolithic cultures
164 The techniques of flaking
185 The working of bone

Part III
211 Dwellings and settlements of Stone Age Man
213 Discoveries of settlements in western Europe
227 Settlements of central Europe
236 Discoveries from the Ukraine and south Siberia

Part IV
275 Art of the Stone Age
287 Palaeolithic art — paintings and engravings
289 Technique and perspective
301 How movement is expressed
317 Abstraction and stylization
320 The technique of Palaeolithic art
339 Themes in Palaeolithic art
339 Animals
351 Fantastic animals and half-men
370 Human figures
401 Jewellery
413 Signs and symbols
441 Hands
457 Dating
475 Art at the end of the Old Stone Age
475 Eurasian art
487 North African art
493 South African art
500 Australian art
529 Conclusion
531 Glossary
538 Bibliography
546 Picture acknowledgements
548 Index

LIST OF COLOUR PLATES

41 *Proconsul major*
42 A cast of *Proconsul africanus*
43 *Paranthropus*
44 *Australopithecus*
69 *Homo erectus modjokertensis*
70 *Homo erectus erectus*
87 Neanderthal-man
88 Neanderthals from Krapina
97 Imprint of Neanderthal-man's foot
97 Cast from the imprint of Neanderthal-man's foot
98 Neanderthal lower jaw
98 Magdalenian harpoon
99 Woman's skull from a Pavlovian burial
99 Lower jaw from a Pavlovian cemetery
100 Three large stone tools
100 Hand-axes of the Abbevillian culture
133 Hand-axes of the Acheulean culture
134 Two crude hand-axes from Sbaika, Algeria
134 Stone points in the shape of small hand-axes
135 Mousterian tools
136 Crystal tools belonging to Magdalenian reindeer hunters
153 Pavlovian stone tools
154 Pavlovian stone tools
155 Stone tools from the Iberomaurusian culture
155 Two cores and one unfinished tool from the Ibero-maurusian culture
156 Microlithic tools
156 Tools from Elora, India
197 Mammoth molars
197 Circular disc made from soft slate from the Pavlovian
198 Primitive bone tools
215 Reconstruction of a tent from Malta, USSR
216 A prehistoric painter completes a painting of a bull
257 Bison from the Magdalenian
257 Bison and ibex from the Magdalenian
258 Three hinds painted in dotted outlines
259 Bone carving of a stylized mammoth
259 Small mammoth modelled in clay
260 Small mammoth modelled in clay
285 Ivory carving of a mammoth

286 Spoon-shaped implement made from a horse's jawbone
303 Small horse's head modelled in clay
303 Head of a cat-like animal in fired clay
304 Bear modelled in clay
313 Animal carved in mammoth ivory
314 A *baton* from the Magdalenian culture
314 Small head of a rhinoceros in fired clay
315 Female figurines
316 Figurine of an obese woman
333 Venus figurine
333 Female figurine
334 Two figurines carved from mammoth ivory
334 Female figurine
335 Head broken off from a human figurine
336 Stylized figurine of a pregnant woman
361 A face carved from mammoth ivory
362 Lower part of a female body
379 The Venus of Dolní Věstonice
380 Stylized female figurine used as a pendant
405 Fragment of a clasp
406 Stylized female figurine
407 Pendant made from mammoth ivory
408 Pendant made from mammoth ivory
425 Swan carved in mammoth ivory
426 Necklace made from fossil snail shell and teeth
427 Necklace made from teeth of arctic foxes
428 Necklace made from teeth and perforated pebbles
461 Necklace
462 Implement with geometric designs
463 Large decorated spoon
464 Pendant made from mammoth ivory
481 Geometric stylized female figurine
482 Prehistoric rock painting of a fabulous animal
483 Sefar, site of the Tassili cave paintings
484 Rock painting of cattle
501 Rock painting of a female figure
502 Human and animal painted figures
503 Cult object. Bark painting from central Arnhem Land
504 Bark painting of a fish

Preface

The development of man and his ancestors was part of a long and complicated process, and many different branches of science were involved in the research. The experts have to rely on discoveries of bones which have often been bedded in rock, river terraces, or loess for millions of years. The arduous work on the sites is often guided by accidental discoveries. Special methods to excavate and prepare discoveries had to be developed. Recent years have brought a number of interesting discoveries, which have often had far-reaching consequences. Many opinions had to be revised, others were substantiated. Numerous discoveries have not yet been evaluated or the results published. At times considerable differences of opinion about interpretations arise. Therefore, there are probably a number of surprises still to come.

Time and dating in the evolutionary process of man

Any line of development takes time. Determining the age of every single discovery and the chronological order is imperative for further investigation and determination of the line of evolution of living creatures. The remains of bones usually rest in the earth and their geological age can be determined from the deposits in which they were found. Here anthropology is dependent on co-operation from geologists and palaeontologists. Remains of other prehistoric animals and plants are also found. The age of the primate discoveries may be worked out from the age of the associated fauna and flora determined by palaeontologists. It is also possible to reconstruct the environment of the primates to a certain extent, if the geological level and the accompanying fauna are known.

Rocks of the Tertiary period began to be laid down about 65 million years ago. The Tertiary is divided into the Lower Tertiary or Palaeogene period and the Upper Tertiary or Neogene period. The Palaeogene period which continued for about 38 million years included three epochs: the Palaeocene, the Eocene, and the Oligocene; the Neogene is divided into the Miocene and the Pliocene. The Quaternary system is the shortest period in Earth's history and has only lasted for about three million years; some experts claim two million years. This system is sometimes taken together with the Tertiary and known as the Cenozoic era or recent time. The Quaternary is often called the Anthropozoic, or time of man, and is divided into the Pleistocene and Holocene.

The Pleistocene can be divided into three parts: the Lower, the Middle, and Upper Pleistocene. During the Quaternary cool phases, the Ice Ages (Glacials), and warmer or interglacial phases alternated. The four Ice Ages in Europe were named after the Alpine rivers Günz, Mindel, Riss, and Würm. The Pleistocene begins with the Villafranchian, a period which stretched from the beginning of the Quaternary to the Günz Glacial phase. The warmer, interglacial Günz-Mindel phase followed and was in turn superseded by the Mindel Glacial and the Mindel-Riss interglacial phase. The third Ice Age was the Riss Glaciation, the last interglacial phase the Riss-Würm. The fourth and last period was the Würm Glaciation. The European terminology of classification is relevant for the geographic areas of the northern hemisphere. Certain deviations, which are detected in some areas, are reflected in the terminology, but are on the whole identical. In recent years the terminology has been simplified to the first, second, third, and fourth Glacial phases, and the first, second and third interglacial phases. These temperature changes did, of course, influence the development of life, including man, on this planet.

New dating methods have become available during the last decades which make it possible to determine the absolute age of organic matter. The radio-carbon, or C 14 method, relies on the estimation of the remaining radioactive carbon (C 14) which is present, at a constant level, in all living organisms. Radioactive carbon stops accumulating at the death of the organism, and radioactive decay begins. Half of the isotope of C 14 has decayed after 5730 years — this is known as the half-life — and only one quarter is left after 11 460 years. Decay continues steadily, and this method can be used to date an object up to 45 000 years old. Older discoveries are dated by the potassium/argon method (K/Ar) because K 40 has a much longer half-life.

It has been possible to determine the durations of geological periods to a certain extent with these methods, and to determine other more exact dates.

A chronological outline of the Tertiary and Quaternary is illustrated here. The numbers refer to the ages of the bases of the periods in thousands of years.

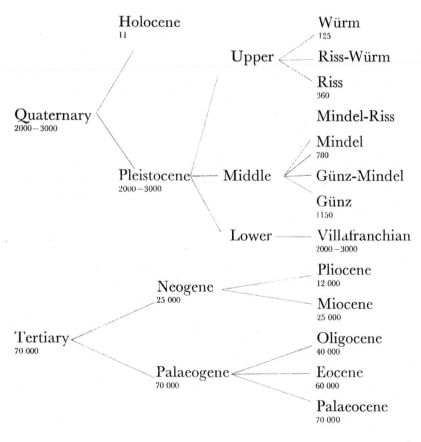

Archaeologists arrived at a different classification of the Quaternary formation based on the cultural development of man. The first stage is the Lower Stone Age (Palaeolithic), the second stage is the Middle Stone Age (Mesolithic), and the third and most recent stage is the Upper Stone Age (Neolithic). By geological standards these periods of time are quite short in duration, and include modern man and his culture, which do not concern us here. If we compare the archaeological chronology with the geological one, it appears that the Palaeolithic corresponds with the Pleistocene, and the Mesolithic and Neolithic to the Holocene.

The process of man's development

The roots of man's development stretch millions of years into pre-history to the Mesozoic era. Then the first primate developed from the most primitive forms of mammals. The most highly organized mammals including man fall into this category. Primates are divided into the Prosimians and the Anthropoids.

The sub-order *Anthropoidea*, which developed from the Prosimians, was in turn divided into three super-families: New World monkeys *(Ceboidea)*, the Old World monkeys *(Cercopithecoidea)*, and the apes and man *(Hominoidea)*. The super-family *Hominoidea* holds the most interest for us because its development leads to man.

This super-family is divided into four groups: the *Pliopithecidae* and *Oreopithecidae* which are now extinct; the *Pongidae* and *Hominidae* including a number of extinct and recent apes, the ancestors of man, and also man himself. The following scheme is developed from above:

Primates

Sub-order: *Prosimii*
Sub-order: *Anthropoidea*
      Super-family: *Ceboidea*
      Super-family: *Cercopithecoidea*
      Super-family: *Hominoidea*
            Family: *Pliopithecidae*
            Family: *Oreopithecidae*
            Family: *Pongidae*
            Family: *Hominidae*

We are mainly concerned here with the family *Hominidae*, which includes modern man, *Homo sapiens sapiens*. The development of this family can only be fully understood, however, if the connections with other groups are understood. Therefore, it is necessary to consider the whole development of the super-family *Hominoidea*.

From the various discoveries which have been made, the palaeoanthropologists distinguish between five stages of development within the family of the *Hominidae*.

The oldest forms, which probably include our first true ancestors, belong to the genus *Ramapithecus*. They come from India, Kenya, and possibly also China and Greece; modern radiometric dating techniques indicate that their age is between 12 and 14 million years.

The genus *Australopithecus* marks another stage in the development of man; it is known so far from several sites in Africa. Quite a lot of material has been found so that we know considerably more about this genus. It was probably more intelligent than other animals but less so than modern man, and it may have used and made primitive tools. *Australopithecus* lived about one to four million years ago.

The earliest *Homo* who lived 2—3 million years ago marks the next stage. He walked fully erect and made the first true tools. His relationship to *Australopithecus* has not been cleared up yet.

The fourth stage in the development of man was occupied by *Homo erectus* who seemed to have lived between 500 000 and a million years ago. All the evidence suggests that this ancestor of man must have made stone tools, knew about fire, hunted, and lived in groups. The discoveries come from Asia, Africa, and Europe. It appears, then, that the development of man took place in many different parts of the world. *Homo erectus* can be thought of as an immediate ancestor of *Homo sapiens*.

The oldest forms of *Homo sapiens*, which are related to *Homo erectus*, have been found in many different parts of the world and are of various ages. Their classification is neither uniform nor complete: there are several sub-species, and Neanderthal-man, *Homo sapiens neanderthalensis*, is perhaps the best known. He was thought earlier to be an independent species, but today experts think that he is just an extinct form of *Homo sapiens*. Modern man, *Homo sapiens sapiens*, appeared about 40 000 years ago.

The cultural development of man

The start of the cultural development of man is marked by his first use of tools, by his first attempts to build shelters, and by his first artistic endeavours. Man's biological development began about 14 million years ago, but evidence of his culture is only about three million years old. It began during the Quaternary, the youngest geological formation. Man's culture was decisively influenced by the way in which he evolved biologically, and the two processes are inseparable.

Tools are the first traces of the activities of man which we find: they were perfected over long periods of time and were used in ever increasing numbers and variations. Of course, the way in which tools were evolved was not a linear process either, and was dependent largely on environmental factors. It is reasonable to expect that at any given time tools from different parts of the world might be more, or less, advanced. Experts have grouped them together according to the way in which they were made, and for what purpose they were used. Evidence of Stone Age technology can be traced through pre-history and history right up to the present day; the Australian Aborigines are an example of a very primitive modern race.

The most primitive tools were made from stone and bone and were used by the African genus *Australopithecus*. Two large cultural groups were already apparent during the phase of development of *Homo erectus;* these were the flake and the core tool cultures with their typical hand-axe industries. They belong to the Lower Palaeolithic period. The cultures of the Middle Palaeolithic period were divided into several groups who developed under the influence of environment and geographical isolation.

Only during the Upper Palaeolithic, about 10 000 to 14 000 years ago, did a wave of cultural activity take place. The more highly developed social life, which now took place in larger settlements with an increasing population, was thriving particularly because of improved hunting methods and the favourable climatic conditions. A qualitative and quantitative development of the tool industry was achieved, and the artistic production as well as the burial rites suggest a rich cultural life. Towards the end of the last Ice Age man had perfected methods of working animal skins, and he was also highly developed artistically.

The changing climate after the Ice Age made a great difference to the life of the Palaeolithic hunter. Art was on a decline at this time, and it serves to point out mistakes which a researcher can make if he assumes that cultural development was a linear process Pictorial expression became often schematized in the Mesolithic, and is less interesting to us today. Of course, this does not mean that a continuing decline in art was to take place. Phases of quick or restrained development can be detected which cannot be taken as a decline or peak, but only as a typical phenomenon of evolution. A number of examples can be cited in which the cultural and biological development of different populations progresses at different speeds.

Man's evolution took many courses, and must be looked at from more than one point of view. There are neither biological nor cultural reasons which would justify leaving out any of the different populations.

Here, we are mainly concerned with the early phases of development of man. We trace human development from its beginnings to the end of the Mesolithic period. It was at this point that some groups of men ceased to live in bands and tribes as hunters and collectors and began to cultivate the land, domesticate animals, make clay containers, and develop other new techniques. They began to group together in ordered social units and live in sizeable permanent settlements.

We are going to concentrate on three main sectors of human activity: making tools; building dwellings; artistic achievement. You should then have a complete picture of man's evolution. We will also give a broad indication of how the process ending with modern man and his civilization began.

I The origin and evolution of Man

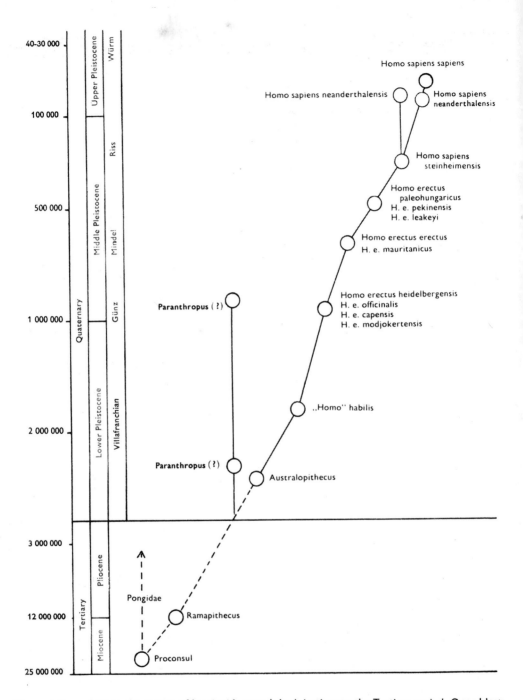

The evolution of Man: the species of hominoids stretch back in time to the Tertiary period. Our oldest direct ancestors belong to the genus *Ramapithecus*. Its age has been estimated at 14 million years. *Australopithecus* – two to three million years old – was already making tools. The unbroken line shows the further development up to *Homo sapiens*.

The development of man — a slow and complicated process

Man, scientifically known as *Homo sapiens*, is the most highly developed of all living creatures. If you wished to trace the development of man into the dark and distant past of his ancestors you would be confronted with a multitude of problems. Anyone studying the development of man has to rely on the most scanty evidence; often only small, carefully excavated fragments of bone. The very special features of man distinguishing him from other animals must also be considered — these features become more obvious as man developed. The time at which highly developed primates became primitive early man began when he started to think. This was clearly connected with the manual tasks which then had to be carried out. From this point on the study of bone fragments alone is not enough to resolve questions of man's social behaviour. We also have to consider the development of human intelligence. It is this intelligence which enabled man to form values about his material needs, and helped him to adapt his environment accordingly.

The question of man's origin has not yet been solved. Often, the discovery of apparently insignificant bone fragments can lead to new ideas and theories. Therefore, it is impossible at this stage to produce a continuous and accurate account of man's development, and to say that it is complete. But let us imagine a time several million years ago, and try to build up a picture of the possible development of man.

The position of man and his ancestors within the zoological system

Man is mammal and belongs to the order of **Primates.** By palaeontological research, it is possible to trace over a long period how the primates have evolved. In the Triassic period, at the beginning of the Mesozoic era, some of the highly specialized reptiles developed into the first mammals. These primitive mammals developed into the insectivores and through a series of sub-primate forms emerged the true primates. This grade of evolution was probably achieved towards the end of the Cretaceous period and at the beginning of the Tertiary. At the dawn of the Tertiary existed small creatures of the genus **Purgatorius** which Szalay (1968) considers the most primitive representative of the primates.

The primates are divided into two subordinate groups: the **Prosimians** *(Prosimii)* and the **Anthropoids** *(Anthropoidea)*. Today there is no doubt that the Anthropoids have developed directly from Prosimians and probably branched off towards the middle of the Tertiary, in the Eocene or Oligocene. Some fossil primates evolved high degrees of specialization only to become extinct, whereas others developed into today's well-known monkeys, apes, and man.

The living higher primates *(Anthropoidea)* are divided into three super-families: the *Ceboidea*, or **New World monkeys**, including the capuchins; the *Cercopithecoidea*, or **Old World monkeys**, including the guenons and baboons; and the *Hominoidea* comprising the **apes and man.** Sometimes the last two super-families are grouped together as the infra-order *Catarrhini*. The first super-family is a quite distinct branch of the primates which developed independently out of the Prosimians and is not important to man's family tree. The second super-family, too, is not immediately connected with man's development. But remember that we should not reject the possibility that the Old

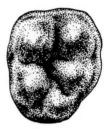

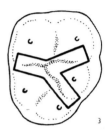

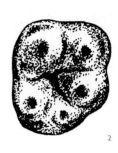

1 Left halves of upper jaws with the corresponding dental formulae: Prosimians 2-1-3-3; New World monkeys *(Ceboidea)* 2-1-3-3; Old World monkeys *(Cercopithecoidea)* 2-1-2-3; and the apes and man *(Hominoidea)* 2-1-2-3. The molars are shown on the right-hand side of the dotted line and the other teeth are on the left-hand side.

2 A comparison between a four-cusped cercopithecoid molar and a five-cusped human molar.

3 A hominoid molar from the right lower jaw with the *Dryopithecus*-pattern (a Y-groove on the chewing part).

4 The gorilla (*Gorilla gorilla*), one of the apes (*Pongidae*) still alive today. A female gorilla is illustrated here.

5 Facial expressions of gorillas suggest an intelligence, which other animals rarely have.

World monkeys *(Cercopithecoidea)* and the apes *(Hominoidea)* may have had common ancestors.

The third super-family, comprising the apes and man *(Hominoidea)*, has had a long development independent of the other two groups of primates. This is indicated by the first signs of Hominoids appearing in the Upper Oligocene, while forms of the Old World monkeys *(Cercopithecoidea)* appeared only much later.

A very long period of time elapsed between the appearance of the primitive mammals and the forms which were to be the origins of man. The first signs of human-like adaptations appeared in these primitive forms, and it is possible to follow them through to the development of man and also to see them in some of the other higher primates.

The particular way in which the first primates lived at the top of trees led to some outwardly visible morphological changes in the construction of the body. Mainly, however, these changes were in the adaptation of the joints which enabled much more flexible movement of the limbs, and in the development of stereoscopic vision. The eyes moved forwards and closer together until their fields of vision overlapped. But the development of the brain is the most notable feature. The nose receded and sense of smell became reduced. There was an increase in the size of the cerebral hemispheres with a consequent development and enlargement of the skull. Of particular importance to the anthropologist are the very noticeable changes in jaw structure because parts of the jaws and teeth are often the only remains of the skull which have been preserved.

The teeth of a Prosimian are simple and primitive. Each row of teeth on the upper and lower jaw is made up of two incisors, one canine, three premolars, and three molars. Consequently, the dental formula is 2-1-3-3 and indicates that each half of the upper and lower jaws has nine teeth, making thirty-six altogether. The higher primates have a dental formula of 2-1-2-3 which means they have one premolar less and only thirty-two teeth. This dental formula identifies most of the members

6

6 Orang-utan *(Pongo pygmaeus)*.

7 Facial expression of a seventeen year old orang-utan.

of the super-family of Old World monkeys *(Cercopithecoidea)* and all members of the super-family of the apes *(Hominoidea)*. The dental formula for the New World monkeys *(Ceboidea)* is like that of the Prosimians. This seems to be further proof of the independent development of this super-family (1).

An important characteristic distinguishing Hominoids from Cercopithecoids is the development of the lower molars. All the Old World monkeys have four cusps on the molars whereas the apes have five (2), which are divided by a characteristic Y-shaped groove (3). This molar surface pattern was called the *Dryopithecus*-pattern by Gregory after the genus **Dryopithecus** which is one of the fossil apes that we shall discuss later. Another important characteristic is the *cingulum* which is a ridge formed around the premolars and molars. This primitive characteristic was lost during evolution, however, and reappears later only rarely and in a stunted form.

The development of the Hominoids is accompanied by a pattern of typical morphological and anatomical characteristics, which are gradually altered during evolution. The body enlarges, the skull enlarges as the brain and brain-case increase in size becoming much more developed than in the monkeys; the jaws become shorter, the dental crowns are lower and the lower molars take on the *Dryopithecus*-pattern, as already mentioned. Stereoscopic vision develops. A lot of monkey-like fossil species lived on plants. The strongly developed canines of a few species were probably used for defensive purposes.

The Hominoids, mostly large animals, had problems moving about in trees. The process of crawling or walking on branches was slow and difficult. Movement was achieved by securing handholds with the forelimbs above the head and suspending the body and propelling the animal forward by swinging with one arm then the other. This way of moving is called *brachiation*. Even today gibbons usually move in this fashion. The first Hominoids showed signs of brachiation and J Napier called them prebrachiators. The structure of their body is slightly specialized and they tend to have long forelimbs and fingers (smaller thumb) which enable them to grasp the branches as if they were using hooks. The hindlimbs are much shorter. Another noticeable aspect was the tail which was mostly invisible externally.

Representatives of the super-family *Hominoidea* which are still in existence belong to three groups: the **gibbons and siamangs** *(Hylobatidae)*, the **great apes** *(Pongidae)* including the orang-utan, the gorilla and the chimpanzee; and the group of **man-like beings** *(Hominidae)*. Extinct forms include some species within these groups, or they belong to independent systematic units (4 to 9).

The development of the apes

The oldest specimen of a higher primate comes from the Oligocene period and was found near Fayum in Egypt. Dr Schlosser and more recently also Dr Elwyn Simons from Yale University discovered numerous specimens of bones and teeth there, especially jaws, from which some primate species have been described.

The genera **Parapithecus** (10), **Apidium** (11), and **Oligopithecus** (12) are among the oldest forms. The placing of the genus *Parapithecus* is problematic. Some authors regard it as an isolated group, but others place it just at the source of the super-family *Hominoidea*. The dental formula of *Parapithecus* and *Apidium* is 2-1-3-3 and indicates a genetic connection with the Prosimians. Both genera are connected with the genus *Amphipithecus* (13) which might be by far the oldest anthropoid and was found in Burma dating from the Upper Eocene. Its dental formula is also 2-1-3-3. The lower molars of all these genera have five cusps.

The genus *Oligopithecus* is thought to be the original form which could have produced the super-family *Cercopithecoidea* (Romer, 1966). Their dental formula is 2-1-2-3, and is the same as most of the dental formulae belonging to Cercopithecoids and Hominoids. According to Groves (1970) *Oligopithecus* probably stood on the border between the Prosimian ancestors of the higher primates, and the primitive Pongids. From the teeth it is possible to distinguish primitive characteristics of the Prosimians, besides those of the apes.

Other discoveries from the upper levels of the Middle and Upper Oligocene of Fayum belong to the genera **Propliopithecus** (14, 15) and **Aegyptopithecus**. Both have the typical dental formula 2-1-2-3 and five cusps on the lower molars. *Propliopithecus* had a smaller skeleton, much smaller than today's gib-

8

8   This expression of the chimpanzee *(Pan troglodytes)* shows contentment.

9   A white-handed gibbon *(Hylobates lar)*, a representative of the sub-family *Hylobatinae*.

9

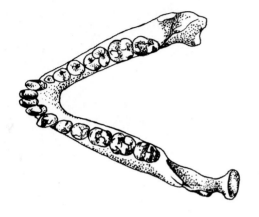

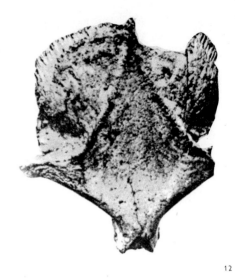

12

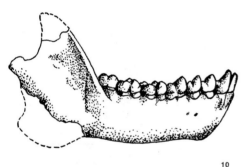

10

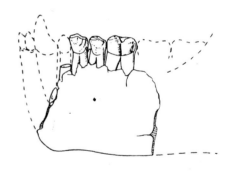

13

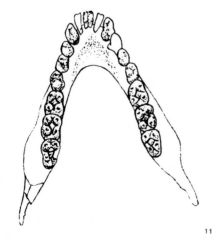

10 Lower jaw o ƗParapithecus from the Oligocene period discovered at Fayum, Egypt (after Schlosser).

11 Lower jaw of the genus Apidium from the Oligocene period in Egypt. The teeth show certain similarities to those of Oreopithecus (after Osborn).

12 A frontal bone, which probably belongs to the genus Oligopithecus. Fayum, Egypt (after Simons).

13 Fragment of the lower jaw belonging to Amphipithecus. The front teeth and the last two molars have been reconstructed (the dotted lines are according to Schlosser).

11

bons. *Aegyptopithecus* was larger, and was about the same size as a gibbon. According to Simons, *Aegyptopithecus* relates directly with the genus *Propliopithecus* and is the nearest relative of today's Pongids. *Aegyptopithecus* is often suggested to be the general forerunner of the Hominoids. Other authors would like to accept the genus *Propliopithecus* as the forerunner of the Pongids, that is, the basic ancestor of the Hominoids.

Both these points of view do not seem to be too far apart; *Propliopithecus* is one of the oldest forms of the Hominoids, older than *Aegyptopithecus*, and a genus with a number of unspecialized characteristics. *Aegyptopithecus* is more specialized, and the known parts of the skeleton suggest connections with the more developed apes, particularly the genera **Proconsul** and **Dryopithecus**. Simons discovered an almost undamaged skull and lower jaw of *Aegyptopithecus* (17). The skull has some primitive characteristics, an inheritance from its Prosimian ancestors which are not closely connected with the Hominoids. This should not surprise anyone, however. Every form, which is taken to be the forerunner in the development of a group should possess generalized as well as primitive characteristics. This is also the case with the genus *Aegyptopithecus*, whose teeth with their five cusp molars and the indication of the *Dryopithecus*-pattern point towards the *Hominoidea*. Simons discovered several tail vertebrae in addition to the skull. It is now known that members of the super-family *Hominoidea* characteristically have no tail, but it could be expected that a primate which was one of the sources of the development of the apes has inherited from his ancestors a tail of some length. Thus, the bodily structure of *Aegyptopithecus* is similar to that of the modern Cercopithecoids, although his jaw structure undoubtedly identifies him as an ape.

At present it is impossible to identify the basic differentiations along the line of development of the Hominoids. *Propliopithecus* and *Aegyptopithecus* date back to the Oligocene beginning approximately 34 million years ago.

Primitive Hominoids from the Lower Miocene include the genus **Limnopithecus** (18, 19) from East Africa and genus **Pliopithecus** from Europe. Until recently *Limnopithecus* was thought to belong to a form which led to today's gibbon (20, 21). Some recent research has indicated, however, that it may be identical with the genus *Pliopithecus* and cannot be thought of as an ancestor of the gibbons.

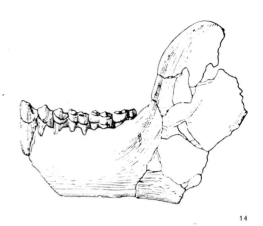

14

15

14 Lower jaw of *Propliopithecus* (after Schlosser).

15 The occlusal surface of the lower teeth of *Propliopithecus*. From top to bottom: canine tooth; two premolars; three molars (after Kälin).

16 Comparisons between the lower jaws of (A) *Parapithecus*, (B) *Propliopithecus*, (C) *Pliopithecus* and (D) the modern gibbon.

17 Partly reconstructed skull of *Aegyptopithecus*.

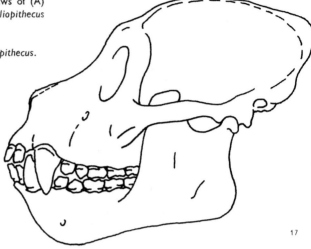

17

16

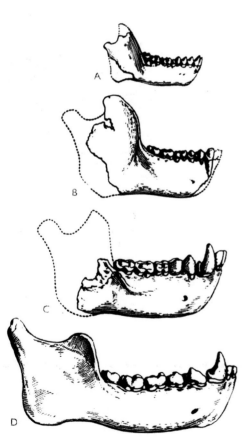

Pliopithecus has been known since 1837 from the Miocene periods in France (22); later sizeable discoveries were made from the Miocene and Pliocene periods. Particularly some of the more recent finds in Czechoslovakia of almost complete skeletons (23, 24) make more accurate information on this genus possible. *Pliopithecus* possessed seven lumbar vertebrae (the other Hominoids, including the gibbons, have only five) and the development of the *sacrum* at the lower end of the spine makes it possible to assume that there was a long tail of fifteen to nineteen vertebrae. The lower molars are differently formed from those of the Hominoids, and the orbital cavities of the skull have a slightly sideways opening (25). The special characteristics, the long-bones of *Pliopithecus*, led eventually to the opinion that they were independent representatives of a family which was called *Pliopithecidae*. This family represents a line of development which had obviously already departed from the line of development of the Hominoids in the Upper Miocene. The last representatives of this family are known from the Pliocene and we can assume at present that they became extinct at that time.

Further discoveries, which could be placed in the line of development of the present day Hominoids, come from the Lower Miocene, from around Lake Victoria in East Africa. In

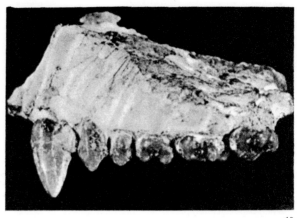

18 Upper jaw of *Limnopithecus* (after Le Gros Clark and Thomas).

19 Lower and upper jaw of *Limnopithecus*. Miocene, East Africa (after Le Gros Clark and Thomas).

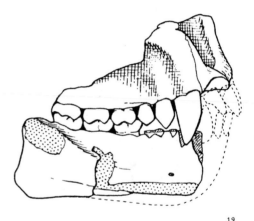

19

the 1930s the remains of a fossil ape were discovered. The discoverers were L S B Leakey and his wife Mary. This find was described in 1933 by the Englishman Hopwood and called *Proconsul africanus* (26,27). It was named after the well-known chimpanzee 'Consul' from London Zoo. When it was ascertained that the newly discovered fossil ape was a predecessor of today's apes and, therefore, also of London's 'Consul', Hopwood decided to call it *Proconsul*. More discoveries followed, particularly in the 1940s, and again by Drs L and M Leakey. They found many skull and post-cranial fragments as well as an almost perfect skull, the first of a Tertiary ape which was in good condition.

The detailed scientific examinations of the complete materials suggested three different species of the genus *Proconsul*: *Proconsul nyanzae*, *Proconsul africanus* (28, 29), and *Proconsul major*, which could be differentiated by their size. *Proconsul africanus*, the smallest, could be compared in size to a small baboon. *Proconsul major*, the largest, was a little larger than a present-day chimpanzee. All three species have common characteristics; the *supra-orbital torus* is usually only poorly developed, their jaws are narrow and protrude forwards (30). Therefore, the mouth-part must have been far more pointed than in today's apes. The lower molars had five cusps showing the faint Y-groove — the basic

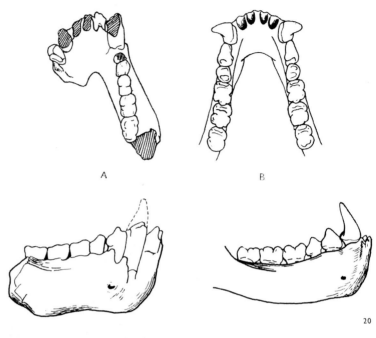

A   B

20

21

20 Lower jaws of (A) *Limnopithecus* and (B) modern gibbons. It was assumed earlier that *Limnopithecus*, *Propliopithecus*, and even *Pliopithecus* were the ancestors of modern gibbons. More recent research has raised doubts in Europe about this hypothesis (after Le Gros Clark and L S B Leakey).

21 Discovery of limb bones belonging to *Limnopithecus* (after Le Gros Clark and Thomas).

22 Lower jaw of *Pliopithecus* from Sansan, France (after Hürzeler).

23 *Pliopithecus* was discovered at Děvínská Nová Ves, Czechoslovakia.

22

23

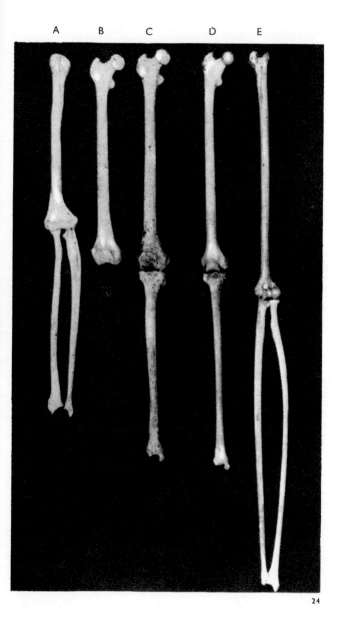

A   B   C   D   E

24

24 Long-bones of (A) the upper, and (B, C) lower limbs belonging to *Pliopithecus*, compared with the long-bones of (D) the lower, and (E) upper limbs of gibbons. The difference in length between the bones of the front limbs (A and E) is obvious (after Zapfe and Hürzeler).

characteristic of the *Dryopithecus*-pattern. They also had a strongly developed cingulum, which is a very primitive characteristic. The *simian shelf*, a characteristic of all recent and fossil apes, served to strengthen the lower jaw. The structure of the limbs leads to the assumption that *Proconsul* moved about on all fours (31, 32) and was only able to take on a semi-erect position with great difficulties. Le Gros Clark and Leakey (1951) came to the conclusion that the foot of *Proconsul* showed certain anatomical evidence which could make development towards a more human-like foot a possibility. But *Proconsul* obviously hardly counts among the ancestors of man; he came to a standstill at a particular time of his development until such time as the higher forms of Hominoids came into evidence. Leakey (1968) for instance, was able to show *Proconsul* evidence in his finds from the Miocene period.

More recent fossil apes are grouped under the collective name of Dryopithecines. The oldest discoveries come from the Middle Miocene and the most recent from the Lower Pliocene. They are mostly teeth, fragments of jaws, and a few bones of the skeleton. The first discovery was made in 1856 in France, and since then many more have come to light. After they were originally rather indistinctly classified under a variety of different genera and species, most of the material has now, since the latest examinations, been classified under the single genus *Dryopithecus*. This genus is known from Europe, Spain, and France, across middle Europe (33 to 36) and the European parts of the USSR as well as North Africa, the Caucasus and Anatolia. *Dryopithecus* seems to be a descendant of the developing type, which originally was near to the *Proconsul* form or even identical to it (Colbert, 1966; Howells, 1967). The teeth are the decisive characteristics, because the chewing surfaces of the lower molars have five cusps and the Y-like groove. Although the *Dryopithecus*-pattern is present in geologically earlier forms like *Aegyptopithecus* and *Proconsul*, specimens of *Dryopithecus* were found before these Fayum forms. Therefore, Gregory named it after the genus *Dryopithecus*. The cingulum of the teeth is clearly developed. The incisors are quite broad, the canines have deep roots. The broadened frontal part of the mouth is clearly distinguishable from the pointed mouth of *Proconsul*. The finds of bones of the upper and lower arm *(humerus, ulna)* in France and Austria are thought by some to indicate brachiation, the arm-swinging form of move-

25

25 Facial view of the skull of *Pliopithecus* from Děvínská Nová Ves, Czechoslovakia (after Zapfe).

ment. When on the ground *Dryopithecus* moved on all fours, probably in a semi-erect position. In more recent forms of *Dryopithecus* the development of the simian shelf is obvious.

To the same systematic domain belong the find from the little town of Udabno, which was originally described as **Udabnopithecus**, the find of a lower jaw from Hungary, which was named **Hungaropithecus**, and finds from Austria, China, and so on. The genus **Sivapithecus** is placed near or within the genus *Dryopithecus*. Remains of *Sivapithecus* have been found in the Siwalik Hills (north India) from the Middle and Upper Miocene, and were classified according to the row of teeth and the fragments of the jaw (37). Leakey discovered traces of *Sivapithecus* also in Africa. Firstly, finds of parts of jaws came to light, and later followed a well-preserved lower jaw with teeth. These discoveries were assigned to *Sivapithecus africanus*, the only one of this kind in Africa. It dated from the Lower Miocene.

Some authors (Simons, 1964, Romer, 1966) put *Sivapithecus* and *Proconsul* with the genus *Dryopithecus*, others (Howells, 1967) see them as

29

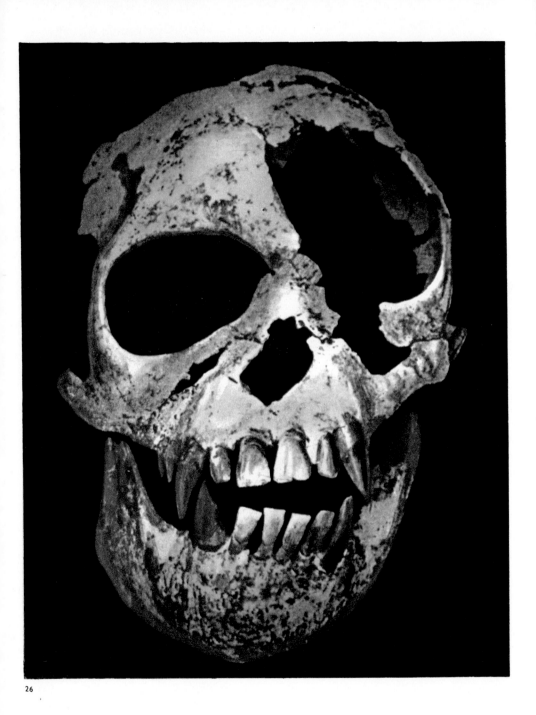

26 Facial view of the skull of *Proconsul africanus*.
The bones were deformed during fossilization
(after L S B Leakey).

30

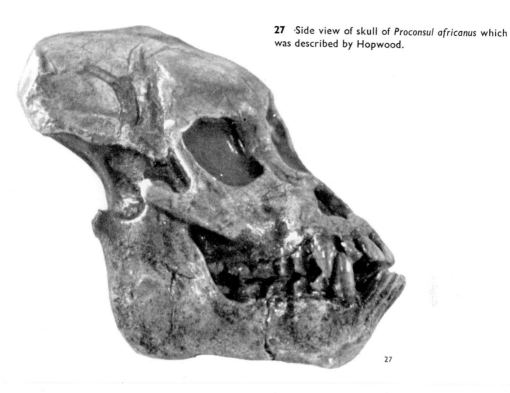

27 ·Side view of skull of *Proconsul africanus* which was described by Hopwood.

27

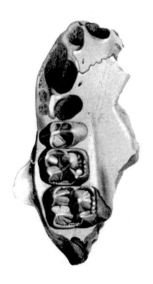

28

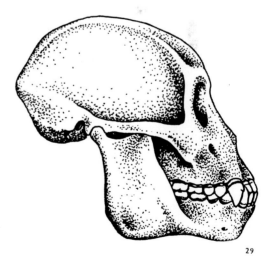

29

28 Upper jaw of *Proconsul africanus* with a premolar and two molars (after Napier and Davis).

29 Reconstruction of skull of *Proconsul africanus* (after Le Gros Clark and L S B Leakey).

31

30 A comparison between the lower jaws of *Proconsul nyanzae* (above) and the chimpanzee (below) (after Le Gros Clark).

31 Thigh bones (femur) of (A) *Proconsul*, (B) *Dryopithecus* and (C) chimpanzee (after Le Gros Clark).

32 The skeleton of the hand of *Proconsul* (after Napier and Davis).

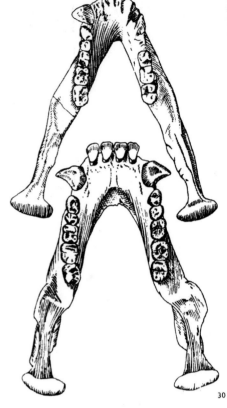

30

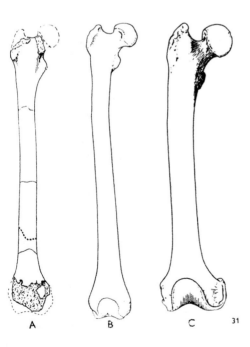

A   B   C   31

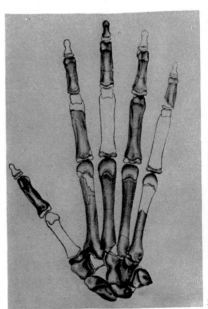

3

33 Side view of the lower jaw of *Dryopithecus* from Saint-Gaudens. The huge canine tooth is clearly visible.

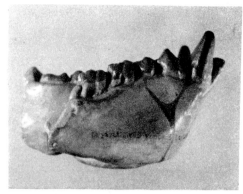

33

independent genera. Leakey (1968) opposes the theory that *Proconsul* could be a form which could be grouped together with *Dryopithecus*. It is, however, definite that they all belong to the sub-family *Dryopithecinae*, which in the systematic grouping, stands as an extinct sub-family next to the recent forms represented in the sub-family of the apes.

Dryopithecus and *Sivapithecus* have ancestors among the apes belonging to the types of *Proconsul* and were probably forerunners of modern apes. It has sometimes been assumed that the genus *Dryopithecus* could be connected with the **gorilla** *(Gorilla gorilla)* (38) and with the **chimpanzee** *(Pan troglodytes, Pan paniscus)*, whereas the **orang-utan** *(Pongo pygmaeus)* has a direct phylogenetic relationship to the family of *Sivapithecus*. *Dryopithecus* was not a highly specialized genus which is why it could develop so freely and diversely. Therefore it is possible to derive the much more specialized types of modern apes from this group.

One of the palaeoanthropological surprises came from China and is connected with the Dutch scientist Professor G H R von Koenigswald. Von Koenigswald searched in drugstores because he knew that 'dragon teeth' were being sold in them. He also knew that they were merely the teeth of ancient creatures, including the teeth of extinct primates. He bought hundreds of teeth and studied them carefully over the period 1935 to 1939. He discovered four molar teeth, which were distinctly different from all the other molars of extinct and living primates. Von Koenigswald was sure that he had found the teeth of a fossil Hominoid because the lower molars showed five distinctly developed cusps with the Y-like groove on the chewing surface of the teeth (39 to 41). But the

teeth were exceptionally large, even gigantic — the circumferences of the crowns of the teeth were six times larger than a human tooth and twice as large as the tooth of a big gorilla. It was impossible to put a date on this discovery because no-one knew where it was found. Eventually von Koenigswald decided to place it in the Middle Pleistocene, and concluded that the teeth must have belonged to a gigantic ape which he called **Gigantopithecus blacki** (von Koenigswald, 1935).

During World War II von Koenigswald was interned by the Japanese. The teeth went to New York where Professor Weidenreich studied them. He came to the conclusion that they belonged to a gigantic primitive man, and he called him *Giganthropus blacki*. Von Koenigswald returned to his work after the war and rejected the theory decisively, and he was later proved to be correct.

There is yet another name associated with *Gigantopithecus*, the Chinese scientist Professor Wen-Chung Pei. During 1955 and 1956 more teeth of *Gigantopithecus* appeared in the Kuangsi Province and later in drugstores in Canton and Nanking. Finally, in 1956 a complete lower jaw was found in the cave called Lintscheng, in the Lan-tschai-schan mountain which lies in the central area of Kuang-si. It was here that Professor Pei began to excavate, and found a second jaw, several teeth, and another complete lower jaw (42, 43).

The research of the Chinese scholar made it possible at last to answer the question about the mysterious *Gigantopithecus*. It was an enormous ape which lived in the Middle Pleistocene. The lower jaw is exceptionally large (44). It also has a well-developed simian shelf, as do the modern apes. The teeth, however, are specific

33

34 *Dryopithecus* has been found at Děvínská Nová
Ves, Czechoslovakia.

and distinctly different. The canines of *Giganto-pithecus* are relatively small, and morphologically similar to those of man (45, 46). Whereas the teeth of the *Pongidae* usually show a space *(diastema)* between the canines and the incisors, in the lower jaw, this is not present in *Giganto-pithecus*. This is why these omnivorous types of teeth could be associated with man rather than with the apes. Apart from this it has nothing in common with man's ancestors. It lived in the steppe or wood-steppe. Professor Pei assumes that *Gigantopithecus* was significantly bigger than the gorilla, and thinks that it might have been approximately 3.5 metres tall. It is hard to say whether this figure is accurate because none of the body skeleton has been found. A comparison of the sizes of the jaws and teeth of *Gigantopithecus* and the gorilla indicates that Professor Pei's assumption may be correct, but instances are known where similar calculations have failed. But if we do assume that *Gigantopithecus blacki* was larger than the gorilla, it would probably be the largest known primate.

The origin of *Gigantopithecus* may probably be traced back to the same point as the origin of the present apes, namely among the Tertiary representatives of the sub-family *Dryopithe-cinae*, possibly from the genus *Sivapithecus*. New discoveries from the Siwalik Hills seemed to

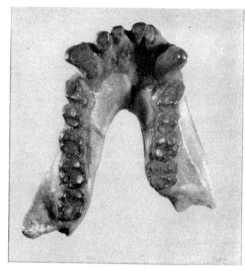

35

36

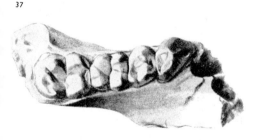

37

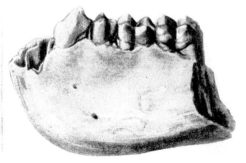

35 Lower jaw of *Dryopithecus* from Saint-Gaudens, viewed from above.

36 Molars of *Dryopithecus* from the Miocene period found at Děvínská Nová Ves, Czechoslovakia (after Glaessner).

37 Fragment of a lower jaw of *Sivapithecus indicus* (after Pilgrim).

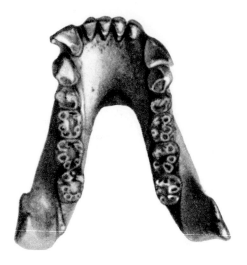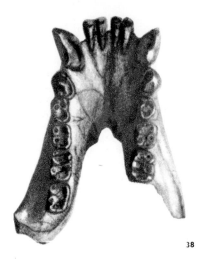

38

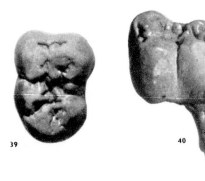

39   40

38 Comparison between the lower jaw of a gorilla and that of *Dryopithecus* (after Gaudry).

39 A third molar belonging to *Gigantopithecus* which was found by von Koenigswald.

40 Side view of a molar belonging to *Gigantopithecus* found by von Koenigswald.

41 Occlusal surface of two teeth belonging to *Gigantopithecus* coming from the Middle Pleistocene of south China.

41

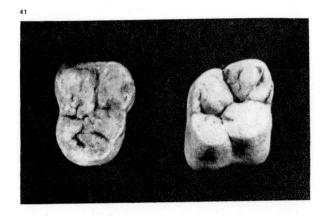

42

42 Three damaged lower jaws of *Gigantopithecus blacki*. It was because of these discoveries that it was possible to identify *Gigantopithecus*, a gigantic extinct ape.

confirm this view. In 1969 Simons and Chopra described a new species from the Pliocene period which they called **Gigantopithecus bilaspurensis** (Simons and Chopra, 1969) (47). Its history of development is connected with *Gigantopithecus blacki*. From the same source the species *Sivapithecus giganteus* was discovered. It is larger than the other representatives of this genus, and the construction of the teeth, and the body size, seem to infer genetic connection with *Gigantopithecus*. *Sivapithecus giganteus* which is now considered as *Dryopithecus indicus*, and the other discoveries which are connected with it come from the Upper Miocene. *Gigantopithecus bilaspurensis* was discovered in the Lower Pliocene and *Gigantopithecus blacki* is known from the Middle Pleistocene. Thus, the stratigraphic evidence does not contradict the acceptance of such a line of development.

The original forms of the sub-family *Dryopithecinae* showed so many common characteristics and had specialized so little, that it was possible for them to develop in so many directions. It is probably because of this that we can search among them for the ancestors of the modern members of the super-family *Hominoidea* — the orang-utan, the chimpanzee, and the gorilla. The development of the highly specialized forms could not continue because they could not adapt to their changing environment, and they became extinct. *Gigantopithecus* met with this fate and disappeared during the Pleistocene.

Oreopithecus bambolii (Gervais, 1872) which was found in Italy represents another line of development which ran parallel to the one above, and which probably ended long ago. About the end of the 1860s a piece of a lower jaw from the Miocene was discovered on Monte Bamboli near Florence (Italy). The four-cusped molars seemed to indicate at first that it belonged to the Cercopithecoids (48) and it was assumed that the jaw fragment was from an extinct form of baboon. Seventy years later the palaeoanthropologist from Basel, Dr J Hürzeler, made another study of this discovery and found that the position of *Oreopithecus* could be disputed. Another discovery of an almost complete skeleton was made in the central region of Italy (49), and it was found to be Pliocene in age. This suggested that Hürzeler was correct, and brought a number of surprises. It proved mainly that, taking into account the overall form of its body structure, *Oreopithecus* was more akin to the apes than to the cercopithecoid monkeys. It looked like a small, stocky chimpanzee with long arms. The skull showed a peculiar structure: the thick protrusions over the eyes (the browridge) were quite large; the facial skeleton, in comparison with all the other extinct and living apes was, however, much more vertical, which eliminated the strongly protruding jaw structure and looked more like a human (50). But this was the only similarity to man. The teeth show a num-

37

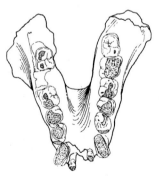

43

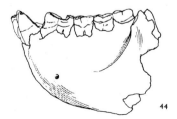

44

43 The site in south China where the jaw of *Gigantopithecus* was found.

44 Drawing of lower jaw of *Gigantopithecus*.

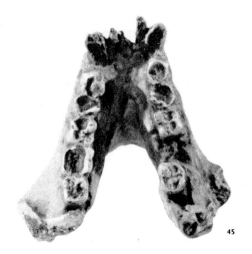

45

46

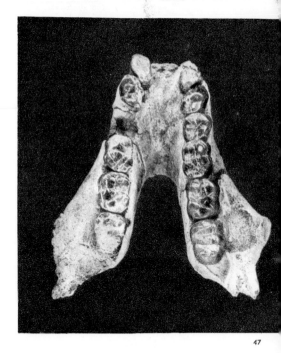

47

ber of characteristics which distinguish *Oreopithecus* from Cercopithecoids as well as from the apes. The typical gap between the canine and incisor teeth which identifies the real apes was missing, and the relatively small canine teeth indicated that *Oreopithecus* was more advanced. The cingulum of the crowns of the teeth seemed to suggest the opposite, however. The lower molars did not show the *Dryopithecus*-pattern. The construction of the cusps was similar to that found in Cercopithecoids.

The fifth cusp is placed near the centre of the lower molars, and is not the same as the *Dryopithecus*-pattern where the cusp is placed sideways along the other two cusps. The structure of the molars indicates that a primate might have been the ancestor of *Oreopithecus* (51). *Apidium*, a primate from the Lower Oligocene of Fayum, was also taken into consideration. Simons thinks that this primitive genus might be a forerunner in a line of development to *Oreopithecus*. *Oreopithecus* is so different, both in body and skull structure, from the other fossil apes that it has acquired the status of a separate family within the super-family *Hominoidea*. The family is called the **Oreopithecidae** and seems to be a branch that did not further develop. The *Oreopithecidae* are next to the other three independent lines of development of the Hominoids, comprising the family *Pliopithecidae* now extinct, the family *Pongidae*, which includes all known fossil and recent great apes, and the family *Hominidae*, to which man and his immediate ancestors belong. *Oreopithecus* probably lived about 12 to 14 million years ago.

45 View of the biggest of the jaws belonging to *Gigantopithecus*.

46 Side view of the jaw belonging to *Gigantopithecus blacki*. We can see the fairly small canine teeth.

47 Lower jaw of *Gigantopithecus bilaspurensis* from India (after Simons).

39

The development of man and his immediate ancestors

While we were looking at the main line of development of the primates which has several branches, we have left the Prosimians *(Prosimii)* by the wayside. We followed the higher groups of primates *(Anthropoidea)* and the actual development of the forms of man (superfamily *Hominoidea*). We have now reached a point at which we want to discuss the family *Hominidae* with its independent branch of development — **man.** It is marked by basic characteristics, which accompany the change of the most complicated and long drawn-out process of the development of man, also called **hominization.**

One characteristic is the straightening up of

48 The last premolar and three molars of the lower jaw (left), and the left half of the upper jaw (right) belonging to *Oreopithecus* (after Hürzeler).

49 The *Oreopithecus* skeleton discovered in lignite deposits in Tuscany.

48

49

Proconsul major, the largest representative of the genus *Proconsul* reached the size of a modern gorilla (Z Burian).

A cast of *Proconsul africanus*'s skull, one of the smaller representatives of the genus *Proconsul*.

Paranthropus was a robust member of *Australopithecinae* (Z Burian).

Australopithecus, a form, which is possibly in the direct ancestral line of man.

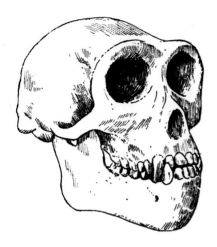
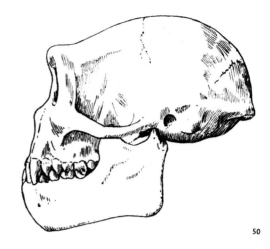

50 Reconstruction of a skull belonging to *Oreo-pithecus bambolii* (after Hürzeler).

51 Last premolar and three molars of the lower jaw of *Oreopithecus* (right), compared with the similar teeth of *Apidium* (left).

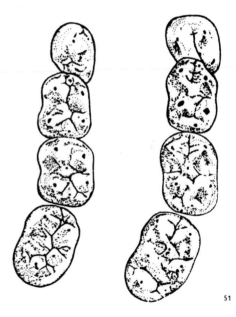

the body, gaining an erect posture, so that changes occurred to the spine, the pelvis, and the long-bones of the limbs. Hands and feet changed considerably. The structure of the sole of the foot changed, and developed a double vault. The facial skeleton became more flattened. The brain and the brain-case grew larger. One of the most important characteristics which accompanies the development of man is the rounded, or parabolic, form of the dental arcade and the hard palate. All known extinct and living apes have a flat, hard palate, and the rows of teeth, premolars and molars are parallel. The teeth are pegged into sockets called the *alveoles*. Towards the front they are connected by the rounded arc of the canine and incisor teeth; the form of the dental arcade is U-shaped, whereas the hard gum or palate of extinct and living man, even their ancestors, is curved and V-shaped. The sharp point of the V was curved by the arcade of the front teeth (52).

The development of man was also determined by climatic and marked environmental changes. Tropical forests were replaced by steppes (grassland), and this seems to have been the point at which man began to adopt an erect posture, because the body had to

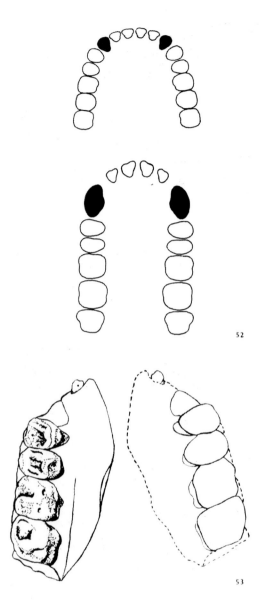

52 Comparison of an arched jaw belonging to modern man (above) and of a Pongid jaw (below) (after Le Gros Clark).

53 Fragment of an upper jaw belonging to one of the oldest Hominids, *Ramapithecus*, with two premolars and two molars. The last molar is missing. The small canine socket and the form of the molars prove that this find ranks among Hominids (after Simons).

adapt to the changed mode of life, of the primates living on the grasslands. The ancestors of man, the herbivorous great apes, had to change their feeding habits to include meat because the vegetation had become reduced. Hunting speeded up the development of the upright posture of the body, stimulated the growth of the brain, and strengthened all other functions. The ancestor of man developed into the omnivorous creature that man is today. Changes in the teeth followed the change in diet. Man's ancestors were neither fast enough nor strong enough to overpower hunting animals easily or to catch up with them. They had to be cunning and use stones and clubs to kill the animals. The hand became an important instrument, and the activities of the brain were stimulated.

The discovery of fossil primates which are presumed to be immediately associated with man began in this century. From the Upper Miocene or Lower Pliocene in the Siwalik Hills (north India) a lower and upper jaw came to light which Pilgrim (1910) decided belonged to the genus *Dryopithecus*, and called it *Dryopithecus punjabicus*. Dr G E Lewis (Yale University) described a discovery of a fragment of an upper jaw, which probably came from the same site as one of the *Dryopithecus* specimens and called it *Ramapithecus brevirostris*. Another fragment of a lower jaw was discovered in the Siwalik Hills. Dr Lewis gave this the name *Bramapithecus*, and included with it the lower jaw discovered by Pilgrim. The upper jaw found by Pilgrim retained its original name of *Dryopithecus punjabicus*.

Dr Elwyn Simons checked these finds again in the 1960s and arrived at new conclusions. He concluded mainly that Pilgrim's first find did not belong to the genus *Dryopithecus* and that Pilgrim's fragments of the upper jaw and Lewis's part of the lower jaw belonged to the same species. *Dryopithecus punjabicus* and *Ramapithecus brevirostris* were both included under the name *Ramapithecus punjabicus*. Simons also checked Lewis's genus *Bramapithecus* and agreed with Pilgrim's opinions. The characteristics of the teeth indicated that the fragments of the upper and lower jaw, which Pilgrim discovered, were definitely related. Therefore, *Bramapithecus* is included in the genus *Ramapithecus*.

The species **Ramapithecus punjabicus** (Pilgrim, 1910) is only known through fragments of jaws, but there is enough evidence to say that *Ramapithecus* cannot be classed with

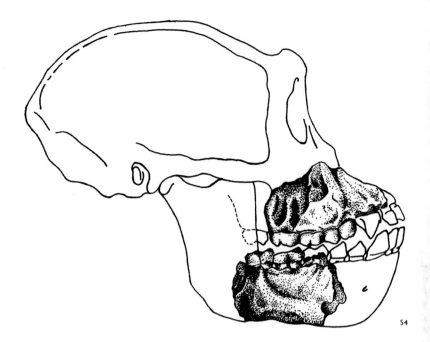

54 Reconstruction of *Ramapithecus*, on the basis of the upper and lower jaws discovered by Lewis. Particularly noticeable are the small canine teeth and the high mandibular branch.

the apes *(Pongidae)*. *Ramapithecus punjabicus* is perhaps the oldest known representative of the family *Hominidae* (53, 54).

The best evidence for this assertion comes from fragments of upper and lower jaws discovered by Lewis. The fragment of the upper jaw is of the left side of the jaw including the first two molars, two premolars, the alveolus of the canine, the root of the second incisor tooth, and a part of the alveolus belonging to the first incisor. The piece of the lower jaw consists of the back part *(corpus mandibulae)* with the second and third molar and the roots of the first molar. All this made it possible to reconstruct the teeth and come to the following conclusions: the structure and proportions of the molars coincide with those belonging to species of early man-like forms; the proportions of the corresponding incisors and molars are similar to man's; the apes have long and strong canines, whereas the alveolus in the upper jaw of *Ramapithecus* proves that its canines were no bigger than the first premolars.

One of the most positive indications that *Ramapithecus* is one of man's ancestors is that the teeth appear to be hominid in shape, right down to the fine detail. It is possible to show that the hard palate was more arched than in the apes. The upper jaw discloses that the profile of the facial skeleton was more upright and more like a man's than an ape's. According to Simons, the upper dental arcade has rounded or parabolic contours and this kind of jaw structure can also be seen in well-developed representatives of the family *Hominidae*, and even in modern man, for instance, in the people of several African tribes. On the other hand, in the new reconstruction made by Walker and Andrews the upper jaw appears much more ape-like. The lower jaw was certainly larger than the one of later forms of *Hominidae*, but the lower molars show similarities with those of man.

The fragments of the skull also gave clues to the body structure of this important genus. *Ramapithecus* was smaller than modern man; the size of the jaw fragments indicates that *Ramapithecus* was 1.1 metres tall. The creature may have moved along on its hindlimbs so that it could be called a bipedal (two-legged) an_ imal. This kind of movement made it possible to use the arms for other tasks. The fauna found in the Siwalik Hills suggests that *Ramapithecus* lived both in the steppe as well as in the wooded steppe which stretched in places far into the tropical jungle.

Ramapithecus has not only been found in north India. In 1961, Leakey announced the discovery of two pieces of an upper jaw from Fort Ternan in south-west Kenya. He called the creature, to which he thought the jaw belonged, *Kenyapithecus wickeri*. The fragment had the two front molars, on both left and right side, a complete left second premolar, a part of the premolar on the left, and the perfectly preserved alveolus of a canine. A little further away a canine and incisor were found. The structure of the upper jaw makes it possible to recognize the same characteristics of the facial skeleton as in *Ramapithecus*. The teeth themselves corresponded with those of *Ramapithecus*. Modern studies suggest that *Kenyapithecus* is a different form of *Ramapithecus*, and should be called **Ramapithecus wickeri** (Leakey, 1961). Another *Ramapithecus* discovery, two single molars, was made in China at a place called Lei-

yaun; it is referable to *Ramapithecus punjabicus*.

The origins of the genus *Ramapithecus* should be looked for in the region of the genus *Proconsul*. We cannot attribute any connections regarding the line of development of man to the *Proconsul* discoveries, but this genus belongs to a particular stage of development which present-day apes and man must have crossed at one point. The ancestors of *Ramapithecus* belonged to some type of *Proconsul*, which lived some time at the end of the Oligocene or the beginning of the Miocene. It has been thought that the genus *Proconsul* and similar forms are derived from the genera *Sivapithecus* and *Dryopithecus*. An African form of *Sivapithecus* which is older than the others has been called **Sivapithecus africanus.** It comes from the lower levels of the Miocene in Kenya. Leakey thinks that this species, despite a number of primitive characteristics, evolves towards man-like forms. The characteristics of *Sivapithecus africanus* such as a broader jaw, smaller canines, and a slightly protruding face are not particularly noticeable. In some aspects *Sivapithecus* is close to *Proconsul*, and Leakey concludes that both forms could have had a common ancestor, which lived at some time towards the end of the Oligocene. Some characteristics of *Sivapithecus* are certainly man-like although they are not strongly represented.

Therefore, the question arises whether or not *Sivapithecus africanus* is the form of *Proconsul* which is the forerunner of the first Hominid, *Ramapithecus*. This assumption is based on the age of this species. If this was the case we could assume that the origin of the development of the genus *Ramapithecus* took place in Africa and from there it spread throughout the Asian continent. Towards the end of the Miocene the development of this genus led into the more distinct forms of *Ramapithecus wickeri* in East Africa, and *Ramapithecus punjabicus* in India and China. Modern dating confirmed that both the Asian and African *Ramapithecus* lived at the same time, approximately 14 million years ago. It seems that the more advanced forms of man underwent parallel evolution over a geographically wide area.

Further discoveries of Hominid primates are associated with the names of Professor Raymond Dart and Dr Robert Broom. Their research programmes began fifty years ago in South Africa.

Raymond Dart (55) was a Professor of the University of Johannesburg. The discovery of a fossil baboon skull in the limestone area near

55

55 R A Dart, the discoverer of the South African Australopithecines.

56 Facial skeleton of a young *Australopithecus* called the Taung baby (after Dart).

56

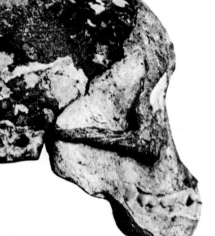

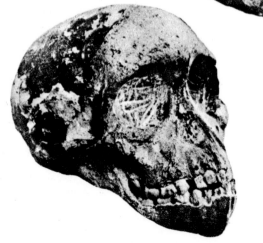

57

57 Two different views of the same skull of *Australopithecus* from Taung (after Broom).

49

58 Comparison between the profile of the skull belonging to *Australopithecus* (unbroken line) and a chimpanzee (dotted line). The distinct differences between the two species are the occipital regions of the skull, the larger canine teeth of the chimpanzee, and the fact that the face of *Australopithecus* protrudes less and has a less prominent brow ridge.

59 R Broom with a skull of *Australopithecus africanus (Plesianthropus)* from Sterkfontein (after Broom and Robinson).

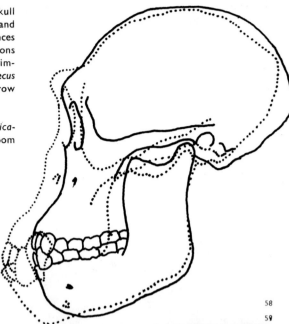

58

59

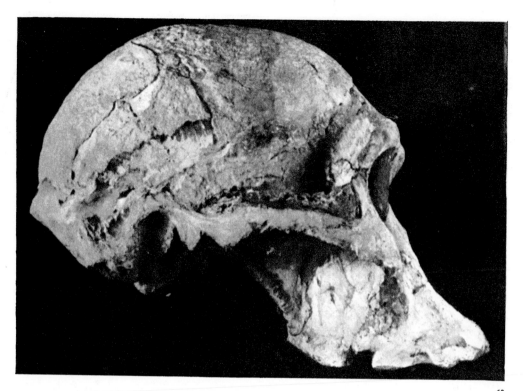

60 The best preserved skull of *Australopithecus africanus (Plesianthropus)* from Sterkfontein (after Broom and Robinson).

Johannesburg aroused his attention. Dart asked the geologists for their co-operation, and in 1924 he discovered, together with a number of fossils from the limestone quarry near Taung, a cast of a brain-case and most of the other parts of a skull. They must have belonged to one individual which could not have been an ape. It is from this skull that we have a complete facial skeleton (56) including the frontal bone *(os frontale)*, the right cheek-bone *(arcus zygomaticus)*, one part of the temporal bone, more or less all of the lower jaw, and all the teeth. Only the brain-case was missing but adequately provided for by the endocast. Therefore, it was possible to reconstruct the skull (57). Dart discovered almost immediately that this was the skull of a youth with its deciduous dentition which was less like an ape and more like a man. Convinced that the fragments belonged to a form which was the original ancestor of man, Dart sent a report and a photograph to the English journal *Nature*. He had made history and his paper was published on February 7, 1925 in the 115th issue; it was entitled '*Australopithecus africanus*: the man-ape of South Africa'.

Professor Dart had named the newly discovered hominid **Australopithecus africanus.** The first response to his paper was unfavourable. Everybody thought that the skull belonged to an ape similar to the chimpanzee or gorilla (58). Only Dr Robert Broom agreed with the discoverer from the very beginning. When Broom became the curator of the Transvaal Museum in Pretoria, he began to search for man's ancestors. His first success came in 1936, and then a number of discoveries followed which were to keep him busy until the end of his life. Broom's first discovery in 1936 came from a lime quarry near Sterkfontein (59). The manager of the quarry, who had previously worked in Taung, handed him the

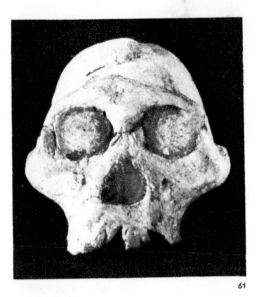

61 Front view of the same skull of *Australopithecus* from Sterkfontein (after Broom and Robinson).

62 Skull of *Paranthropus robustus* from Swartkrans.

61

62

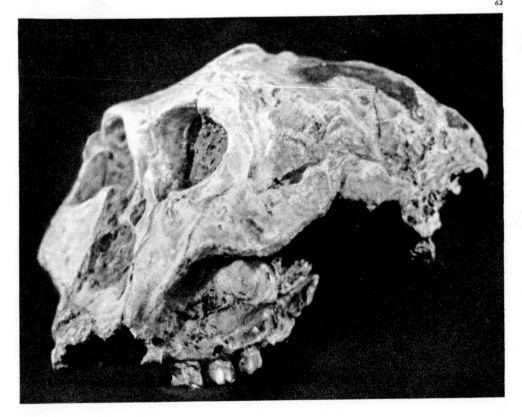

63 *Paranthropus* from Swartkrans. A front view (after Broom and Robinson).

64 Side view of another skull of *Paranthropus* from Swartkrans.

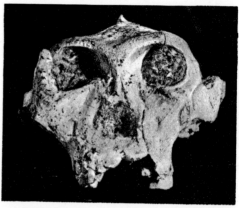

63

64

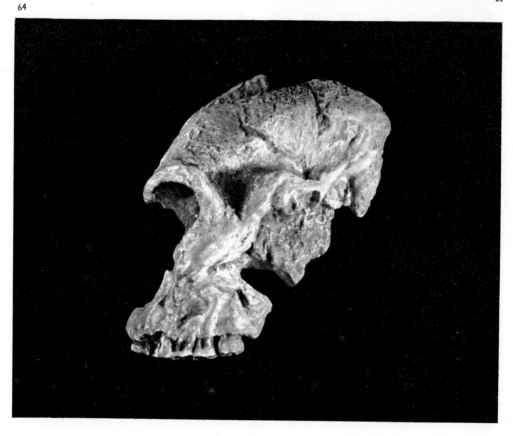

cast of the brain-case of the particular species which the scholar had been searching for so hard. Broom himself found more natural casts in the same place, casts of the brain-case, the base of the skull, parts of the upper jaw with teeth and pieces of the adjoining frontal bone and temporal bone, and other parts of important skull fragments which made the reconstruction of the skull comparatively easy (60, 61). In this case it was an adult.

Broom thought that this skull must be connected somehow with the one from Taung, and called it **Australopithecus transvaalensis.** Later he changed the name to *Plesianthropus transvaalensis* but it has been suggested recently that this was incorrect. Two years later, in 1938, Broom made another discovery, also in the vicinity of Sterkfontein, at a site called Kromdraai. In only a few days Broom had found so many pieces of a skull, that he was able to reconstruct the complete skull and discovered that this new skull was, to some extent, different from that of *Australopithecus africanus*, and *Plesianthropus transvaalensis*. He called it **Paranthropus robustus.**

At this time the wave of unfavourable opinion about Dart's first discovery ebbed away. The world's experts hastened to confirm Dart's research and came to the conclusion that the discoveries from South Africa must belong somewhere between the anthropoid apes and man. Broom made more discoveries, and Dart's opinion was heard once more, after a long silence. New forms of the South African ancestors were described (62 to 64). Skull fragments and parts of body skeletons appeared, and *Australopithecus* became more established.

In 1959 Dr Leakey published a report concerning discoveries from the Olduvai Gorge (65) in Tanzania. This find also belonged to the Australopithecines. A much older fragment, a piece of the upper limb (humerus), was discovered by Dr Bryan Patterson in 1965 in the Lake Rudolf region near Kanapoi in Kenya. Further material, possibly belonging to this group, has been found at Sangiran in Java. Von Koenigswald discovered here in 1941 the fragment of the lower jaw of a hominid, a jaw that was much larger than the jaw of modern man (66). He called it *Meganthropus palaeojavanicus* and placed it in the line of development of man. In 1953 another fragment of the lower jaw was found and von Koenigswald tried to reconstruct the lower jaw. Today he believes that it is connected with the Australopithecines. Robinson placed this discovery in the genus

65 Skull of *Paranthropus boisei* ('*Zinjanthropus*') from Olduvai Gorge. The lower jaw was reconstructed according to the discovery from Peninj (after Tobias).

66 Fragment of a mandible belonging to *Paranthropus palaeojavanicus* ('*Meganthropus*'), a type of *Paranthropus* from Java.

67 Makapansgat, a site where Australopithecines have been found (after van Riet Lowe).

Paranthropus and called it *Paranthropus palaeojavanicus* (von Koenigswald, 1941). His opinion has so far been supported by the existing material.

The latest discoveries belonging to this phase come from Omo in Ethiopia and Koobi Fora near Lake Rudolf. Numerous teeth, six jaws, and a fragmented skull have been found at Omo, which Arambourg and Coppens named *Paraustralopithecus aethiopicus*. Others are of the opinion that the discovery should be placed in the genus *Australopithecus (Paranthropus)*. Other teeth and bone fragments which were found at Omo probably belong to the genus *Homo*. They date back to about three million years ago. Several skulls have been found at Lake Rudolf; most of them are thought to belong to *Paranthropus*. A recent find, skull 1470, belongs probably to the genus *Homo*. Its brain volume is greater than 800 cubic centimetres.

Recent checking of the material brought to light that all the discoveries could be classified into three genera: **Australopithecus, Paranthropus** and **Homo**. The genus *Australopithecus* included the South African discoveries

of Sterkfontein and Makapansgat (67), as well as the materials from Lake Eyasi in East Africa; they all belong to one species, namely **Australopithecus africanus** (Dart, 1925) (68). The other discoveries belong to the genus *Paranthropus*. They come from Kromdraai and Swartkrans and are **Paranthropus robustus** (Broom, 1938) (69). The forms from the Olduvai Gorge, Peninj, and Koobi Fora belong to **Paranthropus boisei** (Leakey, 1959). To complete this we will also include the third species found in Java, named **Paranthropus palaeojavanicus** (von Koenigswald, 1941).

An outline of the Australopithecine discoveries made so far:

Australopithecus africanus (Dart, 1925):

Sterkfontein, South Africa: four skulls, skull fragments, teeth, parts of long-bones, pelvic bones, ribs, vertebrae, and a shoulder-blade. Originally described as *Australopithecus transvaalensis* (Broom, 1936) it was changed later to *Plesianthropus transvaalensis* (Broom, 1936).

Makapansgat, South Africa: parts of skulls, teeth, parts of long-bones, pelvic bones, ver-

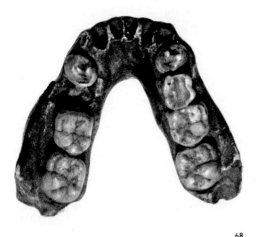

68

69

68 An incomplete lower jaw of a half-grown *Australopithecus* from Makapansgat.

69 View of the occlusal surface of teeth of a lower jaw belonging to *Paranthropus robustus*. The small canine and incisor teeth are clearly visible (after Broom and Robinson).

tebrae. Originally described as *Australopithecus prometheus* (Dart, 1948).

Garusi near Lake Eyasi: fragments of an upper jaw with teeth. Originally described as *Meganthropus africanus* (Weinert, 1939).

Omo, Ethiopia: lower jaw, teeth. Described by Howell as *Australopithecus africanus*.

Lothagam, Kenya: fragment of mandible.

Kanapoi, Kenya: fragment of humerus, *Australopithecus* sp.

Paranthropus boisei (Leakey, 1959):

Olduvai Gorge: skull with teeth. Described as *Zinjanthropus boisei* (Leakey, 1959).

Peninj, Tanzania: lower jaw with teeth.

East Rudolf: fragments of skulls with teeth.

Chesowanja, Kenya: partial skull with teeth.

Paranthropus robustus (Broom, 1938):

Kromdraai, South Africa: parts of skulls, teeth, *talus* (a small ankle bone). Described as *Paranthropus robustus* (Broom, 1938).

Taung, South Africa: juvenile skull. Originally described as *Australopithecus africanus* (Dart, 1925), now as *A. (Paranthropus) robustus* (Tobias, 1973).

Swartkrans, South Africa: skull, parts of skulls, teeth, fragments of long-bones and of the pelvis, vertebrae, a bone of the hand. Described as *Paranthropus crassidens* (Broom, 1949).

Paranthropus palaeojavanicus (von Koenigswald, 1945):

Sangiran, Java: parts of a lower jaw with teeth. Described in 1945 as *Meganthropus palaeojavanicus* (von Koenigswald).

Paranthropus sp.:

Omo, Ethiopia: numerous teeth, six lower jaws and fragments of skull. The material was originally described as *Paraustralopithecus aethiopicus* (Arambourg and Coppens, 1967), now as *Paranthropus* sp.

Homo sp. or **Homo habilis** (Leakey, Tobias, Napier, 1964):

Olduvai Gorge: mandible, cranial fragments, foot and hand bones, clavicle.

Omo, Ethiopia: numerous teeth and mandibular fragment.

East Rudolf: adult skull (1470), juvenile skull, long-bones, cranial fragments.

Swartkrans, South Africa: partial skull.

The dating procedure encountered many difficulties, and a number of changes took place

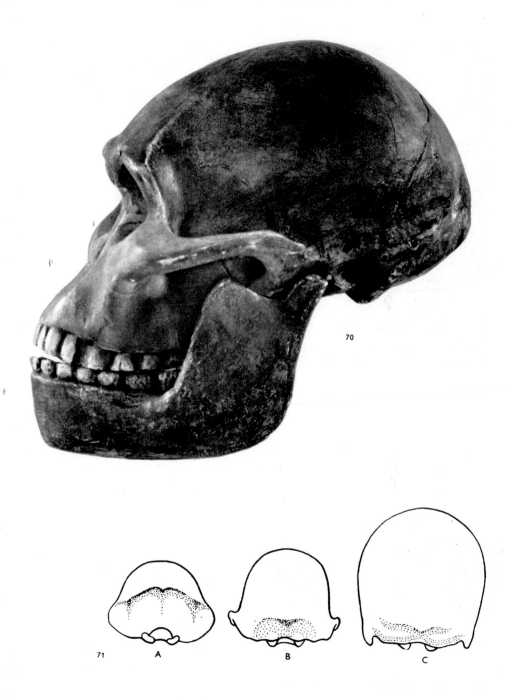

70 A reconstruction of *Australopithecus*, from a discovery made in Makapansgat, of the occipital region as well as parts of the lower jaw and the facial skeleton.

71 View of the occipital region of a skull belonging to (A) a chimpanzee, (B) *Australopithecus* from Sterkfontein, and (C) recent man (after Le Gros Clark).

57

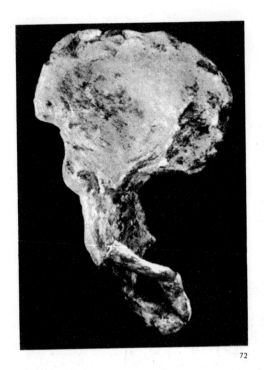

72

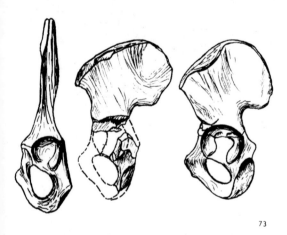

73

72 Pelvic bone of *Australopithecus* from Sterkfontein (after Broom, Robinson and Scheppers).

73 Comparison of the pelvic bones of (from left to right) the chimpanzee, *Australopithecus*, and of modern man (after Dart).

during the years. The forms which have been discussed here are mainly from the Pleistocene. The oldest finds come from Omo, Lake Rudolf, and other places in Kenya. Their radiometric age is as much as three million years. The age of South African discoveries is unknown but may extend from two to three million years. The Olduvai specimens are about 1.75 million years old, and younger. The age of the finds of *Paranthropus palaeojavanicus* from Java is guessed at about a million years. The oldest hominid fossil of this kind is the fragment of a mandible from Lothagam, Kenya. The age of this fragment may be over five million years. All the earlier mentioned discoveries are classified as **hominid,** and within the family *Hominidae* they belong to an independent sub-family called **Australopithecinae.** The second sub-family is the *Homininae* including **man** *(Homo)*.

The dentition of Australopithecines comes closest to that of man, with the *Dryopithecus*-pattern, relative dimensions of the molars, and especially the small incisors and canines, which do not project above the occlusal line. When we study the wear of the teeth-surfaces, and the joint of the jaw, we find that the Australopithecines, unlike the apes, are capable of side to side chewing. The lower jaw of the apes is a much stronger structure than man's.

The profile of the skull has a characteristically shortened face, which is more upright than that of the apes (70); the brow-ridges are quite highly developed, and the vaulted occipital part is not as spacious as man's (71). The brain was not even half the size of man's, although it was larger than that of the apes. The maximum volume of the brain-case of the large anthropoid apes is 480 cubic centimetres, the volume of the Australopithecine brain-case varies between 428 and 530 cubic centimetres, whereas present-day man's has a volume of about 1450 cubic centimetres.

It can be shown that some of the Australopithecines probably moved in an upright posture from the way the spine and skull articulate; indicated by the position of the large opening in the base of the skull, called the *foramen occipitale magnum*. The specimens of the pelvic bones, too, are similar to those of man and suggest an upright posture. The pelvis of both man and the Australopithecines is characterized by the similar hip-bone *(os ilium)*, which is connected to the muscular system of the back, as well as to the muscles leading down into the seat and legs which make the upright posture possible (72, 73). Part of the

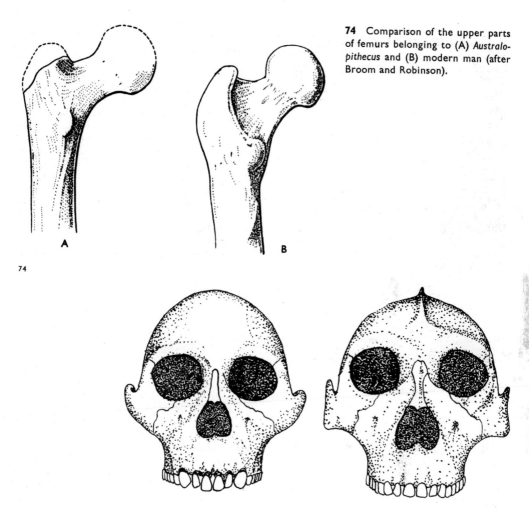

74 Comparison of the upper parts of femurs belonging to (A) *Australopithecus* and (B) modern man (after Broom and Robinson).

A

B

74

75

75 Comparison of skulls of *Australopithecus* and *Paranthropus*. The cranium of *Australopithecus* is more arched, and the face around the cheek bone is more delicate. It is noticeable that, by comparison, the canine and incisor teeth of *Paranthropus* are smaller (after Broom and Robinson).

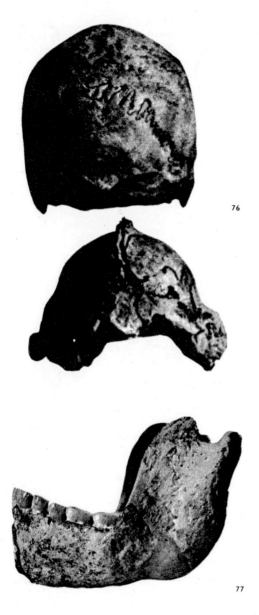

76

77

abdominal muscles begins also at the same level as the other muscles, around the hip-bone, and gives the viscera the necessary support needed for the upright posture. The Australopithecines were already walking on two legs (74).

The sub-family *Australopithecinae* can be divided into two genera, *Australopithecus* and *Paranthropus*. The anatomical, and particularly the biological, differences which exist between the two genera are of special importance, particularly the differences in the ways they lived.

Paranthropus was more robust, and his height is thought to be between 1.5 and 1.55 metres and his weight about 70 kilogrammes. Some characteristics of his long-bones indicate that his posture was not completely erect, and that he carried his head lower than *Australopithecus*.

The big toe of *Paranthropus* may have been strong, short, and widely separated from the other toes, and may have had a strong grasping function. His skull was much larger (75) and his lower jaw stronger than that of *Australopithecus*. Many individuals, particularly the males, had a clearly developed bony ridge across the cranium to which the masticatory muscles were attached (76). The construction of the strong teeth, particularly the molars, suggests that *Paranthropus*, unlike *Australopithecus*, lived on plants (77). The incisors are reduced in size, and are even smaller than man's (78). *Paranthropus* was probably a highly specialized adaptation to his surroundings at the edges of forests. Today, many people believe that *Paranthropus* is an extinct side branch in the development of man. The ages of the specimens suggest that this genus persisted for nearly three million years without any further fundamental development. The highly specialized adaptation to living in closed woodlands with a vegetarian diet leaves little room for further development.

The representatives of the genus *Australopithecus* were more gracefully slight in build; they may have been about 1.2 metres tall weighing 40 kilogrammes. They moved in a more or less erect posture on two legs, although their walk was possibly a swaying one, such as can still be seen in today's apes. The Australopithecines carried their large heads high. The dentition suggests that they were probably omnivorous, with a main diet of meat. It is possible to imagine them living in the steppe and open country, and looking for shelter in caves and rock crevices. They spent most of their time hunting, but they also seemed to understand how to get

76 Comparison of skulls belonging to *Paranthropus boisei* (below) and modern man (above). A sagittal crest is visible on the *Paranthropus* skull (after Tobias).

77 Lower jaw of *Paranthropus* from Swartkrans (after Broom and Robinson).

prey from other predators. They would wait until the prey was left unguarded, and would then take it and carry it off to their hideouts. Thus, the way of life of these two genera — *Paranthropus* and *Australopithecus* — may have been very different. The higher development was made particularly apparent when Dart discovered that the specimen found at Makapansgat could have used primitive tools (79). Many broken animal bones were found at this site, which, after carefully directed studies, Dart believed showed that they had been broken deliberately and for a purpose. *Australopithecus* may have used stones when hunting baboons, and sometimes smashed the baboon's skull to get at the brain. Most of the broken bones are long-bones from which the marrow could have been extracted. Dart also suggested that the long-bones were used as weapons and the jaw with teeth was used as a scraper. Many animal bones had such smooth appearances that they must have been used as tools (80). Dart's opponents objected by saying that the bones found in caves must have been carried there by wild animals. This seems to be unlikely because the modern large beasts of prey do not hide their prey in caves.

The stay in the open country and steppe must have had a decisive influence on the mode of life because of the great shortage of vegetarian food. If our ancestors wanted to survive they had to change and become omnivorous. This change was one of the factors determining the development of the erect posture as well as that of the hand and foot, and considerably influenced the development of the way of thinking.

More species belonging to the pre-human phase were found in Africa (81). L S B Leakey discovered more bones which could be identified as remains of forerunners of man in the Olduvai Gorge after 1960. Leakey has done intensive work in this gorge during the last fifteen years. The gorge is up to 90 metres deep and the hollow basin of the gorge has, during thousands of years, been filled with river and lake sediments, and volcanic ash (82, 83). Originally, these sediments were classified in five different beds, numbered as Beds I to V.

The most important material was found in the lowest two levels (Bed I and Bed II). The deposits of Bed I are up to 30 metres thick, which accumulated during the Lower Pleistocene, and the radiometric age of this deposit is between 1.2 and 2.1 million years. The second level (Bed II) is 18 metres to 24 metres thick

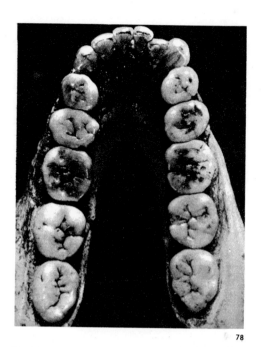

78

78 The dentition of *Paranthropus robustus*.

and dates back from between 0.5 to 1.2 or 1.3 million years ago. The Beds III to V are not as thick, and were deposited during the last 350 000 to 400 000 years.

We have already mentioned that Leakey found a skull of an individual, in the Olduvai Gorge, subsequently named *Paranthropus boisei*. This skull, which is the first one found of an East African *Australopithecus* came from Bed I. Its age was determined by the potassium-argon radiometric dating technique and is between 1.7 to 1.6 million years. Even before this discovery, several primitive but purposefully made tools were found in the Olduvai deposits which included the level from which '*Zinjanthropus*' was discovered. They were chopping tools, mostly pebbles which had been sharpened to a point with a few blows. Besides these, other tools were found which might have been used to shape bones or cut meat. The proof that these tools were made deliberately is found in the recurring types and shapes of the tools.

The tools and the way they were made were studied thoroughly, and they were called *Oldowan-Industry* (84). Initially, experts connected them with the '*Zinjanthropus*' discoveries. After this more discoveries of tools were made in lower deposits, in which no traces of '*Zinjan-*

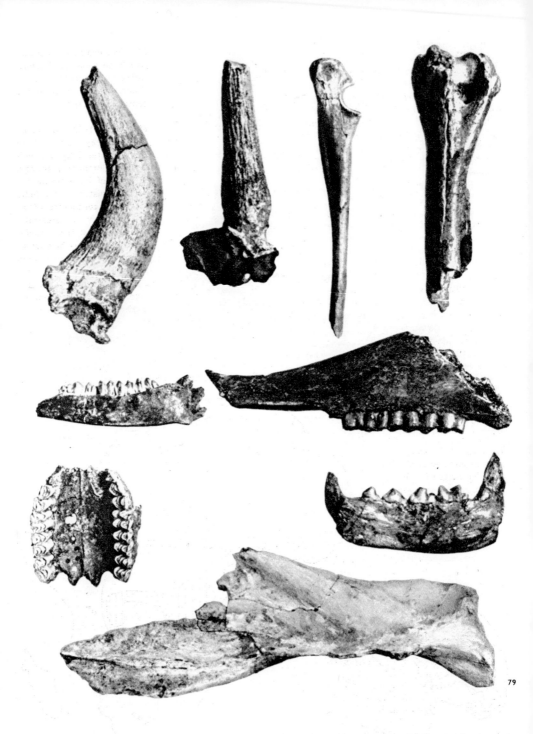

79 A selection of tools belonging to the osteo-dontokeratic culture (bone-tooth-antler culture) which was already flourishing among the Australo-pithecines from Makapansgat (after Dart).

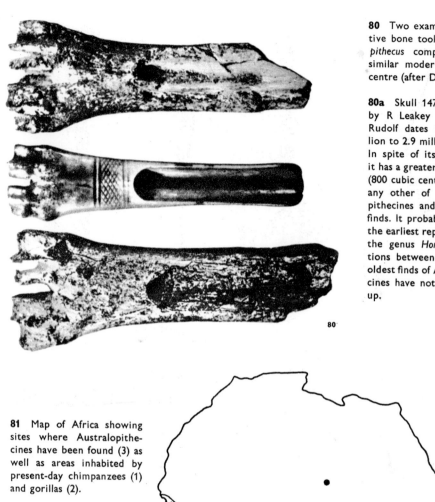

80 Two examples of primitive bone tools of *Australopithecus* compared with a similar modern tool in the centre (after Dart).

80a Skull 1470, discovered by R Leakey east of Lake Rudolf dates back 2.0 million to 2.9 million years ago. In spite of its extreme age it has a greater brain volume (800 cubic centimetres) than any other of the Australopithecines and *Homo habilis* finds. It probably belongs to the earliest representative of the genus *Homo*. The relations between this and the oldest finds of Australopithecines have not been cleared up.

80

81 Map of Africa showing sites where Australopithecines have been found (3) as well as areas inhabited by present-day chimpanzees (1) and gorillas (2).

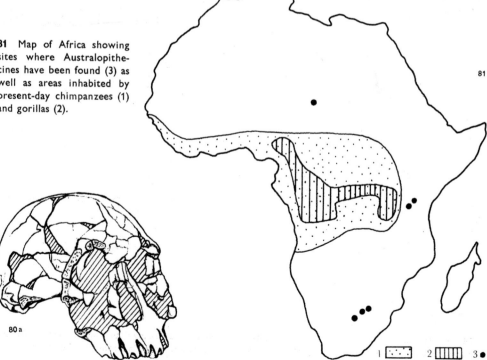

81

80 a

1 ⬚ 2 ⬚ 3 ●

82

83

82 Olduvai Gorge.

83 Layer from the Olduvai Gorge in which fossil remains were found.

thropus' could be found, and speculative explanations had to suffice.

This guessing game ended with a new and important discovery. On November 2, 1960 Jonathan Leakey, the son of Dr L S B Leakey, discovered the first signs of another hominoid. In Bed I, approximately 0.5 metres below the level from which '*Zinjanthropus*' was recovered, a jaw with two teeth, two parts of a well-preserved parietal bone *(os parietale)* (85 to 87) as well as bones of hands and feet were found. These could be distinguished immediately from the skeleton remains of '*Zinjanthropus*'. The first basic research showed that it related to a type which was nearer in the line of development to man than '*Zinjanthropus*'. It was found in an older level, and must have been older than '*Zinjanthropus*'. He was also thought to have made the tools mentioned earlier. More discoveries were made; skeletal remains of the newly discovered hominid were found also in the same level as '*Zinjanthropus*'. Altogether the

84 Two Oldowan stone axes.

85 Lower jaw belonging to *Homo habilis* from the Olduvai Gorge.

86, 87 Parietal bones of *Homo habilis* from the Olduvai Gorge.

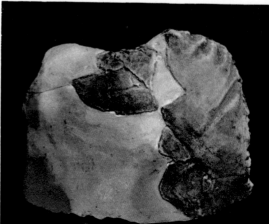

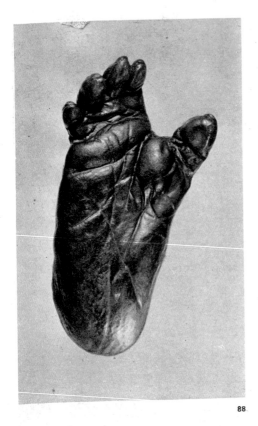

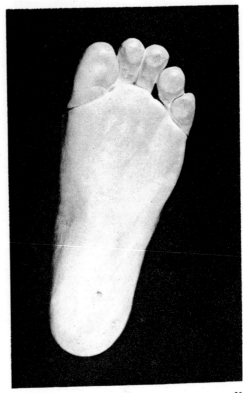

88

89

88 The foot of a gorilla.

89 Foot of modern man.

90 Skeleton of a foot belonging to *Homo habilis* from the Olduvai Gorge (after Napier).

90a Comparison of thigh bones probably belonging to the genus *Homo* and discovered east of Lake Rudolf (left) and *Australopithecus* (right). Noticeable differences appear in the shape and angle of the neck and in the cross-section of the bone. This find clearly shows that *Australopithecus* walked erect, although not to such a degree as modern man; it also proves that the figure and way of walking typical of modern man already existed in that time.

91 Hand of a gorilla.

92 Hand of modern man.

bones found came from at least six individuals.

The discoveries, which Leakey made immediately available to experts, were studied for a long time, and official reports were published in 1964.

One article published in *Nature*, which was written by three eminent anthropologists — L S B Leakey, P V Tobias and J R Napier — renamed 'Prezinjanthropus' and called him **Homo habilis.** Like *Australopithecus* he was perhaps about 1.2 to 1.25 metres tall and weighed 40 to 50 kilogrammes. The accompanying fauna suggested that he lived in open steppe country. According to the dentition he was omnivorous. His cranium is higher and noticeably rounded at the back of the head. The brain volume of *Homo habilis* is larger than that of an Australopithecine. The difference in size was not really considerable, but it played a large part in the developing phases of man. It was more important than any later physical developments. The lower jaw is lightly built. The shape of the jaw, the dental arcade, and

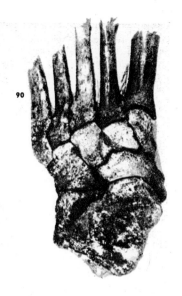

90

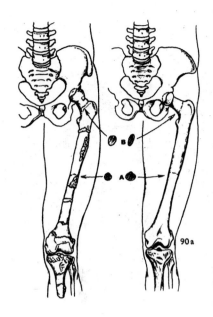

90a

91

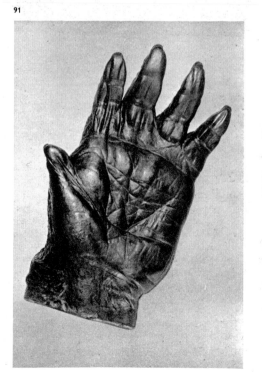

92

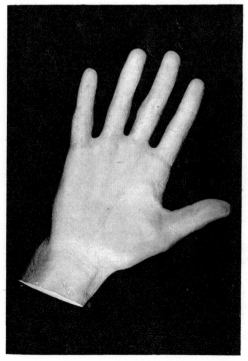

93 Skull cap which was discovered by Dubois in Java.

the separate teeth, which are smaller than the teeth of *Australopithecus*, are similar in size to those of present-day man.

The study of the bones of the foot showed two typical characteristics of man. Firstly, the big toe; this *Homo habilis* was able to move vertically. Secondly, *Homo habilis* possessed a double vault of the sole; a requirement for proper walking which the apes do not have. The human being puts his weight on the whole sole and the double vault softens the shock-waves which are produced when walking. The anthropoid apes when walking in an erect posture put the weight only on the outer side of the sole (88, 89). This showed that *Homo habilis* moved on two legs in an erect position not very different from modern man. His foot (90) was more developed than the foot of the Australopithecines.

A very important piece of evidence, in the evolution of this species is the structure of the hand. According to Dr Napier the hand of modern man is different from any of the other primates. The position of the opposable thumb and index finger is unique to man and also indicates the precision with which man can use his hand (91, 92). The position of the opposable thumb is determined by a number of anatomical characteristics of the bones, muscles, and tendons. *Homo habilis* did not have such a perfectly developed opposable thumb and index finger as man. The thumb was shorter, but he was still capable of making primitive tools. These did not require the special accuracy which was possible with the later development of the opposable thumb and index finger. Therefore, it is possible to recognize the

stages of development of the hand by the precision and method in which the tools were made. Until recently it was assumed that structurally the hand of our ancestors was like that of modern man, even before the brain reached the stage of development which could have made use of this ability. Therefore, the technical quality of the tools was supposed to be a result of improvement in the capability of thought processes and not immediately connected with the construction of the hand. The discovery of *Homo habilis* refuted this argument and confirmed the views of those who maintained that the hand could not have been built on a more advanced level than the brain which guided the work of the hands.

The stone tools found with the skeletal remains of *Homo habilis* are the most primitive of tools, and the hand of the maker must have been very similar to the hand of man. It has been suggested that *Australopithecus* used tools of natural objects of the shape right for the task. He did not make or form them, but may have used them consciously. *Homo habilis*, however, did not only use naturally shaped objects, but he was also able to adapt them for the necessary tasks. He manufactured real tools.

The radiometric dating of *Homo habilis* shows that he is between 1.6 and 1.9 million years old. He lived at the same time as *Paranthropus boisei* in the Olduvai Gorge area; the latter is known to have been a species which persisted for a long time. It is possible that other, more or less highly developed forms, existed which were closely connected with *Homo habilis*. The material available so far seems to confirm this view.

The questions concerning *Homo habilis* have not been completely solved. Some authors assume that this species could be a further developed type of *Australopithecus*, and call him **Australopithecus habilis** or simply 'advanced *Australopithecus*'. The authors holding this view, presume that it is a transitional form which lies between the Australopithecines and the further developed species known as **Homo erectus** which we will discuss later. If we can agree with this classification of *Homo habilis*, we can assume that it is the most highly developed form of this genus both morphologically and biologically. New discoveries of *Homo* in East Rudolf and Omo, however, make this question more complicated. A further stage in the development which led to *Homo sapiens* is the well-known **Pithecanthropus** which is already thought

Homo erectus modjokertensis, Java-man, was an ancient primitive form within the line of evolution of *Homo erectus*.

Homo erectus erectus, also known as *Pithecanthropus*, is a more recent form of *Homo erectus* (Z Burian).

94 *Homo erectus*: a left thigh bone found by Dubois at Trinil on Java. A pathological growth can be seen below the ball-joint (femoral head).

94

95 A reconstructed skull belonging to *Homo erectus* from the Trinil deposits from Java.

95

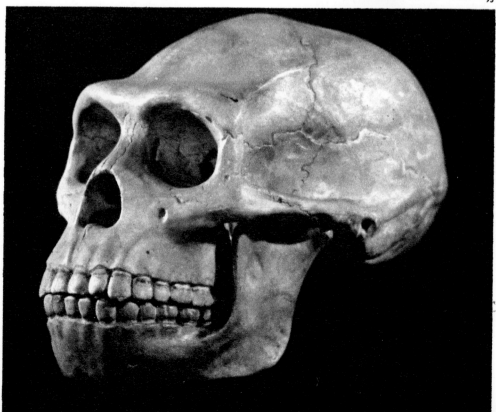

96 Skull of an infant *Homo erectus modjokertensis.*

97 Brain case of *Homo erectus erectus*, the so-called *Pithecanthropus II*, from the Trinil deposits near Sangiran on Java.

98 Reconstruction of a skull belonging to *Homo erectus modjokertensis (Pithecanthropus IV)* from the Djetis deposits on Java (after Weidenreich).

99 Site of Chou-kou-tien near Peking in China, where *Homo erectus pekinensis* was found.

96

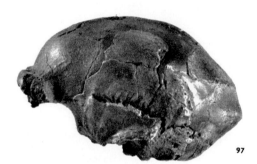

97

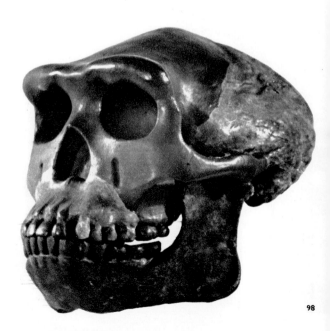

98

of as a primitive man, and is known now as *Homo erectus.*

The discovery of *Pithecanthropus* is connected with the name of the Dutch doctor and anatomist, Professor Eugene Dubois. Dubois was influenced by the natural philosopher Ernst Haeckel, who defended Darwin's theory passionately. Haeckel constructed a family tree of man on a theoretical basis in which he included the hypothetical form *Pithecanthropus alalus* ('the ape-man incapable of speech'). This form should have been the 'missing link' in the line of development between animal and man. Dubois was determined to find this 'link' and was guided by the fact that the development from ape to man must have occurred in the tropical zones, in which anthropoids still live. He visited the great Sunda-Archipelago in 1884, began to excavate and had his first success in 1891. Near Trinil, in central Java, Dubois found a right upper molar and a skull cap of an individual which he at first thought to be an anthropoid (93). A year later he discovered a complete left thigh bone (94) which, as an experienced anatomist, he recognized at once as having man-like characteristics. He compared the remains of the skull with this latest discovery and was convinced that he had found the 'missing link'. The skull cap was thick, heavy, and flattened in front, and the region above the eyes was prominent and ape-

like. The tooth, however, was positively man-like and the thigh bone produced clear evidence that this creature must have moved in an erect posture. These remains were found in deposits attributed to the Middle Pleistocene, about the same age as the second Ice Age of the northern hemisphere; but their age has recently been said to have been 700 000 years. They are called the Trinil deposits.

Dubois published a detailed account in 1894 and called his discovery **Pithecanthropus erectus,** which corresponds to Haeckel's hypothetical term 'missing link'. Since then *Pithecanthropus* also called **Java-man,** was considered to be one of the first classical discoveries of early man (95).

Like Dart, Dubois came across strong opposition. First he tried to fight this, but later he withdrew feeling very bitter and even hid his discovery from the experts. Just as his work began to be recognized, he revoked his earlier opinions. Dubois died during World War II, without being aware of his fame as the discoverer of one of the most important links in the development of man.

More than forty years passed before another trace of *Pithecanthropus* was discovered. This was attributed to the previously mentioned Dutchman of German origin, Professor von Koenigswald. He has been mentioned in connection with *Gigantopithecus* and *Meganthropus.* Von

99

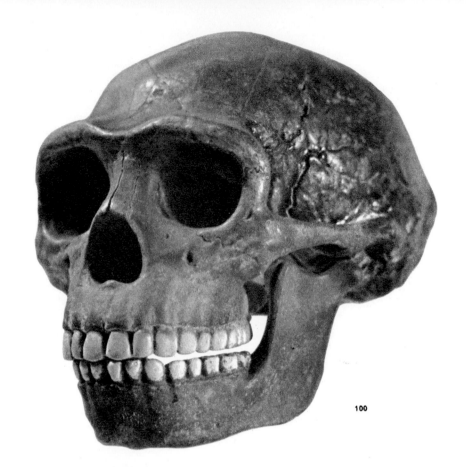

100

100 Reconstruction of a skull belonging to *Homo erectus pekinensis*.

101 Brain case of *Homo erectus pekinensis*.

101

Koenigswald discovered an infant skull at Modjokerto, west Java — near Surabaya — which he was able to identify immediately with Dubois' *Pithecanthropus* (96). This discovery was named *Homo modjokertensis*, and belonged to the genus of man, a classification which is still agreed with by experts today. The infant skull was discovered in the so-called Djetis layer and probably dates back to the period between the Lower Pleistocene and the Middle Pleistocene. The age may be about a million years. Therefore, this infant's skull is older than Dubois' *Pithecanthropus*.

Further discoveries were made; an old and forgotten discovery which Dubois had made in 1890 at Kedung Brubus, east of Trinil, came to light again. The scientist was at first not able to identify it but finally recognized it in 1924 as *Pithecanthropus*. The discovery comprised a small fragment of a lower jaw with a small piece of the root of the first premolar and partially preserved sockets of the second premolar and canine teeth.

An outline of the Pithecanthropus discoveries, in chronological order:

1890 — Dubois, Kedung Brubus, Djetis layer: part of a lower jaw (known as *Pithecanthropus A*)

1891 — Dubois, Trinil, Trinil deposits: skull cap and right upper third molar (known as *Pithecanthropus I*)

1892 — Dubois, Trinil, Trinil deposits: left thigh bone; which together with the discovery from 1891 laid the basis for the description known as *Pithecanthropus erectus* (Dubois, 1894).

1936 — von Koenigswald, Modjokerto, Djetis layer: infant calvaria, originally known as *Homo modjokertensis*, later as *Pithecanthropus modjokertensis* (von Koenigswald, 1936).

1937 — von Koenigswald, Sangiran, Djetis deposits: fragment of a lower jaw (known as *Pithecanthropus B*).

1937 — von Koenigswald, Sangiran, Trinil deposits: skull cap (known as *Pithecanthropus II*) (97).

1938 — von Koenigswald, Sangiran, Trinil deposits: incomplete calvaria (known as *Pithecanthropus III*).

1939 — von Koenigswald, Sangiran, Djetis layer: upper jaw, back of a calvaria (known as *Pithecanthropus IV*) and belonging to the species of *Pithecanthropus modjokertensis* (von Koenigswald, 1936), later re-named *Pithecanthropus robustus*

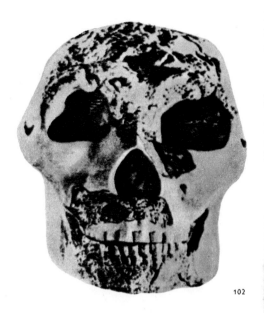

102

102 Frontal view of the skull belonging to *Homo erectus officinalis* from Lan-tian in China.

(Weidenreich, 1945). This name cannot be accepted in the sense of the modern idea of the scientific nomenclature.

More discoveries were made between 1952 and 1974. Scientists from Indonesia made three important discoveries in the Trinil deposits at Sangiran in Java. First a lower jaw was found in 1952. In 1963 followed the discovery of a sizeable fragment of a skull cap and a part of a facial skeleton, and in 1965 more extensive fragments of skulls were found. Other important finds followed: 1966 — cranial base fragments, 1968—69 — calvaria and other fragments, 1970 — numerous skull fragments, 1971 — temporal and parietal fragments. These discoveries have, as yet, not been fully evaluated.

The lengthy research of all *Pithecanthropus* discoveries led to the conclusion that they were undoubtedly man-like skeletons which all belonged to one genus *Homo* and they were described as **Homo erectus** (Dubois, 1894). This **'early man'** was about 1.65 to 1.75 metres tall. The structure of his thigh bone is exactly the same as that of modern man and proves that he had an erect posture when walking.

103

103 Stone tools used by *Homo erectus pekinensis*
from Chou-kou-tien.

Homo erectus did not differ from today's man in the way he moved. This fact is reinforced by the position of the occipital opening at the base of the skull *(foramen occipitale magnum)*. Compared to Australopithecine's the skull itself is more robust. The supraorbital ridge is big and the skull has a more flattened forehead as well as a protruding mouth. The lower jaw is not so high as modern man's but longer. Apart from a few differences in the relative size of the molars, the teeth have a positively human-like appearance. The canines are hardly stronger than in modern man. The upper jaw however, shows just as in the apes, a 4 millimetre wide gap *(diastema)* between the incisors and canines into which the lower canine fits when the jaws are closed. Not even the Australopithecines have this characteristic. The gap was not present in all members of *Homo erectus*. It is possible that this is a secondary sexual characteristic, but it might also be that the teeth in the larger jaws had enough room and did not grow immediately next to one another. These dentitions provided *Homo erectus* with the most powerful set of chewing teeth ever known.

The heavy skull could only have been supported by very strong neck muscles. Proof that these muscles must have been powerful, is shown by the strong bony structures which are at the back of the skull. *Pithecanthropus* must have been a strong, powerful creature. His brain was larger than that of the Australopi-

thecines. Java-man is placed between *Australopithecus* and modern man. The volume of the skull varies from find to find but in general larger differences occur between the forms found in the Djetis and the Trinil layers. *Pithecanthropus I* and *Pithecanthropus II*, from the Trinil deposits, had skull capacities of 900 cubic centimetres and 775 cubic centimetres respectively. The average brain size is 883 cubic centimetres. It was not possible to work out the volume of the skull of any of the older Djetis discoveries except for *Pithecanthropus IV*, and this has the lowest capacity of only 750 cubic centimetres.

Professor Weidenreich recognized the differences between the form of *Pithecanthropus* found in the Djetis and Trinil layers, and described man from the Djetis layers as being the oldest form. The overall differences only came to light during more recent research carried out by von Koenigswald. According to this, 'Djetis-man' was more robust, his skull heavier, and his massive jaws were much more accentuated than in 'Trinil-man'. The supraorbital region was of considerable thickness, the forehead and chin were strongly receding (98). If we then take into consideration that the Djetis

104 This oil painting by Z Burian shows an impression of what *Homo erectus erectus* might have looked like.

105 Geological section of the sand-pit at Mauer near Heidelberg. The white cross on the right-hand side of the picture shows the site at which the lower jaw of *Homo erectus heidelbergensis* was found (after Schoetensack).

discoveries are older, we can only come to the conclusion that 'Djetis-man' developed earlier than 'Trinil-man': on the other hand, the differences are not that important and have not led to two separate classifications. Both can probably be seen as sub-species which followed one another in chronological order, within which the discovery of *Homo erectus modjokertensis* (von Koenigswald, 1936) represents one of the older forms, whereas the typical *Homo erectus erectus* (Dubois, 1894) is a representative of a more recent form.

The story of *Pithecanthropus* from Java was continued in China. Many names of eminent scientists appear in connection with the Chinese discoveries: J G Anderson and B Bohlin from Sweden, O Zdansky from Austria as well as Davidson Black, F Weidenreich, and W C Pei.

It all began in the year 1900 and centred around the Chinese 'drugstores'. Among the 'dragon teeth' sold there, which already played a large part in the discovery of *Gigantopithecus*, another 'man-like' tooth was found. But the site at which this tooth was probably found was only discovered years later. It was a cave near Chou-kou-tien, about 40 kilometres southwest of Peking (99). Anderson, Zdansky, and Bohlin found several teeth during the years 1918 and 1927 at this site. The last lower molar was sent to Professor Black at the Medical College in Peking for inspection. Professor Black described him as belonging to a new primitive species close to the Java *Pithecanthropus*. He called it **Sinanthropus pekinensis** (Black 1927), but it is also well known as Peking-man (100). New excavations which were undertaken by Black and later by Weidenreich and Pei and new discoveries showed Black to be right. Chou-kou-tien had obviously housed a group of early men. Until 1937 when the Japanese invaded China, many skeletal remains, mainly teeth, of over 30 Peking-man males, females, and children were found in this area (101). These remains are probably somewhat younger than those of Java-man found in the Trinil deposits and may belong to a later phase in the Middle Pleistocene. Their actual age is not known, but it is thought to be between 500 000 and 400 000 years, and the correct name is **Homo erectus pekinensis** (Black, 1927). This early man from China was the third sub-species of *Homo erectus* and very similar to *Pithecanthropus*.

Unfortunately, the whole of the *Sinanthropus* collection has been lost. One of the stories

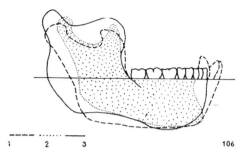

106 Comparison of lower jaws belonging to modern man (2) and *Homo erectus heidelbergensis* (3) with that of a chimpanzee (1).

107 The lower jaw of *Homo erectus heidelbergensis* with markedly wide and massive ascending branch.

claims that the collection was sunk by the Japanese while it was being transported to America; while the other, more probable version, states that the collection was destroyed by Japanese soldiers before it left the mainland. After the war, an extensive search was made by the Americans, Chinese, and Japanese without success. The *Sinanthropus* discoveries exist now only in perfect casts which have fortunately been preserved, together with a detailed scientific description perfectly documented by Professor Weidenreich. There is also some hope that the site at Chou-kou-tien might yield further material, because it has not been fully exhausted.

The Chinese Academy of Science began a new research programme under the supervision of Professor Pei. There are few reports coming from China, but it is known that there has already been some success. Teeth and skull fragments have been found, and perhaps it will be possible in time to replace at least a part of what has been lost.

The *Sinanthropus* discoveries have been evaluated using the latest methods, and have been carefully compared with material from other sites. The body structure of *Homo erectus pekinensis* was similar to that of Java-man. His posture was erect and not significantly smaller; per-

108 This oil painting by Z Burian gives an impression of what *Homo erectus heidelbergensis* might have looked like.

109 A view of the site at Vertésszöllös in Hungary, a settlement of *Homo erectus*.

108

109

haps about 1.55 to 1.60 metres tall. The skulls showed certain differences. Peking-man had a strong skull with a thick brow-ridge, but the occipital muscle tuberosities in the lower part of the occipital bone were weaker. Therefore, *Sinanthropus* could not have been as strong as Java-man.

The lower jaw of *Homo erectus pekinesis* was a little lighter, but the most noticeable difference was the volume of the skull. Three skulls out of four, which had been accurately measured, exceeded 1000 cubic centimetres. Two male skulls measured 1220 cubic centimetres and 1100 cubic centimetres; the third, a female skull measured 1050 cubic centimetres but the fourth, also a female skull, only had a volume of 850 cubic centimetres. The average has been estimated as 1055 cubic centimetres, which is 172 cubic centimetres more than the average assessment of the volume of *Homo erectus erectus* from the Trinil layers and 300 cubic centimetres more than *Homo erectus modjokertensis* from the Djetis layer. Peking-man was already further developed than Java-man.

Another form of *Homo erectus* came to light

through the treasures of teeth found in Chinese drugstores. Among them, Professor von Koenigswald discovered several human teeth which were just like teeth found in Chou-kou-tien, but a little larger. From the evidence of these teeth a new species was described and given the name *Sinanthropus officinalis*. But it was never discovered where these teeth came from. Chinese scientists have recently mentioned another discovery which could be connected with von Koenigswald's *Sinanthropus*. In Chen-chia-wo near the town of Lan-tian in the province of Shen-si a well-preserved lower jaw belonging to a primitive form of man was found in 1963, and only a year later a facial skeleton, a tooth, and a cranium of the same type were found 20 kilometres away near Kung-wang-ling. Both discoveries are believed to be older than those from Chou-kou-tien; their age may be similar to discoveries from the Djetis layer (Java) that is, about a million years. The lower jaw of Lan-tian-man is heavier than the jaw of *Homo erectus pekinensis* and is similar to that of Java-man from the Djetis layers; his skull, too, is more powerful.

The reconstruction made by von Koenigswald showed the skull to be flattened and the brow ridge very prominent. The forehead was only faintly arched. Dr Woo, a Chinese scholar, calculated the volume of the brain cavity as 780 cubic centimetres, which is close to that of Java-man from the Djetis layers which is 750 cubic centimetres. It seems that two forms of development existed consecutively both in Java and China. *Homo erectus modjokertensis* was the predecessor of *Homo erectus erectus* in Java, whereas in China *Homo erectus pekinensis* followed Lan-tian-man, who is today known as *Homo erectus lantianensis* (von Koenigswald, 1952) (102).

Early men from Java, China, and Lan-tian had very similar ways of life. Their dentitions indicated that they were omnivorous like the other hominids. This was confirmed by the remains of animal bones and fruit which were found in their living sites. The men from China used tools made of stone which had been shaped in a primitive way so that they could be used to split objects, to chop, and to scrape (103). These tools were preserved and found in the same deposits as the skeletal remains at Chou-kou-tien (104). The sites in China offered further important evidence about the way of life our ancestors led. It was discovered that some of the skulls, belonging to *Homo erectus pekinensis*, were deliberately broken. It can be concluded that Peking-man was a cannibal. There is similar evidence of this kind in Java, and we can assume that Java-man too had cannibalistic habits. The site at Chou-kou-tien is of particular interest because the cave deposits contained clear evidence of the use of fire. It can be assumed that Java-men also knew how to use fire. This first evidence of fire created a sensation, not only because it was the oldest domestic fire but also because it was so big. The ash layer reached a thickness of six metres which indicated that early men were unsure about lighting a fire, and kept it burning. He must have taken the fire from a natural source and introduced it to his cave. It is hard to imagine the generations of early man who must have tended the fire and made sure that it never went out. It is certain that the use of fire has hastened the development of man and played an important role in furthering his intelligence as well as enabling a higher standard of living.

It has been thought that Java- and Peking-men lived in tribes. The tribes were probably about the same size as the present-day groups of apes and the bands of primitive hunters. We can assume, perhaps, that a *Pithecanthropus* tribe comprised three to six adult men, six to ten adult females and 15 to 20 children of varying ages. Therefore, the group may have consisted of about 30 individuals. Living in a group demands a certain amount of communication. Early man probably began to develop a language with quite a large vocabulary. It was particularly necessary to communicate during hunting, fighting, and any other activities where specific tasks had to be delegated. The process of development in speech manifests itself in the structural changes of the lower jaw. The lower jaw became more refined, the chin receded, and the points of attachment for the tongue muscles became enlarged. *Homo erectus* could not have been fully articulate, but he was able to put his thoughts into words in a similar way to modern man.

Java and Chou-kou-tien were the first sites at which *Homo erectus* was found. Later trails led to Africa and even to Europe. The first European discovery came from the Mauer sand-pit near Heidelberg. On October 20, 1907 a perfect fossil jaw was found in a sand-pit and called '**Heidelberg lower jaw**' or '**Lower jaw from Mauer**' (105). The jaw was described by Professor Schoetensack in 1908, and the species was named **Homo heidelbergensis** (Schoetensack, 1908). The discovery dates back to the Middle Pleistocene but its exact age is unknown. The mandible is large and robust with strong teeth; it was in good condition when it was found. The width of the mandible of modern man is a maximum of 15 centimetres whereas the lower jaw from Mauer is 23.5 centimetres wide. The ascending branch of the jaw *(ramus manibulae)*, which carries the articular process *(processus articularis)* and the muscular process *(processus muscularis)* is comparatively short and very broad. The height of the ascending branch is 66 millimetres and its width 60 millimetres. The corresponding measurements of modern man are 58 to 60 millimetres and 33 to 35 millimetres (106). The chin receded as with Java- and Peking-man and forms a blunt angle of more than 100°; in modern man it is about 70°. The teeth of Heidelberg-man have man-like characteristics; in particular, that the canines do not rise above the other teeth (107).

All these characteristics of the mandible lead to the conclusion that Heidelberg-man must have been similar to the Djetis-type of

110 View of the archaeological excavation at Vertésszöllës in Hungary showing a layer of fossil bones.

Java-man both in the structure of his body and in his appearance (108). The way he lived must have been similar too. The stone tools found in the same layers of the Mauer sandpit were even more primitive than those of Chou-kou-tien. The German discoverer of these tools, A Rust, classifies them as examples of the most primitive Abbevillian culture.

Another European discovery was made in 1965 at Vertésszöllös near Budapest in Hungary (109, 110). Dr Laszló Vertés found several isolated molars and an occipital bone *(os occipitale)* of man (111). Compared to the Heidelberg lower jaw a further development can be seen, and could put the owner possibly on a similar level as men from the Chou-kou-tien site. The full evaluation of the discovery has not yet been concluded. Its age is about 600 000 years. The scientific name of this early man is **Homo erectus palaeohungaricus** (Thoma, 1966). During the last few years other discoveries of *Homo erectus* were made at a site in Přezletice near Prague. In 1968 a small fragment of a molar was found there, which Fejfar described temporarily in the same year as a fragment of a first or second left molar of the lower jaw. It is undoubtedly a human tooth, and tools have been found at the same place. The most impressive thing is the age of this discovery. The fauna discovered at this site shows that it dates back to the Lower Pleistocene, which means that it is older than the discoveries made at Mauer. But definite conclusions have not been drawn yet. If further discoveries were to be made confirming the existence of man at this site, Přezletice would become the site of the most ancient man in Europe. Another promising site is Stránská skála near Brno where excavations are now taking place (112 to 115).

Discoveries which confirm the existence of *Homo erectus* in Africa, come from the northern parts of this continent. In 1954 and 1955 at a site south-east of Oran near Ternifine, three lower jaws were found, one of which was almost complete, as well as a parietal bone. The parietal bone belonged to a young individual and is similar to the comparable discoveries made at Chou-kou-tien. The mandibles, though large, are not as strong as those of Djetis-, Lantian-, and Heidelberg-men. The same applies to the teeth, which are similar in shape and size to those of Java-men from the Trinil layers (116). The Ternifine find is dated from the Middle Pleistocene.

According to the age and structure of the skeletal remains this must be a form of *Homo erectus*. The archaeological finds belong to the Abbevillian-Acheulean culture and mean that this discovery belongs to an advanced stage in man's development (117, 118). Professor Arambourg, the discoverer of the Ternifine site, called this species *Atlanthropus mauritanicus*. Later, however, it was assigned to the group *Homo*

111

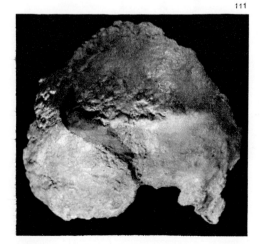

111 Occipital bone of *Homo erectus palaeohungaricus* from Vertésszöllös in Hungary.

112 Stránská skála near Brno (Czechoslovakia) where *Homo erectus* has been found. The excavations have not been completed but so far bone and stone tools have been found.

erectus and is now known as **Homo erectus mauritanicus** (Arambourg, 1954).

Another important discovery comes from Swartkrans in South Africa, from the same deposits in which *Paranthropus* was found. The age is estimated to be about a million years, which may be approximately the same age as the Djetis layers. Professor Broom and the experienced palaeoanthropologist Dr J T Robinson both took part in the excavations. They discovered a more or less complete lower jaw, with three molars on the left side, but only the second and third ones on the right side; as well as fragments of the upper jaw. Broom and Robinson described this form in 1949 as *Telanthropus capensis*. The fragments of the upper jaw suggest that the structure of the facial skeleton must have been similar to that of Java-man. The lower jaw is as powerful as the jaw of Djetis- and Heidelberg-man. Robinson later placed the specimen in the species *Homo erectus*. Its full scientific name is **Homo erectus capensis**.

Homo erectus was also found in the Olduvai Gorge, which seemed to be the goldmine of palaeoanthropology. It was again Dr L S B Leakey and his wife who, one month after the discovery of *Homo habilis*, found a well-preserved skull without a facial skeleton in the upper layers of Bed II. Its structure left no doubt that it was connected to Java- and Peking-man. The discovery included the typ-ical tools belonging to the Abbevillian (Chellean) culture which further confirmed the dating and classification.

The skull has a powerful brow-ridge, and its volume is about 1000 cubic centimetres, from which we deduce that he is connected to the more advanced type of Peking-man (119). Professor Heberer named him *Homo leakeyi*, in honour of his famous discoverer. According to today's standards, however, the scientific name is **Homo erectus leakeyi** (Heberer, 1963).

Another discovery belonged, until recently, to the group of *Homo erectus*. It concerns skull fragments discovered in Lake Eyasi (Tanzania) during the period 1935 to 1938. Professor Weinert described the material and named this species *Africanthropus njarasensis*. But the classification and dating are not completely worked out. It is probably a more recent individual, and the first dating of 250 000 years has been reduced to approximately 40 000 years (Howells, 1967). Most of the experts, however, are convinced that it is an advanced form of man.

We have reached the end of our short accounts and descriptions of the *Homo erectus* discoveries. The known forms can be put into two groups. The first group would include the more primitive forms of approximately a million years old. *Homo erectus modjokertensis* from the Djetis layers in Java, *Homo erectus lantianensis* from Lan-tian in China, *Homo erectus*

113–115 Stone tools belonging to *Homo erectus* from the site of Stránská skála near Brno, Czechoslovakia.

capensis from Swartkrans and *Homo erectus heidelbergensis* from Mauer in Germany belong to this first group. More recent and further advanced species are included in the second group. Their ages range from about 700 000 to 500 000 years. These include *Homo erectus erectus* from the Trinil deposits of Java, *Homo erectus pekinensis* from Chou-kou-tien in China, *Homo erectus mauritanicus* from Ternifine in North Africa, *Homo erectus leakeyi* from the Olduvai Gorge in East Africa and *Homo erectus palaeohungaricus* from Vertésszöllös in Hungary.

This phase in the development of early man — the emergence of the group of *Homo erectus* — is undoubtedly one of the most important developments. Early man is the direct ancestor of these species. At first glance they appear quite different, but a close study of their structure and build, their way of life and culture, shows that they belong to the same lineage as present-day man.

Thus, the oldest forms of **Homo sapiens** are directly connected with **Homo erectus**. They come from all parts of the world, and various geological horizons. They also differ considerably, from a morphological point of view. This leads to controversies in which scientists differ as to where a species belongs and at what level it appears in the family tree of man.

Species which are classed today with *Homo sapiens* were first discovered before 1891—92 when Professor Dubois discovered the first signs of *Homo erectus*. In 1848 a very old manlike skull was found in the fortifications of Gibraltar. The skull was handed over to Lieutenant Flint, who in turn passed it on to experts. But the importance of this find was not recognized at this time and was only later appreciated by the experts. This was brought about by a scientific discussion regarding another discovery, which has since become very famous. A discovery was made at Neanderthal — a valley near Düsseldorf — of fragments of a skull and skeleton. These fragments were found in 1856 by workers in a cave filled in with clay. Later they came into the possession of C Fuhlrott (120). Unfortunately, it was not possible to determine the original horizons from which these bones came, nor was it possible to reconstruct the way in which they lay. Meanwhile, the experts became very interested and arguments abounded. Only a few experts recognized all the implications of this incredible discovery of Neanderthal fragments. Thomas H Huxley dared to contradict the eminent

Neanderthal-man represents one stage of development in the ancestral line of man (Z Burian).

Neanderthals from Krapina were undoubtedly cannibals (Z Burian).

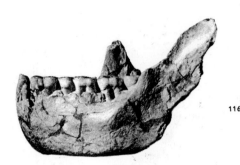

and famous anatomist and anthropologist Professor Rudolf von Virchow. Virchow maintained that these remains of Neanderthal-man belonged to a feeble-minded being. Virchow said that this could be deduced by the pathological characteristic visible on the skull. These and other arguments continued over many years, and only through further discoveries which showed the same characteristics was it eventually agreed that these remains belonged to the ancestors of modern man.

More and more discoveries of Neanderthal-man were made during the next decades. There are some differences between various discoveries, but the name **Neanderthal-man** has always been used. There have been so many discoveries that it would be impossible to list and discuss them all here. Therefore, we have decided to mention only the most important in order to show the connection between Neanderthal-man and *Homo erectus*.

The discoveries show that the transitional stages between *Homo erectus* and this primitive species of *Homo sapiens* covered a wide area, and over a long period of time he adapted to different conditions. This can be seen by the fact that the Neanderthal discoveries from different areas show different characteristics, some of which are very like **Homo sapiens**.

Two female skulls are among the oldest

116 Lower jaw of *Homo erectus mauretanicus* from Ternifine, Algeria (after Arambourg).

117 Simple stone tool from the North African Acheulean culture.

118 Acheulean hand-axe from Sbaika, North Africa.

119 A skull cap found in the Olduvai Gorge, which has been described as *Homo erectus leakeyi* (after L S B Leakey).

120 C Fuhlrott, the discoverer of Neanderthal--man (after Packenberg).

120

finds: the first and nearly complete skull was found by Berckhemer in 1933 at Steinheim in Germany; the second was put together from parietal and occipital bones found in 1935, 1936, and 1955 in Swanscombe in Kent (121, 122). Both skulls come from the second interglacial period and their age is about 250 000 to 300 000. Unfortunately, no lower jaws or even parts of lower jaws could be found for either skull. A lower jaw (123) was, however, discovered at Montmaurin in France in 1949 and its shape suggests that this jaw belongs to the same species as the skulls from Swanscombe and Steinheim. This material made it possible to reconstruct this early type and determine the characteristics of early *Homo sapiens*.

The brain-case is quite small but vaulted. The forehead, which was low and receding in early man, is now far more arched than the forehead of *Homo erectus*. The prominent brow-ridge is a noticeable characteristic and is similar to that of Peking-man, *Homo erectus pekinensis*. Steinheim skull has a well-rounded occipital and its facial skeleton is vertical. The lower jaw (as shown by the discovery at Montmaurin) with its ascending branch is similar to the lower jaw of *Homo erectus heidelbergensis* found at Mauer. The chin protrudes further, however, and the third lower molar is larger than the first and second molars. Everyone believes that this is a primitive characteristic. The capacity of the skull is fairly small — only a little more than that of some of the later finds of *Homo erectus* (for example, *Homo erectus pekinensis*).

121 The occipital and parietal bones found in Swanscombe, England. This belongs to an early *Homo sapiens*.

122 A skull which was discovered in Steinheim by Berckhemer. It belongs to one of the oldest forms of *Homo sapiens*.

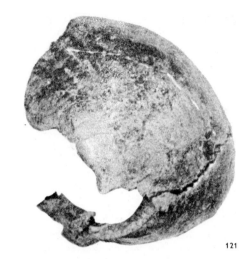

121

122

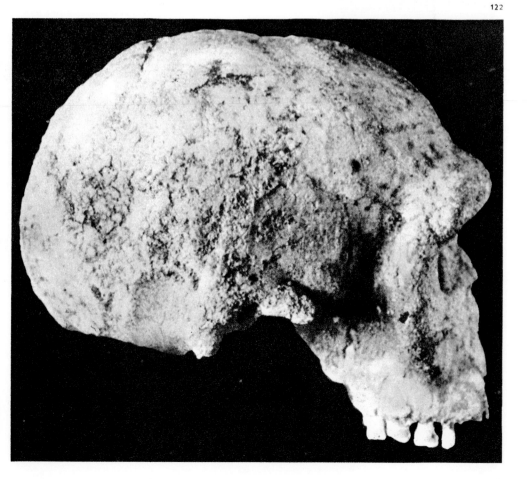

123

The capacity of the Steinheim skull is about 1150 cubic centimetres (Howells, 1967), and the Swanscombe skull is between 1250 and 1300 cubic centimetres.

As already mentioned, these discoveries date from the second interglacial period. The climate then was mild as the fauna found in these deposits indicates. In addition to the remains of bones, these sites also yielded tools of the Acheulean culture.

The early man found at Steinheim, Swanscombe, and Montmaurin was not identical to Neanderthal-man. Nevertheless, it was described as the Steinheim-Neanderthal for a considerable time. Today, it is generally known as Steinheim- or Swanscombe-man but its scientific description is **Homo sapiens steinheimensis** (Berckhemer, 1934). There is also an important new discovery of a facial skeleton from the Arago Cave in the Pyrenees (124), belonging to a similar type but showing more robust character of a male's skull.

Then at the beginning of the last Riss-Würm interglacial phase the true neanderthal form appeared; it belonged to the group of **Homo sapiens neanderthalensis** (King, 1864) which is the scientific name for the world-famous discovery in Neanderthal which was made more than 100 years ago.

From more recent research is has become increasingly obvious that there are two lines of development; one is called the 'early Neanderthal' or '*Preneanderthal*' the other 'extreme' or 'classic Neanderthal'.

The early Neanderthal type comes from the warm Riss-Würm interglacial phase and lived about 150 000 years ago. The most important discoveries of this phase of development come from Ehringsdorf near Weimar in Germany (125), and from Saccopastore near Rome (126). Skulls have a flattened facial skeleton with an occiput similar to those of the Steinheim skull. The brow-ridge is moderate, the forehead is slightly more arched, and the dentitions show less primitive features. The third molar is no larger than the first and second molars. The capacity of the skull found at Ehringsdorf (Germany) is between 1400 cubic centimetres and 1450 cubic centimetres as in modern man whose skull capacity is usually between 1350 and 1500 cubic centimetres. The female skull found at Saccopastore, however, had only a low capacity of about 1200 cubic centimetres. In this respect there is little difference between this skull and the Steinheim skull whereas the Swanscombe skull had an even larger cubic

123 A lower jaw found in Montmaurin, France. Together with the discoveries from Steinheim and Swanscombe, this probably belongs to one of the earliest forms of *Homo sapiens*.

124 A skull from Tautavel, the Arago cave in the French Pyrenees. It is nearly 200 000 years old and the morphology of the facial skeleton suggests that it belongs to one of the oldest forms of *Homo sapiens neanderthalensis* (after de Lumley).

124

capacity. One other interesting discovery comes from travertine deposits at Gánovce, Czechoslovakia; it is an endocranial cast from the beginning of the warm Riss-Würm interglacial phase (127, 128). It belonged to one of the most primitive Neanderthal-men in Europe.

The discoveries of 'classic' Neanderthals come from the last glacial period — the so-called Würm Glaciation. What is known of the age of the 'classic' Neanderthal indicates that he must have appeared 80 000 years ago and remained for a long time, because traces can still be found as little as 35 000 years ago. The very first Neanderthal-man discovered belongs to this 'classic' group. The earliest skull of Neanderthal-man was found in Gibraltar (129). Other discoveries came from La Chapelle-aux-Saints, Le Moustier, La Ferrassie, La Quina (130 to 134) and Arcy-sur-Cure in France, from the Island of Jersey, from Spy sur l'Orneau and La Naulette in Belgium, from Bañolas in Spain and the Guattari Cave on Monte Circeo near Rome in Italy.

If we compare early Neanderthal-man with the 'classic' type it is clearly seen that the latter has a prominent brow-ridge, a low forehead, broad nose and powerful molars with large pulp cavities. The back of the head has a chignon or bun-like swelling with a bony ridge running across it. The chin is either missing altogether or only weakly represented. The capacity of the skull is remarkable, however; it is not only larger than the capacity of the early Neanderthal-man, but often larger than that of modern man. The capacity is between 1350 and 1700 cubic centimetres with the average at about 1400 to 1450 cubic centimetres. This is the average capacity of the skull of modern man. At some sites, as well as skulls, other fragments of bone were found (135). These parts of skeletons gave scientists the opportunity to determine what 'classic' Neanderthal-man looked like. He must have been strong, and well-built, but fairly small at about 1.55 to 1.65 metres tall. In comparison to modern man the lower limbs were shorter, and the thigh bones were slightly arched (136), a characteristic which does not appear in either modern man or *Homo erectus* (137).

Skeletal finds of 'classic' Neanderthal-man were often accompanied by tools showing a rich Mousterian culture.

Sites where 'classic' Neanderthal-man was found in Europe show that he lived during the Würm Glaciation. Unlike the earlier Neander-

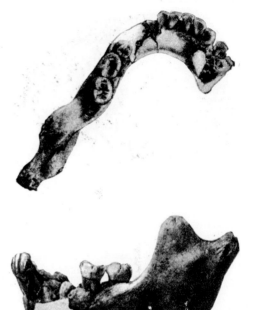

125

125 Lower jaw of a young Neanderthal-man from Ehringsdorf near Weimar, Germany (after Virchow).

126 Frontal view of an early Neanderthal skull from Saccopastore near Rome, Italy (after Sergi).

126

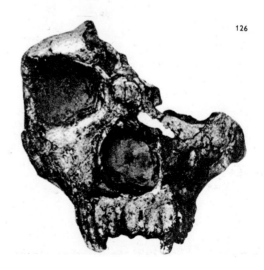

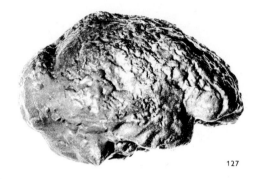

127 Endocranial cast of an early Neanderthal-man from Gánovce, Czechoslovakia.

128 The travertine hill at Gánovce, Czechoslovakia, another site of Neanderthal-man.

129 The site in Gibraltar where the very first discoveries of Neanderthal-man were made.

127

128

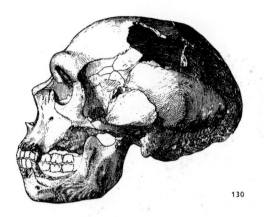

130

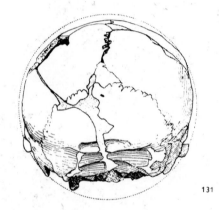

131

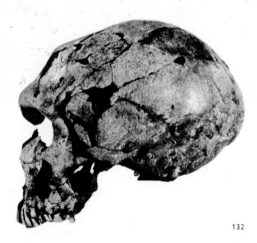

132

thal-man this 'classic' type existed in a rough and cold climate.

We are left with two important questions. First, what are the genetic connections between these two types of Neanderthal-man? And second, at what stage do they appear in man's ancestral family tree? The experts have not been able to reach any definite conclusions and these questions cannot be answered fully.

The early type of Neanderthal-man, found at Ehringsdorf and Saccopastore, seems to be connected to *Homo sapiens steinheimensis*, whom we believe was found at Steinheim, Swanscombe, Montmaurin, and Arago Cave. The genetic connection between early Neaderthal-man and the Steinheim skull can be suggested by an examination of the structure of the skulls. Preneanderthal-man shows several *sapiens*-like characteristics which suggest that there is a continuous line of evolution to the later types, which belong to the basic structure of modern man. This type appears for the first time in the middle of the Würm Glacial phase and is called **Homo sapiens sapiens** (Linnaeus, 1758). The remains of early Neanderthal-man skeletons also point to genetic connections with the 'classic' form. Therefore, it is possible to assume that early Neanderthal-man might be the ancestor of both modern man, *Homo sapiens*, as well as of the 'classic' Neanderthals. 'Classic' Neanderthal-man reached his acme during the last Würm Glaciation, and modern research shows that he had adapted to the climatic conditions of the Ice Age (Hemmer, 1967). It is, of course, not impossible with regard to the lines of development of early Neanderthal-man, that one line led to 'classic' Neanderthal-man and another to modern man. This theory is strengthened by the fact that certain blade-like tools, characteristic of later cultures of *Homo sapiens sapiens*, have been found in parts of central Europe and the Near East, together with the usual stone tools of 'classic' Neanderthal-man. In addition, some

130 Drawing of 'classic' Neanderthal skull from La Chapelle-aux-Saints, France (after Boule).

131 Rear view of the skull from La Chapelle-aux--Saints, which can be distinguished by the characteristic circular outline of 'classic' Neanderthal--man.

132 Skull from La Ferrassie.

Footprint of a Neanderthal-man from a cave in northern Italy.

Cast from the footprint of a Neanderthal-man. Northern Italy.

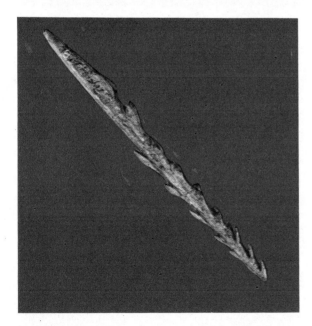

Neanderthal lower jaw from the Hortus cave, France.

Magdalenian harpoon with three rows of points from the Pekárna cave, Moravia, Czechoslovakia.

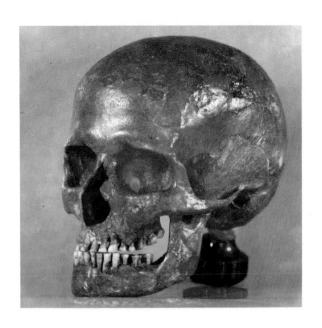

Woman's skull stained with red ochre from a Pavlovian burial at Dolní Věstonice, Moravia, Czechoslovakia.

Lower jaw from a Pavlovian burial at Dolní Věstonice, Moravia, Czechoslovakia. The bone on the left has been deformed due to arthritis.

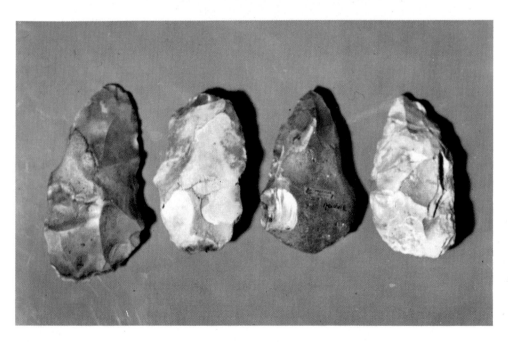

Three large ancient stone tools from inner Arnhem Land, northern Australia.

Hand-axes of the Abbevillian culture found at the French site of Abbeville.

133 The site of Le Moustier (France), after which the Mousterian culture of the western European Neanderthal-man was named (after Eppel).

134

135

136

bones show intermediate characteristics which present the experts with difficulties when trying to classify these bones according to this or that type.

Discoveries of Neanderthal-man in southern Europe, as well as some outside Europe, are of interest, particularly the discovery made in 1899 in the so-called 'cannibal cave' at a little town called Krapina near Zagreb in Yugoslavia. Some of these remains (138) seem to be more like early Neanderthal-man, although they also show characteristics belonging to the classical prehistoric man. The Neanderthal-man from Krapina lived around the turn of the last interglacial phase and the last Glaciation; he could have been at the source of the development leading to 'classic' Neanderthal-man.

Other interesting discoveries have been made in Morocco. One site at Temara near Rabat was discovered in 1958, another at Djebel Irhoud was discovered in 1962, and a third at Haua Fteah in the Cyrenaica was discovered between 1952 and 1954. All the remains found on these sites have been dated within the period of 'classic' Neanderthal-man. There are also some morphological traces which would confirm this.

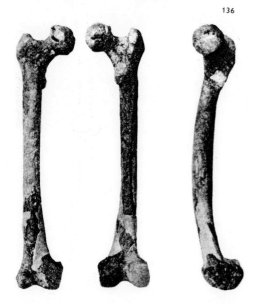

134 A skull from La Quina, which was discovered by H Martin. It belongs to the 'classic' Neanderthal--man from western Europe.

135 Skeleton of a foot belonging to Neanderthal--man from the cave in La Ferrassie (after Boule).

136 Thigh bones of 'classic' Neanderthal-man from La Chapelle-aux-Saints. The slight bend is easily recognized.

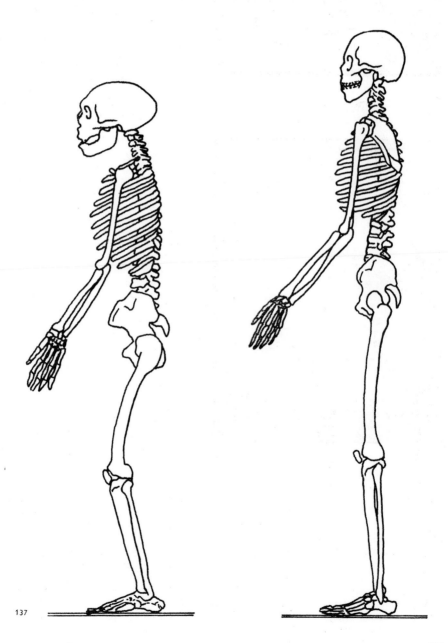

137 A comparison between the skeleton of a 'classic' Neanderthal-man (left) and modern man (right). The skeleton of Neanderthal-man was reconstructed using the discovery from La Chapelle--aux-Saints as a model (after Boule).

137

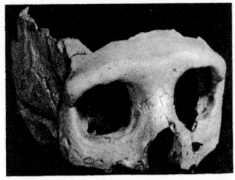

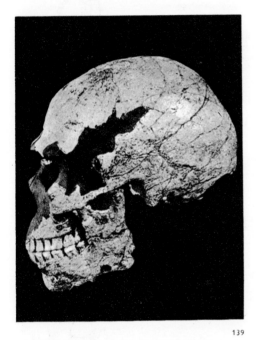

Particularly important are the remains found at Mugharet et-Tabun and Mugharet es-Skhul near Mount Carmel in Israel. From these and other sites in Israel have come a number of skeletons since 1931, which showed positive characteristics of both *H. s. sapiens* and Neanderthal-man (139, 140). These are thought to have lived during the time of the Würm Glaciation. If the oldest Neanderthal-man can be seen as being the first part in the chain of development leading to classic prehistoric man, the discoveries from Israel can be thought of as being basically progressive Neanderthal-man and provide a genetic link between early Neanderthal-man and modern man. Many skeletal remains from the sites in Israel show clearly developed characteristics similar to those of modern man. The thigh bones are straight, quite long, and can easily be distinguished from the short, slightly bent thigh bones of 'classic' Neanderthal-man. The brow-ridge is still fairly prominent, but there are already signs indicating that this species is changing and starting to take on characteristics of modern man. The brow-ridge of *Homo erectus* was very prominent and stretched across in one continuous line. A slight change is already often noticeable in Neanderthal-man where the brow-ridge, though still prominent, is slightly indented above the nose and seems to connect the two brow-ridges on either side of the root of the nose. Modern man has two independent ridges above the brows, much less protruding and divided above the root of the nose. The vault of the skull of some of the Israel Neanderthal-men is high, the occipital region is full and rounded, and the lower jaw shows signs of developing a chin. This type was slightly taller than 'classic' Neanderthal-man. The volume of the best preserved skull from Mugharet es-Skhul is about 1500 cubic centimetres.

138 Part of a skull belonging to Neanderthal-man from Krapina, Yugoslavia.

139 Skull of Neanderthal-man from Mugharet es-Skhul, Mount Carmel in Israel. The characteristics of both Neanderthal-man and *Homo sapiens sapiens* are clearly visible.

The remains discovered in the years from 1933 to 1974, in Djebel-Kafzeh near Nazareth (141) belong to a similar type of man. A particularly well-preserved male skull has a volume of 1560 cubic centimetres and new discoveries proved strong similarity to *Homo sapiens sapiens*.

Another remarkable site outside Europe is the Shanidar cave (142) which lies in the mountains of north Iraq. The site dates back to the middle Würm period and the remains found there, unlike the ones found in Israel, are more similar to 'classic' Neanderthal-man (143).

An interesting point was that the right lower arm was amputated on one of the males. The wound was healed, but because his teeth were worn in a special way it has been suggested that he used his teeth to compensate for the loss of his hand.

More discoveries were made in the USSR. The first one was a skeleton of a boy found in a cave at Teshik-Tash (144). The ibex horns with attached frontal bones which were found in a circle around the skeleton show that a burial took place. Another discovery was made in the Kiik Koba cave on the Krim peninsula. Here a shin-bone (tibia) and fibula as well as a skeleton of a foot all belonging to a Neanderthal-man were found.

Other important discoveries of Neanderthal-man come from Hungary. A skeleton of an infant and a lower jaw of an adult were found in a cave at Subalyuk. Other discoveries were made in Moravia in Czechoslovakia. The sites at Moravia (Švédův stůl cave, Kůlna cave, and Šipka cave) contained fragments of skulls showing transitional changes which make it difficult to class these as either early or 'classic' Neanderthal-man. The same applies to discoveries made at Šala, Slovakia. They prove, however, that the sites in Hungary and Czechoslovakia were also occupied by Neander-

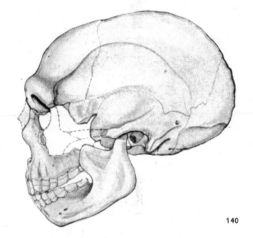

140

140 Drawing of a woman's skull from Mugharet et-Tabun, Mount Carmel, Israel. This skull is rather like a 'classic' Neanderthal skull from western Europe, although a lower jaw of a man has been found in the same deposits showing a number of advanced characteristics (after McCown and Keith).

141 Skull from Djebel Kafzeh near Nazareth, very similar to that of a *Homo sapiens sapiens*.

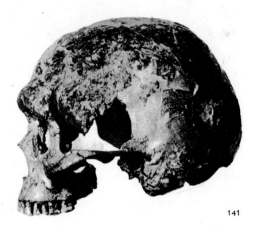

141

142

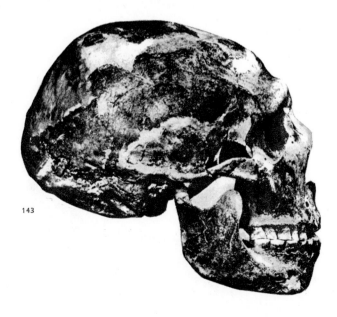

143

142 Shanidar cave in northern Iraq where skeletons of Neanderthal--man have been found (after Solecki).

143 Skull belonging to Neander-thal-man from the Shanidar cave. This skull looked somewhat like that of a Neanderthal-man from western Europe (after Solecki).

thal-man during the last interglacial phase and the following Glaciation.

In 1958 a single skull was found in a cave near Mapa in the Chinese province of Kwangtung, but it has not been possible to classify this skull. It has 'Neanderthal-man features' but we do not know whether he was closer to the equivalent of European early or to 'classic' Neanderthal-man. This find seems to suggest, however, that in eastern Asia too, early man, *Homo erectus*, was replaced by a type which was similar to Neanderthal-man, a subspecies which could be placed in the early stage of development of *Homo sapiens*.

Particularly interesting discoveries of parts of skulls belonging to various types of ancestors of modern man have been made in Java in south-east Asia. A large number of skulls have been found at Ngandong by the river Solo (145). The way in which these remains were found seems to suggest that they had been victims of cannibals. It is difficult to classify Solo-man, because he is not only different from the European and Near East type of Neanderthal-man, but also from the Chinese discovery at Mapa. Reconstruction shows Solo-man to be well built, with powerful browridges, and characteristics very similar to *Homo erectus*. The age which dates back to approxi-

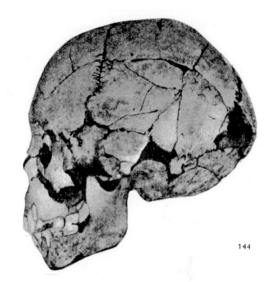

144

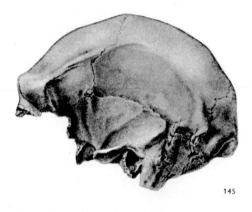

145

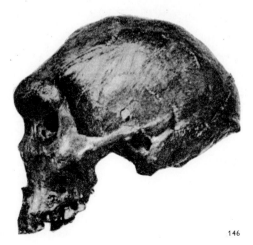

146

144 Skull of a Neanderthal-boy from the cave at Teshik Tash in south Uzbekistan, USSR.

145 One of the skulls from Ngandong on Java (after Weidenreich).

146 The skull from Broken Hill, Zambia.

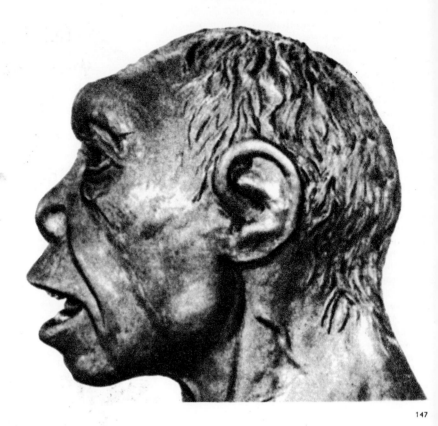

147

147 Reconstruction showing what the inhabitants from Broken Hill might have looked like (after Schultz).

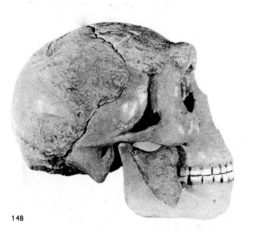

148

148 Reconstruction of a skull from Saldanha Bay, South Africa.

149 Reconstruction of Cro-Magnon-man (after MacGregor).

mately the first phase of the last European Glaciation is, however, considerably less than all other discoveries connected with *Homo erectus*. It seems that Solo-man belonged to a type which in south-east Asia immediately followed the advanced type of Java-man *Homo erectus erectus*. It is interesting that Solo-man's skull capacity is only 1035 to 1255 cubic centimetres. The skull capacity is larger than that of *Homo erectus erectus*, but it is not very different from the Chinese *Homo erectus pekinensis*, although *H. e. pekinensis* is much older. The extraordinary structure of the skull of Java-men from the river Solo suggests that their development might have been delayed in south-east Asia, so that the European type from Steinheim is comparable in development — not in morphology — to Java-man from the river Solo. The name of *Homo sapiens soloensis* (Oppenoorth, 1932) should be used for this type of man.

Similar questions are posed by two discoveries from Africa. One is the famous skull

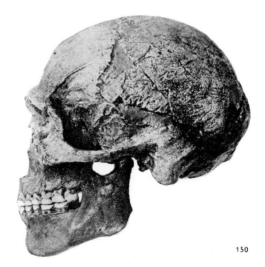

150 Skull from Předmostí, Moravia, Czechoslovakia which must have belonged to an exceptionally robust man *(Homo sapiens sapiens)*.

151 A female skull from Dolní Věstonice, Moravia, Czechoslovakia. Upper Pleistocene dolichomorphous type.

152 A male skull from Afalou-bou-Rhummel, North Africa (after Boule and Vallois).

from Broken Hill in **Zambia** (146, 147), the second was found near Saldanha Bay (148) about 128 kilometres north of Capetown. The latest research shows that these two skulls are Middle Pleistocene in age. They bear strong resemblances to *Homo erectus* who was in Africa, represented on the one hand by *Homo erectus capensis* and on the other by *Homo erectus leakeyi*: they could be the descendants of these forms. The capacity of the skull from Broken Hill was about 1300 cubic centimetres and is slightly above the capacity of the skulls from Ngandong, but well below the average of early Neanderthal-man. The remains from Broken Hill and Saldanha should be thought of as *Homo sapiens rhodesiensis* (Woodward, 1921); because together with Solo-man from Java they obviously represent a branch of development running parallel to the Near East and European Neanderthal-man. Von Koenigswald viewed all these types as 'tropical Neanderthal-man'.

We believe that both *Homo sapiens soloensis* and *Homo sapiens rhodesiensis* belong to an early form of *Homo sapiens*, which developed at a different rate. What happened to this early man cannot yet be determined. During this period evolution towards the early form of *Homo sapiens sapiens* was very rapid. This is shown by the discovery from the cave at Niah (Borneo), and it could be assumed that the less developed species of *Homo sapiens soloensis* and *Homo sapiens rhodesiensis* were ancestors of the races which now live in these areas, and that they have either become somehow integrated with these forms or have been exterminated by them.

We are nearing the end of our study of the descent and development of man. The example of Neanderthal-man from Israel has shown us how *Homo sapiens neanderthalensis* developed and changed into the present day form of *Homo sapiens sapiens*, which first appeared at the end of the first Würm Glaciation about 30 000 to 40 000 years ago. This early type of man shows no marked differences in the skeleton, including the structure of the skull, from modern man. Even the capacity of the skull had reached the same level as that of modern man. The only noticeable morphological differences can be found in the geologically early discoveries, which in comparison to modern man had a more robust body structure. The most famous sites of this man are: **Cro-Magnon**, Cro-Magnon-man (149), and **Combe Capelle** in France; **Oberkassel** in Germany, **Předmostí** (150), **Mladeč** and **Dolní Věstonice** (151)

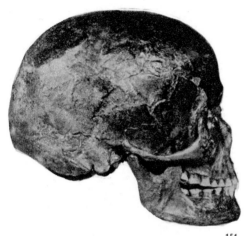

151

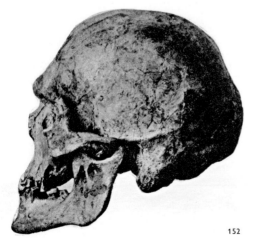

152

153 A concentration of bones (Pavlovian culture) in Dolní Věstonice, Moravia, Czechoslovakia.

154 Long, rounded lance-point. It was found at Předmostí, Moravia, Czechoslovakia and belongs to the Pavlovian culture.

155 Sharp point made of bone, with groove and rough base for easier hafting. It comes from the Magdalenian culture and was found at Pekárna cave, Moravia, Czechoslovakia.

156 Bone dagger (Pavlovian culture) from Předmostí, Moravia, Czechoslovakia.

154

155

156

157

157 A hook made of bone for catching fish (Pavlovian culture); Předmostí, Moravia, Czechoslovakia.

in Moravia, as well as a number of other sites (152).

The various cultures considerably influenced the biological development of man, but played a much larger part during the later phases of evolution. We can appreciate the important changes that took place, as man began to eat meat, as he started using a fire to prepare meat and warm himself, as he constructed his first homes, and made his tools. Towards the end of the Stone Age a series of constantly improving tools appeared and settlements emerged which throw light on to the social order of the species. The activities of these early Palaeolithic hunters can be deduced from the remains of the most common prey which could be found near larger settlements (153). The remains of more than 1000 mammoths were discovered in Předmostí (Moravia); in Solutré (France) numerous bones of wild horses were found, and in Ambrosievka (Ukraine) remains of hundreds of bison have been discovered. Obviously these discoveries suggest that large organized hunts have been operating in these areas. The hunting tools and the stage of their perfection give valuable information (154 to 158). The spear is still the most important weapon. As well as perfectly developed spearheads of stone, other implements appeared: spearheads of bone, of mammoth ivory, or of antler; and in the Magdalenian culture bone tools and harpoons with barbs have been found. Unfortunately, wood or other organic material has only rarely been preserved. Primitive wooden spears with points hardened by fire have been known from the Upper Palaeolithic, but discoveries like this from the Lower Palaeolithic are extremely rare. Undoubtedly, the Palaeolithic hunters knew of several kinds of wooden traps. Fishing nets, and several different kinds of hooks have been discovered in Upper Palaeolithic settlements. It is also at this time that the first stone arrowheads appear, showing that the bow must have been used. The large antler or bone clubs and various, often artistically decorated bone daggers which have been unearthed can probably be counted as hunting or defensive weapons.

Towards the end of the Palaeolithic the bone tool culture received a boost. The preparation of skins must have reached a peak even at that time. If we examine similar tools of modern cultures such as Eskimos or Siberians who are supposed to be experts in preparing skins, it becomes quite clear that they do not

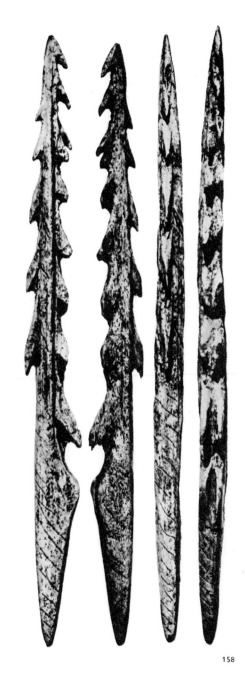

158

158 Harpoons made of bone (Magdalenian culture), Moravia, Czechoslovakia.

113

159 Skulls, which have obviously been broken at the base to extract the brain to eat it. These are signs of cannibalism. Above left: a skull from Steinheim; right: a skull belonging to Neanderthal-man from Monte Circeo; below: a modern Papua skull from New Guinea and a prehistoric discovery (Bronze Age) from Moravia (after Gieseler and Jelínek).

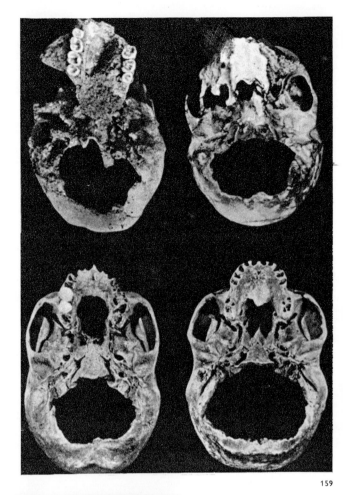

160

159

160 A collection of skulls dating back to the middle Stone Age (Mesolithic); proof of head-hunting. Ofnet cave, Bavaria, Germany (after Saller).

161 Burial from the Grotte du Cavillon in Grimaldi, Italy.

have such a wide variety of tools as did the reindeer hunters of the Magdalenian culture.

Evidence dating back that cannibalism existed has been found in the remains of settlements, and that parts of human bodies — particularly skulls — have been used as trophies (159). This applies to *Sinanthropus* as well as to Steinheim-man, and to Neanderthal-man at Monte Circeo and Krapina where skulls have been found with parts of the base broken away indicating that the brain had been removed. This same technique is still used by cannibals who live in the mountainous regions in New Guinea. Human long-bones, too, were often split in the same way as animal bones to get to the marrow. The unique Mesolithic discovery of thirty-six skulls in the Ofnet cave in Bavaria (Germany) shows that ritual head-hunting existed (160).

The first known burials are from the Middle Palaeolithic, as discoveries of Neanderthal-man from Le Moustier and La Ferrassie in France prove. The skeleton of a foot from Kiik Koba on the Krim peninsula in the USSR, and the burial of a youth in the cave at Teshik Tash also in the USSR confirm this. The arrangement of skeletons in bowl-shaped rocks, the flexed position of the deceased and the sepulchral accompaniments leave no doubt that even Neanderthal-man had some conception of a life after death. It is thought today that Neanderthal-man was not so primitive as described in earlier anthropological publications. As efficient hunters they well understood how to use the skins of animals, and how to build sound dwellings (Molodova). The burials suggest that they had a developed community spirit, and that cultural religious rituals took place.

Complicated rites were performed at burials as far back as the early Upper Palaeolithic

(161, 162). The communal grave of twenty individuals in Předmostí was covered with large bones and mammoth shoulder-blades. At several Pavlovian (eastern Gravettian) burial sites mammoths' shoulder-blades and other large bones have been used to cover graves, like the ones of an infant and woman in Dolní Věstonice (163), and of men in Brno II as well as the communal grave in Předmostí. It is interesting to note that the Pavlovian graves in Ukrainian settlements (164) were often built with the same material as their dwellings. We can also get some idea of Upper Palaeolithic man's state of health by looking at skeletons (165). The average age was about thirty years and individuals aged above fifty were rare. The life expectancy of people of the early Middle Ages was no higher, so that it is safe to assume that the state of health of the Palaeolithic hunter was good. This is confirmed by the fact that diseased bones are rare but evidence of death by accident is quite common. The condition of the teeth was almost always good showing very little sign of tooth decay (166). Older people sometimes seemed to have arthritic joints, which may have been genetic or caused by the rough conditions of life (167).

From the anthropological point of view our study of development of man ends here. From now on we shall be dealing with the development of human activities; we shall follow the culture which eventually leads to modern civilization. All discoveries of Palaeolithic men showed that they did not accept their environment as being unchangeable, but that they used all their strength to make it fit and change it to their advantage. If we want to know the cultural background of our ancestors we must find out what tools they used, how they made them, and how they produced the first works of art. This is what we shall discuss in the following chapters.

162

162 Double burial from Grotte des Enfants in Grimaldi, Italy (after Verneau).

163 Excavation of a Pavlovian burial place of a woman in Dolní Věstonice, Moravia, Czechoslovakia. The skeleton was covered by a mammoth shoulder-blade above which a part of a pelvic bone belonging to a mammoth was found. The skull is visible on the side below the shoulder-blade (after Klíma).

164 Burial in a deep grave covered by a mammoth shoulder-blade. Kostienki, Ukraine, USSR.

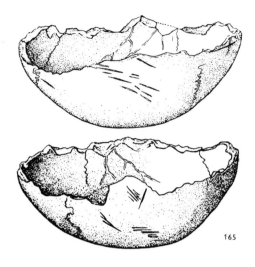

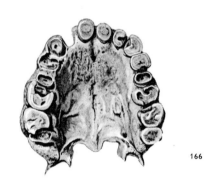

165

166

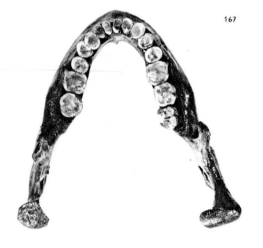

167

165 A bowl made of a human skull, which points to a well-developed ritual in the Upper Palaeolithic. Le Placard, France (after Boule).

166 Upper jaw of Rhodesia-man. The teeth show signs of decay and dental abscess formation, which is very rare in such early finds.

167 Lower jaw from Dolní Věstonice, Moravia, Czechoslovakia. The joint shows signs of arthritic process.

II Stone tools — their manufacture and use

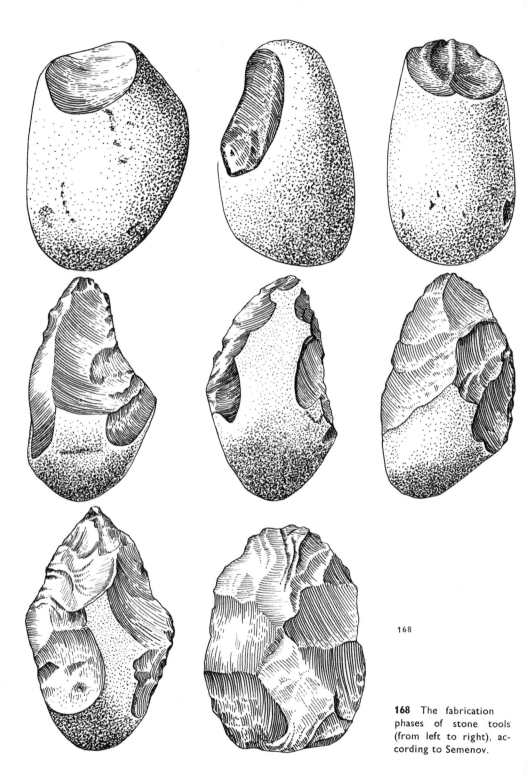

168

168 The fabrication phases of stone tools (from left to right), according to Semenov.

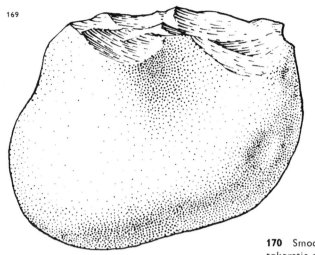

169 Chopper from Villafranchian layer in the Vallonet cave in southern France (after de Lumley).

170 Smooth point of a bone tool of the osteodon-tokeratic culture (after Heberer).

Stone tools provide the most prolific source of information about the activities of man. The tools are divided into characteristic forms, and grouped and named according to their use. There are scrapers, points, knives, flakes, and hand-axes. Recent research has shown that many tools were used for more than one purpose. For example, scrapers were often used as knives, and not every flaked edge was a cutting edge; sometimes, Stone Age man used the rough edge as the working edge and held the other in his hand.

Stone tools are, of course, not the only relics left by Palaeolithic man, nor the most important. Often, however, the tools are the only evidence left for the archaeologist to work on. With the help of these tools the development of the various cultures can be established, which gives us a chronological view of prehistoric man, as well as indicating his way of life. At the end of the 1800s experts thought that stone tools dated back not only to the Pleistocene, but even to the Tertiary period proving that man existed at that time. But it now appears that such tools (called eoliths) are to be found even in the Lower Tertiary, although no trace of our human ancestors can be found there. Such 'tools' were obviously formed by natural physical processes such as erosion; on beaches and in rivers, for instance, stones are constantly rolling together and breaking. It is now believed that the oldest known tools are the **Abbevillian** axes, the development of which took place over a very long period of time (168). Only

170

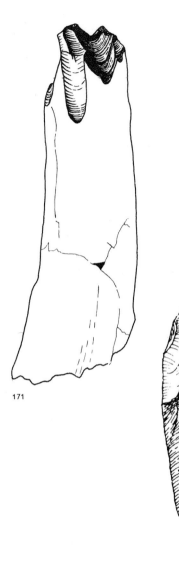

171 A worked rhinoceros bone from the Acheulean layer (osteodon-tokeratic culture) in the Grotte du Lazaret, France (after Octobon).

172 A worked rhinoceros bone from the Acheulean layer (osteodon-tokeratic culture) in the Grotte du Lazaret, France (after Octobon).

towards the middle of the 1900s were stone tools discovered in Africa, India, and later Europe which dated back to the Upper **Villafranchian** (169). They are pebbles which have been flaked in one or two directions only. L S B Leakey found them in the same layers as *Homo habilis*, which has been described in the previous chapter.

Raymond Dart was the first to say, in 1949, that a period — before the development of stone tools — existed in which prehistoric men used tools made from animal bones and teeth. Dart called this the osteodontokeratic culture ('bone-tooth-antler-culture') (170, 171), and backed his assertion with a study of split bones and teeth belonging to Australopithecines from sites in South Africa. His research was criticized, but it seems today, after further discoveries and their evaluation, that Dart's findings were basically correct. The split bones, which were found in the oldest sites, were clearly chosen to a pattern. Primitive man preferred long-bones and skulls of animals. Further research showed that the method of splitting the bones was always the same. Also, bones damaged by use suggest that these were very primitive tools (172 to 175).

The period in which primitive man made simple stone tools was obviously preceded by a period in which he used similar tools which had been shaped naturally. They were probably branches which were used as clubs and levers, or stones which were used for throwing or striking. Some primitive races still use naturally formed stones for such tasks.

How can we distinguish between a naturally formed stone and a stone which has been flaked by man? If a stone has been split by either extreme heat or frost a bulb does not form, although natural flaking occurs (176 to 179). The basic difference between natural and artificial flaking lies in the way man uses flaking to create a special form of tool (180). When flaking was done by man, special materials were chosen, and often the method of flaking shows clearly for what task the tool was intended (181). Natural flaking never shows these characteristics. The tools are not so well shaped, and the bulbs if they exist at all, occur in irregular places.

The place in which tools are discovered is also an important point. If stones different from the local material are found, it is a clear indication that they could only have been brought there by man.

Man of the Old Stone Age soon learned how

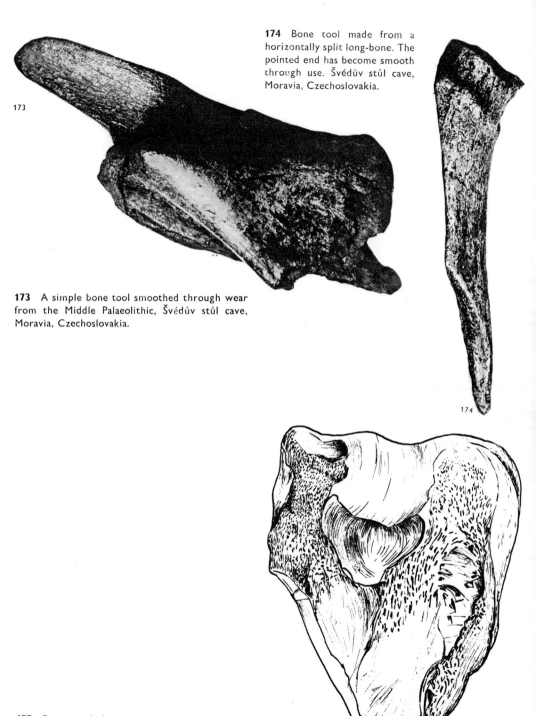

174 Bone tool made from a horizontally split long-bone. The pointed end has become smooth through use. Švédův stůl cave, Moravia, Czechoslovakia.

173 A simple bone tool smoothed through wear from the Middle Palaeolithic, Švédův stůl cave, Moravia, Czechoslovakia.

175 Bone tool from the Lower Palaeolithic, shaped like a hand-axe. Stránská skála near Brno, Czechoslovakia.

176

177

178

179

180

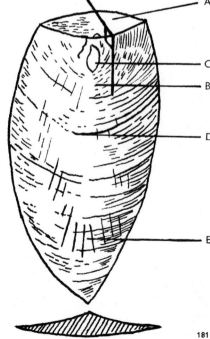

176 Natural eolith, which is rather like a tool made by man.

177 A flint fractured by natural forces so that it looks as if it has been made by man.

178 A flint split through intense heat.

179 Frost can cause 'pot-lid' splitting on a flint.

180 Chopping tool from In Amenas, Sahara desert.

181 Characteristic features of a flake produced by man. (A) striking platform and point of percussion, (B) bulb of percussion, (C) bulbar scar, (D) ripples, (E) fissures.

181

183

184

182 Tools made of rock crystal belonging to the Magdalenian culture have been found in the Žitný cave, Moravia. This raw material is rarely found in prehistoric sites, but many tools of this kind were found here.

183, 184 Crude tools made of a stone which is difficult to flake. Pavlovian culture, Dolní Věstonice, Moravia, Czechoslovakia.

to distinguish different types of stone and preferred those which were easily made into tools.
Particularly suitable were flint, quartz, jasper,
rock crystal, obsidian, and so on. These stones
are easily split, and yet they are hard enough
to give sharp edges.

In the Lower Palaeolithic tools were made
mostly from materials found locally. Later,
expeditions further afield were undertaken to
find suitable raw materials such as flint, rock
crystal, and obsidian which were probably
also used as objects for exchange (182). Occasionally tools were produced from a local
and unsuitable material, so that they were
usually rougher than well-made typical tools
of that period; the larger tools were sometimes
made even from limestone (183 to 185).

The Aborigines of modern Australia provide

us with confirmation that early man probably
used any suitable material for his tools. Shortly
after telephone lines and overhead cables were
erected in Australia, the Aborigines discovered
that it was easy to split the glass insulators to
make useful tools; they also made tools from
broken bottles using the same techniques that
they used for working stone (186).

Obviously, the availability of the raw material played a large part in the final form of
the tool. It was, for instance, impossible to
make large tools if only small pebbles could be
found. Changes in tool types did not always
occur because of the disappearance of a culture
but often through the interchanging and mutual
influence of various cultures.

When trying to assess the choice and pro-
cessing of materials used in prehistoric times,

185 Quartz and flint flakes from a site in Ondratice, central Moravia, Czechoslovakia.

186 Glass point from Kimberley, Australia. The Aborigines made them from bottle glass.

187 A spearpoint made from an unretouched quartz blade. North-east Australia.

we can often find clues by observing today's primitive societies. Daniel Wilson (1889) pointed out that the Red Indians of North America not only chose suitable material when making their arrowheads, but also placed emphasis on beautiful material, particularly if the article was to be something special. J R B Love also mentioned in 1936 that the Aborigines in Australia preferred beautifully coloured stones for their spearheads. A number of examples suggest that the properties and the 'look' of the raw materials played an important part. Spencer and Gillen (1904) explained that it was not very surprising that in one Australian tribe tools of various degrees of perfection could be found. Spencer pointed out in a report on central Australia that the technique for working the tool was to some extent determined by the properties of that material. In places where only quartz could be found the tribes produced mainly flaked tools, but where diorite occurred the tools were often smoothed (187 to 190). In prehistoric times man usually collected his raw material from easily accessible sites, either from river gravel deposits or where he could find deposits of rocks suitable for the task. Only later do we come across sites where materials were dug up from some depth. This happened for the first time in the Middle and Upper Palaeolithic (the extraction of red ochre at Lake Balaton in Hungary, or the mining of hornstone from Stránská skála in Czechoslovakia). Other examples, taken from ethnology, show that the extraction of raw materials was done by special methods. The Red Indians of North America knew of sites where a special stone occurred which was used to make particularly good arrows. The way to these sites was just as clearly indicated as the method used to extract the raw material. Howitt (1904) reported that the Australian Aborigines jealously guarded their sites of raw materials which were used for making axes. If a stranger entered the site a dispute would break out immediately.

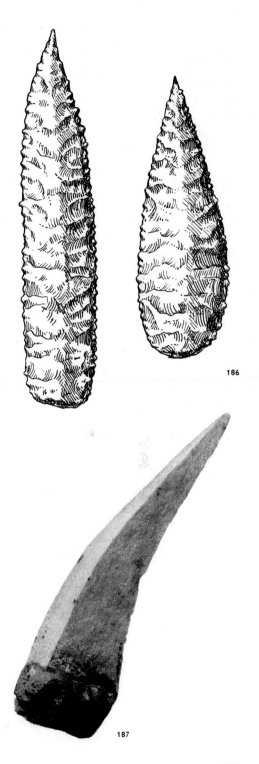

186

187

188

189

188 Aboriginal multipurpose stone tools from central Australia.

189 A stone axe made of diorite. Arnhem Land, northern Australia.

190 A discus-shaped stone tool from Tasmania.

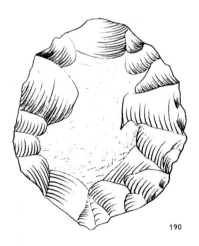

190

Stone tools — manufacture and Palaeolithic cultures

In the Lower Palaeolithic, man had to make his own individual tools; proper workmanship developed only later. There are reports from North America which, in describing modern Red Indians, mention that the making of tools from stone has for a long time been almost a profession. Most members of a tribe could make stone tools, but the most talented would be held in high esteem. The men of the Australian Worrora tribe near Kimberley make spearheads as their main occupation (Love, 1936), while the women collect the food. The spearheads are between 30 and 50 millimetres long and have serrated edges, obtained by pressure-flaking with a bone or wooden tool. During a hunt the men from the Worrora tribe often pick up a stone and check it by striking it against another. If it proves to be suitable the hunter will shape the stone roughly and then put it in a bag so that he can finish it off when he returns home (191, 192). These and other

reports made at the beginning of the 1900s
provide us with valuable information about
the manufacture of stone tools, and help us
reconstruct the way of life of Stone Age man.
It is likely that the same methods of making
stone tools were used by Stone Age man as are
used by the primitive tribes of today. It seems
also that Stone Age man and modern primitive
men extracted the raw materials in a very
similar way.

Two methods of making stone tools were
used during the Lower Palaeolithic. The tools
were either shaped from a suitable stone by
flaking, chipping off until the tool was formed
(**core industry**); or the flakes of the parent
core would be altered to form a primitive tool
(**flake industry**). But tools for flaking were
known in both industries. Larger flakes can
themselves be worked like cores and made into
tools. If the flake is longer than it is wide in a
ratio of at least three to two, and if it is flaked
from a cylindrical core, which often happened
in the Upper Palaeolithic, it belongs to the
blade industry (193, 194). The oldest known
tools from the Lower Palaeolithic are **axes** and
chopping tools, which can easily be produced by a few simple blows (195, 196). The
greatest number of these tools were found in

191 An Aborigine from Arnhem Land, making
a stone tool. The core from which he is striking his
flakes rests on his heel.

192 An Aborigine from Arnhem Land retouching
a stone tool. He holds a hammerstone in his right
hand and in his left hand the flake on which he
works.

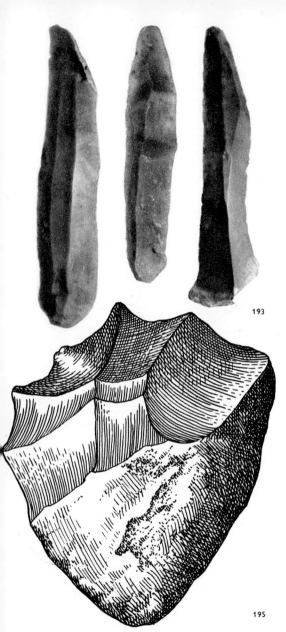

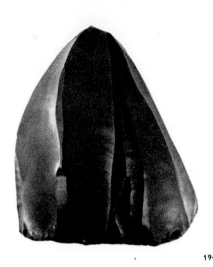

193

194

the oldest sites although sometimes they were also found in small quantities in the Upper Palaeolithic living sites. The core and flake industries which existed during the Lower Palaeolithic were confined to particular areas. The core industry is found in Africa, western Europe, and India; the flake industry in eastern Europe and south-east Asia. The reason for this is not yet known.

The stone hand-axe is a typical and versatile tool used for cutting, splitting, and other similar tasks. Usually it was made from pebbles or core-like stones, and sometimes even from large flakes. The oldest stone axe tools were crudely shaped and often show remains of the original surface of the pebble which was not flaked (197). They are from the **Abbevillian** or **Chellean** culture, and crude hand-axes with oval or pear-shaped outlines belong to this culture. Acheulean tools of better workmanship follow this period. Knives, points, drills, and scrapers in a crude form were introduced which were later to be fully developed during the Upper Palaeolithic cultures. The **Acheulean** culture (198), as we know from sites in North Africa, is associated with *Homo erectus* and shows characteristic but simple signs of cultural development. In addition to the core industry, the flake industry from the Lower Palaeolithic, called the **Clactonian** culture, is also known to have developed. Typical tools from the Clactonian culture have the striking plane at an obtuse angle to the ventral side of the flake (199 to 203). This technique occasionally appeared also in later cultures.

195

193 Blades made from cylinder-like cores. These blades were either shaped further or used like this as knives or points.

194 Cylindrical stone-core from which blades were struck in the Upper Palaeolithic.

195 A large stone tool of the Acheulean culture from Yashtush, Sukhumi, USSR.

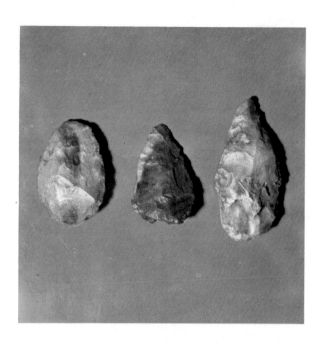

Hand-axes from the Acheulean culture found at the type area of Saint-Acheul, France.

Hand-axes of the Acheulean culture found at Sbaika, Algeria.

Two crude hand-axes from Sbaika, Algeria.

Stone points in the shape of small hand-axes from the late Mousterian deposits in the Kůlna cave, Moravia, Czechoslovakia.

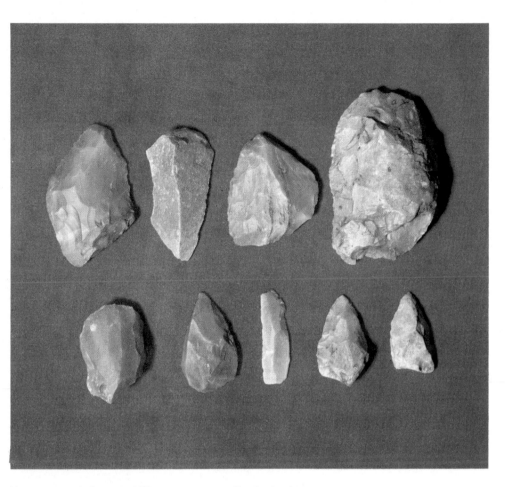

Mousterian tools from the Kůlna cave, Moravia, Czechoslovakia.

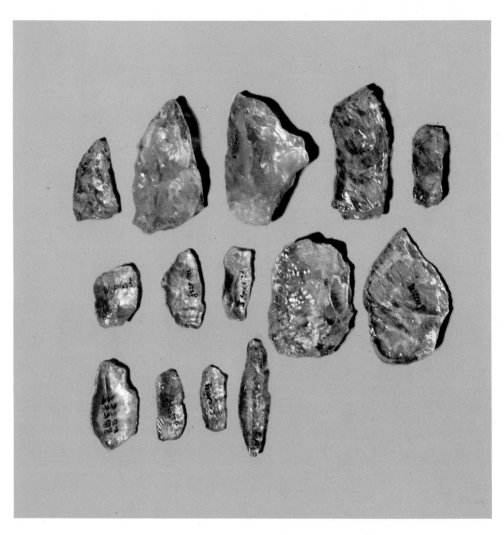

Rock crystal tools belonging to the Magdalenian reindeer hunters from the Žitný cave, Moravia, Czechoslovakia.

The following period in the Lower Palaeolithic is characterized by tortoise-cores and flakes made from prepared cores. This was called the **Levalloisian** technique (204 to 208). It is a technique which made it possible to produce tools with sharp edges and of several shapes and sizes suitable for different activities, and it can be dated to 250 000 to 100 000 B.C. Some prehistorians are convinced that it was a technique used during different periods of time and in different areas, and not related to a specific culture. The **Mousterian** culture (209) belongs to the Middle Palaeolithic (100 000 to 30 000 B.C.), but there is still some controversy here between scholars. The different groups within the Mousterian culture used basically the same types of tools, but in some ways they do differ from one another. Tools produced in the **Mousterian** with an **Acheulean** tradition include axes, small axes as well as scrapers, knives, hand-drills, blades, and points (210), and so tend towards the Lower Palaeolithic cultures. Different again is the **Charentian** — or **Mousterian** culture of the so-called **La Quina** type — which is confined to the area around Charente in France. Then there is the **Mousterian** of the **La Ferrassie** type which is close to the La Quina type, but is distinctive because of

196 Simple stone tool from the Lower Palaeolithic. Mlazice, Bohemia, Czechoslovakia.

197 Crude hand-axes of the Abbevillian culture, Abbeville, France.

196

197

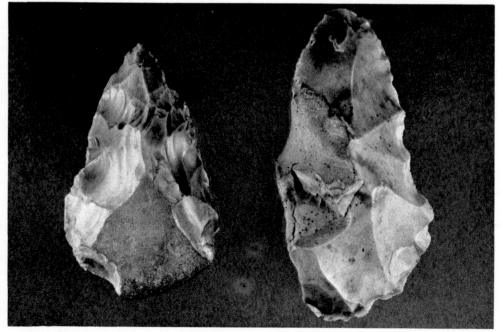

137

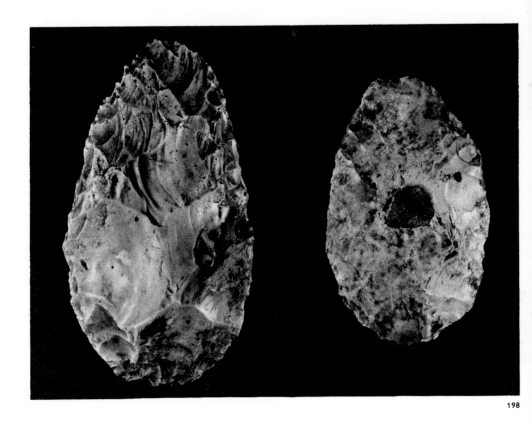

198 Almond-shaped Acheulean hand-axes from St Acheul, France.

199 Lower Palaeolithic Clactonian flakes with characteristic wide angles between the ventral side and the striking platform. Clacton-on-Sea, England.

its use of the Levallois technique. Then, again, some Mousterian cultures did not have hand-axes; and the so-called **Micromousterian** culture had leaf-like blades among its other tools. The separate groups of the Mousterian cultures developed quite independently from one another, and they can be found in various stratigraphical layers in the caves.

Just as we can detect connections between the tools of the Mousterian culture and the preceding Acheulean culture, the influences on Upper Palaeolithic cultures are also evident. The Mousterian culture, together with primitive man, *Homo sapiens neanderthalensis*, is geographically concentrated in Europe, the neighbouring areas of North Africa, and Asia. The Upper Palaeolithic cultures of western Europe have been closely studied by prehistorians who have used these findings as guidelines in dividing them. There can be no doubt, however, that these rules cannot be applied for the evaluation of areas outside Europe (211, 212). The **Perigordian-Aurignacian** (30 000 to 12 000

B.C.) is the oldest cultural complex of the Upper Palaeolithic in western Europe. Backed knives, points, and double points and other 'Mousterian-like' tools occur at the beginning of the **Perigordian** period (213). There is no trace of any artistic development. Small Venus-like figurines dating from the Perigordian period, as well as some low reliefs, have been found. The first traces of cave paintings also belong to this period and are found in the caves of Gargas, Pair-non-Pair, and Abri du Poisson. Among the stone tools of the **Aurignacian** culture special types of scrapers have been found as well as end scrapers on blades and gravers (214 to 216). This culture also marked the beginning of bone tools, mostly various types of spear-points (217), as well as the first black and red cave paintings and crude engravings. The bone tools found in these layers sometimes show simple engravings.

The **Solutrean** culture which was largely confined to southern and south-western France produced perfectly made, typically west-Euro-pean tools (218). As well as the beautiful laurel-leaf blades — large implements perfectly bi-facially flaked and remarkably thin — this culture also produced the first bone needles. Characteristic are the reliefs which are often found at cave entrances.

The Solutrean of western France is a rela-tively late culture in the Upper Palaeolithic. From this springs another western European culture, the **Magdalenian**, which is divided into six different phases. This culture produced a remarkable abundance of bone and antler tools, many of them used for working on leather. Various hand-drills, saws, and microlithic stone tools are also worth mentioning.

The Epipalaeolithic (formerly called Meso-lithic or Middle Stone Age) in Europe emerged about 9000 to 5000 B.C. This period produced a large number of microliths which are small, geometrically formed stone tools made from flakes or parts of flakes. Microliths were made from small cores and were often used together to form composite weapons such as blades of

200 Clactonian technique of flaking stone: the preparation of the core. The scar is clearly visible on the stone after it has been struck.

201 Clactonian technique of flaking stone: this is a core with negative traces of flaking.

202 Clactonian technique of flaking stone: the finished flake.

200

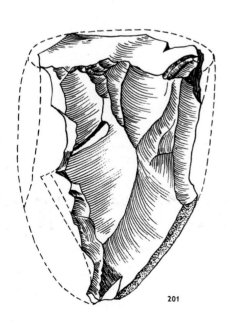

201

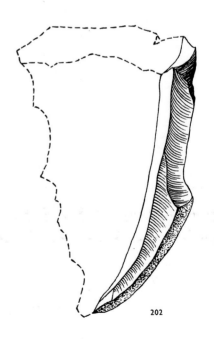

202

spear-points (219). An important feature of this period's tools are handles made of wood or bone.

This is basically how the cultural phases of the Lower, Middle, and Upper Palaeolithic, as well as of the Epipalaeolithic, are divided in western Europe. Deviations within these phases occurred not only on other continents, but also within Europe itself. This is why the Upper Palaeolithic culture of central Europe is now called the **Szeletian**, and not the Solutrean as it was earlier mistakenly thought to be. The Szeletian is much older than the west European Solutrean and shows many traces of the Mousterian. It is obviously one of the oldest of the Upper Palaeolithic cultures, and only shares the technique of pressure-flaking with the Solutrean. The western European Magdalenian culture stretched as far east as Moravia, northern Austria, and south Poland. Eastern **Gravettian** cultures, now called **Pavlovian** (220) are then found beyond this moving further eastwards.

The Soviet discoveries of the arctic Palaeolithic are also of great importance, and cover the area of European Russia nearly to the northern polar circle. These discoveries prove that Stone Age hunters must, for at least a

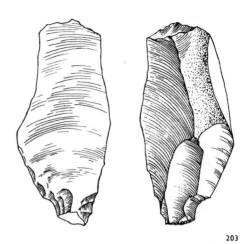

203

203 A blade made by the Clactonian technique. The blunt angle at the bottom of the blade is clearly visible.

204 Tools made by the Levalloisian technique, based on a tortoise-core. Levallois, France.

204

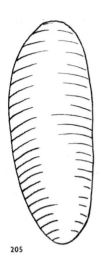
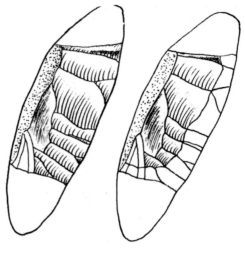

205 Levalloisian technique of flaking stone: preparation of the tortoise-core.

206 Levalloisian technique of flaking stones: the tortoise--core before and after flaking.

207 Levalloisian flake. The dorsal side of the flake showing flaking, the ventral is an unworked surface.

205

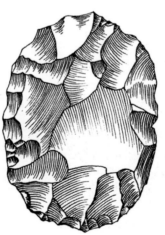
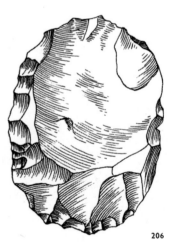

206

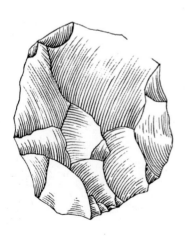
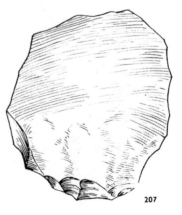

207

short period, have been living in these regions.

Noticeable differences in the development of the Upper Palaeolithic are obvious between Africa, Siberia, south-east Asia, Australia, and America. These large geographic areas have their own characteristic cultures and different time scales.

Comparisons between African and European discoveries are difficult, because the climatic conditions of the African Palaeolithic were not only much less changeable but also of a different pattern. The question arises, in what respect might it be possible to compare the African rain seasons (pluvials) and the dry seasons (interpluvials) with the European Ice Ages (Glaciations) and the interglacial phases? This might only be possible for North Africa. It is thought that the periods of rain in eastern and southern Africa called the Kagerian and Kamasian could be compared with the Lower Palaeolithic of Europe and the early pluvial, called the Gamblian, could be compared with the Upper Palaeolithic of Europe.

The well-known discoveries of Dr and Mrs Louis Leakey at the Olduvai Gorge contri-

208 Levalloisian technique of flaking stone: making a flake.

209 Two characteristic Mousterian side-scrapers. La Quina, France.

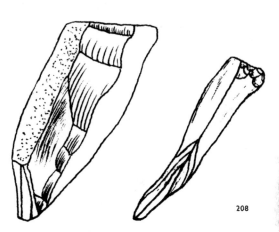

208

209

210

210 Characteristic side-scraper-like Mousterian point. Le Moustier, France.

buted much to the research on African pre-historic tools. They found tools in clearly defined stratified deposits together with skeletal remains belonging to *Paranthropus*, which Leakey called *Zinjanthropus boisei*, and an advanced hominid, called *Homo habilis*. These oldest stone tools are chopping tools and hammerstones made from pebbles which we recognize as the **Oldowan** culture. They originate from between two and one million years B.C., and are proof that the process of development of man, which has been accompanied by stone tools from the earliest phases, must have begun much earlier than was originally thought. Above the layer of the Oldowan culture were found deposits of the **Chellean-Acheulean** (221), a culture which is thought to have been associated with *Homo erectus*. Discoveries of pebble tools come not only from Olduvai but also from sites in eastern Africa, from Abyssinia, from South Africa, from the Sahara desert and also from North Africa.

The basic tool of the Chellean-Acheulean period, the hand-axe, seems to appear later in Africa than in Europe. At the Kalambo Falls in northern Rhodesia hand-axes have been found dating from 55 000 B.C. This is a period which in Europe coincides with the Mousterian culture. Among the tools from the Acheulean period in Africa cleavers made from large flakes have been found, while similar discoveries made in Europe show tools made from cores only. This culture had not spread far in Africa. The chronologically latest finds come from sites in the Kalahari desert in South Africa. Proof of the earliest use of fire in Africa comes from the Acheulean levels in the Cave of Hearths, South Africa, and from the Kalambo Falls in Rhodesia. But you must remember that Africa has not yet been fully explored.

Olduvai Gorge plays a pre-eminent part in prehistoric research in eastern Africa, and gives a good chronological support to discoveries. In South Africa, the Vaal river terraces play a similar role. The gravel deposits of the Kagerian Pluvial contain pebble tools, and the later gravels of the Kamasian Pluvial yield discoveries from the '**Stellenbosh culture**', which corresponds to the Chellean-Acheulean.

While evidence of the Lower Palaeolithic is spread quite evenly across Africa, the Middle Palaeolithic shows a clear cultural zone in the north; a cultural development closely connected with that of the Mediterranean and the Middle East, and a cultural zone to the

144

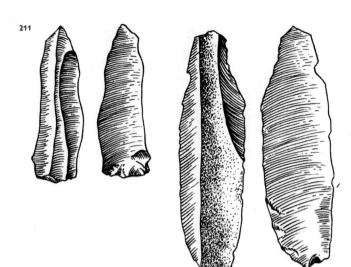

211 Blades which show clearly the negative traces where other blades have previously been struck from them. The original surface can still be seen on the larger blade.

212 A characteristic flaking technique from the Upper Palaeolithic. If the ends have been struck off the flint the striking platform appears on the core; negative traces of flaked off blades are clearly visible.

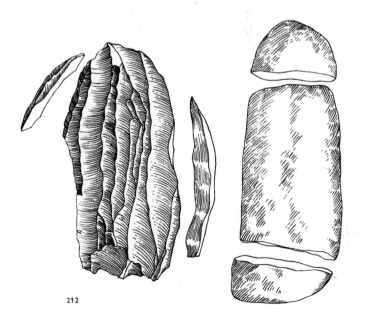

212

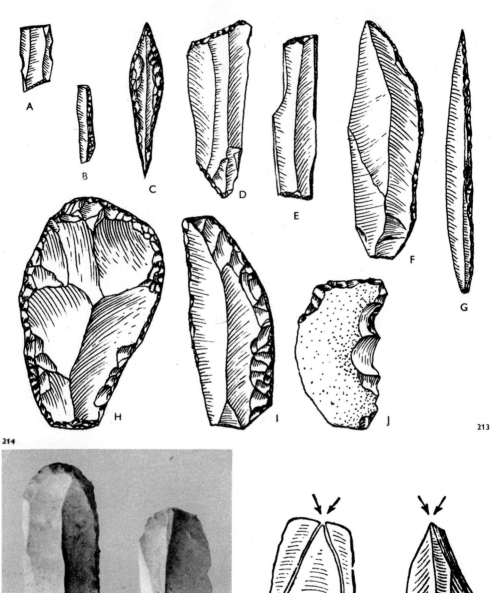

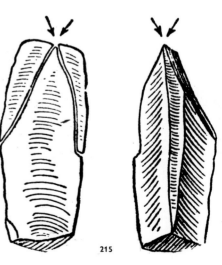

213 Perigordian tools: (A) graver, (B) backed blade, (C) point of the Font-Robert type, (D) geometric blade, (E) fourfold graver, (F) Chatelperonian type backed blade, (G) Pavlovian point, (H) a side scraper made from a flake, (I) side scraper, (J) denticulated flake (after Bordes).

214 End scraper on a blade and burin-scraper (on the right). Aurignacian.

215 A graver is made from a blade-like flake which is struck twice on the top part of the stone to produce the point.

216 A graver-like point; graver and an end-scraper on a blade. Aurignacian.

south, which relates to Africa south of the Sahara desert. The cultural zone of southern Africa, in comparison to that of northern Africa, has developed far slower.

As well as the Mousterian culture which used the Levalloisian technique, another typically African culture, called the **Aterian**, appears in North Africa. This culture is very similar to the Mousterian. Some tools, however, especially points, are tanged (222, 223). They are accompanied by bifacial points in the more recent sites. This Mousterian-like culture corresponds chronologically with the Upper Palaeolithic in Europe. The areas of the Maghreb have the **Capsian** and **Ibero-maurusian** cultures which follow the Aterian culture. Both these cultural periods, which lie in the Epipalaeolithic period of North Africa, correspond in time to the Mesolithic period in Europe (224 to 227).

The slow development of the Middle Palaeolithic industry south of the Sahara is so noticeable that it is difficult to compare it with the culture of North Africa. The South African

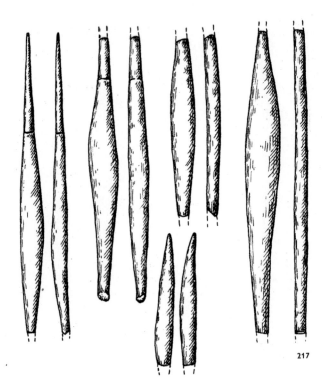

217 Flat bone points. Willendorf II, Austria.

218 Three typical Solutrean points. Western France.

217

218

cultures have many archaic tools (axes, points, and so on) which are the equivalent of the tools from European Lower Palaeolithic. It seems as if the environment, particularly the vegetation, played a decisive role in the development of these tools. The tools of the **Sangoan** and **Lupembian** cultures point to a tool industry mainly used for rough woodwork. These cultures come from Uganda and the Congo, and show that eastern and southern Africa have a number of local Middle Palaeolithic cultures which seem to be much later than in Europe.

The cultures of Asia are equally heterogeneous. The development of such a large continent could not, of course, be uniform. While the Middle East compares chronologically with the Mediterranean area, the chronological system in India is based on four periods of glaciation in the Himalayas. The chronological order of the sites in south-east Asia is based on palaeontological discoveries and terra-rossa deposits of the Villafranchian, while the loess deposits belong to the later periods.

The richest sites of the old pebble industries are to be found in the Siwalik mountains in north India. There they are called the **Soan** cultures, named after the river which flows through this region. The oldest discoveries come from the **Pre-soan** and probably belonged to the second Glaciation. The 'pebble' cultures of south-east Asia also show a few hand-axes and Levalloisian flakes. This is very typical of the **Patjitanian** culture of south Java. Among the most ancient sites in China, at Chou-kou-tien (228), pebble tools were found associated with a quartz industry. But no hand-axes were found; these appear in China only rarely. While primitive pebble tools do appear in northern Malaysia, the **Anyathian** culture of Burma shows only a poor flake industry. Sites in central and southern India have yielded rich finds of Abbevillian and Acheulean hand-axes. New discoveries of these Acheulean tools have been made in Afghanistan and Iran. Soviet scientists have discovered rich Abbevillian and Acheulean sites in Armenia and Transcaucasia. One of the most important sites in the Middle East, dating to the Lower Palaeolithic, is at el Ubedyia in the Jordan valley; this belongs to the Villafranchian culture. Many of the Lower Palaeolithic discoveries and sites in Jordan, Israel, Syria, and the recently discovered sites in Turkey belong to the late Acheulean culture. Remains of the Mousterian culture also are often found

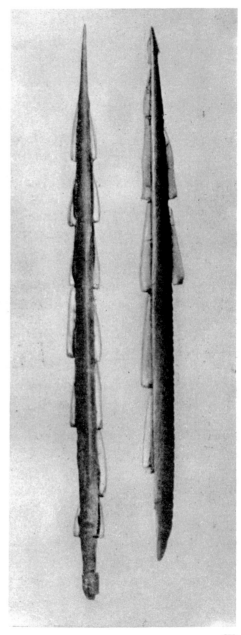

219

219 This is an example of a composite tool. The microlithic blades were fitted into a wooden shaft, forming an elongated blade. Mesolithic, Denmark.

220

220 Characteristic Pavlovian tools. Moravia, Czechoslovakia.

in the Middle East and it is possible that they
are more recent in these regions than their
counterparts in European sites. One of the
most important characteristics of these sites is
the rich variation of tools.

Mousterian sites in the USSR have been
found on the eastern shore of the Caspian Sea,
in the southern Caucasian mountains and in
central Asia. Uzbekistan is another area in
which the Mousterian culture can be found
producing evidence of both hand-axes and
pebble tools. Cultures and sites comparable to
the Mousterian are practically unknown in
India, and east and south-east Asia. This might
be explained by the fact that large parts in this
area have only been explored superficially. It
is also very difficult to compare chronologically
the discoveries of the various well-known sites

221

221 Acheulean cleavers from North Africa.

222 Tanged stone point. Aterian culture of the Middle Palaeolithic in North Africa.

with those of India and south-east Asia; often it is impossible. But the interesting fact is that Neanderthal-man, who is usually associated with the Mousterian culture, is missing throughout.

Rich discoveries dating from the Upper Palaeolithic have been made in the Middle East, but there are far fewer of these finds in Siberia and hardly any in south-east and east Asia.

The Aurignacian culture is only rarely represented in the Middle East, and is characterized by an atypical bone industry — Perigordian types are missing altogether. This culture has numerous scrapers, and also from its earliest period, tools of the Mousterian type, including the characteristic Emiran-points. The industry which followed, and produced the backed blade, continued into the Mesolithic period.

222

223

223 Tools from the North African Aterian culture (after Balout).

Stone tools from the Pavlovian settlement at Dolní Věstonice, Moravia, Czechoslovakia.

Stone tools from the Pavlovian settlement at Dolní Věstonice, Moravia, Czechoslovakia.

Stone tools from the Ibero-maurusian culture found at Ushtata. Tunisia.

Two cores and one finished tool from the Ibero-maurusian culture, Ushtata, Tunisia.

Microlithic tools from a site at Elora, India.

Tools from Elora, India.

224 Characteristic Capsian tools from North
Africa (after Balout).

225

225 Tools of the developed Capsian (after Balout).　**226** Tools from the North African Ibero-maurusian.

The Siberian sites with their numerous tool types are probably comparable to European cultures of the Palaeolithic. The sites of the Yenisei area produced besides Mousterian tools, an Upper Palaeolithic blade industry, together with bone awls and needles. Around Lake Baikal settlements have been found dating back to the Upper Palaeolithic. Their blade industry produced scrapers, gravers, hand-drills, and bone tools. This period also produced some art consisting of engravings and ivory sculptures of women. As already mentioned, the cultures of the Upper Palaeolithic are practically unknown in eastern Asia, except for the few tools of the Mousterian type discovered in the cave at Chou-kou-tien.

Australia was thought to have been a conti-nent without early settlements. This view, how-ever, was changed by discoveries made in New South Wales. These discoveries have been radiocarbon dated (C 14), and this has proved conclusively that the southern part of Australia was inhabited in the Upper Palaeolithic. The fire remains found at Menindee (New South Wales) is approximately 17 000 years old. Another discovery was made in north Austra-lia, where edge-ground axes were found in deposits approximately 23 000 years old (Oen-pelli, Arnhem Land). The recent discoveries in New South Wales (Lake Mungo) revealed the remains of a partially cremated human skeleton about 30 000 years old. These im-portant discoveries together with recent dat-ings, one from Keilor (8500 to 15 000 years)

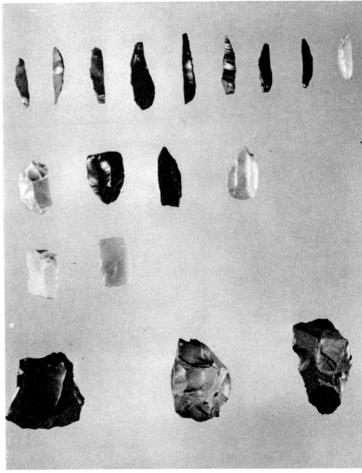

227 Stone and bone tools. North African Ibero-
-maurusian (after Balout).

228 Two quartz tools made by *Sinanthropus (Homo erectus pekinensis)* from Chou-kou-tien, China.

and one from Talgai (12 000 years) show that *Homo sapiens sapiens* had existed in Australia since the Upper Palaeolithic and knew the technique of grinding stones earlier than his counterpart in Europe. The above-mentioned discoveries also throw light on the remains found in the Niah cave in Borneo. A skeleton of *Homo sapiens sapiens* found in this cave at a depth of 2.5 metres was dated as 40 000 years old. If the method of the dating is correct, this skeleton then represents the oldest discovery made of modern man.

For a long time it was thought that America had only 'recently' been inhabited. The discovery made in 1926 of a so-called '**Folsom-point**' refuted this opinion. At Folsom further discoveries of points underneath bison bones have been made which confirm the existence of early man. Most of the American Stone Age discoveries do not come from proper settlements but from the 'killing-sites' where the Palaeolithic hunter killed his prey, a mammoth or bison. Judging by the sites so far discovered the Folsom hunter seemed mainly to kill bison. According to radiocarbon dating these hunters

lived about 8000 B.C. The tools which come from the Lindenmeir site, discovered between 1934 and 1938, consist not only of fluted points but also of scrapers, hand-drills, bifacial leaf-like points and, less abundantly, gravers, choppers, grinding stones, and pieces of haematite. The points found in the Sandia cave in New Mexico, which come from a lower deposit than the Folsom points, are older. The **Sandia points** (229) are bifacially flaked and show slight traces of a tang. The **Clovis points** (230) might be as old as the Sandia points. Clovis points, which have been found in New Mexico among mammoth bones, are elongated and flaked on both sides, slightly fluted, with a somewhat concave base. The Folsom points, which are better made, are more deeply fluted. It is thought that America was first inhabited during the last Würm interstadial, between 15 000 and 14 000 years B.C. It is possible, however, that the original inhabitants of America arrived during the last but one interstadial, which would mean about 30 000 years ago. According to recent research they must have crossed the Bering

Strait and originated from eastern Siberia. The population must have spread rapidly towards the southern parts of America, because discoveries have been made in south Patagonia which is the southernmost part of this continent. In the Palli Aike and Fell caves, settlements have been discovered in deposits dating from about 8000 to 7000 B.C.

It is characteristic of the American cultures that the Amerindians went directly from the Palaeolithic period, which had existed for a long time, and, without entering an intermediate Mesolithic stage, they entered an epoch which is marked by its ceramics, grinding and sharpening stones, and other typically Neolithic techniques. The development in America took a somewhat different turn from that in Europe and many other parts of the world.

229

230

229 A point of the Sandia type from North America.

230 A point of the Clovis type from North America.

231 Hammerstone showing numerous traces of percussion all around it. Magdalenian, Pekárna cave, Moravia, Czechoslovakia.

232 Hammer tool made from an antler. Pavlovian, Předmostí, Moravia, Czechoslovakia.

233

234

235

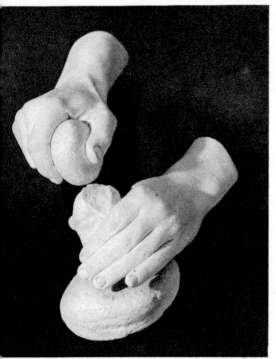

The techniques of flaking

Stone tools were either made by **percussion** or **pressure-flaking**. There are two different methods of percussion — direct and indirect. The most common tool for flaking was the hammerstone, usually only an ordinary stone of the right size and strength. Two characteristic features can be detected on stone flakes and also on some tools if they have been struck by another stone. First, if a stone is struck by another stone the point of impact forms the apex of a cone when the flake breaks off, and secondly, a clearly visible bulbar scar forms on the bottom part of the flake. The traces of percussion can, of course, be removed by further retouching. Some flaked tools, particularly delicate bifacially worked points and knives, were made through indirect percussion; for instance, by using a wooden or bone punch, or sometimes through pressure-flaking.

236

The original crude flaking with the hammerstone would have been made initially by a direct blow. If an implement of hard wood was used for flaking a harder raw material, such as obsidian or flint, a **diffused bulb** would occur which is much less visible than that made when two stones are struck together.

The hammerstone (231) — usually a pebble — was used for the direct percussion method. It was often harder than the raw material it shaped. But the implement of hard wood, ivory, or antler (horn) used for flaking was usually softer than the raw material upon which the flaking took place (232).

Stone Age man would hold the flint in his left hand and the hammerstone in his right. With the hammerstone he struck the core stone with strong, direct, and precise blows. Cores (tools of the core type) were mainly used; or sometimes a flake struck off from a parent core (flake tools). It is comparatively quick to make tools in this way. More primitive tools such as choppers and hand-axes can be made entirely with hammerstones. The crude

233 A pebble which has been used as an anvil on which to make stone tools.

234 A flat stone slab which has been used as a working platform. Magdalenian, Moravia, Czechoslovakia.

235 Flaking with a hammerstone by direct percussion on a hard working surface.

236 Delicate retouching done on a hard working surface. The left hand is holding the tool which is to be retouched.

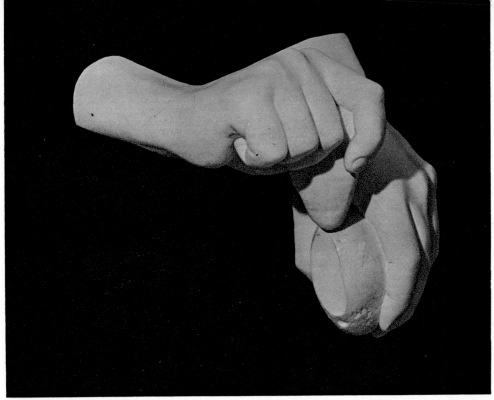

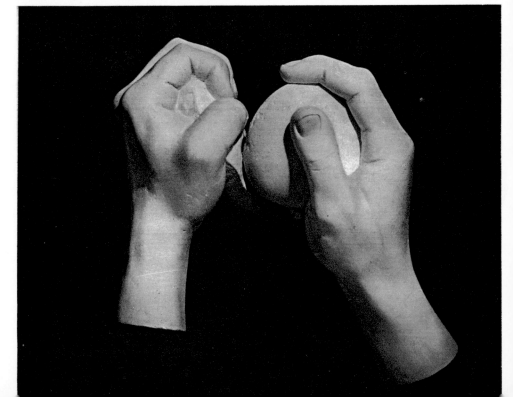

237 The first stage in making a bifacial point: removing flakes with a pebble.

238 Making a point with a hammerstone. The right hand holds the hammerstone while the left hand holds the worked stone.

239 A badly made point with a large hump. The point was not finished and was thrown away unused; Szeletien, Ořechov, Moravia, Czechoslovakia.

240 Three types of point. The two points (centre and right) show indications of having been hafted. The shape of the left-hand point indicates its probable use as a knife. Aurignacian, Szeletien.

239

240

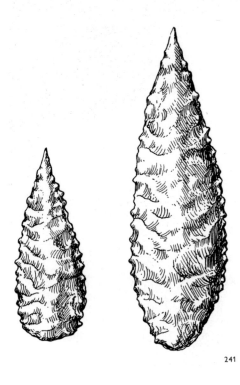

241

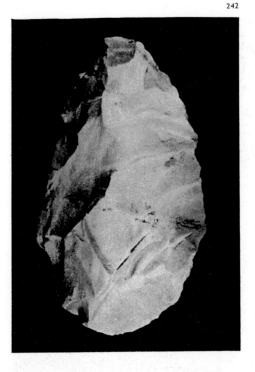

242

241 Glass points from Kimberley, Australia; they were made from broken bottles.

242 A bifacial point made by Australian Aborigines from Arnhem Land.

243 Flaking a tool which is held in one hand while the punch made of bone or hard wood is held in the other.

244 Retouching a side scraper using a hard wood punch. The hand holding the stone to be flaked is protected by a piece of leather.

shape of smaller tools was also achieved by this method and only later improved by delicate retouching to their ultimate shape. Usually a hard surface was used on which to strike the stone. Stone Age man used two methods to break a stone. He would either strike the stone against a larger, harder stone placed on the ground (the 'block-on-block' technique), or he would hurl it against a stone wall or rock. The stone would break into several pieces and suitable flakes could then be chosen and shaped. If he used the latter method he would place the stone on a stone surface and work on the tool with a hammerstone (233 to 235). Naturally, the hammerstone would often be damaged or broken.

When retouching a tool (236) every blow was struck with care in a particular way, and the direction and force used were important for the final shape of the tool. Reports from modern primitive peoples give us an insight into the respect gained by an accomplished toolmaker. The Shasta Indians of California are one such example. All members of the tribe make stone arrowheads, but only a very few became proficient in this art. Snyder, in his book *The Method of Making Stone Arrow*

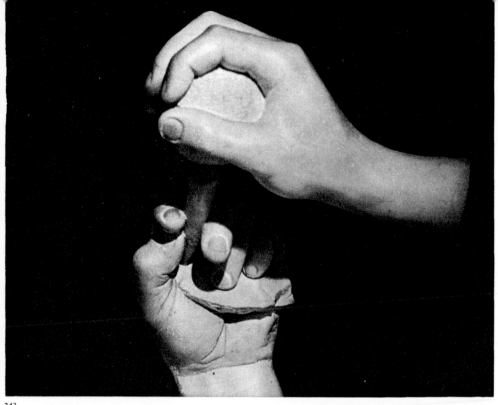

243

244

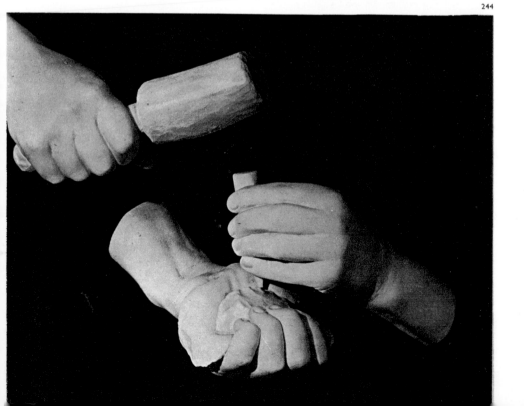

245 Flaking a stone by indirect percussion. The stone is held between the knees (after Semenov).

246 Retouching using a hammerstone.

245

246

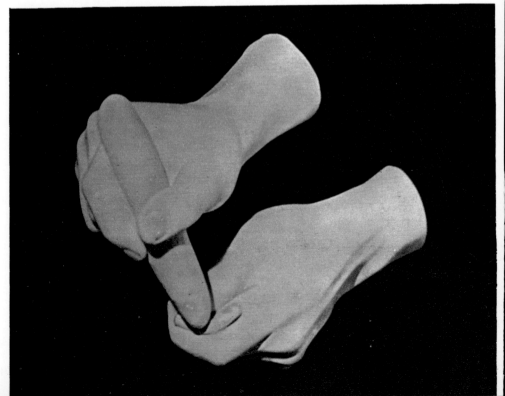

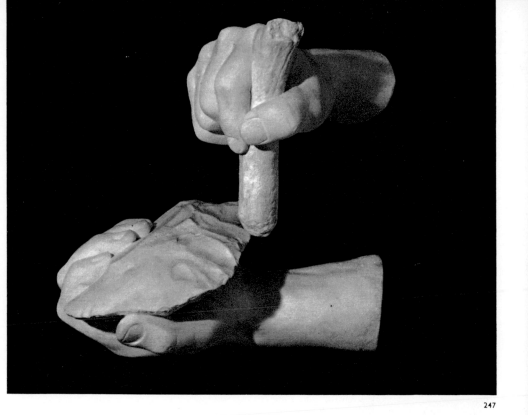

247 Working a stone tool with a bone hammer.

248 The humerus of a kangaroo, sharpened at one end, was used by the Aborigines to pressure-flake or retouch stone points. Northern Australia.

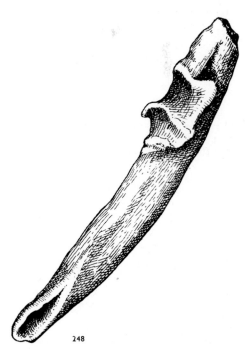

248

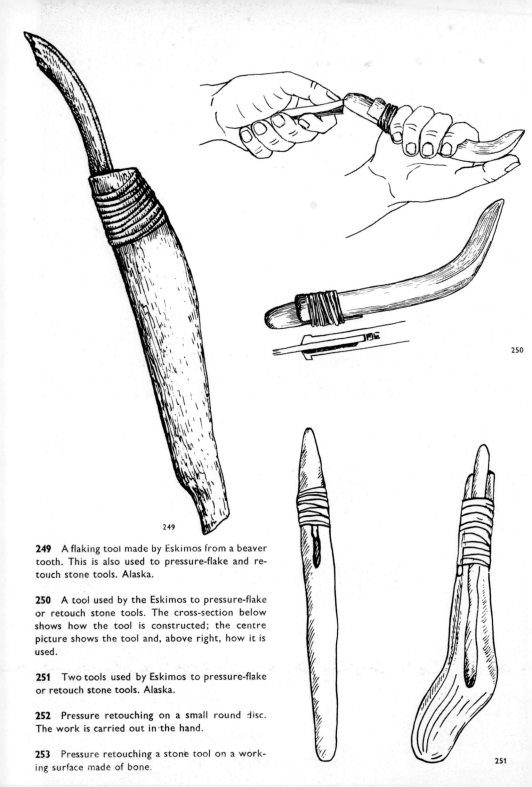

249 A flaking tool made by Eskimos from a beaver tooth. This is also used to pressure-flake and re-touch stone tools. Alaska.

250 A tool used by the Eskimos to pressure-flake or retouch stone tools. The cross-section below shows how the tool is constructed; the centre picture shows the tool and, above right, how it is used.

251 Two tools used by Eskimos to pressure-flake or retouch stone tools. Alaska.

252 Pressure retouching on a small round disc. The work is carried out in the hand.

253 Pressure retouching a stone tool on a working surface made of bone.

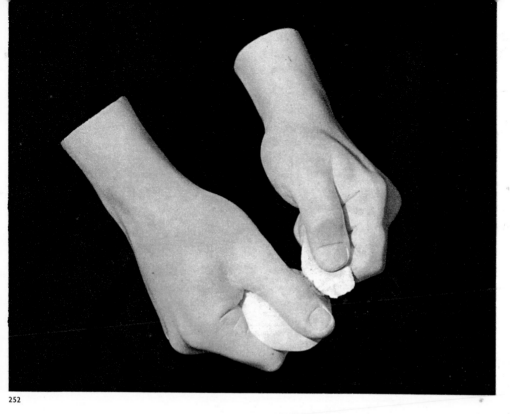

252

253

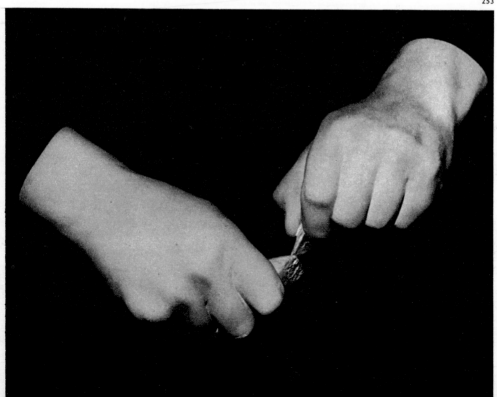

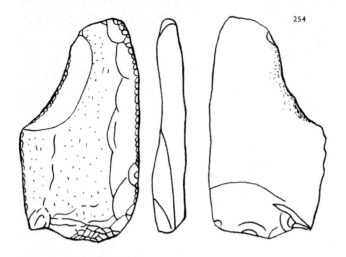

254

254 Stone tool used for retouching. Mousterian period, Roshek, USSR (after Semenov).

255 Pressure retouching on a bone support; modern Australian Aborigine.

255

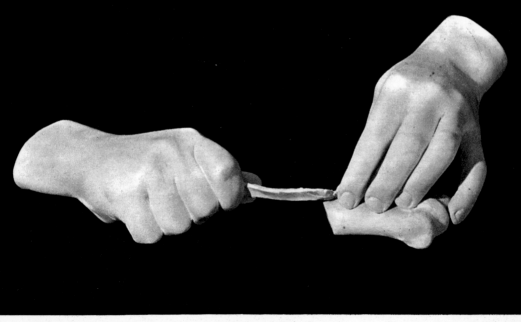

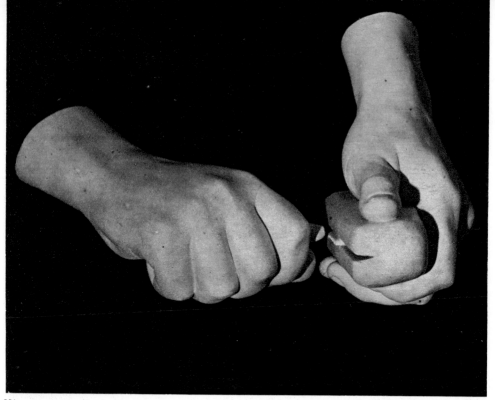

256

256 A microlith set in a wooden shaft being worked on by a bone tool.

Points, talks about the method of making leaf-like flint tools. The flake is placed on a smooth piece of rock and held firmly in the left hand. The hammerstone is held in the right hand and the flake then struck with deliberate and precise blows, first on one side and then on the other, removing small flakes. Then begins the retouching which these Indians do by using a bone point which is pressed on to the flake. The first phase of working this tool is the same as is used to produce a bifacially worked tool, that is, made by holding it in the palm of the hand. Flaking the raw material on a stone surface leaves less choice in working the stone. One of the disadvantages of flaking on a stone surface is that the flake might be chipped at the point of impact between the hammerstone and the core, or the core and the stone surface on which the core was placed. Retouching is made impossible when using this method.

The **leaf-like point** was a tool which could be made with a hammerstone. The pebble from which the tool was made was held in one hand and the hammerstone in the other. The first blow, which is directed at the edge of the pebble, produces a flake (237). Further blows struck at the same angle follow on one side of the pebble. In this way a tool is formed which shows one side of the stone totally untouched and the other side with a mosaic pattern of negative flake traces (238). Then another part of the stone would be worked on. In this way a bifacial disc-shaped or pointed tool was formed. Often the tool would not be completely flat, however, but had humps in the middle (239). If it proved impossible to refine, it would just be thrown away. Very often the point would break off and such points can be found in the sites where stone industries flourished. If the broken plane of the point looks the same as the surface of the tool, it can be assumed that they are of similar age and that the tool must have been broken at the time at which it was made. We can assume that these tools were not only representative of the European Upper Palaeolithic because leaf-like tools and the technique used to make them is also known from later periods and found in many different parts of the world (240 to 242). Another method of making tools is by 'indirect

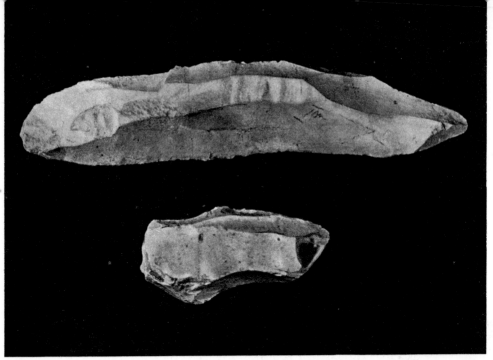

257

258

259

257 Blades used for cutting stone.

258 Small oblong cut pieces of soft stone (slate). Pavlovian culture, Dolní Věstonice, Moravia, Czechoslovakia.

259 A flat stone disc cut from soft stone. Pavlovian culture, Předmostí, Moravia, Czechoslovakia.

260 Stone disc of slate with a segment cut out. Pavlovian culture, Předmostí, Moravia, Czechoslovakia.

260

261 Ground stone from the Pavlovian settlement at Předmostí, Moravia, Czechoslovakia. A rare discovery, and proof that stones were occasionally ground in the Palaeolithic period.

262 Methods of fastening a stone blade to wooden shafts. Reconstructed according to Upper Palaeolithic discoveries from Luka-Vrubleckaya, USSR, and from Lucerne, Switzerland.

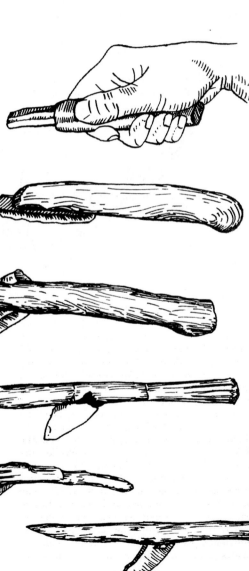

261

262

percussion'. The stones were usually flaked with a bone or wooden punch. The wooden punch and the worked stone are held in one hand while the other hand uses the hammerstone (243). If the toolmaker is inexperienced another method can be used; the stone is held in one hand, the punch in the other, and a second person uses the hammer (244), which can be made from stone, bone or wood. One or two men can also make tools in another way by placing the stone on a flat surface and, without using a punch, flaking the stone directly with a hammerstone. If the worked stone is big enough it can also be held between the knees (245).

Catlin (1868) described the method of indirect flaking which he had observed among the Apaches. The hand used for holding the stone is protected by a piece of leather with an opening for the thumb. The man would sit on the floor with the stone in his hand. The other hand positions the punch which is usually made out of bone. The punch is placed against the part of the stone from which a flake is to be removed and a second person strikes the punch with a hard, wooden club. The stone is first flaked on one side, then turned around and flaked on the other. This method is repeated until the desired shape is achieved. If the stone is held in the hand the blow is softened and diminishes the possibility of breaking. The punch is between 140 and 160 millimetres long and 20 to 25 millimetres wide. In cross-section two sides are flat and the third is rounded.

B B Redding reported a similar technique used by the Wintoon Indians, where only one person carries out this task. He held the obsidian core in his left hand, using the index and middle fingers of the same hand to hold the punch made from bone or antler. According to the size of the flake required, he placed the punch a certain distance away from the edge of the stone. The Indian struck the first blow but the flake broke; he then replaced the punch firmly and with great care on the obsidian. This time he was successful and the flake had a desired form and a shell-like surface. With the combination of different kinds of punches, and stone or bone hammers, precisely shaped tools can be made (246). The flakes are small and flat and leave a mosaic pattern of corresponding negative traces on the tool. The bulbs on the flakes are diffuse. Soft hammers were used for making long, fine blades from obsidian, for example. These are

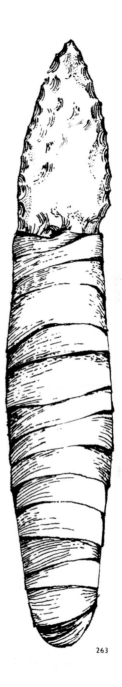

263

263 Stone knife bifacially flaked and attached to a shaft which had a strip of untreated leather wrapped around. Alaska.

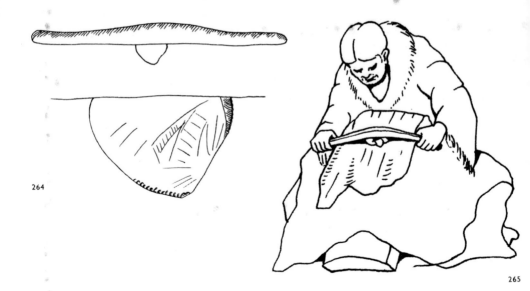

264

265

264 Stone scraper set in a wooden handle for two--hand use in working on skins. This picture does not show a typical scraper but a flake. A fine retouch is visible on the flake, caused through the work (detail below). Chuckchee, east Siberia.

265 A stone scraper being used to clean a skin. Chuckchee, east Siberia (after Semenov).

266 Knife bifacially flaked and socketed in a bone shaft. North American Indians.

267 Horse-phalanges which have been used as shafts or handles for stone tools. Magdalenian culture, Pekárna cave, Moravia, Czechoslovakia.

268 An atypical stone blade, socketed in a reindeer antler which was used as a shaft. Magdalenian culture, Pekárna cave, Moravia, Czechoslovakia.

266

267

268

ideal to work on; the material is easy to flake to achieve delicate retouching (247). Stone Age man probably used a similar technique for flaking with soft hammers in his hand, as he did for flaking with a hard hammerstone.

Pressure-flaking was mainly used to retouch tools or for very delicate work. Using this technique, however, only small flakes were obtained, often no longer than fish scales. For this kind of work mostly tools made from bone, antler, or wood were used. They were pointed and sometimes had handles similar to those which can still be found in use by some primitive peoples such as the Eskimos (248 to 251). Pressure-flaking can also be achieved by reversing the process, that is, by pressing the tool or flake against a suitably hard surface, such as a bone or a small pebble (252 to 255).

Small, delicately cut and ground pieces of stone which were used for retouching are known from the Ukraine and Czechoslovakia and belong to the Pavlovian culture.

Other small retouched microlithic tools are known which would have been too small to work in the hand. Therefore, Stone Age man must have used a piece of wood or antler with a groove (256) into which the microlithic tool was placed; and pressure retouching could be done in this way.

We sometimes find the technique of **stone cutting**. Thin, rectangular pieces of soft stone

269 A burin-like tool held in a bone socket. Magdalenian culture, Pekárna cave, Moravia, Czechoslovakia.

270 Antler shaft with a fixed burin. The numbers 1, 2, 3, and 4 refer to the shape of the cross-section of the shaft and are also marked on it. Malta, Siberia (after Gerassimov).

271 An atypical stone blade socketed in a reindeer antler, Magdalenian culture, Pekárna cave, Moravia, Czechoslovakia.

272 Two stone tools (a scraper and blade) in shafts made from antler, Malta, Siberia.

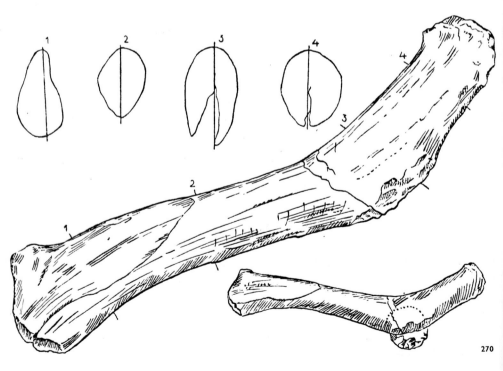

270

— obviously unfinished tools — have been found in Dolní Věstonice in Czechoslovakia. The edges were cut with stone blades and thin pieces of stone split off (257, 258). Thin stone discs from the early Pavlovian have been found which were approximately 200 millimetres in diameter and had a central hole varying between 50 and 80 millimetres (259, 260).

Discoveries of Palaeolithic polished stone tools are very rare. They were ground using a technique known only in the later Neolithic period. Edge-ground axes were found recently near Oenpelli in northern Australia and dated as 23 000 years old. The oldest polished tools, which are very rare (25 000 years), come from Předmostí in Czechoslovakia (261).

Discoveries of tools with handles or sockets made of bone prove that man did not hold all his stone tools directly in his hand; this is especially so in the Upper Palaeolithic. It is almost certain that by then most tools had wooden handles or sockets which have unfortunately not been preserved (262 to 268). Only occasionally have tools with microlithic blades in a socket been discovered. It is possible, however, to reconstruct the implement according to the position in which the different parts have been found. Discoveries of empty bone sockets are fairly frequent, and short hollow handles made of horse's digital bones are also known. One such discovery was made in the Pekárna cave (Czechoslovakia) where a large, but rather atypical burin was found hafted into a bone that had been specially hollowed to receive it (269). Three other finds of antler hafts are known with stone tools in them. They come from Maita in Siberia and the Pekárna cave (270 to 272).

These rare discoveries of stone tools hafted into bones not only threw light on the activities of Stone Age hunters but also gave a further insight into the variety of tools available at that time. The spear was the usual weapon of the hunter, and stone tools used for hunting always had some kind of pointed end. Two interesting discoveries have been made in Czechoslovakia. The skull of a bear found in Moravia had a wound on the top, but a bone ridge had formed around the deep gash showing that the bear did not die immediately from the injury. The shape of the gash shows that an atypical heavy stone tool, with a burin-type point, must have been the weapon used. The other discovery was the skull of a wolf found in a Pavlovian settlement at Dolní Věs-

272

273

tonice; it was lying among many other animal bones, obviously the remains of some of the food of the Palaeolithic hunters. A flint flake was stuck in the nose of the animal (273). The wound did not seem to have healed, and the X-ray showed that the flake used was broad, flat and atypically shaped. From these two examples it seems apparent that the Palaeolithic tools just discussed were used to kill or hunt animals even if they did not fully correspond to modern typological classification.

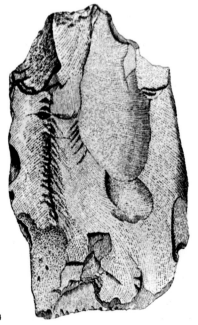

274

273 The skull of a wolf with an atypical stone flake stuck in its nose. Pavlovian culture, Dolní Věstonice, Moravia, Czechoslovakia.

274 A broad chisel made from a bone flake. Magdalenian, Pekárna cave, Moravia, Czechoslovakia.

The working of bone

In sites of the Middle and Upper Palaeolithic period many bones can be found which have been deliberately broken or split. This proves that man must have tried to get at the marrow of the bone and the brain to eat it. Long-bones predominate because these, of course, have the most marrow. Also, the split bones could easily be made into tools. The technique of working a bone or mammoth tusk often differs very little from flaking stones. If large bones were broken, not only to extract marrow but also to be made into tools, traces of flaking by hammerstones can be seen (274, 275). These bones were probably flaked by using a hard anvil. Heavy hammerstones were used also for flaking mammoth tusks. It was obviously not easy to remove the tusks from the sockets, let alone try to split the tusks diagonally because they were often 200 millimetres thick. Similarly to stone flakes, crude flakes of bone were used as scrapers, knives or further retouched to form other tools (276, 277).

275 Double-ended chisel made from bone. Magdalenian culture, Pekárna cave, Moravia, Czechoslovakia.

276 Blade-shaped bone tool. Traces of some kind of retouching can be seen on the upper edge of the blade. Pekárna cave, Moravia, Czechoslovakia.

275

276

277

277 Flaking a mammoth tusk with a hammerstone and a small chisel. Pavlovian settlement, Dolní Věstonice, Moravia, Czechoslovakia.

278

278 Fragment of a stone wedge, which was used to split mammoth ivory and broke during the process. Pavlovian culture, Předmostí, Moravia, Czechoslovakia.

279

279 A mammoth tusk split lengthwise. Pavlovian culture, Dolní Věstonice, Moravia, Czechoslovakia.

280 Two blades made from mammoth ivory. Pavlovian culture, Moravia, Czechoslovakia.

281 A part of a mammoth tusk which was shaped and used as an abrasive tool. Pavlovian culture, Předmostí, Moravia, Czechoslovakia.

281

280

282

282 A flaked and cut piece made from mammoth ivory. Magdalenian culture, Pekárna cave, Moravia, Czechoslovakia.

283 Two flakes, fragments produced while working mammoth ivory. Pavlovian culture, Dolní Věstonice, Moravia, Czechoslovakia.

284 Unfinished spoon or scoop from mammoth ivory. Pavlovian culture, Dolní Věstonice, Moravia, Czechoslovakia.

285 Unretouched large bone flakes. Pavlovian culture, Předmostí, Moravia, Czechoslovakia.

283

284

285

The longitudinal splitting of bones has occurred a little more frequently, but only a few tusks have been found showing clearly the small stone wedges which got stuck in the tusk indicating the technique used for working these tusks (278, 279). It was certainly more difficult to split bones or tusks diagonally. In such cases, there are traces of blows with an axe-like tool to weaken the tusk at the point where it should break. Discoveries of stone tools which look like small wedges or chisels often show traces of battering by a hard object on their upper surface. It is possible that these tools were used to split tusks or bones both diagonally and lengthwise.

Crude flakes of tusks or bones could be used in exactly the same way as stone flakes (280 to 285). They show traces of blows received, often a bulb is visible, and the edge sometimes has worn smooth through use. Sometimes they also show traces of damage on

the blade edge which occurred through long use. The bones were sometimes first deeply grooved and then flaked with a chisel.

So-called pseudo-artefacts have been found in excavations; they give the impression of tools intentionally made, but in fact are not — invariably they are debris or waste material. If a long-bone is split from both ends a characteristic boat-like shape is formed by the middle piece of the bone. This shape is quite unusual and if an archaeologist finds several of these shapes in one place he could easily believe that he had found a strange bone implement. Such small remains of bone are often called 'toggles'.

Another interesting pseudo-artefact occurs if the bone is split from one side only. In places where Stone Age man split large numbers of bones, and cut off the epiphyses (the end pieces of the long-bone) they could be mistaken for properly made tools. But only definite traces of these tools being used for

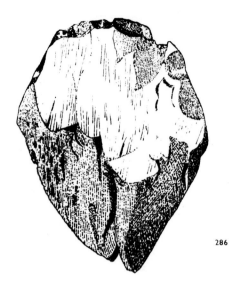

286

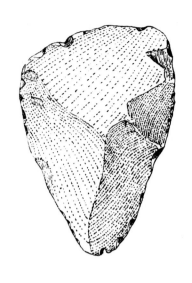

287

286–289 Four bone flakes showing indications of use. Pavlovian culture, Předmostí, Moravia, Czechoslovakia.

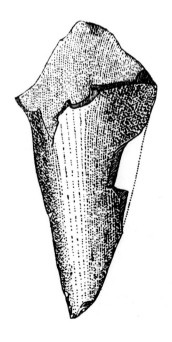

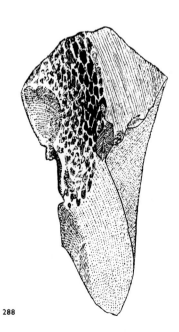

288

specific purposes are proof of their being proper tools (286 to 289). It was, of course, possible to make use of bones or teeth which were conveniently shaped without any further working (290, 291). Proper tools are distinguished by scratches, smoothed edges or surfaces, and by the damage to blades or points which would be caused through constant use (292).

Anvils form a special group of bone implements. Large bones, or parts of bones, with blow marks and cuts indicate that they have been used to work other bones, meat, or skins on them (293, 294). Particularly on large bones, such as the shoulder-blades of a mammoth or rhinoceros, long scratches can often be found; they were probably used as a base on which to cut skins to make straps and clothes.

Metacarpal and metatarsal bones of large mammals, particularly of mammoths, were used as anvils for making bone tools. This is evident from the traces left by hard blows.

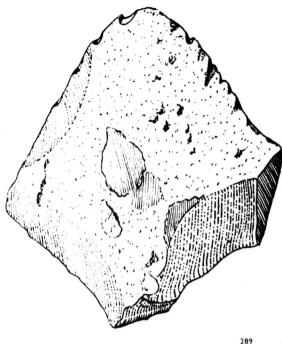

290 Scrapers made from mammoth molar teeth used for cleaning skins. Pavlovian culture, Dolní Věstonice, Moravia, Czechoslovakia.

289

290

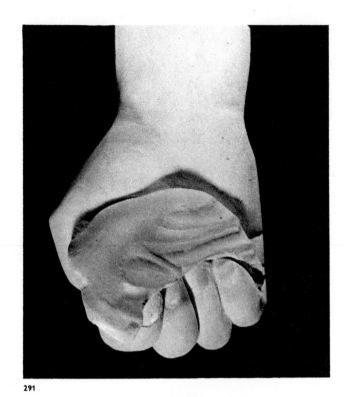

291

291 A scraper is held like this.

292 A bear's jaw. The edges have become smooth through use. Mousterian culture, Kačák cave, Bohemia, Czechoslovakia.

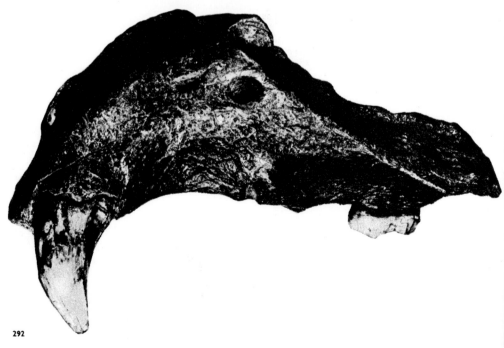

292

293 An anvil made from mammoth ivory. Pavlovian culture, Dolní Věstonice, Moravia, Czechoslovakia.

294 Fragment of a bone shaft or handle which was used as a working surface. Pavlovian culture. Dolní Věstonice, Moravia, Czechoslovakia.

With the constantly rising number of bone, tusk, and antler tools in the Upper Palaeolithic, more stone tools, particularly burins and hand-drills for bone working, were made. The burin was capable of making deep grooves in solid materials such as bone, antler, or mammoth tusks, and was used in the same way as in the modern lathe cutting tool (295). Sometimes it was possible to undercut the surface layer and the piece cut could then be eased out with either a cylindrical or chisel-shaped bone wedge.

When Palaeolithic man cut antler lengthwise he often scraped or chopped out the porous layer of bone, which is clearly indicated by the chisel marks left on the bones (296, 297). Where mammoth tusks or bones had been cut diagonally with a burin the sectional plane was relatively smooth. The cuts reached different depths, and the bone or tusk was then broken off either through indirect pressure or a blow.

The grooves of lengthwise cuts are usually straight, although it is possible at times to detect several grooves on the surface of the bone or antler which indicate that some grooves had been incorrectly made. The cuts are usu-

ally smooth but it is sometimes possible to see faint parallel scratches on the wall of the groove, traces of irregular blade of the stone tool (298). Some bone plates bear traces of the chisel blows on their sides. The Magdalenian culture is noted for large numbers of tools made from antler. Antler is tougher than bone, and it is only rarely cut diagonally. In such cases it was covered with short, lengthwise, deep cuts leading from one end to another. The cut antler was then broken diagonally in the desired place (299), and useless portions were broken off and discarded. Sometimes the pieces were prepared for breaking by striking the shaft of the antler with heavy blows (300, 301). If Stone Age man wished to achieve a smooth and accurately cut antler he would give it the greatest attention (302). He would cut the tines with the burin by making deep grooves on both sides. These tines have a kind of socket at the base and look like tools, but they are nothing more than rejected waste material.

Pieces of bone which have been either cut off or chopped out are often cut or scratched into the final shape both on the soft inside as well as the hard outside of the bone. Deep

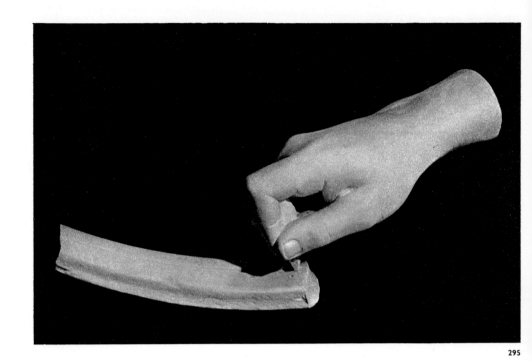

295

296

297

298

295   A stone burin cutting a bone.

296   The marrow in the bone of a reindeer antler has been removed. A long incision was made first with a burin and the marrow removed with chisel--like tools. Magdalenian culture, Pekárna cave, Moravia, Czechoslovakia.

297   An antler cut lengthwise with the soft marrow removed.

298   A reindeer antler cut lengthwise. Grooves can be seen along the cut edge.

299

299   Traces of incisions can be seen on this reindeer antler. The upper and supraorbital tines of the antler were first deeply cut and then broken off. A small piece of the skull which is attached to the antler shows traces of having been struck several blows. Magdalenian culture, Pekárna cave, Moravia, Czechoslovakia.

300   A piece of worked antler. Both ends show traces of blows made with a blunt object.

300

301 Antler which has been cut with a blunt object. The marks left by several blows can be seen at the point at which the antler broke.

302 Cut off antler tines, so-called sockets. These appear to be tools, although, in fact, they are waste pieces.

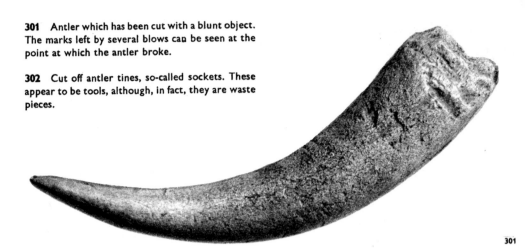

301

302

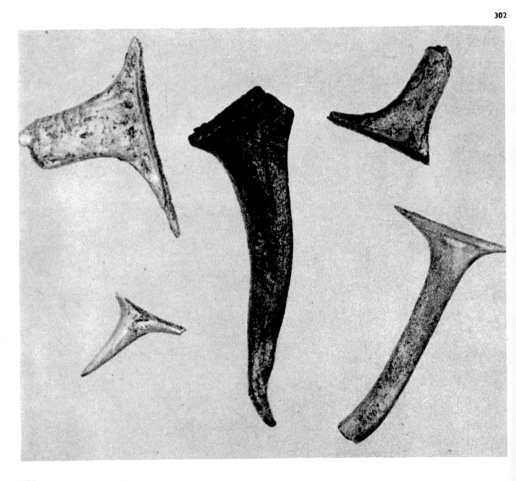

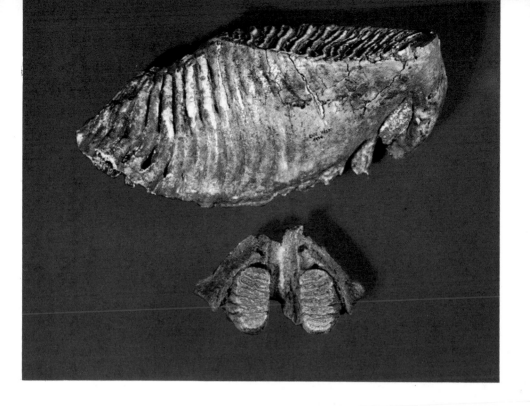

Molar of a mature mammoth and that of a young one. These animals were welcome prey to the prehistoric hunter because they provided him not only with food, but also with the material for making tools.

Circular disc made from soft slate with a segment cut out; Pavlovian culture, Předmostí, Moravia, Czechoslovakia.

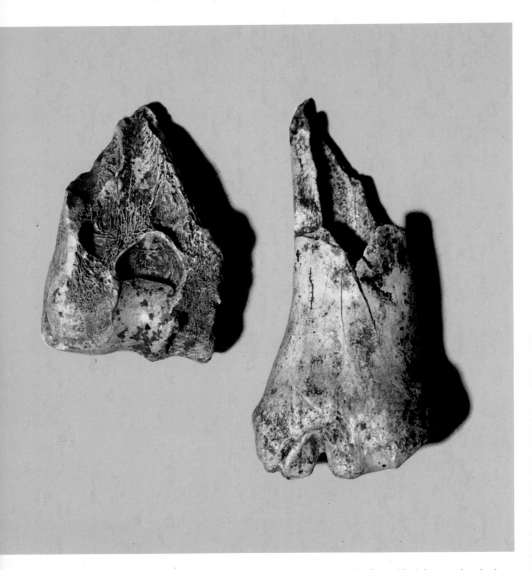

Primitive tools made from the bones of large mammals belonging to the Günz-Mindel interglacial phase. The tool on the right is similar in shape to the later developed hand-axe; Stránská skála, Moravia, Czechoslovakia.

grooves are visible on the sides of these flakes; sometimes they are the marks of the chisel which prised them out. The blade or point of the stone tool always had an irregular or serrated edge. This was advantageous when cutting meat or leather because it had the effect of cutting as well as tearing it.

Small bones and especially bones of birds could not easily be worked on, because the methods were too crude. If it was desired to cut such bones, knives or small saws had to be used (303). These smaller tools were used for greater precision work. They were also used to cut or saw holes in teeth, snail shells, or shells which would be used as pendants and necklaces (304). Some diagonally cut or saw: off teeth (305, 306) have been found in Magdalenian settlements. Often they are large bear canines with wide grooves on the lower part of the teeth (307), where they have obviously been strung and worn as a pendant. Hollow

303 Upper Palaeolithic saws and drills, finely retouched. Magdalenian culture, Pekárna cave, Moravia, Czechoslovakia.

303

bones of birds were cut diagonally and often used as needle boxes or pipes. If Stone Age man wanted to achieve a clean cut he would make several incisions right round the bone. Scraping as a technique appears also in this connection which made it possible to be very accurate particularly if the scraping was to remove the soft inner parts of the bone (308). This technique can be recognized by the scraping lines which can be seen running parallel and close together (309). The scraping of an implement would often be carried out last in order to remove any small holes, bumps or other irregular features showing on the surface.

The technique of bone cutting and splitting was also used for making harpoon and spearpoints. The shape of the harpoon or spearhead would be scratched deep into the porous layer of the bone using a burin, and then the rest would be broken away (310). Then the porous layer was scraped off, the basal part of the point cut flat on both sides, and the surface of the base would be grooved to give a rough but firm grip when fixing the point to the haft of the weapon. An interesting discovery of three spearpoints in the Nová Drátenická cave (Moravia, Czechoslovakia) showed the rough functional grooving of the bases of points

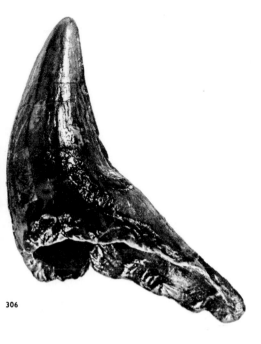

306

307

304 Palaeolithic hunters collected snail shells, drilled holes through them and used them as jewellery. Pavlovian culture, Dolní Věstonice, Moravia, Czechoslovakia.

305 The tooth of a bear with a hole drilled through it.

306 A retouched canine tooth of a bear which was used as a scraper. Magdalenian, Pekárna cave, Moravia, Czechoslovakia.

307 The tooth of a cave bear which has been used as a pendant. A groove was made at its root, and a thin flake was cut off along its length.

308 Flat bone spatula.

308

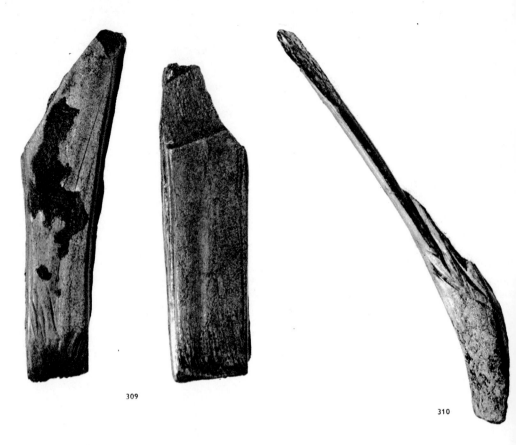

309

310

309 Examples of scraped bones. Magdalenian culture, Pekárna cave, Moravia, Czechoslovakia.

310 Almost finished bone point. Magdalenian culture, Pekárna cave, Moravia, Czechoslovakia.

311 Detail of the basal part of the bone point shown in 312. The base has been originally roughened to obtain a good grip; from this a decoration with a zigzag pattern developed. Magdalenian culture, Nová Drátenická cave, Moravia, Czechoslovakia.

311

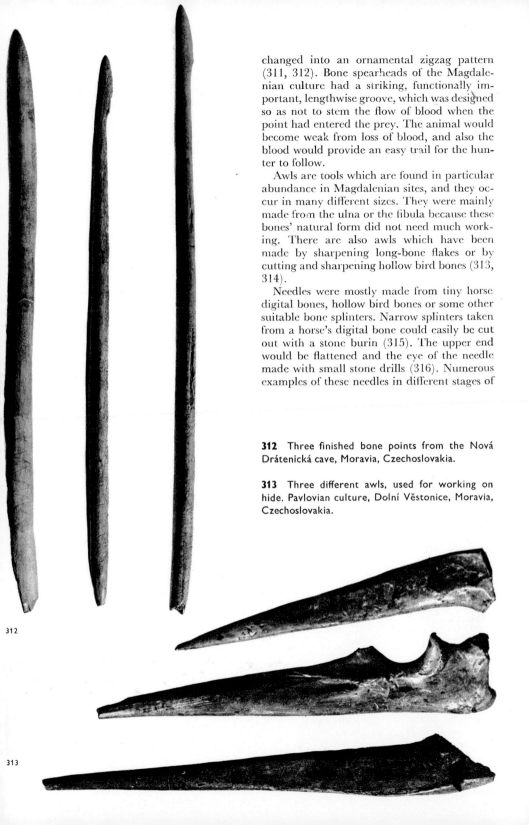

changed into an ornamental zigzag pattern (311, 312). Bone spearheads of the Magdalenian culture had a striking, functionally important, lengthwise groove, which was designed so as not to stem the flow of blood when the point had entered the prey. The animal would become weak from loss of blood, and also the blood would provide an easy trail for the hunter to follow.

Awls are tools which are found in particular abundance in Magdalenian sites, and they occur in many different sizes. They were mainly made from the ulna or the fibula because these bones' natural form did not need much working. There are also awls which have been made by sharpening long-bone flakes or by cutting and sharpening hollow bird bones (313, 314).

Needles were mostly made from tiny horse digital bones, hollow bird bones or some other suitable bone splinters. Narrow splinters taken from a horse's digital bone could easily be cut out with a stone burin (315). The upper end would be flattened and the eye of the needle made with small stone drills (316). Numerous examples of these needles in different stages of

312 Three finished bone points from the Nová Drátenická cave, Moravia, Czechoslovakia.

313 Three different awls, used for working on hide. Pavlovian culture, Dolní Věstonice, Moravia, Czechoslovakia.

312

313

314

314 Various types of bone bodkins.

315 Needles were made from horse bones; the metatarsals (these bones show the traces left after cutting out the bone slivers).

316 Stages in the manufacture of needles from slivers of bone.

317 Bone needles of varying sizes. Magdalenian culture, Pekárna cave, Moravia, Czechoslovakia.

315

manufacture give a very accurate picture of the way they were made. The finished needles vary from 20 to 200 millimetres in length (317, 318). If the needle was particularly small the burin would be used to start the hole off and the drill would complete it (319).

Drilled holes are not only known in needles, pendants, snail shells, and teeth (320, 321), but also in stone objects. Stones with holes drilled through are known from the Upper Palaeolithic where they were used as pendants or costume ornaments (322). Larger holes often give the impression that they had first been made with stone points and then been cut or drilled to shape. On the other hand, many of the small, smooth holes prove beyond doubt that they have been made with some kind of

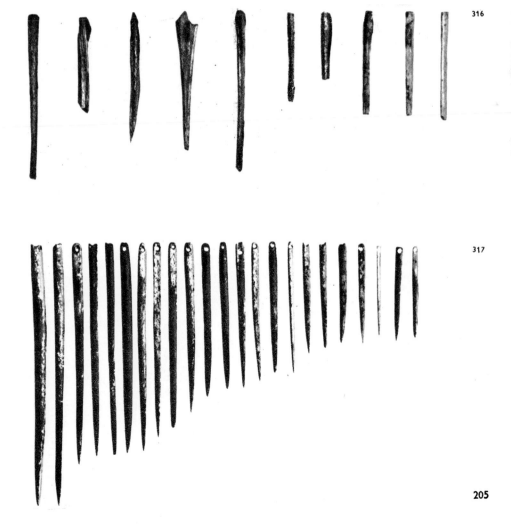

316

317

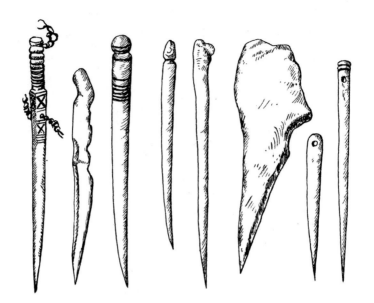

drill. Finds from burials associated with Brno II, dating from the beginning of the main Würm Glaciation (oldest Pavlovian culture) show that this technique is very old. This grave produced small round discs made of bones, mammoth ivory, and stone with dents or holes all made by stone drills (323, 324). Malta, in Siberia, yielded round rings which, as well as the fine ivory rings from Pavlov in Czechoslovakia show great skill and some kind of mechanical method used (325, 326). The holes, however, do not give the impression that com-

318 Various types of bodkins and needles; from the left the first five and the eighth are Eskimo needles, and six and seven are Magdalenian (after Hauser).

319 Fragment of a bone needle from Yeliseievitchi, Ukraine. Details of how the hole was made using a small burin, are clearly visible (after Semenov).

320 Canine teeth of cave bears with holes drilled through them. Before drilling, the roots were cut to become thinner.

321 Canine teeth of cave bears and stags were much prized hunting trophies in the Palaeolithic period. It was quite possible, at that time, to drill perfect holes through such hard material as tooth.

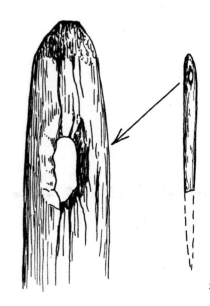

plicated drills existed at that time (327); obviously simple drills which were easy to handle had been used (328, 329).

It can be said that within particular defined areas certain stone tools from the Lower, Middle, and Upper Palaeolithic are particularly characteristic of these periods. If we compare modern primitive peoples and only observe their stone industry we come to the conclusion that the Tasmanians, who became extinct during the 1800s, were technologically equivalent to the European Stone Age. Several Australian and South African tribes have not developed their technology beyond the Upper Palaeolithic or Epipalaeolithic period. Typical Aurignacian scrapers of the European Upper Palaeolithic type were still in use with the Tasmanians and some Australians in the 1880s. Therefore, our classification of stone tools can only help us in a comparative typological study, not in stating an absolute chronological scale.

Some types of tools were used for longer periods by certain groups of men, or some tools appeared earlier than expected. In this latter case they would be atypical and would differ in shape and form from the classical models of the typological system devised.

The development of man was influenced by many different aspects, such as climate, the environment, and living conditions, as well as

320

321

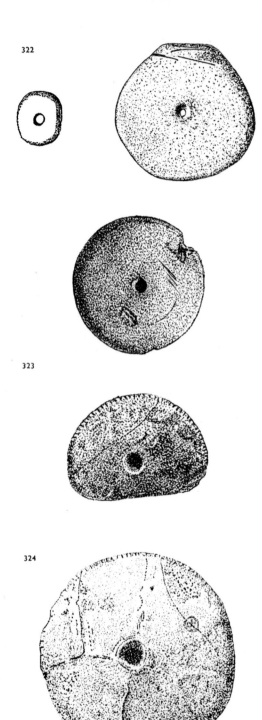

various isolating factors so that differences must appear between different groups. This fact is as much in evidence today as in prehistoric times.

We are at present at a stage of strong cultural change and widely spaced cultural contacts between very unequally developed races, and we have witnessed many times how this change has often brought about the extinction of lesser developed peoples. One of the most devastating examples is that of now extinct Tasmanians who have been exterminated by the ruthlessly advancing European civilizations. They were among the most primitive men in the modern world. How informative it would have been to have studied the way of life of these people, quite apart from humanitarian reasons for saving them; their industry, their methods of hunting, their social life, their art, mythology, and their whole world of thoughts and ideas could have been studied. The bushmen of South Africa, the Indian tribes like the Onas, Alacalufs, and Yaghans in South America, as well as the inland Eskimos from North America suffered the same fate. These races are also either extinct or are threatened with extinction.

Fortunately, not all contacts with modern civilization have had such catastrophic results. There are, for instance, the Indians of south-

322 An antler bead cut to size, polished, and with a hole drilled through it (left); polished pebble with a hole drilled through (right). Magdalenian culture, Pekárna cave, Moravia, Czechoslovakia.

323 Round stone disc with drilled hole (above) and a bone disc (below), from a Pavlovian burial. Brno II, Moravia, Czechoslovakia.

324 Round stone disc with a hole in the middle and decorated with fine lines around the edge. Pavlovian culture, Brno, Moravia, Czechoslovakia.

west North America, a number of Australian tribes, and several Siberians of the USSR. These people left behind on a level of primitive culture of hunting and collecting, have come into contact with modern civilizations. This does not mean that they will die out, however, because they have preserved their language and even attended special schools to improve their knowledge. There are several examples today which prove that primitive people have and can achieve high academic, artistic, and athletic standards. If favourable conditions exist, these groups will one day be capable of jumping certain intermediate periods of cultural phases. In order to achieve this, however, it does call for national compatibility to make it possible for people with different cultural backgrounds to live together.

Lastly, if we consider that it is possible for a Stone Age culture, like the one in New Guinea, to exist in the highly developed 1900s, how much more possible must it have been for many cultures of widely differing levels to have existed in the Palaeolithic period, when small groups of people were far more isolated. One question still remains unanswered. To what extent can we judge the importance of so many obviously different stone tools and their function in cultural developments?

325

325 Method of cutting a 100 millimetre diameter bracelet from a piece of mammoth ivory. Malta, Siberia.

326 Thin rings made from mammoth ivory. Pavlovian culture, Pavlov, Moravia, Czechoslovakia.

326

209

327

328

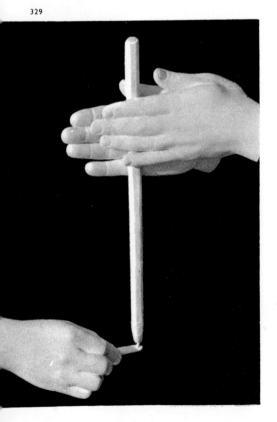

329

327 Crudely cut holes in phalanges (toe bones). Magdalenian culture, Moravia, Czechoslovakia.

328 Bone point showing traces of drilling in a hard material at the end. Magdalenian culture, Pekárna cave, Moravia, Czechoslovakia.

329 A hafted stone drill showing its working position.

III Dwellings and settlements of Stone Age Man

330

330 Hut at Terra Amata near Nice, France. A fireplace was found in the centre of a bowl-shaped depression in the sand (after de Lumley).

The hunters of the Stone Age built their settlements on flat or very gently sloping ground near a river or lake, the locations of most Upper Palaeolithic settlements known to us today. The countryside has not basically changed since the Upper Palaeolithic.

A large number of settlements from the Middle and Lower Palaeolithic, however, are found on river banks or in caves. Only rarely have they been found in open country, although we must assume that this would be preferred, and the caves were only used for protection in rough climates. Climatic conditions obviously played an important part in the choice of a settlement or dwelling. This can be observed even in primitive races of today who use — in tropical regions — only simple shading covers during the dry season to protect themselves from the heat and sun. Only in the rainy season will they build waterproof dwellings or retreat into caves.

If the Palaeolithic hunter lived in flat country with no caves in the vicinity, he often would dig a subterranean or semi-subterranean dwelling and cover it with a securely fastened vaulted roof. In warmer periods tents were used, especially in periglacial Europe. The tent was easily moved and its primitive construction was suitable for the nomadic way of life of Stone Age man. There are three main types of dwelling of Palaeolithic hunters and hunting peoples in general; there were various kinds of protective roof or awning, tents, and solid dwellings. The awnings gave seasonal shelter, often against the cold; the tents were used for shelter mostly during the summer months, and the solid dwellings as living quarters in the winter. This way of life can still be observed today among the hunting peoples of Siberia and the Eskimos.

The material available obviously played a large part in the choice of a particular shelter. In the areas where wood was rare (in periglacial areas of Europe) dwelling constructions were made from mammoth tusks, antlers and large bones. Parallel examples come from present-day eastern Siberia where the lower jaws and ribs of whales were still used to build houses in historical times. Subterranean dwellings still existed in the 1880s, in which the above-ground constructions were covered up with clay to protect them against cold. In grassland areas dwellings are still covered with grass, which is piled on to a simple roof structure, and many prehistoric dwellings must have looked very similar.

Light protective roofs and tents were also erected inside caves too large for Palaeolithic man to inhabit as a single dwelling place, and could be divided into several living quarters.

Discoveries of Palaeolithic dwellings are very rare. Only a very few settlements of this period have been discovered. The only complete settlement known at present is of the Pavlovian culture at Dolní Věstonice (Czechoslovakia), and its absolute dating according to the radiocarbon method shows that it is about 25 000 years old. Sites discovered in the Ukraine, Kostienki I, and Avdieievo, may also belong to the same period. The first Stone Age settlement in the USSR was found by S N Zamjatnin in 1927 near Gagarino in the Ukraine (S N Zamjatnin, 1929).

The archaeological work in the first half of the 1900s was hampered on two accounts: firstly because of the condition of the deposits, and secondly because excavation techniques at that time were much less advanced. It was then thought sufficient to excavate a few large areas, and no overall view of the site was obtained, nor were connections between the finds clearly realized. The finds were usually not properly catalogued, plans of the site often do not exist, and the excavated areas were often described only very briefly. A change took place as archaeologists began to uncover vast areas and excavate whole settlements. This technique made it possible to retrieve large numbers of objects and complex information which could be compared with other discoveries.

As already mentioned, the condition of the deposits covering a site is very important. It is clearly preferable to excavate a settlement covered with loess which reveals every detail and gives better results, than a settlement that is covered with debris. This might be one of the reasons why more evidence has been found in Palaeolithic settlements in central Europe, the Ukraine, and Siberia, where loess deposits are quite common. The earliest discovery of the remains of a Stone Age dwelling is probably that found by L S B Leakey in the Olduvai Gorge in East Africa. It is a circle of stones in a deposit belonging to the Lower Pleistocene period. This find is nearly 1.8 million years old, and if it definitely constituted a dwelling it would have been most probably the work of *Homo habilis*.

Discoveries of settlements in western Europe

The oldest remains of a hut from the Acheulean culture were found by de Lumley near Nice on the French Riviera. The site is called **Terra Amata** (330). The **Grotte du Lazaret** is situated nearby, and one of the oldest discoveries of a Palaeolithic dwelling has been made there. During excavations in 1957 the remains of a hut measuring 3.5 metres by 11 metres were discovered in the Acheulean deposits (331). The hut stood against the cave wall near the entrance and could be easily identified because of the concentration of stone tools and bones which are typical of such sites. Outside the area of the hut discoveries were rare. The stones delineating the hut could not have fallen from the roof of the cave and it is clear that they were placed there to give more stability to the construction of the hut. The hut was using the cave wall for support, but

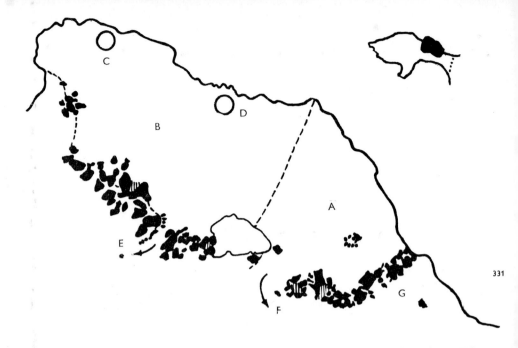

331 An Acheulean hut found in the Grotte du Lazaret near Nice, in France. Its outlines are marked by deliberately placed stones, and also by the implements found inside the dwelling. It consisted of an anteroom (A), a living space (B), two small fireplaces (C, D), and large and small entrances (E, F). Opposite the cave entrance a pile of stones acted as a wind-break (G). Above is a drawing outlining the cave with the hut marked in black (after de Lumley).

the wall was not part of the hut. This was evident because a narrow path ran beside the cave wall in which no implements were found. The wall of the hut was separated from the cave wall to keep out the water running down the inside of the cave. No remains of posts or other constructional material were found. But seven piles of stones about 0.8 to 1.2 metres apart, which could have been used to prop up posts, were found. If the posts stuck in the stones had been leaned against the cave wall the dwelling would have been extremely low. The piles of stones gave the impression that the posts must have been standing upright holding and supporting cross-beams which would rest on a ledge on one side of the cave wall and on the upright post on the other to give the structure greater stability. The upright posts could have been split at the top and the horizontal posts would have rested in the fork.

The stones outlining the hut had a gap in one place, obviously forming the entrance. This is confirmed by its being the only place where finds of stone tools and bones spill over the edge of the hut. The entrance was not large — only about 0.8 metres wide (332).

332 View of the reconstructed Acheulean hut inside the Grotte du Lazaret (after de Lumley).

Reconstruction of a tent from the Siberian site of Malta in the USSR.

A prehistoric painter completes the painting of a bull on the cave wall at Lascaux, France (Z Burian).

333

The biggest concentration of stones opposite the entrance of the cave must have acted as a wind-break against the winds blowing in from the sea.

The hut was probably covered with animal skins. They would be protection against the cold and winds and also from the water which dripped down from the cave walls. The skins were held down by stones which surrounded the hut. This method seems to have been used by all primitive hunting peoples when building such dwellings. The distribution of charcoal and bones indicated that the hut was divided into two sections by a leather curtain. One room was small, without a fireplace and directly within the main entrance. Here only sparse discoveries were made. The other room, a living room, was larger with two fireplaces and many tools and bones. The only access to the living room was through the smaller room (333).

The two fireplaces in the living room were very small and their clay bases hardly burnt. In all probability they were secondary fireplaces with the main fireplace located outside the cave.

333 Reconstructed interior of the Acheulean hut in the Grotte du Lazaret (after de Lumley).

334 The excavated area of the Acheulean hut in the Grotte du Lazaret. The surface is divided into metre squares. In the foreground, towards the right of the stones, the entrance is visible; the rock wall of the cave is seen in the background (after de Lumley).

334

On the hills around the cave pine trees formed more than eighty per cent of the forests during the Riss Glaciation, yet the charcoal deposits in the fireplaces indicated only forty per cent of pine wood. This shows that the inhabitants must have known of the different heating potential of various woods.

In front of both fireplaces some interesting finds were made. The deposits revealed sea snail shells, but they were so small that they could not have been used as food. Therefore, this suggests that they must have been brought in with seaweed. The snail shells were mainly found around the two small fireplaces, in places where other discoveries were rare. One group of them was between the two fireplaces and

335 A Perigordian settlement with traces of a tent construction in Corbiac, France (after Bordes).

336 A square tent marked out by stones which cover the floor. Magdalenian culture, Plateau Parain, France (after Bordes).

335

336

another was found to the right of the main entry and behind the protective stone wall. These spots could have been sleeping places made up from dried seaweed. Of course, the 'beds' could also have been covered with animal skins, which could explain the small bones found here. These could have been parts of the feet and toes of only partly cleaned animal skins. Larger bones were absent. Tools were only rarely found around the sleeping places, but did occur elsewhere in the room (334).

The fact that there was little light, and that only few implements were found, seems to show that the hut must have been used mainly as a resting place. The daily life of the inhabitants was probably spent outside the cave. It was here that the spoils of the hunt were divided and implements were made. The huts were used during the long winter evenings and at night, and tools were probably retouched here, which would explain the existence of small stone flakes.

The remains of the hunted animals may indicate the time of year in which the hut must have been used. The bones of young — approximately five months old — ibex (these animals are born in mid-June) suggest the beginning of winter. Remains of marmots indicate spring. Therefore, it can be assumed that these were basically winter quarters, which the inhabitants would leave as soon as the warmer weather began. Remains of similar seasonable dwellings which belong to the Upper Palaeolithic period have been found in other sites in France (335 to 338).

Another dwelling discovered at **Fourneau du Diable**, France (339), had an irregular oblong layout, the sides measuring 7 and 12 metres. On the northern side were a number of stone blocks and on the southern side the remains of a stone wall; the rock face formed a natural recess on the western side. The main entrance, about 4.2 metres wide, was in the corner of the south-east wall of the hut, behind the rock wall. It was possible to rest wooden poles against the wall, cover them with skins and the living room would be finished. The cultural layer was found directly on the rock, and where the hut was not surrounded by stones a low wall of clay was found, beyond which no tools or bones were recovered.

In 1945, a site belonging to the Hamburgian culture (c 15 000 B.C.) was found by Rust at **Borneck**, north Germany, which showed traces of a double tent (340). It consisted of one

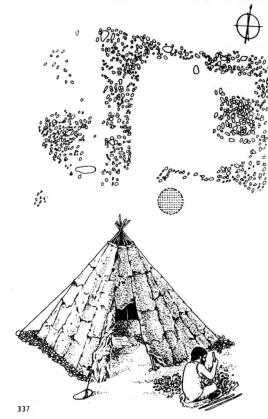

337

337 Outlines and reconstruction of the square Magdalenian tent from Plateau Parain. The large stones were used to hold the tent down. An area for making stone tools is just outside the tent (after Bordes).

338 Small, bowl-shaped fireplace lined with stones. Early Upper Palaeolithic; Metharnis, de Gramar I, France (after Bordes).

338

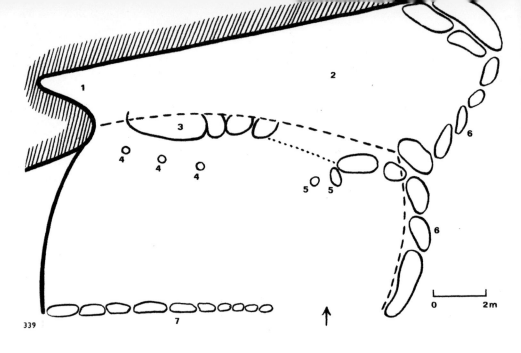

339 Plan of an Upper Palaeolithic dwelling beneath an overhanging rock in Fourneau du Diable, France (after Peyrony).

⇢→	entrance
– – – –	hut area
. . . . .	steps
1	cave
2	wall

3 painted rock
4 holes in the hut floor
5 worked stones
6 built-up wall
7 stone wall

circle of stones which would have held the edges of the tent down and a larger stone circle outside it which reflected the horseshoe shape of the inner wall. The curve of the outer tent was placed so that it could protect the inner tent from the prevailing wind. Right round the horseshoe-shaped layout large pieces of rock were found at intervals which were obviously used to anchor the tent ropes. The inner tent measured 2.5 metres by 3.5 metres and the outer horseshoe-shaped tent was about five metres long (341). Outside the tent a concentration of about 2000 small flakes were found.

Three other tents were discovered at Borneck with implements of the Ahrensburgian culture. Unfortunately, the remains of two of the tents were almost completely destroyed. The third tent, which was only 2 metres in diameter, was surrounded by a circle of small stones with a gap for the entrance (342). Remains of a fireplace, and several hundred stone flakes were also found. Rust dated this Ahrens-

burgian site at about 8500 B.C., and interpreted the dwelling as a summer tent. Another horseshoe-shaped tent belonging to the Hamburgian culture was found at **Poggenwisch** in north Germany (343). In front of the main entrance was a fireplace, a 'workshop' where tools had been made, and a little further away stones were found that held down the tent which had been surrounded by a sand wall. The basic length of the tent was 5 metres (344) — similar to that found at Borneck.

The second tent found at this site was larger and more complicated, and belonged to the Magdalenian culture (345 to 347). The larger, pear-shaped part measured 4 metres by 7 metres, and was obviously the living quarters. A kind of hall surrounded by stones was in front of this room. This hall was about 1.2 metres in diameter and had a kind of double floor made of stones weighing up to 60 kilogrammes as a protection against the damp. Quite large stones formed an inner circle to steady the outer sand wall. Another partly

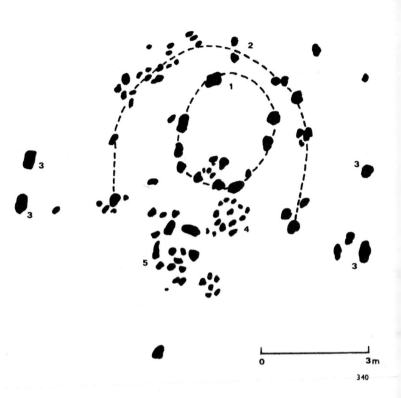

340 Plan of the construction of a double tent erected by Hamburgian hunters at Borneck (northern Germany). 1 stones outlining the inner tent; 2 stones outlining the outer tent; 3 stones used for anchoring the tent; 4 fireplace; 5 place for making stone tools (after Rust).

341 Reconstruction of the double tent built by Hamburgian hunters. Borneck, north Germany (after Rust)

340

341

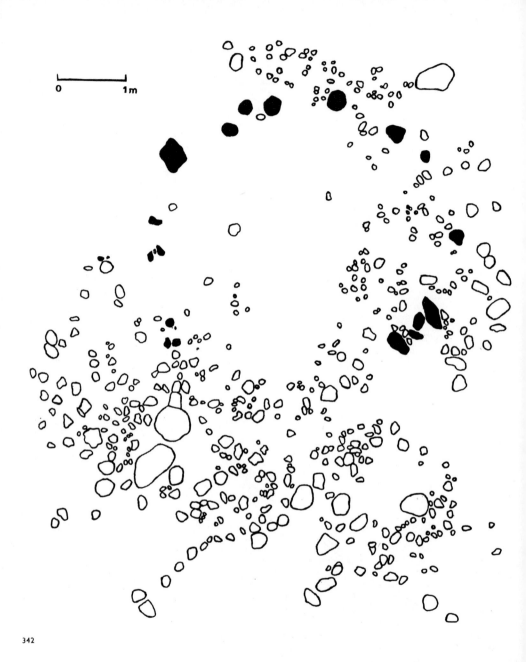

342

342 Plan of the stone distribution found at an Ahrensburgian settlement of reindeer hunters. The stones indicated in black probably weighed down the covers of the tent. Borneck-east, northern Germany (after Rust).

343 Occupation level with remains of a tent. The large anchor stones are clearly visible as is the low clay wall, surrounding the tent and the fireplace. Middle Stone Age, Poggenwisch, north Germany (after Rust).

343

floored passage led into a further tent. This
was round and about 4 metres in diameter.
Rust identified this site as a winter quarter.
He found nearly a thousand flakes, mainly in
the large main tent which also had a fireplace.

During 1937 and 1938 Rust discovered another site of the Lower and Middle Mesolithic
periods with outlines of six huts near **Pinneberg**, north Germany. The outlines were clearly marked by the much darker earth of the
huts which contained charcoal. Every hut was
surrounded by a ditch of between 250 and
400 millimetres deep in which traces of six
deeply embedded, approximately 100 millimetre thick, posts could be seen. The walls of
the huts were probably made from reeds and
moss. The entrance to these very small huts
which measured only 1.5 metres by 0.5 metres
inside faced south. According to the vertical
holes in which the posts stood and the thickness of the posts, we can assume that the lower
parts of the walls were vertical. The construction of the hut could hardly have been of a
simple dome shape, but it was probably built
so that the roof rested on the vertical posts

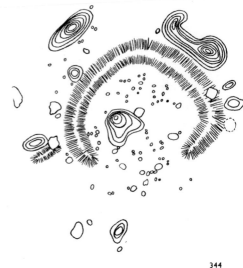

344

344 Plan of a Hamburgian culture tent with post-
-holes, clay wall and anchor stones. Poggenwisch,
north Germany (after Rust).

345

345 Reconstruction of a double tent from Poggenwisch. Magdalenian culture (after Rust).

346 The stones which anchored the Magdalenian tent at Poggenwisch (after Rust).

347 Plan of a double tent from the late Upper Palaeolithic. The black stones mark the outlines of the tent (after Rust).

346

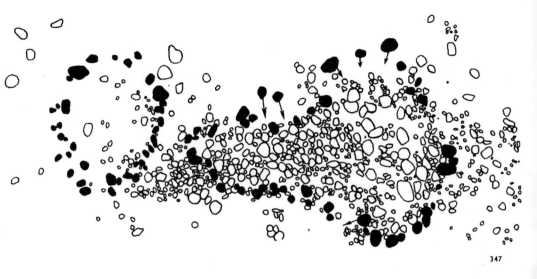

347

standing about 0.5 metres apart. The entrance opened into a short passage and there was no sign of a fireplace either inside or outside the huts. Hut number one produced a large number of stone tools and was thought to belong to the Dryas period (348). The largest number of implements was found to the south-west of the hut and we can assume that the inhabitants spent most of their time here.

The layout of the second hut (349), which was built a little later, was similar. A ditch surrounded the hut, and holes for the posts were found in it approximately 300 millimetres apart. Four post-holes were located in the broader part of the ditch, and the fifth was by the entrance. The posts were about 50 to 80 millimetres thick, and the post at the entrance was a little thicker. The outline was somewhat pear-shaped, measuring 1.5 metres by 2 metres. A ditch about 1.5 metres long ran from the broader part of the hut and vanished in the sand. No post-holes were found in this ditch. It could have been the foundation of a wall which functioned as a windbreak to shelter the first small room, although this is unlikely because no evidence of long-term occupation was made in hut number two nor hut number three. There was no fireplace inside or outside of hut number two.

Hut number three (1.5 metres by 2.5 metres) stood a little further away and also had a pear-shaped layout and post-holes. Its entrance was to one side and faced south-east (350).

The outlines of huts numbers five and six overlapped in parts. They were the most recent huts, and were larger (2.4 metres by 3 metres) than the older huts numbers one, two, and three. Traces of working areas beside the huts (as in huts two and three) could not be found, but otherwise the layouts were the same as in the other huts. The ditch which surrounded the huts was not as deep nor as evenly excavated as in the earlier ones (351).

Therefore, it can be assumed that the huts from the Lower and Middle Mesolithic periods at Pinneberg were small, had no fireplaces, and favoured irregular oval or pear-shaped forms (352).

During 1921 and 1922 at **Mainz** concentrations of stones were found in deposits of loess 2.72 metres deep. They were placed about 0.5 to 1.0 metre apart and grouped around one or two fireplaces. One of the fireplaces was in a bowl-shaped depression, 200 to 300 millimetres wide, which was filled with pieces of limestone the size of a fist, and burnt pieces of bone and charcoal. The second fireplace was circular, 700 millimetres across, also filled with stones, but not sunk in the ground. E Neeb (1924) discovered a firmly flattened clay surface about 0.6 metres by 1.8 metres which was surrounded by a 50 millimetre high clay rim. There were no traces of posts or other supports but many split bones and stone tools were found. Today, it is quite clear that Neeb had discovered a settlement, but un-

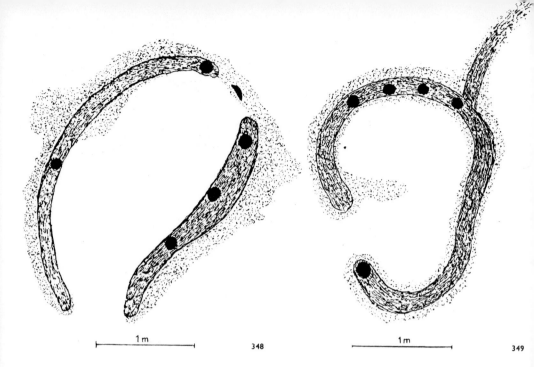

348 Pear-shaped outline of a Mesolithic dwelling from Pinneberg, Germany (after Rust).

349 Plan of two huts running into one another. Mesolithic period, Pinneberg, Germany (after Rust).

350 Plan of a Mesolithic dwelling with easily distinguishable post-holes. Pinneberg, Germany (after Rust).

351 Outline of a pear-shaped Mesolithic dwelling with posts fencing it in. Pinneberg, Germany (after Rust).

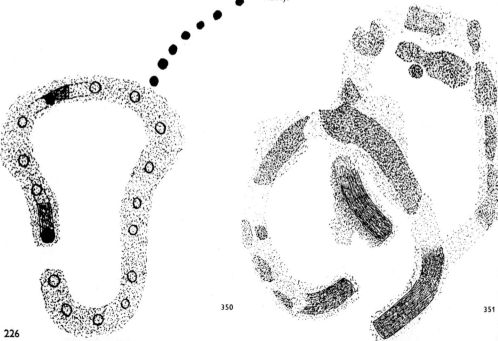

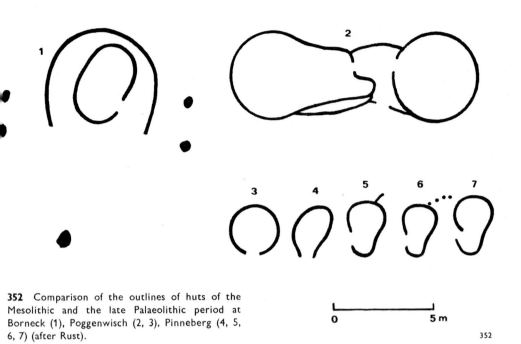

352 Comparison of the outlines of huts of the Mesolithic and the late Palaeolithic period at Borneck (1), Poggenwisch (2, 3), Pinneberg (4, 5, 6, 7) (after Rust).

0   5 m

352

fortunately this was not excavated by the methods now used, and the importance of this discovery was lessened.

In 1964 a research project at a Magdalenian settlement was started at **Pincevin** near Montereau on the banks of the Seine in France (353). Leroi Gourhan and M Brézilon excavated the remains of a settlement and were able to ascertain that, according to the animal remains, this must have been a summer and autumn settlement. The dwellings were not sunk into the ground, but the outlines were clearly defined by the numerous finds. Three elements were present in every dwelling. Each had a fireplace, a cleared surface with only a few implements; a working area with bone and stone tools as well as other fragments; and an entrance. In front of two of the three fireplaces were large stones used as seats.

The evidence of the finds was very clear and this, together with the study of the locations of the implements, made it possible to deduce that there were three connected tents either covered with bark or more probably with animal skins. Based on the clearly visible sleeping places it could be estimated that the tents housed between ten and fifteen people. The tents were probably built by placing poles together to form a basic cone shape.

This site near Montereau shows what the temporary settlements of Stone Age reindeer hunters in the Magdalenian culture of western Europe must have looked like. By comparison with Upper Palaeolithic dwellings found in Czechoslovakia and the USSR these tents must have been much more recent.

Settlements of central Europe

One of the best known prehistoric sites of central Europe is that of **Dolní Věstonice** in Czechoslovakia. The Czechoslovakian palaeoethnologist Absolon (1945) searched intensively for a long time for traces of dwellings but nothing was found. He found only a large pile of mammoth bones which he described as waste material. Then, in 1950, Klíma published a report describing an artificially made hollow, 5 metres by 9 metres, which appeared to be a kidney-shaped outline of a hut. There was a 400 millimetre-thick Pavlovian layer

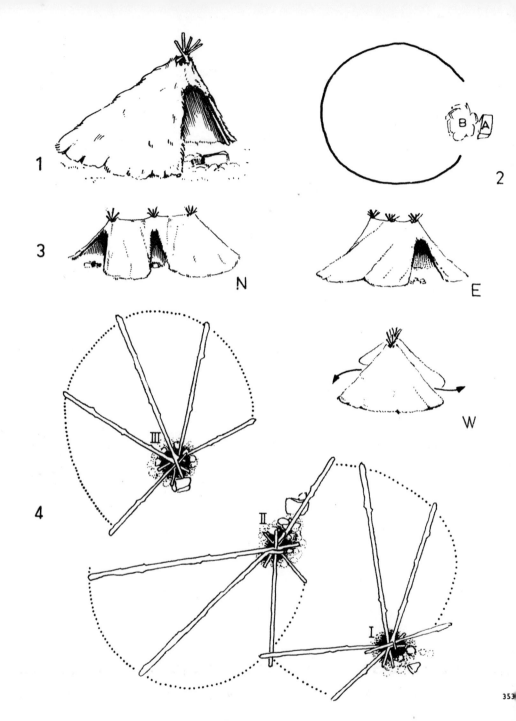

353 Reconstruction of the first Magdalenian tent from Pincevin, France: 1 isolated, semi-circular part of one end of the dwelling; 2 its outline with stone seat by the entrance (A) and fireplace (B); 3 overall views seen from the north, east, and west. The arrows indicate entrances; 4 plans of three connected tent constructions with three fireplaces (I, II, III) (after Leroi Gourhan).

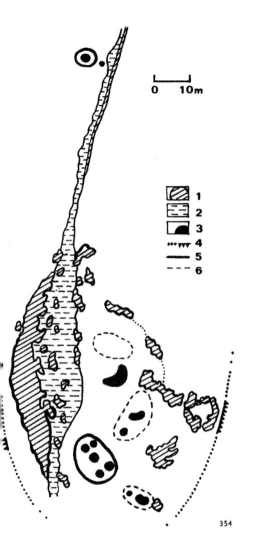

which thinned out towards the edge of the site. The dwelling itself was situated on slightly sloping ground, and the deposits found within it contained some limestone blocks and stones which were probably of a collapsed stone structure. Five fireplaces, each 1 to 1.3 metres in diameter, were found in the dwelling in depressions in the ground, and often surrounded by stones. The deposits produced rich finds, among them some 30 000 stone tools. At the western edge of the site the skeleton of a woman was found covered with mammoth shoulder-blades. Most of the finds came from the area of the central fireplace and nearby. There, in an area of about 1.5 metres square more than 1000 tools and flakes were found; this was obviously a working area. On the surface, depressions of 200 to 300 millimetres were traced similar to ones found in settlements in the Ukraine. These are not post-holes but are storage pits. A spring was found next to the dwelling which is today covered by large loess deposits. Further along from this dwelling a whole settlement was later uncovered (354, 355).

354

354 Pavlovian settlement in Dolní Věstonice. Hut number II, a circular hut, stands a little way off from the main settlement and is connected to it by a silted up ditch. A pile of waste mammoth bones was found near hut number II. 1 pile of bone waste; 2 silted up ditch; 3 fireplace; 4 limit of the settlement; 5 outline of the dwellings; 6 assumed outlines of dwellings (after Klíma).

355 General view of the excavation of a round hut at Dolní Věstonice. Ruins of a stone wall and the remains of the fireplace are visible in front of the figure. Pavlovian culture, Moravia, Czechoslovakia.

355

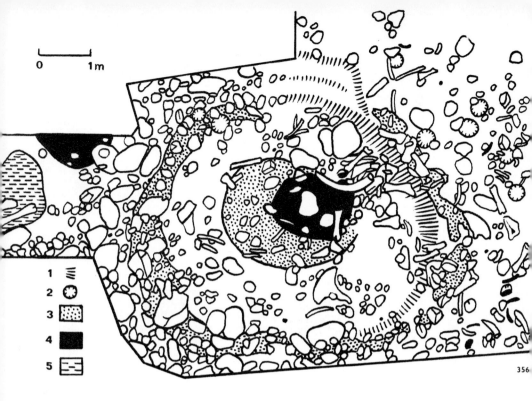

356 Plan of round hut number II discovered by B Klíma in 1951 at Dolní Věstonice. 1 depression in the ground; 2 post-holes; 3 remains of the circular wall around the dwelling and the fireplace; 4 fireplace; 5 spring (after Klíma).

357 Cross-section of the Dolní Věstonice hut number II. A deep hollow with the spring is visible on the right. To the left are the remains of the stone wall, a fireplace, an artistically made depression, and a clay wall. The occupation level is marked in black, with other deposits above it (after Klíma).

In 1951 a second hut was discovered about 80 metres away from the first one and described as Dolní Věstonice II. It was again on slightly sloping ground and also near to the now underground spring (356, 357). A single, oval-shaped fireplace was found in the middle of the almost circular dwelling which was 6 metres in diameter. This fireplace had a blackened clay step around two-thirds of it. Several rough pieces of clay were found in the ashes, and also parts of clay animals and human figurines. The living room and fireplace had been levelled by extending one side into the slope for about 0.8 metres, and building up the other with stones (358).

At the edge and within the surface area two types of post-holes have been discovered. Four larger holes were vertical, lined with stones

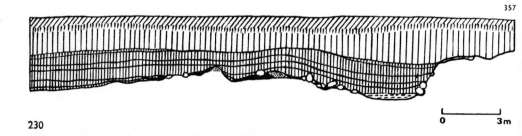

and placed in the remains of a stone wall. They were 200 millimetres deep, 100 to 150 millimetres wide, and carried the main posts of the construction (359). No holes could be found at the opposite side. The roof of the dwelling must have had a distinct slope. One side of the roof rested on the poles, the other on the ground (360). The post-holes of the second type were sunk at an angle; about 100 millimetres deep and 50 to 70 millimetres wide. These three holes were located in the inner part of the dwelling, and obviously supported extra props for the roof. The layers found in the hut are of importance. The lower deposit was the same as the deposit surrounding the hut, but yielded more finds. The upper layer was only present inside the dwelling and a little just outside it. It contained stones, mammoth tusks and bones which were part of the construction, and also the original cover remains of the sloping roof. The last covered the original cultural layer inside the hut when it collapsed.

The second hut at Dolní Věstonice revealed some unusual discoveries. Numerous pieces of modelled clay in the fireplace made it clear that this was not only living quarters but also

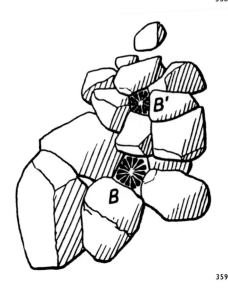

358 Part of a stone wall. Hut number II, Dolní Věstonice, Moravia, Czechoslovakia (after Klíma).

359 Post-holes (B, B') found in hut number II, Dolní Věstonice, Moravia, Czechoslovakia (after Klíma).

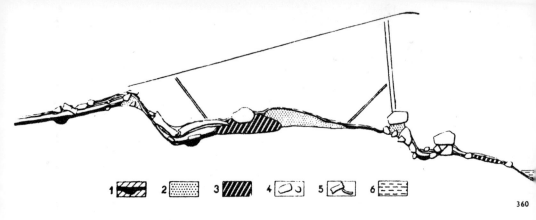

1 ▨ 2 ▦ 3 ▥ 4 ⬭ 5 ◁ 6 ▤

360

360 Reconstructed cross-section of hut number II at Dolní Věstonice. The roof is based on the evidence of the post-holes. 1 occupation level; 2 wall around the hut and fireplace; 3 fireplace; 4 limestone; 5 bones; 6 water (after Klíma).

361 General view of the' reconstructed round hut number II at Dolní Věstoñice, Moravia, Czechoslovakia.

362 Outline plan of an Upper Palaeolithic Pavlovian settlement at Pavlov, with huts and fireplaces (the numbers indicate the outlines of excavated huts); Moravia, Czechoslovakia (after Klíma).

a work room. The hut stood apart from the others and could have housed a high ranking person such as shaman or medicine man (361).

Eight metres away from the first hut a 12 metre-wide and 45 metre-long pile of bones was found. This proved that the site must have been occupied for a long time.

Another Pavlovian settlement was discovered in 1952 approximately 400 metres away. The settlement was called **Pavlov** and had a 100 millimetre-thick cultural layer. Year after year thousands of tools and implements were found there. After 700 square metres had been uncovered, it was possible to see that the settlement was about 40 metres by 20 metres. The scatter of tools stopped so sharply that we could almost assume that some kind of a wall or fence limited the area of the set-

361

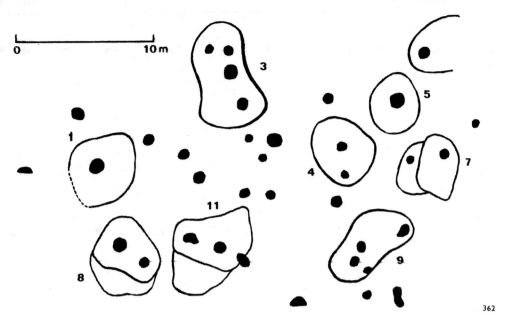

362

tlement. Slowly, eleven dwellings were uncovered with round, kidney-shaped or irregular outlines (362 to 364).

In 1955 Klíma uncovered remains of a Pavlovian settlement at **Ostrava-Petřkovice** in Czechoslovakia. This settlement was not deeply dug into the ground. Because of the way in which the fireplaces were built and the stone tools left around them, Klíma was able to identify three kidney-shaped outlines of 6 to 8 metre-long huts which each had two fireplaces (365).

Another Old Stone Age dwelling which had two fireplaces was discovered at **Tibava** in Czechoslovakia in 1956 (366). The outline was irregular and kidney-shaped; it measured 3 metres by 5.25 metres and was 150 to 350 millimetres dug into the ground. Inside the hut two post-holes were found, probably to support the horizontal roof beam. Outside stones were found at the south and north sides. They were obviously remains of a supporting construction to hold up the poles. A small pit in the ground contained thirty-five tools and they prove that this site must date back to the Middle or Lower Aurignacian culture.

In a loess site of the Magdalenian culture near **Račice** in Czechoslovakia seventeen hollows measuring 0.54 metres by 2.2 metres and 100 to 250 millimetres deep were found. They

were placed around an empty room in which only a few post-holes could be seen. Only in the hollow could the remains of a fire be discovered. Several burned pebbles were found and these were obviously used as pot-warmers to cook on. The hollows were probably used for various purposes, because in addition to stones and charcoal, stone tools were also found. In 1953 Mazálek tried to reconstruct this dwelling as an oblong-shaped tent with the rafters of the roof forming a ridge. From the position of the various holes, workplaces, and fireplaces, it was possible to deduce that the tent was probably entered from the south side. This discovery can be compared with Magdalenian huts found in the loess sites of Germany by Rust.

In Czechoslovakia semi-subterranean dwellings from the Mesolithic period are rare, and only a few have been found during the last few years. It was thought that this area was probably sparsely populated during the Mesolithic period, although recent research has proved that Mesolithic settlements do exist.

At **Putim** near Ražice (Bohemia, Czechoslovakia) the outline of a long pit with a flat bottom was uncovered. It measured 5.5 metres long, 1.8 metres wide and was about 0.7 metres deep. It contained numerous pieces of charcoal and five pebbles of which one was

233

363 Plan of Pavlov hut number VIII with two fireplaces. 1 stones; 2 bones; 3 fireplace and ash deposits; 4 pits and man-made hollows; 5 area of hut (after Klíma).

364 Plan of Pavlov hut number V with a single, central fireplace, objects and shallow depressions (after Klíma).

365 Plans of three Pavlovian huts from Ostrava-Petřkovice, Moravia, Czechoslovakia. 1 mammoth molars; 2 fireplaces and ash deposits; 3 pits and depressions (after Klíma).

366 Plan of the Aurignacian hut at Tibava, Czechoslovakia. There are two fireplaces and two post-holes in the centre of the hut, and piles of stones, to the north and south of the hut left over from its building (after Bánesz).

367 Plan of the Upper Magdalenian layer from the Děravá cave, Czechoslovakia. The fireplaces are indicated in solid black; one of them lies outside the hut. Other discoveries indicate that the inhabitants carried out most of their activities in front of the hut (after Prošek).

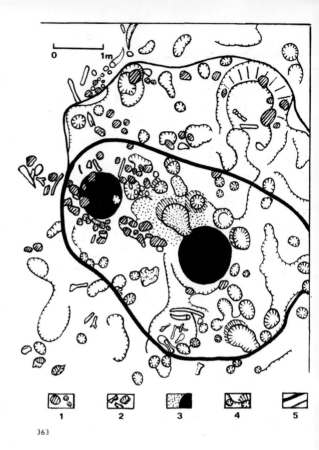

363

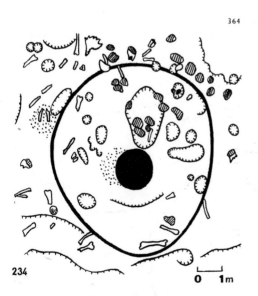

364

very smooth. Stone tools were found only on the outside of the pit. No remains of the hut construction or its post-holes were discovered.

Mazálek discovered more Mesolithic living sites not far away from the Pikarna hill. In front of one of the pits with two small post-holes at the side, a bowl-shaped fireplace 1.05 metres in diameter and 250 millimetres deep was found. Further open fireplaces were found in this settlement together with a number of flint stone tools.

Cave dwellings of the Palaeolithic period are also known in Czechoslovakia, although it is difficult to distinguish them in stony areas. Often we are entirely dependent on the discovery of tools of which the existence and distribution suggest that there must have been walls. This was the case in the **Dzeravá Skála** cave in western Slovakia which was found by Prošek in 1951. Implements from the Pavlovian culture were found by the north wall of the cave in an area measuring 6 metres by 11 metres. It was here that the construction might have been supported against the wall of

234

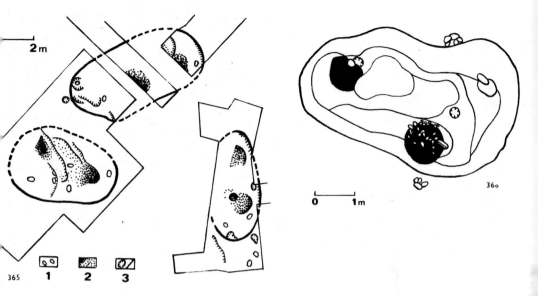

360

365

1 **2** **3**

the cave. The ceiling of the cave which measured 18 metres by 2 metres was up to 11 metres high in places.

In the large **Kůlna** cave (about 1600 square metres) at Moravia in Czechoslovakia, Palaeolithic dwellings could not be clearly identified because their actual position was not easy to trace. It could only be assumed that the dwellings were placed along the cave walls, because it was there that most of the Upper Palaeolithic implements were found.

Another type of dwelling was a small cave which was lived in with no additions being made except for a small wall to close it off. Prošek discovered two Upper Palaeolithic occupation layers in the **Děravá** cave, Bohemia, Czechoslovakia (Prošek, 1952) (367). The upper layer stretched 4 metres into the cave and was bordered by three large rocks. It seems as if the actual cave was shut out by a wall which rested against the ceiling and cave walls. The living space was about 4 metres by 10 metres and had two fireplaces. The lower layer reached about 2 metres into the cave, where it was bordered by a small stone wall.

367

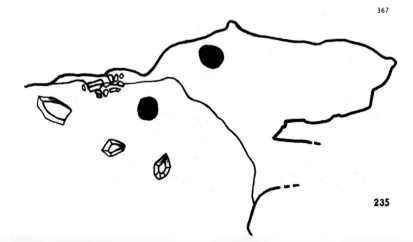

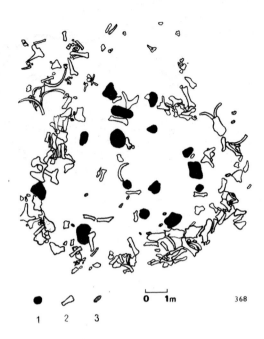

0   1m   368

1   2   3

368 Plan of a circular dwelling of the Mousterian culture. Molodova, Ukraine, USSR. 1 fireplace; 2 large bones; 3 stones.

369 Reconstruction of a Mousterian hut at Molodova, Ukraine, USSR (after Tchernysh).

Discoveries from the Ukraine and south Siberia

Discoveries of Stone Age settlements in the Ukraine and south Siberia have yielded much information. Both areas belong to the loess regions which bear so many Palaeolithic remains. The dwellings can be divided into two groups. There are round dwellings with a diameter of about 5 to 6 metres, and there are dwellings which are very large and are thought to have been inhabited by whole tribes. These dwellings usually have many fireplaces running down the middle. Today, ideas have changed and it is not clear whether the settlement was made up of separate dwellings with the fireplaces in the middle, or whether they represent a single construction.

The oldest Ukrainian dwelling was excavated during 1955 to 1961 and 1963 in **Molodova** on the banks of the river Dniester, USSR. Large mammoth bones from the Mousterian layer were found lying in a circle. The circle was 6 to 8 metres in diameter (368) and consisted of twelve skulls, fifteen tusks, thirty-four hip and shoulder-blade bones, five lower jaws, and fifty-one mammoth long-bones. The circle was broken in two, diametrically opposed places, which must have been the entrances. Inside the dwelling fifteen small

369

fireplaces were found, their size varying from 0.4 by 1.0 metres and 0.3 by 0.4 metres. They contained burned bones and charcoal and this latter proved that the inhabitants had used wood to make their fires.

There is not much evidence of what this dwelling looked like inside. It is probable that the basic structure was made of wood and was covered with animal skins which were held down at the edges by bones. The large mammoth bones were obviously part of the building material. This type of construction is also found in Upper Palaeolithic settlements in the Ukraine, and seems proof that man was already able to build large dwellings in the Middle Palaeolithic, and that he was no longer dependent on caves. The remains of the dwelling found at Molodova, however, could not have been arrived at without many years of prior development because such a dwelling cannot be called primitive any more (369).

The site of **Telmanskaya** at Kostienki (Ukraine) was discovered by P P Yefimenko and A N Rogatchev in 1937. In the upper cultural layer a round hut-pit with a diameter of 5.2 to 5.6 metres and 500 to 700 millimetres deep was found. The walls were upright and

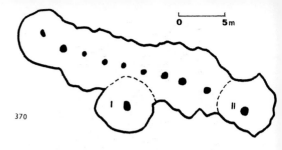

370

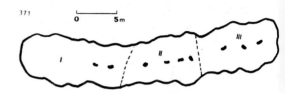

371

370 Plan of a long hut. Kostienki IV, Ukraine, USSR. The fireplaces form a single row down the middle. Two separate sections, marked I and II, each contains a fireplace (after Rogatchev).

371 Plan of a long hut, divided into three sections with two, four, and three fireplaces respectively. Kostienki IV (after Rogatchev).

372 Reconstruction of two long huts. Kostienki IV, Alexandrovka, Ukraine, USSR (after Yefimenko).

372

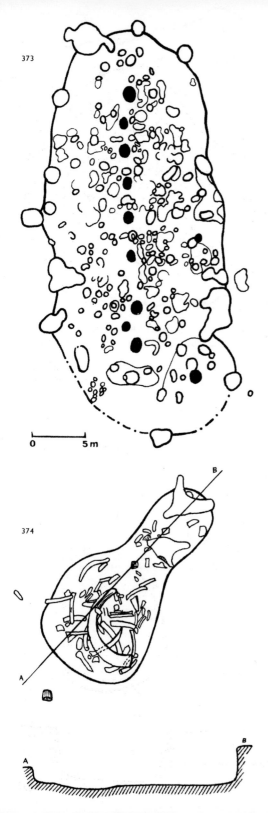

the bottom flat. A 2 metre-wide passage led out of the hut in a westerly direction. The only bowl-shaped fireplace lay right in the centre of the hut. It measured 750 to 800 millimetres in diameter, was 150 to 200 millimetres deep, and contained ash and burned bones. Opposite the entrance three depressions in the ground were noticed. These were probably used as storage places. Rogatchev continued the research here in 1949 and 1950 and found further pits. If they had all been built simultaneously the dwelling could not have been habitable. It can be assumed that several layers representing continuous periods must have contributed to the positions of the various pits and holes. This settlement is similar in size and in the shape of the small pits to the settlement of Alexandrovka which lies only a little further away.

Rogatchev discovered second, third, and fourth occupation layers. The second layer revealed a complete settlement and part of a round dwelling six to seven metres in diameter which stood out as being different from the surroundings by kind and number of tools. Several quartz flakes were found here, but hardly any mammoth tusks, bones, and bone flakes, although these were found in abundance outside the hut, while no quartz flakes were found outside at all. A fireplace was in the centre of the round hut, and it contained charcoal and burned bones. It is not a rare occurrence at Kostienki to find more than one occupation level, which must mean that this was a very favourable place, situated as it is along the banks of the river Don on clay ground.

The site of **Alexandrovka** is known as Kostienki IV and was excavated in 1937 and 1938 by A N Rogatchev. He discovered two kinds of settlement which he later attributed to two different cultures. He uncovered two round huts in the upper layer which were overlapping on one side with huts of the lower layer, and which presented a number of fireplaces. A loess deposit, completely sterile, separated the two layers: this loess deposit was found opposite the two round huts of the upper layer. The lower deposits also showed outlines of round huts and contained large dwellings. Rogatchev felt that the two occupation layers must have intermingled at a later date, as there were different types of dwellings as well as differences in other objects. The upper layer contained several quartz, slate, and mammoth ivory flakes, and typical burins and bifacial

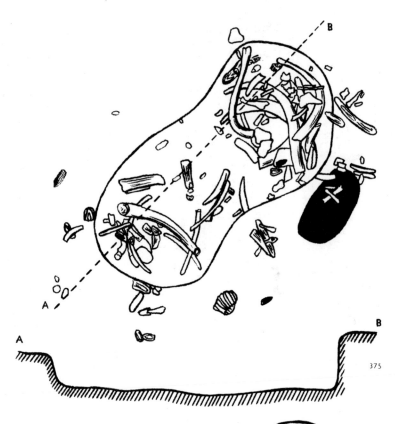

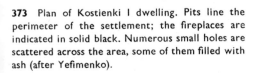

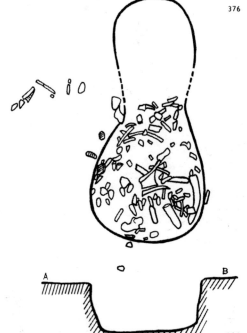

373 Plan of Kostienki I dwelling. Pits line the perimeter of the settlement; the fireplaces are indicated in solid black. Numerous small holes are scattered across the area, some of them filled with ash (after Yefimenko).

374 Plan and section (below) of a small semi-subterranean hut-pit towards the perimeter of the settlement. Kostienki I, Ukraine, USSR (after Yefimenko).

375 Plan and section (below) of a small semi-subterranean hut-pit towards the perimeter of the settlement. Kostienki I, Ukraine, USSR (after Yefimenko).

376 Plan and section (below) of a small semi-subterranean hut-pit towards the perimeter of the settlement; Kostienki I, Ukraine USSR (after Yefimenko).

239

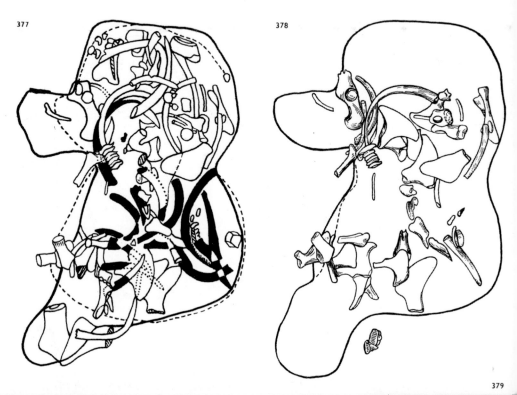

377   378

379

stone tools which were all totally absent in the lower layer.

The outlines of the two round huts of the upper layer were only 100 to 400 millimetres deep, and each had a bowl-shaped fireplace in the centre of the floor. Many more implements were discovered inside the hut than outside. On the northern edge of the dwelling situated to the west the thinner cultural layer did not reach far beyond the hollowed-out space of each hut. This did not happen on the southern edge where the two round huts were connected by an ochre-coloured substance. The area was sloping slightly at this particular point, and it can be assumed that the upper deposit had slipped down at a later date.

The hut on the western side was more interesting. It was 400 millimetres deep towards its northern edge but only 100 millimetres on its eastern side. There the floor of the hut was on a level with the ground outside. Six enormous tusks were found inside; the larger part of a humerus bone, a lower jaw, part of a shoulder-blade, and parts of the spines and ribs of mammoths. At the edge of this deposit twenty large sandstone slabs and pieces of sandstone were found. They lay at the very top of this deposit and may be considered to be building material.

Particularly interesting was the discovery of

377 One of the large pits at the edge of the settlement, hut-pit A. The tusks, here shown in black, formed the arch of the first room. The solid black line indicates the upper outline, the broken line indicates the ground outline of the hut-pit. Kostienki I, Ukraine, USSR (after Yefimenko).

378 Upper layer of hut-pit A, Kostienki number I, Ukraine, USSR (after Yefimenko).

379 Concentration of bones near a circular hut in Kostienki-Anosovskaya. The use of the upturned lower jaws of the mammoth as building material is characteristic (after Rogatchev).

380 Part of an Upper Palaeolithic settlement at Kostienki-Anosovskaya showing the remains of a circular hut and three storage pits (after Rogatchev).

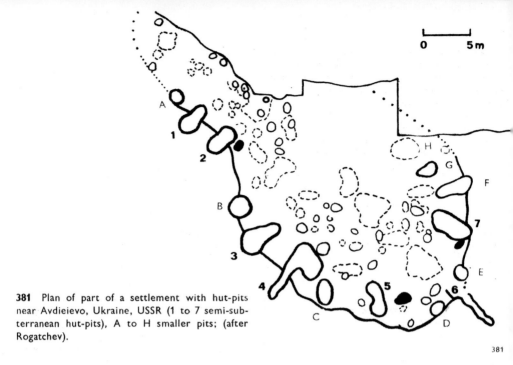

381 Plan of part of a settlement with hut-pits near Avdieievo, Ukraine, USSR (1 to 7 semi-subterranean hut-pits), A to H smaller pits; (after Rogatchev).

381

a lion's skull, found in the upper levels of the layer. Rogatchev thought that the skull might have been kept on top of the roof as a kind of decoration or that it might have had some ritual significance. Yefimenko made an interesting discovery of the skull of an aurochs in dwelling 'A' at the site of Kostienki I, which might be a parallel.

The fireplace which was in the centre of the settlement was surrounded by about twenty holes, about 200 millimetres deep. They were probably used to store or prepare food, because pots or similar containers were unknown at this period. The tusks and bones of mammoths in the eastern dwelling were found at the bottom of the layer, not at the top. It can be assumed that they were not part of the construction (with the exception of the two tusks which were found in a somewhat higher level). The fireplace which was almost round, measured 1 metre in diameter, was approximately 100 millimetres deep, and slightly tilted in a westerly direction. It had a flat base and was bordered by a very small rim, only slightly protruding above the normal surface of the hut. Five medium-sized holes were found nearby, and from their position it would appear that they were of different periods. On the southern edge of the settlement a clay wall in good condition was found, it was 50 to 90 millimetres high and 400 to 500 millimetres

wide. The clay was obviously deposited there when the living area was dug out and was then used either to stabilize the huts or to form a retaining border. The flat stones found at the western side must also have been used in the same way.

The lower layer of this site revealed two large, long dwellings. The one on the southern side was 33.5 metres by 5.5 metres and was distinguishable by the reddish colouring of its cultural layer. The other one was situated between 17 and 20 metres further north and measured 5.5 by 2.3 metres (370). The first dwelling had more than ten centrally placed fireplaces in it and the plan shows that there must have been three different parts which are separated from one another by steps about 100 millimetres high (371). The first part, to the west, was 14 metres long, the centre part was 9 metres long, and the eastern section was 10.5 metres long, and also contained the richest finds. The dwelling was constructed along the slope obviously to protect its shortest side against the rain and water from melting snow. All fireplaces were built along the longitudinal axis of the dwelling, and it can be assumed that the structure must have had a roof which was highest in the middle. The roof was obviously anchored to the ground and cross-beams were connected to the ridge. This is also substantiated by the way in which

it was found. The middle of the dwelling
produced more material probably because all
activities were carried out there. On the north
end of the western section was a kind of passage
which was obviously the only entrance and
faced the valley of the Don. Most of the stone
and bone flakes were found around the fireplaces which means that meals were prepared
here, and tools made. All activities were
obviously carried out inside the dwelling. Most
of the bones found here belonged to hares;
other animals are rarely found. On the north
and south-east sides of the dwelling two smaller
areas were found; they were not dug out,
but were covered with flaked stones and
bones. In the warm season people obviously
used to sit outside and work (372).

The outlines of the second dwelling were
clearly marked by the tool-finds. This dwelling,
too, was divided into three parts and had
altogether nine bowl-shaped fireplaces. There
were two fireplaces in the western part, four in
the central section, and three in the south-

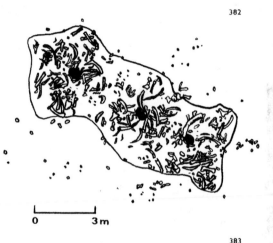

382

382 Plan of a hut in three sections, with three
fireplaces and large quantities of bones and tusks.
Pushkari, Ukraine, USSR.

383 Reconstruction of a hut divided into three
sections from Pushkari.

0   3 m

383

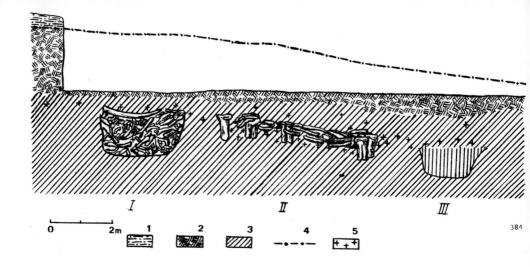

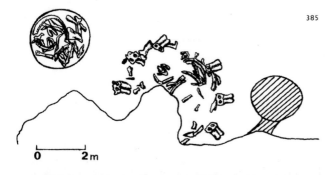

384 Cross-section of a hut (II), storage pit (I), and a pit for ashes (III) at Dobranitchevka, Ukraine, USSR. 1 later deposits; 2 recent clay; 3 loess; 4 original land surface; 5 archaeological finds (after Shovkoplias).

385

385 Plan of a dwelling from an Upper Palaeolithic layer in Dobranitchevka, Ukraine, USSR. The remains of the settlement were partly destroyed during earlier excavations. A storage pit filled with bones is on the left, a pit for ashes on the right (after Shovkoplias).

386 Remains of mammoth skulls, the main material of the construction. Dobranitchevka, Ukraine, USSR (after Shovkoplias).

387 Storage pit filled with large bones. Dobranitchevka, Ukraine, USSR (after Shovkoplias).

386

astern part. Three cooking pits and twenty-five smaller holes were found around the fire-places, they were 200 to 400 millimetres across and of the same depth. There were no holes outside the dwelling. Three upright mammoth flakes of long-bones were found on the western part 600 millimetres away from the edge of the dwelling, and they obviously were used to strengthen the clay wall around it.

Kostienki I is sometimes also called **Polyakovo**. P P Yefimenko did some research there during 1931 to 1936, and A N Rogatchev researched during 1938. Yefimenko uncovered an oval-shaped settlement measuring 14 to 15 metres by 36 metres (373), where numerous tools were found in the deposits inside the dwelling, although only a few implements occurred outside. It is possible that the living room was surrounded by some kind of walls. At the edge of this settlement Yefimenko found four large pits filled with deposits, and he called them the winter hut-pits. He also found twelve smaller ones which were used to keep bones in. If the building covered the whole area, as Yefimenko assumes, the pits at the edge could then be remains of the construction. It is more likely, however, that only part of the area was covered, a fact indicated by the finds (374 to 376). Semi-subterranean hut-pit

'A' could be described as one of the larger dwellings (377). It is about 2 metres by 3.5 metres and has a small terraced passage leading to the outside. A mammoth tusk and two shoulder-blades were found here (378) with which the entrance could be covered up. Mammoth shoulder-blades were also used in the Upper Palaeolithic to cover graves, so that it is not surprising that they were also used to build huts. A similar entrance at the back of the hut was also found; it was shorter and steeper. But this could have been some kind of light shaft.

The floor of the hut-pit was more or less flat and showed outlines of two circles. One of them was larger and had a fireplace in the centre. The smaller circle had two layers of bones. The upper layer consisted mainly of shoulder-blades, hip-bones, and tusks of the mammoth. The lower layer, which was level with the floor of the hut, consisted mainly of tusks which were laid with the points turned inwards towards the centre of the room. They were fairly regularly spaced. This was presumably the supporting framework of the dome-shaped roof which collapsed once the hut-pit was empty. The floor of the hut was approximately 1 metre below the ground and the top of the hut rose 0.8 to 1.0 metres.

388

389

388 The same storage pit as 387 with large bones at the Upper Palaeolithic settlement at Dobranitchevka, Ukraine, USSR (after Shovkoplias).

389 Part of a mammoth skull firmly wedged into the ground. Mammoth skulls were used as building material for the outside wall of the circular hut at Dobranitchevka (after Shovkoplias).

390 Another mammoth skull from Dobranitchevka, also firmly wedged into the ground. It is part of a structural outside wall of a hut (after Shovkoplias).

391 Plan of a large Upper Palaeolithic settlement at Yudinovo, USSR. The mammoth skulls are mostly placed along the edge of the dwelling. The area is divided into squares which enabled detailed research.

390

These facts led Polykarpovitch to believe that these pit-huts must have been used for sleeping and somehow were kept warm; otherwise they would not have been sufficient protection against the cold. They showed no traces of typical fireplaces; one layer of coal and ash could be found and there was only a little space left around the remains of embers. It could be that the main fire was kept somewhere else and that the inhabitants collected the hot ash and bone 'coal' in rolled up animal skins and took them back to their huts and slept on them. This hypothesis is strengthened by the fact that no traces of stone nor large bones could be found inside the huts. Rogatchev also assumed that sick people could have been cured there. But an answer to this suggestion can only be given after further research has been carried out.

Along the middle of the large settlement eleven fireplaces were found; two of them a

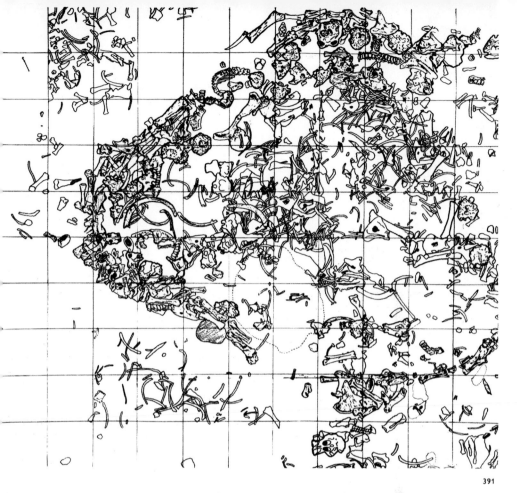

little further away, towards the edge of it. Several irregular, bowl-shaped depressions and small holes were found inside the dwelling which might have been used as storage places. Beside some of the depressions large mammoth bones had been stuck vertically into the ground. According to Yefimenko they were used as working tables or anvils, and the pits — which contained numerous implements — could be thought of as the working places. Rogatchev also discovered well-preserved remains of hut constructions in Kostienki-Anosovskaya (379, 380) with several deep store pits, where large bones were used in their construction.

Research was also carried out at another important site in the Ukraine called **Avdieievo**. This was a Palaeolithic site at which M Vojevodski worked during the years 1946 to 1948, and A N Rogatchev in 1949. They uncovered the remains of a settlement measuring about 500 square metres, which was partly destroyed by the small river Rogosnaya (381). This oval-shaped site, 15 metres wide and 19 to 20 metres long originally covered an area of about 800 square metres; it was even larger than the Kostienki I settlement. At the edge seven hut-pits were discovered (I to VII) measuring between 4 and 8 square metres and between 0.6 to 1.0 metres deep. Within the settlement some thirty to forty flat, irregular-shaped depressions were found, and large mammoth bones were found standing upright around some of them. The depressions contained not only mammoth bones but also a large number of bone implements which were otherwise rare in the settlement. Rogatchev assumed that the pits must have been inhabited. One of the hut-pits, labelled 'P', was particularly interesting. This hut was situated in the north-west part of the settlement and measured 1.6 metres by 3.1 metres. It was

392

built on a slope but had a horizontal floor, and was 0.7 metres deep on the eastern side but only 0.4 metres deep on the south-west side. The hut was made up of two broad parts which were linked by a narrow passage. Mammoth tusks and rib-bones as well as other bones, were found indiscriminately piled up in the broader areas, and on some traces of cutting could be found. Just beside the hut a fireplace measuring 0.5 by 0.9 metres was found which was level with the ground and contained a large amount of 'bone coal'.

The circumstances surrounding the discovery of the site raised many questions which could not be answered. The large tusks and bones, also found in Kostienki I, were probably parts of the roof. It is not known, however, why the fireplace, which obviously belonged to these hut-pits, was outside. The various discoveries, particularly the way in which the mammoth tusks were placed, suggest that this hut must have been one of a settlement. The size of the settlement could not, however, be determined. This hut was one of the largest of its type, but it would, nevertheless, have been too small to house a whole family, and in trying to heat it, room for only one person would have been left.

The large dwelling on this site was probably occupied by a single large group. Yefimenko assumed that this was a summer dwelling and that hut-pits were used in the winter, but this has not been proved. It would have been very

difficult at that time to put a roof on a dwelling of that size, but on the other hand, it seems impossible that the same people could have fitted into these small hut-pits during the winter, while they occupied a space of about 800 square metres in the summer.

One of the most prolific sites was **Pushkari**, a Ukrainian site located on the banks of the river Don near Novgorod-Seversk. The upper layers are even and piles of bones are only visible at a depth of 150 to 200 millimetres. These piles mark the outlines of a Palaeolithic pit dwelling. The settlement was 12 metres long and 4.5 metres wide, and oriented northwest to south-east. It covered about 50 square metres. Only mammoth bones were found; mostly tusks and molars but also shoulder-blades, hip-bones, and long-bones, 150 bones in all. Eighteen upper jaws and one lower jaw of mammoths were also discovered. The tusks had been broken away and used (382). These skeletal remains belonged mainly to mature mammoths.

There was no evidence that the bones found had been worked on. It is interesting, however, that a kind of red dye was found between the tusks and bones. A comparison may be drawn between these discoveries and those made at Mezin which revealed large painted bones and are discussed a little later. The layers varied; the one in the depression, which was 200 to 300 millimetres deep, was different from the surrounding layer. The walls, particularly in

392 Lower jaws of mammoths, pointing downwards, forming part of the reinforcement of the outside of a hut at Mezhiritch, USSR (after Pidoplitchko).

393 Plan of the west side of the settlement at Mezin, Ukraine, USSR. 1 bones; 2 ash-pits; 3 fireplaces (after Shovkoplias).

394 Circular hut with two fireplaces (shown in black); other fireplaces and ash-pits as well as stored bones, surround the hut. Mezin, Ukraine, USSR (after Shovkoplias).

395 Circular hut at Mezin just before it was lifted (after Shovkoplias).

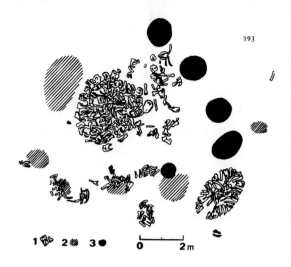

1   2   3   0   2 m

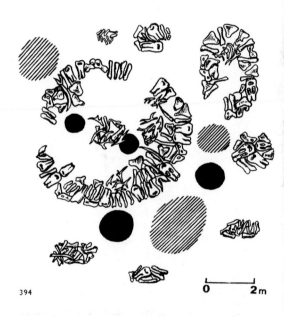

394   0   2 m

the central part, were leaning over slightly, whereas they stood upright in other parts. Upper jaws with molars were found stuck in the ground in four places. The sockets of the tusks were empty and the grinding surface of the molars stood upright. It is most probable that the upper jaws and the long-bones which were rammed into the ground at an angle could have been the supports of the dwelling. The bones in the lower layer belonged to mammoths, horses, wolves, bears, and arctic foxes. Along the length of the dwelling three fireplaces were found. The first, on the western side, was 0.8 by 1.2 metres and oval-shaped. 'Bone coal' and stones blackened by fire were found in it. In the outer ring, the layer of ashes was about 20 to 50 millimetres thick. The middle of this fireplace was between 600 and 700 millimetres across, 150 to 170 millimetres deep and had a layer of ashes of about 100 millimetres deep. The second fireplace in the centre measured 1.2 by 2.5 metres and had a layer of ashes 40 millimetres deep. In its middle was a hole 800 millimetres across and 200 to 250 millimetres deep with a layer of ash between 150 and 180 millimetres. The upper layer of the depression revealed slightly blackened stones, and on two sides of the fireplace some bones were stuck upright. They were each 100 to 120 millimetres long; it was one sharpened bone, a piece of a mammoth tusk, and a long-bone. The third fireplace was the largest, 2.2 by 2.5 metres, more or less circular,

396

397

396 Circular hut at Mezin. The fireplace and vertically standing bones are clearly visible (after Shovkoplias).

397 Hut at Mezin. As an experiment tusks were placed in the upright skulls which formed the outer wall (after Shovkoplias).

398 Reconstruction of Upper Palaeolithic huts from Mezin, Ukraine, USSR. The lower part of the building is made from large bones and mammoth skulls. Two skulls, with tusks formed the arched entrance. The upper part of the arch was completed by a hollow long-bone. The antlers were used mainly for making the roof (after Pidoplitchko).

and had a depression of 500 to 800 millimetres. The layer of ash in it was 70 to 100 millimetres deep. Fifty small holes were found in the site which were all grouped around the three fireplaces, their concentration being densest around the centre fireplace.

Another three fireplaces were found outside the dwelling in the upper layer. They contained a smooth layer of ash. Around the three fireplaces inside the dwelling mammoth tusks were found with tips pointing inwards. None were found between each of the fireplaces. Therefore, it could be assumed that they were part of the roof construction. The smaller holes around the fireplaces were probably used not for preparing food but to store implements. Other holes were found which had been used to hold the poles and supports of the dwelling. They are distinguished by their straight sides, the fact that they are not very deep, and that they only rarely contain stone flakes. The pieces of bones found in these holes were probably used as wedges. The remains of the buildings make it possible to assume that this was a tent-like construction with three dome-shaped roofs (383).

In 1952 a concentration of bones and charcoal was found at **Dobranitchevka**, in the upper loess deposits, on the left bank of the river Supoi, a tributary of the river Dniepr. Work in this area had destroyed parts of the newly discovered site (384, 385). By 1963 200 square metres had been uncovered producing a pit for storage and a round hut with a bowl-shaped fireplace. Most of the bone and stone tools were found here. The hut was 3.8 metres in diameter and was surrounded by mammoth skulls and other large mammoth bones (386). Some bones stood upright and sunk up to 300 millimetres deep into the ground. They were obviously still in situ, and formed a base at the edge of the dwelling supporting the wooden construction above. This dwelling is like those of today's tribes of east Siberia, who call them *tschum*. Four thousand stone flakes and several hundred scrapers, burins, and drills prove that these tools were made inside the dwelling. Twenty-four mammoth tusks and other bones were found in the upper cultural layer. Shovkoplias, the excavator, thought that these bones held down the animal skins and fixed them to the wooden construction. After the dwelling had collapsed they would then be in the upper level of the deposit. No fireplaces were found inside the dwelling, but remains of one was found outside. It was a round pit 900 millimetres deep, 2 metres wide at the top and 1.3 metres wide at the bottom. A passage 900 millimetres wide and 450 millimetres deep led into the destroyed part of the settlement. Both pit and passage were filled with ash and 'bone coal', and also contained

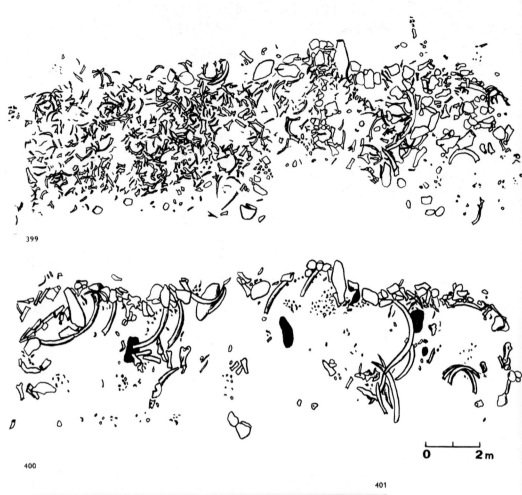

399

400

401

0   2 m

bones and broken stones which lay on top. It may be assumed that this pit was not a firepit but rather intended to take the ash and coal of a fireplace from the destroyed part of the settlement with which it was connected by the passage. Therefore, there must have been two units; one of the fireplaces containing the red-hot coal, the other providing heat. Another pit was found on the opposite side of the dwelling 2 metres away from the edge. It was 2 metres wide and 1.2 metres deep (387), and filled with bones, probably used for 'coal', and stored there (388). Similar pits are known from Palaeolithic sites in the Ukraine, such as Kostienki.

During the excavations in this locality Shovkoplias discovered two further round dwellings. Each one measured 4 metres in diameter and was bordered by facial bones from mammoth skulls stuck into the ground (389, 390). The first hut contained a small round fireplace. A larger fireplace with four storage pits filled with bones lay outside, together with concentrations of stone flakes which indicated that tools were made here. The second hut had a fireplace let slightly into the ground and which was hemmed in by parts of mammoth skulls. A mammoth bone stuck upright into the ground obviously constituted one of the two supporting posts for a spit. The wall of clay which surrounds so many dwellings in the Ukraine was not present here. Only two storepits were found outside the dwelling. Were these huts inhabited by single families?

In **Yudinovo**, site in the Ukraine, a round hut 5.6 metres in diameter was uncovered, around which pairs of mammoth skulls were grouped spaced at regular intervals. A third of this circle was also hemmed in by lower jaws and long-bones of mammoths. The bones found inside the hut indicated that it must have been divided into two parts, one larger with faint traces of a fireplace, the other smaller and without the fireplace (391). Storage pits were placed around the hut. Below this occupation layer another older layer was found also containing the remains of a round hut which had been partly destroyed by the construction of the later hut above.

399 Remains of an Upper Palaeolithic long-hut from Malta, Siberia (after Gerassimov).

400 After the roof debris had been removed hollows in the ground were clearly recognizable as well as the division into three chambers with three fireplaces. Flat stones and tusks form the outside wall (after Gerassimov).

401 One of the dwellings at Malta, Siberia, before being lifted (after Gerassimov).

402 General view of the excavated area of Palaeolithic settlements at Malta, Siberia, USSR (after Gerassimov).

403 Plan of the uppermost layer of the remains of a circular dwelling with three fireplaces. Malta, Siberia, USSR (after Gerassimov).

404 Circular dwelling at Malta, Siberia. Flat stones form the outer circle; reindeer antlers, which were obviously part of the roof, lie in the centre (after Gerassimov).

405 Circular dwelling after the remains of the roof had been removed. It has a central fireplace and is surrounded by flat stones. Malta, Siberia, USSR (after Gerassimov).

403

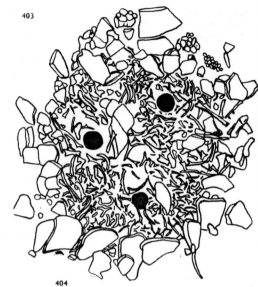

404

405

406 View of the circular dwelling at Malta, Siberia. Remains of the entrance are visible in the foreground (after Gerassimov).

407 Horseshoe-shaped outlines of a dwelling from Malta, Siberia, USSR (after Gerassimov).

408 Horseshoe-shaped and circular dwellings at Malta, Siberia (after Gerassimov).

406

407

408

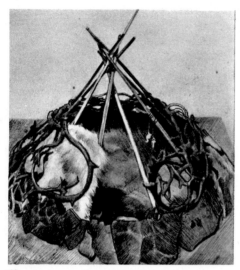

409

410

One of the most interesting new discoveries comes from the Ukraine and was uncovered by J G Pidoplitchko at **Mezhiritch**. It is a round hut, 5 metres in diameter and covers an area of about 40 square metres. The lower part was in perfect condition because it was covered by sediments shortly after it had been destroyed. The upper part had been left exposed for some time and was not so well preserved. The foundations of this construction were made up of the lower jaws of mammoths. Two to four, sometimes five lower jaws were placed one on top of the other so that they would make quite a high construction (392). Lower jaws of mammoths have also been found used as building material in other sites in the Ukraine, although not to such an extent, and not in the same state of preservation as found at Mezhiritch. In places, shoulder-blades were used which were cut and flattened in such a way that they would be suitable for construction. Only on rare occasions have hip-bones and other mammoth bones been used for building.

The roof structure was made of mammoth tusks, and the entrance flanked by two mammoth skulls. The sockets were turned upwards and the bones of the forehead showed traces of red dye. New tusks were fitted into the sockets of mammoth skulls so that they formed an arch above the entrance. The arch was most probably covered with animal skins, and in front of it a wall, used as a wind-break was built from large mammoth bones which had been pushed into the ground closely set next to each other. The rear of the hut had a small entrance which was later closed up with parts of mammoth spines. The whole construction was supported by four poles which were wedged into the ground with suitable bones. Shovkoplias and Pidoplitchko assumed that the frame of the building was made of branches. A fireplace was found in the centre of the hut and another mammoth skull with traces of dye on the forehead was found nearby. The storage pits lay outside.

At **Mezin**, near Tchernigov, concentrations of bones were discovered in 1912, 1913, and 1916 which, according to the original description, were thought to be the first Palaeolithic dwellings found. Unfortunately not all of the settlement was excavated. The discoveries were centred around a depression 1 metre deep and 4 metres wide, the full form and true measurements of which are unknown. Only during 1954 and 1955 was another circular, 5 metre-large area of mammoth bones and

409 Reconstruction of a circular tent from Malta, Siberia. Flat stones are used as outside reinforcement and reindeer antlers form the roof construction (after Gerassimov).

410 Reconstruction of the same tent from Malta, Siberia (after Gerassimov).

Bison. Painting from the Salon Noir, Magdalenian culture, Niaux, France.

Bison and ibex. Painting from the Salon Noir, Magdalenian culture, Niaux, France.

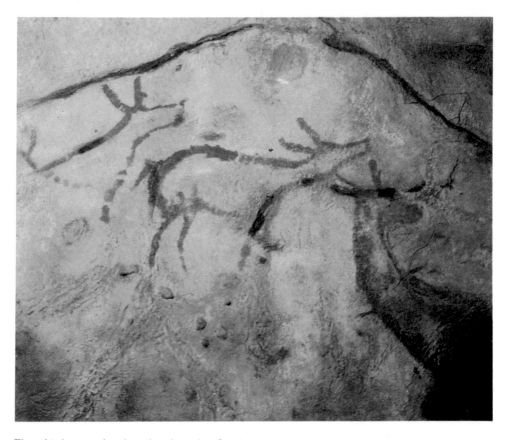

Three hinds painted in dotted outlines. Las Covalanas, Spain.

Bone carving of a stylized mammoth. Avdieievo, USSR.

Small mammoth modelled in clay (× 3). This discovery originated the research at Dolní Věstonice,Moravia, Czechoslovakia, which turned out to be one of the largest prehistoric sites in Europe.

Small mammoth modelled in clay from Dolní Věstonice. Pavlovian culture, Moravia, Czechoslovakia (× 3).

reindeer antlers uncovered (393 to 395). The largest bones, fifteen skulls, hip, and long-bones of mammoths, lay side by side forming a circle which was only once broken — in the south-east (396). The bones became smaller in the interior of the circle; they were shoulder-blades, lower jaws, tusks, and so on. The edges of the shoulder-blades were removed in almost all cases, so that they would fit more easily. Several reindeer antlers were found in the centre which originally formed the vault of the roof and had fallen on top of the layer when the dwelling had collapsed.

According to the positions of the bones the hut must have stood on a slight slope and was let into the ground on one side (300 to 500 millimetres) to make the floor even (397). Three relatively small fireplaces were found in the centre of the hut (500 to 700 millimetres in diameter), all set into the ground. Mammoth bones stuck upright into the ground were found in four places which, according to Shovkoplias, had been wedged in to hold the wooden supporting beams of the structure. It seems that the hut was dome-shaped, which is still a characteristic of huts and tents belonging to some of the present-day tribes of northern Siberia (398).

It has been known since the 1800s that a Palaeolithic site existed at **Honcy** beside the river Udai. Excavations began only in 1914 and were carried out by the Moldavian Museum. Later, in 1935, the archaeologist, Levickij, carried on with the work. Remains of mammoths were discovered which indicated, by their positions, a definite plan. Obviously this was a dwelling measuring 4 by 4.5 metres, oval-shaped and surrounded by twenty-seven mammoth skulls. Apart from three skulls, the dwelling was hemmed in by them on three sides. On the outer edge thirty mammoth shoulder-blades were found standing upright in the ground, while towards the middle of the circle thirty mammoth tusks were found. The rather smaller number of other bones includes six lower jaws, three hip-bones, a whole pelvis, some long-bones, and spinal bones: this suggests a deliberate selection. The floor was 700 millimetres deep in the ground, and the tusks carried the weight of the roof. Levickij also reported that smaller pits surrounded this dwelling rather like the settlement at Dobranitchevka. The fireplaces contained bone-ash and burnt bones; charcoal was not found. As in most settlements most of the discoveries of bones and tools were made inside the hut.

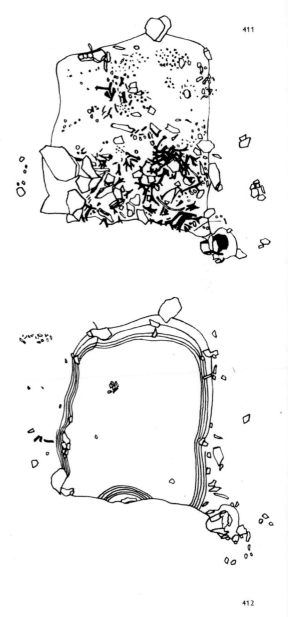

411 Plan of the dwelling shown in 401. Numerous reindeer antlers are scattered around, obviously remains of the roof (after Gerassimov).

412 A plan of the layers of a partly destroyed dwelling (see 401 and 411). Malta, Siberia, USSR (after Gerassimov).

413 Part of a dwelling with a clearly visible surrounding wall. The section across the middle shows a raised fireplace. Malta, Siberia, USSR (after Gerassimov).

414 Upper Palaeolithic dwelling. The clay wall surrounding it is strengthened with flat stones on the inside. Malta, Siberia, USSR (after Gerassimov).

415 Clay wall on the inside of a dwelling, strengthened with flat stones. Malta, Siberia, USSR (after Gerassimov).

416 View of the clay wall (415) from a different angle. Malta, Siberia, USSR (after Gerassimov).

Let us now turn to the sites discovered in Siberia. One of these sites was in **Malta**, and Gerassimov found two types of hut there. One was a long, oval-shaped hut measuring 6 metres by 14 metres which was open on one of the long sides and slightly set into the ground (399, 400). Three fireplaces were found inside, and the dwelling was hemmed in by a clay wall which was created when the hut was dug out. Further research showed that the wall was made from large clay blocks and large mammoth bones. The structure itself was probably made of wood which has, of course, not been preserved. Reindeer antlers were also used. The second dwelling was also very interesting; a smaller round tent which was painstakingly reconstructed and described by Gerassimov. He thought it was probably used as winter quarters. The fireplace was slightly north of the centre of the hut and outlined with stone slabs. This dwelling was also dug out and surrounded by a clay wall secured by heavy stone slabs. The construction was basically made of wood and reindeer antler, most of which Gerassimov found in the middle and on the top of the layer. The larger proportion of stone and bone discoveries made inside the dwelling were found at the edge; there were fewer discoveries made in the centre and around the fireplace. Several of the stone slabs surrounding the outside wall were still in their original positions,

413

414

slanting and standing on the edge. It can be assumed that the wooden construction must have been dome-shaped and covered with animal skins (401 to 419).

The site at Malta is dated back to the end of the Würm Glaciation. It would probably prove interesting if it could be compared with other European sites and the chronological dates examined.

At **Buret**, another Siberian site, situated on the river Angara near Malta, a similar concentration of mammoth bones was found (Okladnikov, 1941) as at Dolní Věstonice, Czechoslovakia. Buret dwelling, however, lay in flat depression and had a bowl-shaped fireplace with partly burned wood in it. Some experts think that this site must have been a dwelling or at least a roofed structure for sheltering against the weather.

Okladnikov reconstructed the hut found at Buret and came to the conclusion that the basic construction consisted of wooden poles, rods or branches and that the roof was either dome- or cone-shaped. The interlacing supports were provided by reindeer antlers (420). The depression was surrounded by a low clay wall which was covered with large stone slabs and bones. The hut measured about 5 to 6 metres long and 4 metres wide; the outline was almost oval. A short entrance passage pointed towards the Angara river. Okladnikov

417

418

417 During the lifting the wall disintegrated into the clay blocks with which it was originally built. Malta, Siberia.

418 This wall, put together from separate clay blocks, shows the well-thought-out construction of a clay wall surrounding a dwelling. Malta, Siberia, USSR (after Gerassimov).

419 A fireplace lined with stone slabs. Malta, Siberia, USSR (after Gerassimov).

420 Reconstruction of three Upper Palaeolithic huts from Buret, Siberia, USSR. The middle hut has a narrow, arm-like entrance.

points out that this site is similar to the sites at Gagarino on the river Don as well as the Chuckchee dwellings, known as *valkar*, which were all made from large bones. Reports from travellers show dwellings like this existed in Siberia even in the 1800s.

We have reached the point at which we should look at each discovery and make comparisons. Even if we do not take Leakey's discovery into account which described stone circles found in the Olduvai Gorge, it is quite clear that for a long time prehistoric man had been able to erect dwellings.

Cave dwellings are already known from the Acheulean culture, and circular dwellings, up to 5 metres in diameter, and of complicated construction containing several fireplaces, are known from Molodova, and prove to have existed in the east European Mousterian culture. The dwellings of the Aurignacian and Pavlovian culture have oval, kidney-shaped, irregular, and sometimes even circular, outlines. Round dwellings are found in the Ukraine as well as many oval-shaped ones up to 35 metres long. At Dolní Věstonice a pile of mammoth bones was uncovered (421) by Absolon and later by Klíma. Both scientists described them as piles of waste material. The discoveries from the loess regions in the USSR prove that such piles always revealed the remains of dwellings and were not just piles of waste. This could be further proved by the fact that fire-places were found beneath the bones and also that the so-called 'waste piles' lay in bowl-shaped depressions. Besides, there is no proof that prehistoric man regarded bones as useless waste. The sites in the Ukraine (Dobrani-tchevka, Mezin, Mezhiritch, Honcy) showed that the round huts each had several storage pits filled with bones. These bones were obvi-ously used for the fires, for building material, for making tools, and so on, and were carefully stored. Many dwellings in the Ukraine with circular outlines belonging to the Palaeolithic period have been carefully examined, and show that bones of mammoths and other large mammals were used as building materials. Sites such as Kostienki and Avdieievo in the USSR, as well as Dolní Věstonice in Czecho-slovakia, give many clues to the structure of whole Palaeolithic settlements. The discoveries were usually closely confined to a particular site, and give the impression that the whole settlement was surrounded by a construction of some kind. Some scholars think that there were fences made of twigs and branches which functioned as a protection against wild ani-mals. Sometimes they also mention that set-tlements could have been fenced in by skins

stretched between two poles which acted as wind-breaks and again as protection against wild animals. None of this is, as yet, substan-tiated. Some of the huts within large settlements in the Ukraine, such as Kostienki could not be identified, and outlines of irregular, kidney- or oval-shaped layouts at Dolní Věstonice can often only be noted as bowl-shaped, flat de-

419

420

421

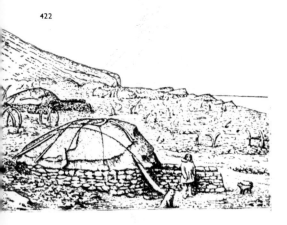

422

423

421 View of a vast concentration of bones from Dolní Věstonice, Moravia, Czechoslovakia. A fireplace was discovered, and it can be assumed that these bones were part of the hut's construction which belonged to the Pavlovian culture.

422 Drawing of a dwelling of the coastal Chuckchee people from the 1800s. A stone wall constitutes the foundation. A comparison may be drawn with the huts from Malta, Siberia, with their flat stones, or with the large mammoth bones and skulls used as foundation walls in the Ukraine. The long, narrow entrance is also comparable with that of the hut at Buret. The roof was held down by large stones and bones (after Vrangel).

423 The construction of a hut belonging to the coastal Chuckchee people. It consists of a foundation wall, an outside construction and a cone-shaped roof (after Potapov-Levin).

424 The construction of a temporary dwelling of the Chuckchee people. It consists of an outside wall and roof (after Potapov-Levin).

425 A 'tschum' – a seasonal dwelling of hunting people from the Siberian interior. The cone-shaped tent construction is covered with pieces of bark stitched together.

426 Another type of an east Siberian 'tschum'.

pressions. Fireplaces and other discoveries are found inside as well as outside these depressions, and concentrations of smaller bones do not constitute the outlines of these depressions.

The Siberian sites show tent constructions made from reindeer antlers, covered with skins and anchored by clay walls and stone slabs.

Circular dwellings from the Upper Palaeolithic period in Czechoslovakia and in the Ukraine were probably dome-shaped, although cone-shaped constructions would also have existed. Sites in southern Siberia seem almost only to have cone-shaped tent constructions. Dome-shaped constructions are less common in periglacial areas with a scarcity of wood. The fireplace is usually the main proof of this because only the ash of bones and singed bones are found; hardly ever charcoal. If wood was not available for building, Stone Age man had to use tusks and bones of mammoths or other animals, as well as reindeer antlers. Therefore, the size of the dwellings was restricted. If skulls, tusks, and long-bones of mammoths, as well as stones, had been used to erect the outer walls, we could expect to find a number of reindeer antlers in the centre of the dwelling. They would be bound to one another to make the framework of the dome. Large dome-shaped constructions were only made with difficulty even if the settlements of the colder periods of the Upper Palaeolithic did lie near the northern border of the wooded area.

Wooden dome-shaped roofs are made more easily from deciduous trees than from conifers. In areas around the northern tree limit only low, knarled, crook timber grows, which does not yield the long, flexible wood needed to build larger domes.

The tents of the Palaeolithic period in southern Siberia are similar to the European tent dwellings of the Magdalenian culture and the Upper Palaeolithic period. The cone-shaped constructions are very similar and the only difference is that until now, on European sites, neither clay walls and stone constructions, nor reindeer antlers used to make a dome framework, have been found. The Mesolithic period is characterized by smaller and irregular huts.

Pavlovian sites of central and eastern Europe show bowl-shaped depressions and pits in various sizes scattered across a site. If they had been used all at once the surface of the area would have been impossibly crowded to live on. Thus, we can assume that only a certain

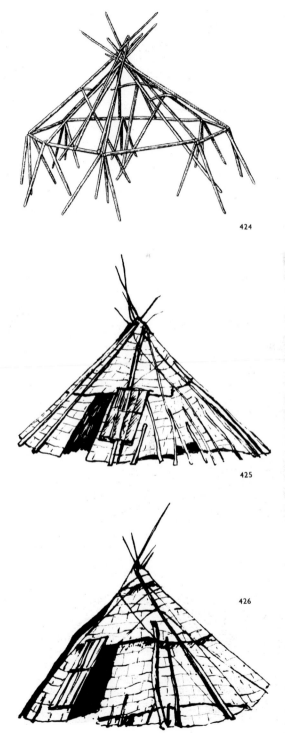

424

425

426

427

number of them were in use at the same time, and that the older ones would be filled in. They were probably used for different things; some might have been used for storage, others for cooking. At the edge of large settlements, such as Avdieievo and Kostienki, pits were found of about 1 metre in diameter, and these could only have been used for storing or to extract clay for as yet unknown purposes. It is not known to what use the larger pits were put. They did not often appear and they were not big enough to be used as dwellings.

The construction of the hut, as well as the contents of the fireplaces, show that Old Stone Age man, like some present-day Eskimos, was not deterred from moving into inhospitable regions like the polar tundra although he was dependent on the easily available raw material.

The fireplaces are an important part of the settlement. In large settlements pits in which the ash might have been kept have been found in addition to the proper fireplaces. These 'ash-pits' could not have been used to make a fire because the ground is not burnt and the ash and coal deposits are flat, of different size, and irregularly shaped. It is possible that if the proper fireplace needed cleaning, the ash and burning material would be carried to these other places. They might even have used the hot ash to distribute warmth somewhere else. A cleaned fireplace was found in Pincevin (Montereau, France).

Fireplaces are sometimes found lined with flat stones to isolate the walls and bottom as well as making them more secure. In other places blackened stones or pebbles occur which had generally been used as pot warmers, and which were also used to cook meat, as still happens among present-day hunting peoples. The hunters would heat the stones in the fire and when they were hot, fry the meat on them.

Fireplaces of considerable depth are known from the Upper Palaeolithic period (at Dobranitchevka, for example) which had long channels to protect the fire from draught. A very unusual fireplace was found in a round hut at Dolní Věstonice, dating from the Pavlovian culture, which had a low, round clay wall. This fireplace contained parts of small clay figures and this presents the problem of to what use this fireplace might have been put. But it does prove the high technical standard of the Pavlovian culture.

Let us now turn to the ethnological connections and comparisons. Particularly comparable are those cultures which are on a similar level of development, and people who share the same climatic and living conditions. Most suitable for comparative studies are tribes from present-day periglacial zones. The Chuckchee living in eastern Siberia constructed dwellings from whale bones until quite recently (422). As in Palaeolithic settlements the floors of the dwellings were set below ground level, and the whale bones — mostly jaw bones — were wedged by smaller bones or stones. The dwellings of the Chuckchee were covered with grass and a small passage led into the hut. Their small summer huts were covered with animal skins and not sunk into the ground.

There are various differences between the summer and winter quarters even in Palaeolithic sites. The constructions of present-day dwellings of Siberian hunters, too, show definite characteristics and identical traces; the upright posts on the outside correspond to the large bones which surrounded many Palaeolithic sites (423 to 426). The leather cover is

427 Eskimo tent in Alaska. The skins covering the tent are held down by boulders on the outside. (Photograph by Jean Gabus.)

428 View of an Eskimo tent, Alaska. (Photograph by Jean Gabus.)

429

430

429 Eskimo tent combined with a modern tent shelter which replaces the long entrance. (Photograph by Jean Gabus.)

430 Eskimo tent construction, Alaska. (Photograph by Jean Gabus.)

held down by stones and is also secured with straps which have stones on their ends. If the dwelling is destroyed these stones must fall into the interior of the dwelling and be in the upper layer of the deposit. The sloping holes for the posts found in a hut at Dolní Věstonice (hut II), are without doubt similar to the constructional supports of Chuckchee dwellings. Not only this people, but also Asiatic Eskimos, use bones as building material where there is no wood. If driftwood is present both materials are used. The layout of the huts is usually irregular or oval-shaped; not circular as some authors thought earlier. The grass or leather covering changed the original shape and also covered up some of the irregular features. This is why the oval outlines of dwellings were often thought to have been circular. The Eskimos living in the arctic region (427 to 430), who suffer from a shortage of wood, have built dwellings set into the ground and supported by whale jaws or ribs which rested on a wall made from the smaller parts of the skull or ribs. Dwellings made of whale bones and stones were used originally in the whole area occupied by the Eskimos from Greenland to Cape Diezhnev in Asia. These dwellings were later superseded by igloos.

In contrast to the Eskimos who with a few exceptions built their dwellings entirely without wood and of whale bones, the Stone Age inhabitants of the periglacial areas did not, even at the height of the glaciation, move far away from the edge of the wooded zone. This is why they were able to use a combination of building materials. They not only had the use of large bones, tusks, and stone, but also wooden posts as well as rods and branches. The varieties of wood in the fireplaces prove that wood was constantly used for the fire and that it could neither be far away nor rare. The constructions were obviously covered with grass or animal skins, because no other material was available.

The description of a pit-hut by Jochelson is very interesting. He discovered a semi-subterranean hut of the Siberians which was 15 metres long, 12 metres wide, and 7 metres high with a single entrance passage. This dwelling shows very obvious similarities in its construction to Palaeolithic dwellings. Archaeological reports often reveal that some North American Indians, too, lived in dwellings slightly let into the ground, circular or oval-shaped, and with tubular entrances.

The inhabitants of the southernmost part of

431

431 Circular, dome-shaped dwellings of the Alakaluf Indians who live in the coastal areas of south Chile. The light construction is covered with skins, sometimes recently replaced by pieces of textile, and is not dug into the ground.

432 Vedda camp, Sri Lanka (formerly Ceylon) beneath an overhanging rock (after B Allchin).

432

433 Dome-shaped South African bushmen's hut made of woven branches as a protection against the sun (after B Allchin).

434 A lightly built hut of pandanus leaves, which are supposed to protect against the heat. North Australia.

435 Light protective roof made from eucalyptus bark. Central Australia.

436 Structure of a dome-shaped hut of the central Australian Aborigines.

America had simple wind-shelters, or dome-shaped huts with irregular, oval, or circular outlines made with twigs or branches which were stuck into the ground and bent in towards one another (431). The dwelling was covered with moss or grass and sometimes with animal skins. These dwellings were very primitive. More stable dwellings set into the ground were found further north built by the inhabitants of the pampa. Some of the dwellings in the south were let into the ground but they were not true subterranean dwellings, they were only huts placed over a hollow, bowl-shaped depression similar to those at the Palaeolithic settlement found at Dolní Věstonice.

Material for comparative studies can also be found in primitive races which live under very different climatic conditions (432). The bushmen (433) and Australian Aborigines (434) of the dry and hot zones make shelters against the wind and sun by sticking branches or pieces of bark in a line into the ground (435 to

434

435

436

438). Sometimes they build simple huts made of grass or bark with no definite layout. Of course, it is not necessary for these peoples to take cover from the climatic conditions as the hunters of the Old Stone Age had to do. Therefore, it is only possible to compare these huts with other dwellings on a very basic level. There is no doubt that Palaeolithic hunters also erected shelters or protective wind-breaks, but they were not used as proper dwellings, and were used only for short periods, perhaps to shelter men during a hunt.

When we turn to ethnological studies we can see that the similarity between the dwellings of Old Stone Age man and present-day primitive races living in periglacial areas, are remarkable. The similarities are based on living conditions and environment, and on the necessity and possibility of a secure existence. The living conditions of recent primitive races living in the cold regions are similar to those of our ancestors, the hunters of Palaeolithic period.

437

438

437 Aboriginal dwelling in the interior of Arnhem Land, northern Australia. The sun-shade roof made from leaves and bark is carried on four posts. It is a typical example of a tropical protective hut.

438 Light structure for a dome-shaped Aborigine hut in central Australia.

IV Art of the Stone Age

439 Bone with an engraving of two hinds from Chaffaud cave in France; it is the first discovered Stone Age engraving.

440 Marcelino de Sautuola, who discovered the cave paintings of Altamira, Spain (after G Guinea).

441 Outline plan of the cave at Altamira. The famous Palaeolithic paintings are situated in the first large bay (1). The entrance to the cave is indicated by an arrow (after G Guinea).

The first discoveries of Palaeolithic cave paintings and engravings came so suddenly in western Europe that they were viewed with great suspicion because these discoveries would have changed the ideas generally held about the development of art. In the mid-1800s only classical, Ancient Egyptian, and Celtic art were known, and it was assumed that prehistoric discoveries could only have consisted of much more primitive artefacts. It was obvious, therefore, that the idea of a remarkable art-form of a very high standard existing 10 000 to 30 000 years ago, could only be accepted slowly. The cave paintings, engravings, reliefs, and statuettes found one after the other provided the proof that prehistoric man had reached a high level of cultural development. None of it was as primitive as had been thought till then. It was almost the opposite in fact; the mammoth and rhinoceros hunters of the Ice Age had laid a foundation of culture with their art on a level which was not to be reached again for many millennia. Of course, there is no contemporary documentation of any kind to accompany the Palaeolithic, and archaeologists and art historians have to try to reconstruct the meaning and message of Palaeolithic art, taking the existing discoveries and assessing them according to style, theme, and technique used in their archaeological context.

First, artistically decorated objects were found; these came to light during the excavations of caves. The dating produced no more difficulties than the assessment of the deposits in which they were found. The first discovery was made in 1843 in the Chaffaud cave (France); it was a bone which had two female deer engraved on it, and was thought to be of Celtic origin (439). Only later discoveries by E Lartet from La Madeleine and the Vézère valley in France proved without doubt their Palaeolithic origin. This was different, however, as far as the paintings and engravings found on walls of caves in western Europe were concerned. The first discoveries were made about 100 years ago, but it was only in the early years of the 1900s that the conclusion was reached that this must have been cave art of the Palaeolithic period.

The name of Marcelino de Sautuola, the discoverer of the incomparable cave paintings at Altamira, is deeply printed into the annals of the history of art. Sautuola (440) studied the surrounding caves of Santander where he lived, and had visited Altamira as early as 1875. He saw a prehistoric collection consisting of figurines and ornamental engravings on bones in 1878 in Paris and decided to return to Altamira to study the cave more closely (441). It was his nine-year-old daughter who in 1878 discovered on the low ceiling of a side cave, paintings which caused great surprise (442). But only two years later, when he was absolutely sure, did Sautuola tell the world that he had discovered cave art dating from the Old Stone Age. He stuck to his beliefs until the end of his life. Only Professor Vilanova, a geologist from the University of Madrid, supported his arguments, the rest of the experts were in the fiercest opposition. How could it have been otherwise? At the time of the discussions especially concerning the theories of Darwin, nobody expected to find such highly developed art from prehistoric times which could prove the talent and high cultural level of man from the Ice Age. It was always assumed that they were primitive wild creatures

441

442

443

442 Sketch of the paintings on the ceiling at Altamira (after Breuil).

443 Painting of a hind from Altamira (after Breuil). Length 220 centimetres.

444 Paintings of bison on the ceiling at Altamira.

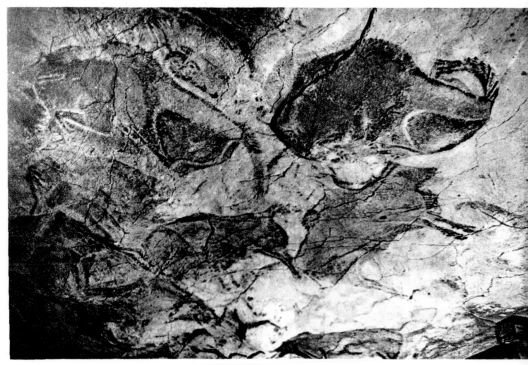

444

and that their level of development was little advanced from their animal ancestors. Altamira, however, proved that even among mammoth hunters great artists could be found. But this view was created so suddenly, without any warning, that some went as far as accusing Sautuola of fraud. These cave paintings, it was said, could have been made by a French painter who was a friend of Sautuola and who had been invited to stay there. To settle the argument the French palaeontologist Harlé was sent to Santander to examine the authenticity of these cave paintings. The result was crushing: Harlé announced that the paintings had obviously been created between the dates of their alleged discovery and Sautuola's announcement of it! This opinion supported the original views of leading historians, and Carthailac in particular. The Altamira discovery was put aside without any further research (443, 444).

In the meantime further reports of more cave paintings appeared in western Europe. Chiron reported one such discovery in 1878.

It was an engraving from the Chabot cave in France and he even enclosed a photograph of it. His report did not stir any interest. Rivière discovered paintings in the La Mouthe cave (France) in 1895 and declared them to date back to the Palaeolithic period. Unfortunately, he too was ignored. Further discoveries were made in the same year in the Pair-non-Pair cave (Gironde, France). Rivière received more or less the same treatment as Sautuola. It was said that he had made a mistake and even that he had become a victim of a fraud. At this time Carthailac himself visited both caves and in La Mouthe he uncovered an ochre painting beneath a Palaeolithic stalagmite deposit. But the authenticity of these discoveries was not accepted either. In 1897 the Marsoulas cave was discovered, and here too cave paintings were found, despite the fact that this cave had always been completely covered and no-one had previously been able to enter it. Even in 1901 Capitan and the Abbé H Breuil, two recognized experts, were criticized when they published reports about Palaeolithic paintings

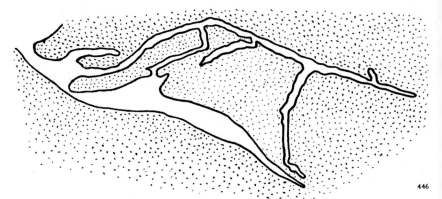

445 The rocks at Font de Gaume, France, with their well-known rock paintings.

446 Outline plan of the Font de Gaume cave (after Breuil).

in the Font de Gaume cave, and engravings in Les Combarelles (445, 446).

Further paintings and engravings including three-dimensional figures were found in the same cultural deposits. Carthailac was forced to alter his view in 1902 and published an essay which he called 'Mea Culpa d'un Sceptique' and in which he admitted his mistakes. Unfortunately Sautuola did not live to hear this apology. Altamira was visited again by experts, including Harlé. He too had to admit his mistake.

The following years brought many more cave paintings to light. In Spanish caves such as El Castillo, La Pasiega, Las Covalanas, and Hornos de la Peña. In France there have been Teyjat, Bernifal, La Grèze, Niaux, Gargas, Tuc d'Audoubert, Les Trois Frères, and Le Portel. Among the great discoveries of the last thirty years are the particularly well-known caves of Lascaux (1940), Roufignac (1956), Del Romito (1961), Kapova cave (1959) in the southern Urals (447 to 449), Ekain (1969),

447

447 View of the river Bielaya from Kapova cave, Urals, USSR.

448 Painting of a mammoth in the Kapova cave (after Bader).

448

and the recent discovery of Ait Tsenker cave in western Mongolia.

The largest number of Palaeolithic cave paintings and engravings was 'concentrated in France and Spain. The richest discoveries were made in the Cantabrian mountains, in northern Spain, the Pyrenees and the Dordogne in southern France. The great similarities found within this art have led to it being called 'Franco-Cantabrian art' (787).

Most of the caves with paintings and engravings are in the Vézère valley and the surrounding area in the Dordogne. The most famous and important are the bison and mammoth paintings in the Font de Gaume cave,

449 Outline of the Kapova cave in the southern Urals. The paintings are indicated with the numbers I, II, and III (after Bader).

450 Painting of two bisons. Lascaux, France. Length 240 centimetres.

451 Mountainous rocks at Niaux, France. The entrance to the cave is in the middle of the slope.

450

the engravings in the Les Combarelles cave, a large number of paintings from the Lascaux cave (450), and the sculptured horses at Cap Blanc and so on. Other major caves included in this group are Pair-non-Pair, Teyjat, Gabillou and the caves at Charente and Vienne.

The second group is in the Cantabrian mountains in Spain. It includes Altamira, the classic painted cave, and Hornos de la Peña, La Pasiega, Pindal, and El Castillo.

The caves of Niaux (451), Marsoulas, Les Trois Frères, Tuc d'Audoubert, Bédeilhac, Le Portel, Gargas, and so on, are on the French side of the Pyrenees.

In addition to these three large areas there are also smaller ones, mostly in western Europe, in southern Spain and the surrounding area of Malaga, in southern France along the lower Rhône, and some isolated sites in central Spain, Portugal, central France, southern Italy, and Sicily.

No cave paintings or engravings are known from the Palaeolithic period in central Europe. The geometric murals from the Domica cave in Czechoslovakia only date from the Neolithic period. Outside western Europe only two sites

are known with paintings dating undoubtedly from the Palaeolithic period; this is the Kapova cave in the southern Urals (USSR) and the Ait Tsenker cave in Mongolia. Many other discoveries which have been described as Palaeolithic paintings or engravings are from later periods.

The paintings found in south-east Spain are different from Franco-Cantabrian Palaeolithic art both in style and themes. Human figures are depicted throughout, often including whole scenes, and they are executed in a highly stylized form. They were once thought to belong to the Palaeolithic period, but now they have been included in the Mesolithic, the Neolithic, and even later periods. Most of the engravings from the so-called 'arctic art' of Europe found in Norway, Sweden, and the northern parts of Russia, are undoubtedly from more recent periods. It is possible, however, that some of the more primitive engravings of animals date from the Mesolithic period, or even from the Upper Palaeolithic. The same could be assumed about the discoveries from North Africa and the Sahara desert. Simple engravings of animals long extinct in these

452

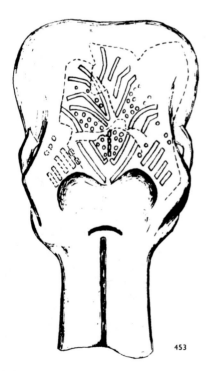

areas such as giant buffalos, elephants, hippopotamuses, and others could also date back to the Epipalaeolithic period.

The dating is so far based on estimations, and should be checked by more modern and exact methods.

Some of the most recent publications have come from Okladnikov and Dikov. They concern engravings from east and north-east Siberia, and some discoveries have even been made beyond the Arctic Circle. Dikov has already published material about the first Palaeolithic discoveries from inner Kamchatka, and both authors think that some of the engravings are of exceptionally great age. Many of the engravings recently found in South

452 Rocky cliff with the Grimaldi cave at the Italian Riviera. The first Palaeolithic Venus figurine was discovered here.

453 Mammoth skull with red painting on its forehead. Mezhiritch, Ukraine, USSR (after Pidoplitchko).

Ivory carving of a mammoth. Pavlovian culture, Předmosti, Moravia, Czechoslovakia. Length 11 centimetres.

Spoon-shaped implement made from a horse's jawbone and engraved with a horse's head. Pekárna cave, Moravia, Czechoslovakia. Length 35.5 centimetres.

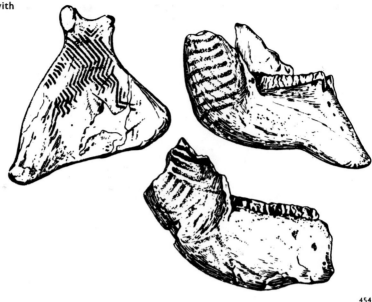

454 Mammoth bones with red decoration. Mezin, Ukraine, USSR (after Shovkoplias).

454

Africa or India are by comparison much more recent. The latest Palaeolithic discoveries — circular engravings — were found under closely datable deposits in northern Tasmania. Every single area and every site obviously needs a detailed study carried out using modern methods.

There are far fewer reliefs or three-dimensional works of art in existence than paintings and engravings. We know of them only from France and from the relief found in northern Tasmania. There is, however, a difference in Palaeolithic works of art which are found in some cultural deposits. In addition to the classic sites in western Europe (452) discoveries of this kind have been made in other areas, mainly in central Europe, with the richly productive sites in Czechoslovakia, West and East Germany. In these areas a more ornamental style can be observed. Unlike the natural, realistic style typical of western Europe, the ornamental style is particularly often found in sites in the Ukraine. A host of artistically ornamented implements and sculptures have been found there. They are rare, but some enormous mammoth bones and skulls have been found decorated with red paintings on them at Mezhiritch and Mezin, (453, 454) which were obviously parts of dwellings. A few discoveries have been made north of the

Ukraine, such as a small sculpture of a horse from Sunghir, east of Moscow. A large site on which small Palaeolithic works of art were found lies in southern Siberia and in the area around Irkutsk, where many engravings on bones were found, as well as sculptures of birds and humans.

Compared to the area in which Palaeolithic cave paintings occur, small works of art have been discovered over far larger regions. They reach from western Europe to southern Siberia in the Upper Palaeolithic periglacial zone.

Palaeolithic art — paintings and engravings

Cave paintings are usually found in easily accessible places, and at a height of about 1.4 to 2 metres, which means that the artist could easily reach the surface on which they occur. They are either on ceilings or other horizontal surfaces, and on walls. Sometimes they are found in places not so easily accessible, which the Stone Age artist could not have reached without some help or special construction to support him. In other places, however, the

455

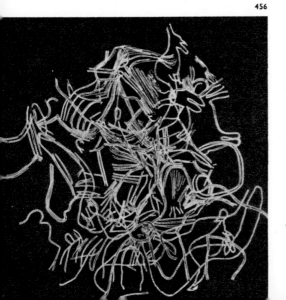

456

455 Drawing of a large bison and a small ibex; their comparative sizes out of proportion. Magdalenian culture, Niaux, France. Length 90 centimetres.

456 A typical example of superimposed engravings in the cave Pech Merle, France (after Lemozi).

457–458 Drawing and photograph showing the simple outlines of an engraved ibex. The horns are seen from the front and the crossed legs indicate movement. Aurignacian culture, Ebbou, France (after Lemozi). Length 40 centimetres.

paintings are so low that it is difficult to appreciate them from the necessary distance. Palaeolithic man obviously did not consider the overall composition of a picture important. This is also proved by the fact that many large complicated paintings are not clearly arranged. It is sometimes impossible to get even an idea at first glance, either because it is too large or because it might have been put on the wall of a narrow winding cave entrance.

In some of the caves the paintings are high up, and the artist had to use some kind of ladder, probably a notched tree trunk, which he could lean against the wall. In the Spencer Mountains of northern Australia the author discovered recent paintings high on a rock wall above a deserted dwelling site. Not far away from it a tree, found lying on the ground with roughly broken off branches, was probably used as a ladder.

Technique and perspective

While it is clear that there are many widely different styles of cave paintings and engravings, it is possible to make a few generalizations concerning their features held in common. The main point is that no real relationship of sizes in individual animals is observed when they are brought together in groups (455); smaller animals, such as stags, lions, and ibexes are depicted as being exactly the same size as the mammoths and bisons they accompany. In Lascaux, a gigantic aurochs is painted next to a miniature horse; in Cap Blanc, a horse is engraved between the legs of a bison, and so on. Again, it is common for animals to be drawn one on top of the other in a haphazard way (456). Because of this, and because the artists did not present the animals in their proper proportions they did not seem to concern themselves too much with how their pictures would look as a unity on the wall. The paintings are not in any way *compositions*. A single animal may often be seen to be drawn from several vantage points: if, for example, we look at the ibex in 457, we see the horns from a frontal position, and the body in profile (458). In this drawing the artist has attempted to give some idea of the depth of the scene by crossing the front legs, but on the whole animals are generally portrayed in a flat plane, with no sense of perspective or background. There is no sense of depth with the Irish elk which has been drawn into clay at Pech Merle (459). On the other hand, the engraved antler club from the Teyjat cave (460, 461) shows a horse which has a very sophisticated sense of depth achieved by superimposing one leg over the other. Such a sense is more forcibly conveyed in the relief of a resting woman from La Madeleine (462), and in the carving of the bison, which is licking

457

458

459

459 Crude finger engraving of an Irish elk in the clay deposits on a rock wall. The running animal looks rigid, and the significance of the vertical lines down the drawing is not clear. Pech Merle, France. Length 120 centimetres.

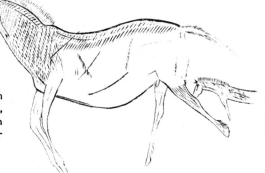

460–461 Engraving of a horse on a pierced baton from Teyjat, France. Length 30 centimetres. Right, a copy of this perfect Magdalenian engraving which shows the movement of the legs clearly (after Breuil).

460

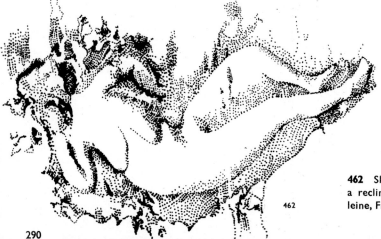

461

462

462 Sketch of the relief depicting a reclining woman from La Madeleine, France.

463 A bison turning its head to lick its flank. The movement is perfectly captured. Magdalenian sculpture, La Madeleine, France. Length 10 centimetres. (Photograph by Musée des Antiquités Nationales, St Germain-en-Laye).

463

its flank (463). On this bison we may trace several real levels — obtained mainly by literally setting the head as an overlay on the body. This gives a heightened sense of depth, and a three-dimensional effect: we see, for example, one horn carved on the raised part of the head, and another horn set back on the receded body.

In more ancient paintings and engravings a different technique can often be found which is attributed to the Aurignacian and Perigordian cultures. The artist portrayed an animal from the side except for the horns, ears, and sometimes also the hooves, which he presented in frontal view. The late Magdalenian culture, the peak of Palaeolithic art, reveals some conception of depth. The way in which depth was indicated in art cannot, however, provide a chronological guide line, which was assumed by the Abbé Breuil.

While it is true to say that the lack of unified composition is noticeable, and probably springs from the fact that the pictures were built up over many centuries of overpainting, there is still a strong feeling of unity which emerges from the majority of the caves. In particular

we could mention the horse paintings from Lascaux (464), the bisons of Font de Gaume (465, 466) and Le Portel (467) and, of course, Altamira and Pech Merle as well as the group of bisons from the Salon Noir in Niaux (468), or the composition from Lascaux (469). Apart from ideas of unity it is clear that any idea of depth and space in Palaeolithic art is different from our own. Our modern thinking and visual experience is conditioned by a cultural insistence on verticals and horizontals, and with these we surround our lives, and from them we derive our special sense of space. No such experience entered into the lives of the Old Stone Age artists, and for this reason it would be rash of us to claim that we can properly 'read' or interpret what they say. When we attempt to appreciate these pictures and carvings from our own point of view, we may feel that the Palaeolithic paintings are chaotic — yet, even so, their mysterious beauty and power filters through.

It might be easier to understand if a comparison is made with the mode of painting of present-day primitive races such as the Eskimos or Australian Aborigines. The artistic

464

465

466

work of these primitive groups also lacks the unity of a system consisting of vertical and horizontal lines, particularly if we just take figures into account and not the geometric ornaments. Primitive people are not perturbed by different orientation in a picture, and they do not think it necessary to view every picture from a central focal point. It is typical of the European to turn a transparency of one of these works of art around in order to look at it from all sides and work out the various details in that way.

Variations in the technique of some of these works are also very interesting. A systematic process is used to develop the human or animal body. The European artist sketches the main

proportions of head, body, and limbs first. This, however, is mostly unknown to primitive races. Some figures in Australian rock paintings done by the Aborigines have no heads. The author was able to watch an Aborigine paint a large crocodile on a rock face. He started with the tail (470), followed this with the hind legs, the body (471) and its details, the front legs, and then the head (472) with all its features. It is quite obvious that the artist had a very clear idea of what he was going to paint and it was not necessary for him to work in a particular sequence. There are other interesting discoveries depicting only parts of the body; the limbs of an aurochs in the Bédeilhac cave, a female figure without head in Garé de Couze (473, 474), torsos of the so-called magicians at Pech Merle and Cougnac (475 to 478) as well as many unfinished pictures of animals from different sites. We sometimes come across Palaeolithic paintings and engravings in which the artist has not only expressed what he can see but also what he knows to be there. The mammoth depicted in the Pindal cave in northern Spain has a red heart (479). The engraving of a fish in Abri du Poisson (480) shows its intestines. Pictures like that are common in certain forms of nordic European art and the spine and intestines of the animals are also shown (481). In northern Australia

464 Painting of horses at Lascaux, France. Consisting of a single scene, it was obviously created by one artist only.

465–466 Drawing and sketch of a scene depicting bisons and mammoths. Font de Gaume, France (after Breuil). Length 500 centimetres.

467 Two fighting bisons at Le Portel, France. Length 150 centimetres.

467

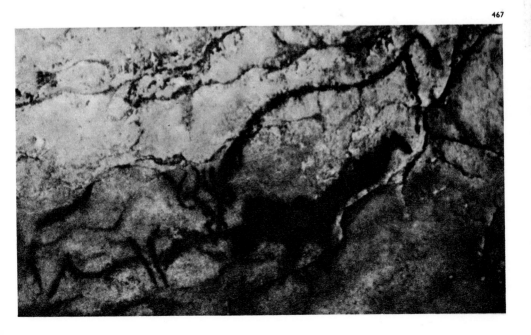

468 Main wall with the cave paintings at Niaux,
France.

469 The great frieze of horses, deer, and aurochs
at Lascaux; a well-conceived, uniform composition.
Magdalenian culture, France.

a style of drawing and painting animals developed which is nowadays called the X-ray style (482, 483), which shows fish, kangaroos, and even human beings with parts of their bone structure, intestine, and muscles. The author asked an Aborigine painter to explain the shading on his paintings, 'Surely flesh is flesh,' he said. During the evening, while the artist was cleaning out a dead kangaroo, he pointed out the various muscles as proof that the animal had different 'flesh' on its body, and to indicate this the artist showed different shadings on the drawing. There are few pictures in Palaeolithic art which could be considered to be descriptive or narrative scenes. The most famous, though still problematic scene, is at Lascaux (484), which shows a dead man lying in front of a bison. A broken spear is seen in the body of the animal and the intestines protrude from the wound. A bird is perched on a pole next to the man and in the foreground a rhinoceros shown in a completely different style, is just leaving the scene. Some archaeologists argue that the rhinoceros does not belong to the scene. Opinions differ but it seems almost certain that this is an account of an event that took place. In Font de Gaume a picture of two reindeer is always thought

to be one scene. One reindeer is grazing and looking at the other one which is lying down (485). An engraving of a cow followed by a bull (Teyjat cave, France, 486) must also be interpreted as a single scene, or the fight between two bison found engraved on a horse's rib-bone from the Pekárna cave, Czechoslovakia (487). The heads of several stags at Lascaux are usually interpreted as a scene of 'swimming stags' (488), which is supposed to explain why the Palaeolithic artist painted only the heads. We should expect, however, that in a picture of swimming stags, with their noses above the surface of the water, the antlers would have been leaning backwards, whereas the stags from Lascaux carry their antlers upright on their heads as if walking on firm ground. One of the most famous engravings is a scene with a figure and two extraordinary animals depicted on the walls of Les Trois Frères. The figure is half human, half bison and standing in an upright position. It holds a bow in its hand, which looks like a primitive musical instrument. The lower half of the figure is human except for the tail which ends in a brush-like point. The human arms end in bison hooves and the figure has a bison head. Walking in front of this 'centaur-like figure'

469

470

471

472

470 An Australian Aborigine painting a large crocodile on a rock face. The work is started at the tail end.

471 Painting of the crocodile; the body is seen from above, the tail from the side.

472 The head of the crocodile has been drawn in profile and the eggs shown in the body are fertility symbols.

297

474

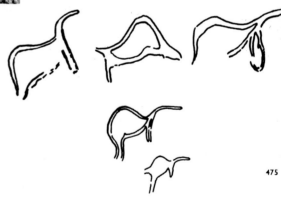

475

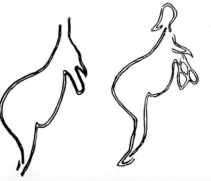

473–474 Rock engraving and sketch of a female figure without a head. Engraving at Gare de Couze, France (after Bordes). Height 15.7 centimetres.

475 Silhouettes of bison and women. Finger drawing at Cougnac, France.

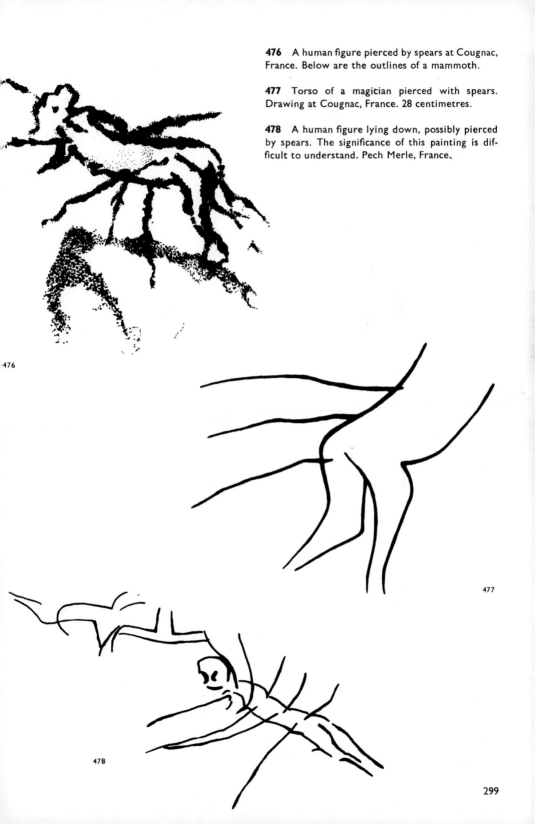

476 A human figure pierced by spears at Cougnac, France. Below are the outlines of a mammoth.

477 Torso of a magician pierced with spears. Drawing at Cougnac, France. 28 centimetres.

478 A human figure lying down, possibly pierced by spears. The significance of this painting is difficult to understand. Pech Merle, France.

476

477

478

479

480

481

479 Mammoth with its heart. Pindal cave, Spain (after Breuil). Length 44 centimetres.

480 Fish with its intestines indicated; a deep engraving from Abri du Poisson, France. The dark hewn lines above and below are traces of an attempt to steal this relief. Length 100 centimetres.

481 Elk with its intestines indicated; engraving from Kloftefoss, Norway. An example of the 'X-ray' technique in nordic art.

is an animal looking back at it. It has a deer's body and a bison's head. The third figure represents a reindeer with limbs, having paws. The most general, although not quite satisfactory, interpretation is that the male figure is a hunter wearing a skin as a disguise to get near to his quarry (489). These three engravings are on one level and form a scene.

How movement is expressed

If we look closely we realize that the Palaeolithic artist in fact managed to create far more movement than it at first appears. The movement in the oldest paintings and engravings is

482

482 Typical bark painting made by a north Australian Aborigine in the 'X-ray' style. The Aborigine not only paints what he can see, but also what he knows to be there, such as the intestines and parts of the bone structure.

Small horse's head modelled in clay. Note the interesting lines running lengthwise along the neck, and the short mane. Pavlovian culture, Dolní Věstonice, Moravia, Czechoslovakia.

Head of a cat-like wild animal of fired clay. Pavlovian culture, Dolní Věstonice, Moravia, Czechoslovakia. Length 6 centimetres.

Bear modelled in clay. Pavlovian culture, Dolní Věstonice, Moravia, Czechoslovakia. Length 7.5 centimetres.

483 Rock painting of a kangaroo in the 'X-ray' style. The heart, lungs, diaphragm, spine, and joints on the neck and legs are clearly visible. Arnhem Land, northern Australia.

484 Shaft of 'The Dead Man' at Lascaux, France. A broken-off spear is stuck in the bison's body and blood flows from the wound, or the intestines are protruding. The schematically drawn man has a beak-like face and lies on his back; below him is a symbol of a bird on a pole. Length 275 centimetres.

485 Painting of two grazing reindeer. Font de Gaume, France (according to a reconstruction by the Abbé Breuil). Length 245 centimetres.

486 Sketch of an engraving of a bull following the cow. Teyjat, France. Length 105 centimetres.

487 Scene of fighting bisons; engraving on a horse's rib. Magdalenian, Pekárna cave, Moravia, Czechoslovakia. Length 30 centimetres.

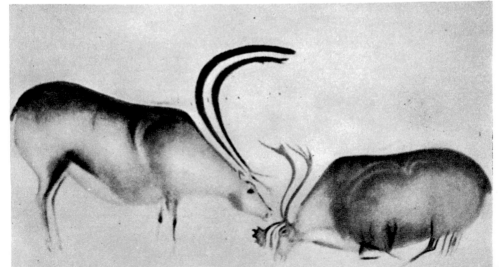

486

ressed by the position of the legs, the lines
he body, or the turning of the head. Por-
als of rigid or static figures are very rare.
eady in the Aurignacian culture, animal
ravings such as in the Ebbou cave, were
ited giving the impression of movement by
ssing the limbs.

f all four limbs of the animals are painted,
y are almost always so arranged as to sug-
movement. There are many examples:
engraved and coloured horses from Las-
x; the large black bulls and the small
ured horses from the same cave; the trot-
horse from Le Portel (490), or the bison
n Le Mouthe. Particularly interesting is the
er drawing in clay of a galloping Irish elk
ch Merle). The galloping is conveyed by
limbs stretched out in front and behind,
so-called 'flying gallop'. The same style
sed by the Palaeolithic artist to convey the
ing of running or jumping. We find an
mple in the horse at Font de Gaume (491).
he pierced baton from Teyjat shows a
ectly realistic engraving of a galloping
se. The bent forelegs are portrayed at the
nent of leaving the ground, the hind legs
straddled far apart, the right one in front,
left one behind (460). The sculpture on the
of a spear-thrower from Abri Montastruc

is shaped like a jumping horse, the front legs
are tucked under the stretched body; head,
neck, and body are in one line with the hind
legs in a position ready for jumping (492). On
the cave ceilings at Pech Merle in the so-called
'macaroni' style is a drawing of a running
hunter without a head (493). This was interpreted by the Abbé Lemozi. He carries a bow
and arrow under his arm, his body is bent
forward, one leg is stretched out in front almost
horizontally, the other leg is only hinted at.
This interpretation corresponds basically with
numerous Mesolithic and Neolithic drawings
from Spain. A reindeer antler is known from
Lorthet in the Pyrenees with an engraving
showing a stag turning around.

A fine example is the sculpture of a female
bison looking back over her shoulder from La
Madeleine. By comparison, the head is larger
than the body and better finished, the artist
obviously thought it to be of great importance.
One horn in front is protruding like a relief,
while the other horn is incised into the animal's
body. The mouth area too is expressed in relief
form, whereas the tongue of the animal is
deeply incised into the body, indicating that
it is licking the flank.

A line drawing of the basic outlines of three
female deer occurs at Las Covalanas. All three

487

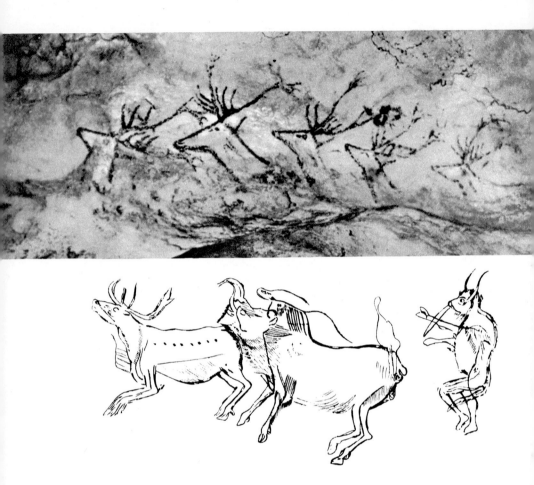

are looking in the same direction which is rare in Palaeolithic art. The animal in the middle is complete, with outstretched neck and uplifted head, as if sniffing the air suspiciously; it steps forward while doing so. The other two deer have only a head and neck. The one on the left has her head lifted too, the right one has turned her head in such a way as to give the impression that she was looking in the same direction as the other two (494). From Laugerie Haute cave comes an antler with two mammoths incised on it facing each other; the legs of the mammoth on the right are pressed into the ground and the animals are pushing against one another with their heads (495). This is presumably a picture of two mammoths fighting. Then there is a model of a horse's head from Mas d'Azil. This is supposed to be neighing horse with its ears pointing back (49 Moving figures and animals are also depic in Altamira (497). At Pech Merle the sim outlines of a bison with its head lower preparing to charge, can be seen on a wall the cave (498). A half human, half anim figure is portrayed at Les Trois Frères. carries a bow in one hand and, lifting its leg, is stalking a strange animal with a bi head. There is a second such figure engrav in the same cave.

Movement was quite often portrayed in laeolithic art. This is not only true of Magdalenian culture; classic small figuri and multi-coloured paintings range from Aurignacian to the Mesolithic period.

490

491

Stag heads, generally sug-
~~ed~~ as being shown swim-
~~g~~ a river. Lascaux, France.
~~gth~~ 500 centimetres.

Drawing of the scene with
~~nasked~~ magician. Les Trois
~~es~~ cave, France (after Breuil).

Trotting horse at Le Por-
France. Length 45 centi-
~~res.~~

Galloping horse at Font de
~~me,~~ France (after Breuil).
~~gth~~ 115 centimetres.

492 Sculpture of a jumping horse. Magdalenian culture, Abri Montastruc, France. (Photograph by Musée des Antiquités Nationales, St Germain-en--Laye).

493 Torso of a running hunter. Painting from Pech Merle, France (after Lemozi). Length 28 centimetres.

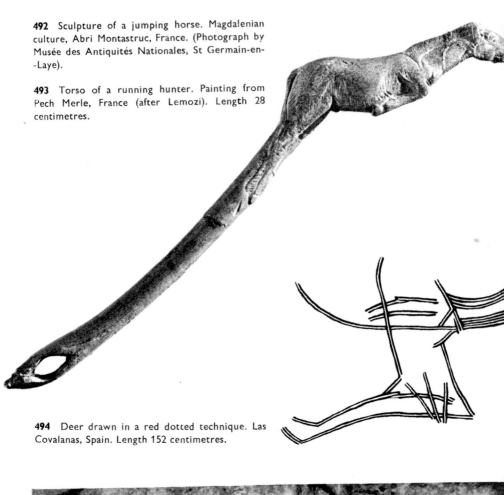

494 Deer drawn in a red dotted technique. Las Covalanas, Spain. Length 152 centimetres.

495

495 Fighting mammoths. Engraving at Laugerie
Haute, France.

496 Head of a neighing horse. Carving from Mas
d'Azil, France. Length 5.5 centimetres.

496

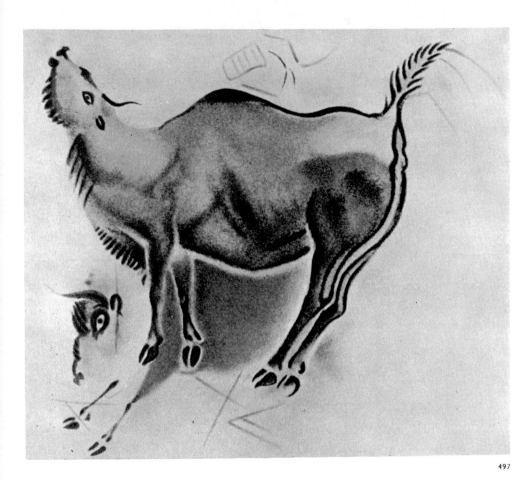

497

497 Bellowing bison. Magdalenian culture, Altamira, Spain (after Breuil).

498 Simple drawing of a bison preparing to charge. Pech Merle, France (after Lemozi). Length 60 centimetres.

498

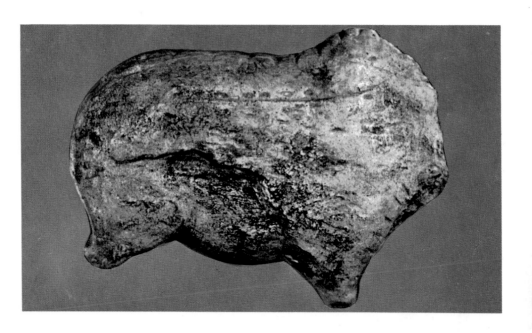

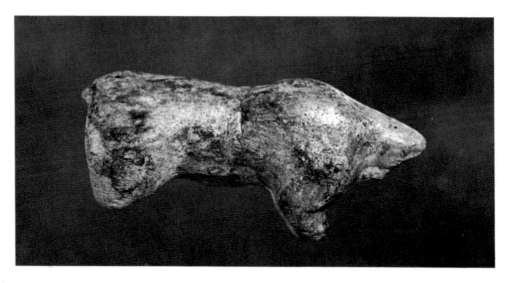

Animal carvings made from mammoth ivory. Early Aurignacian culture, Vogelherd, Germany. Length 7.5 and 6 centimetres.

A pierced bone club decorated with a simple engraving of a bear. Magdalenian culture, Pekárna cave, Moravia, Czechoslovakia. Length 17 centimetres.

Small head of a rhinoceros made of fired clay. Pavlovian culture, Dolní Věstonice, Moravia, Czechoslovakia. Length 4.2 centimetres.

Female figurine made from mammoth ivory and with a faint indication of a face. Malta, Siberia, USSR.

Female figurine from Malta, Siberia, USSR, with clearly visible facial features and a distinctive hairstyle. Height 8 centimetres.

Figurine of an obese woman from Gagarino, Ukraine, USSR. Height 5.8 centimetres.

bstraction and
ylization

stract pictures usually just catch the char-
eristics of an object and are not concerned
h portraying something naturally. There is,
vever, some connection between the ab-
ict and the symbol. The abstract portrayal
isually concerned with the important char-
eristics and leaves all the unimportant de-
ls aside. If we look at the symbol as an
stract, we can differentiate between two
ds of abstraction: the simplifying and the
nbolizing picture.

The symbol is a sign indicating a particular
ject or concept. The sense is not immediately
own to the uninitiated, because the abbrevi-
on has reached such a degree that it is often
possible immediately to connect it with the
ginal model. Sometimes a symbol would be
ated without being an abbreviation or sim-
fied sign of an actual model. Abstract sym-
lism and art was particularly well-developed
ring the Magdalenian period but it existed
ght from the beginning of the Palaeolithic
riod.

Abstract animal drawings among red dots
n be seen at Pech Merle. Only the simple
ltlines of a mammoth can be recognized (499).
bove this drawing and the red dots, a simple
ttline drawing of a bison can be seen. Experts

think that this is a stylization of a bison preparing to attack, with a robust chest which
gravitates down into a sharp point and symbolizes the head. Other interesting pictures
are on the same wall slightly below the previously mentioned picture. Also of interest is the
picture of a bison in the large cave. Here the
head of the bison is merely a continuation of
its neck, and only barely hinted at. The other
drawings too are probably stylized bison. If
this is the case, the tail is turned upwards and
the legs form a rectangular, and in one case an
oval shape which looks like a woman's breasts.
The point symbolizing the head is practically
parallel with the hind legs. These drawings
show considerable differences from a bison,
and when the picture is turned around it shows
a remarkable likeness to the outlines of a stylized figure of a woman from the same cave.
The tail of the bison could be taken as the
woman's head, the hind legs could be taken
as the breasts, and so on, but it is extremely
difficult to work it out.

The most interesting site is Pech Merle
where among other clay drawings, three simple,
slightly forward-bent figures of women with
hanging breasts and protruding hips can be
seen. This is a step towards stylized female
figures as we know them from the engravings
at La Roche Lalinde, the carvings from Vogelherd, or the well-known Pekárna cave (500).

Two other examples illustrating the stylization of mammoth and bison drawings can be
seen at Pech Merle. The outline of the mam-

499

99 Schematic mammoth
Ihouette from Pech Merle,
·ance.

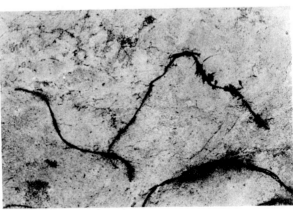

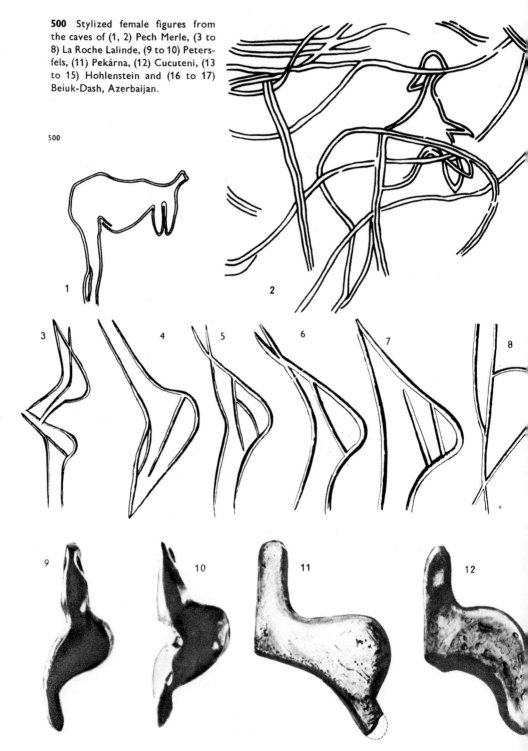

500 Stylized female figures from the caves of (1, 2) Pech Merle, (3 to 8) La Roche Lalinde, (9 to 10) Petersfels, (11) Pekárna, (12) Cucuteni, (13 to 15) Hohlenstein and (16 to 17) Beiuk-Dash, Azerbaijan.

500

1

2

3

4

5

6

7

8

9

10

11

12

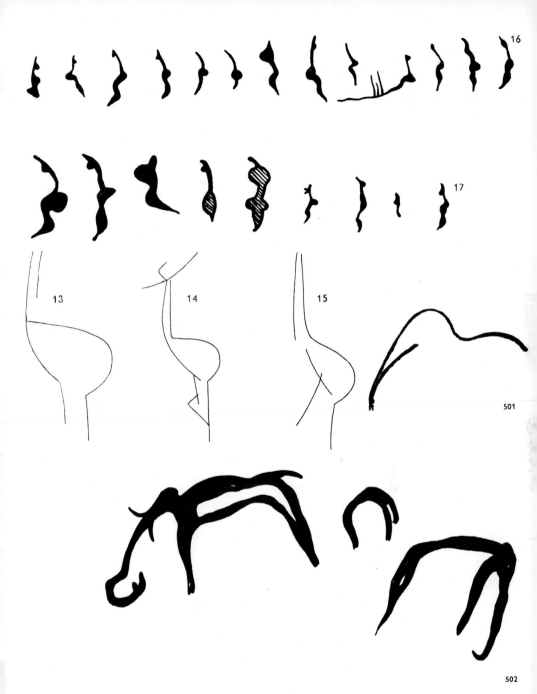

501 Schematic mammoth silhouette from Pech Merle, France.

502 Mammoths; schematic finger drawing in clay. La Baume Latronne, France.

moth was first reduced to a simple, characteristic line, a line showing only the contour of the head and back (501). The wavy line indicating the line of the back, with a high front and a low tail end, is typical of the bison also. Leroi Gourhan described the stylization of a mammoth drawn in clay consisting of three simple lines: the tusks, the trunk, and outline of the head or body (La Baume Latronne) (502).

The engraving of a reindeer herd on a bone from Teyjat (France) indicates the simple stylization of a large number of individuals or, as in this case, a herd. The first reindeer is drawn in full; the other animals of the herd are only indicated by their legs and antlers. When observing such a herd of animals their bodies would merge together and only an indefinable mass of antlers and legs would be seen (503).

The stylization of several identical objects in one cluster or row is best indicated by repeating the characteristics of the object. This has been practised by other primitive cultures too. In northern Australia the author discovered at the Cadell River a picture of a shoal of fish. Some fish were drawn fully, others only indicated by their tails (504).

The technique of Palaeolithic art

Tools such as burins were used for most engravings, particularly for the deep rock engravings. The discoveries of large stone burins at Le Roc leave no doubt about the technique of this work. Finer engravings are typical of

504

503 Reindeer herd engraved on a bone found at Teyjat, France. The first and last animals are completely drawn while the rest of the herd is indicated only by their legs and antlers. Length 20 centimetres.

504 Fish and fish tails which are drawn instead of the whole fish. This painting shows how symbols were created. Arnhem Land. northern Australia.

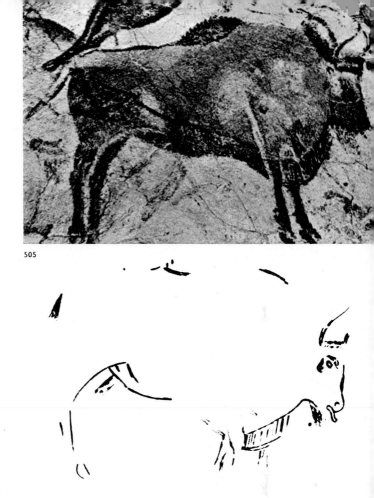

505 A combination of an engraving and a painting. Below the engraved portion of the animal is sketched in outline. Altamira, Spain (after Graziosi).

505

the Middle and Upper Magdalenian culture; their outlines consist of several fine lines. This technique is also used in engravings combined with paintings (505), at Altamira for example, and also for engravings on bone, ivory, antler, or stones. Details are often indicated by hatching, for example, for manes (506) and the hair of animals. It seems that this technique is more recent than most of the outline engravings, and it is more graphic than three-dimensional in appearance. Pictures engraved in clay on the cave floors are rare; they probably do not survive because they were at greater risk than those cut in the rock. The two carved bison from Tuc d'Audoubert (507, 508) are a remarkable find. The Palaeolithic artist did not model these bisons in the clay, but used a sculpture-like technique more usual for stone to get the result. These two clay 'sculptures' lie on a slab of stone with only one side

worked in a three-dimensional form, whereas most of the other side which rests on the stone is hardly formed or carved. Associated with these 'sculptures' is a smaller, crude model, and next to it a deep clay engraving of a bison (509, 510), which indicates the technical development from engraving to relief work.

Solutrean reliefs at cave entrances and on cave walls are often accompanied by deep engravings and the marks made with pointed stone tools (511), which were also found beside the horse relief at Cap Blanc in Dordogne, France. We sometimes come across dotted outlines or crude engravings like the lioness at Les Trois Frères (512, 513). It is difficult to find out whether these dotted lines have later been connected together by engraved lines. In Europe not only dotted lines are known but also larger areas of dots. This is, however, mostly the case of post-Palaeolithic periods.

506 Drawing of the sculpture of a horse from Lourdes, France. The fine hatching indicates the fur, mane, and tail (after Breuil). Length 7.2 centimetres.

507 Clay sculpture of two bison modelled lying on one side. Tuc d'Audoubert cave, France.

508 One of the modelled bison. Tuc d'Audoubert, France. Length 61 centimetres.

One of the simplest techniques is that of the finger drawing in clay. Breuil thought that this was the oldest technique but was not able to prove it. Finger drawings with clay are known from cave walls at La Baume Latronne, and finger drawings in clay are known from Gargas. Some of these pictures just seem to be scribbles, but others are perfectly composed pictures. There is a finger engraving of a fish (514), and another of a bison in Niaux which

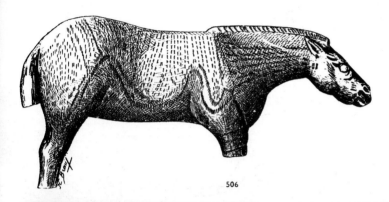

506

507

508

s engraved on the clay floor of the cave with
sharp implement. Sometimes combinations
paintings and engravings occur. Many multicoloured paintings, in places already enhanced
simple engravings, were found in Altamira.
mbined techniques were often used in Palaeo-
hic art. The bison standing on its hindlegs
m the El Castillo cave is one example of the
mbined technique which also makes use of
e natural shape of the rock (515). Other
amples of engraved and painted objects are
e ibex heads at Lascaux; a picture of a run-
ng horse crossed by engraved arrows; and an
graved and painted bison (516). A man-like
ure engraved and painted red occurs at
gles-sur-l'Anglin. The reliefs at the entrances
caves were often colourfully painted, many

of them show traces of red paint (for instance,
at Le Roc and Laussel). These colours, exposed to all weather conditions, did not last,
and today only a few traces of them can be
found.

The cave sculptures from Europe which
made use of the natural form of rocks are very
interesting. One such example is the bison
from El Castillo which has already been mentioned. The lower part of the rock with its
different indentations and protruding parts
looks like the legs, tail, and belly of the bison.
The hooves of the hindlegs and the horns are
engraved, and the body, mouth, and mane
were blackened. The artist at Niaux made use
of the little holes made by dripping water. He
incised a bison around these holes in the clay

509 Unfinished ...son from the ...d'Audoubert ca... France. (Photogr... by H P Herdeg ... A Weider, Zurich.

510 Human foot... prints made arou... the sculpture of ... bison in the T... d'Audoubert cave... France.

511

511 Strong burins which were used to carve the reliefs at Le Roc, France.

512 Crude engraving of the outlines of a lioness. Les Trois Frères cave, France. Length 75 centimetres.

513 Lioness. Sketch of an engraving from Les Trois Frères, France (after Breuil).

514 Engraving of a fish on the clay floor. Niaux, France. Length 30 centimetres.

515 Bison from the El Castillo cave in Spain. An example of a combination of a painting and an engraving which also makes use of the rock surface in modelling the rear of the bison.

513

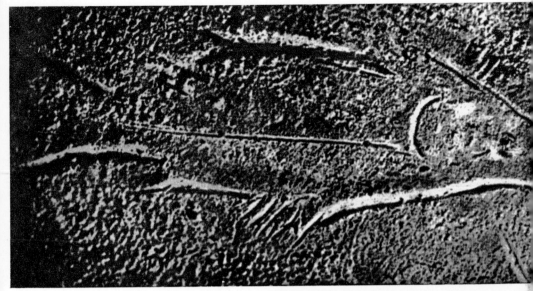

514

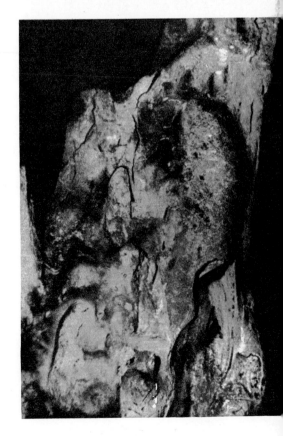

515

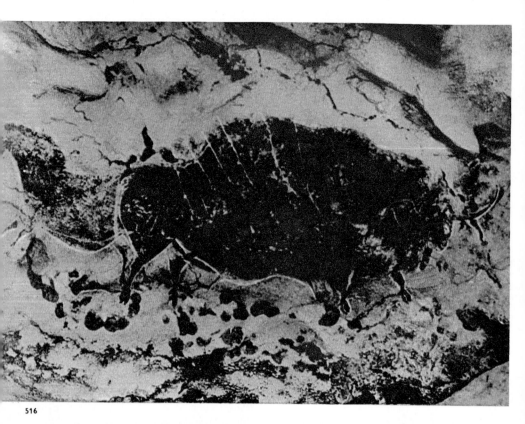

516

517

floor and added arrows to the holes indicating the wounds of the bison (517). A strange natural opening in the rock wall was found at Salon Noir, which looks like a stag head. A Palaeolithic artist must have noticed it and painted antlers on both sides (518). A hornstone protrusion from a limestone wall at Roufignac cave has been used for the eye of a mammoth engraving. The unevenness of the ceiling at Altamira has also been used, together with a few engraved lines here and there, and combined into a perfectly shaped bison lying down. A great number of examples could be given to illustrate the extraordinarily vivid imagination of the Palaeolithic artist. These artists knew

how to make use of the natural shapes and forms of the rock surface, but mostly did not compose pictures planning the 'scene'. They engraved, painted, or drew on stone without preparing the surface, and sometimes they would draw with their fingers on cave walls covered with thin clay deposits (519). Only at Font de Gaume was the surface prepared with red paint by the artist (520).

Some artifical light must have been provided in order to paint in the caves, and lamps have been found in west European caves (521 to 523).

Coloured earth was used to make paint. Yellow, red, and brown came from ochre, black and dark brown came from manganese dioxide. White paint made from kaolin has also been found, in addition to limonite and haematite giving orange, red, and brown tones, and charcoal used for black paint. Water was used for binding, but sometimes also fat. On some sites rare discoveries of paint containers have been made. Sea shells were used at Altamira, and a decorated bone bowl (524) was found at Les Côttés. Red paint was also found in deposits belonging to the Mousterian culture, although there was no evidence of artistic objects. Perhaps this paint was used to paint the body for ritual purposes.

516 Bison from Lascaux with engraved arrows across its body.

517 A bison incised on the clay floor of the Niaux cave. The small hollows caused by dripping water indicate wounds.

518 A natural hollow in the rock with painted antlers which gives the impression of a stag's head. Niaux, France.

518

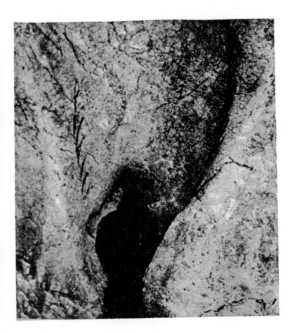

519 Finger drawing of a horse with many wounds on its body. Clay engraving from Montespan, France. Length 45 centimetres.

520 Drawing of a wolf on a red painted background. Font de Gaume, France (after Breuil). Length 120 centimetres.

521

522

Other dyes or paints have been found in Palaeolithic deposits; for instance, at Arcy-sur-Cure. Small lumps of pigment were discovered here which were used like crayons, and at Laugerie Haute in the Dordogne (525). Palaeolithic ochre mines were uncovered in western Hungary.

In Australia, modern Aborigines make paint powder by scraping a lump of earth on a flat stone (526). The Aborigines use water to mix their paints, and add a small amount of resin to make it more durable. It is possible that the European Palaeolithic hunters used a similar technique. The paintings were usually made in clear outlines with simple lines which become broader in places. Animals were only exceptionally coloured but some coloured surfaces are known such as a picture of a horse at Le Portel. At Lascaux and Font de Gaume a surface had been painted in two colours, and at Altamira with three different colours. The body of a bison at Marsoulas is covered with red dots (527, 528), and at Niaux the body of a horse can be seen covered with black hatchings (529).

Paintings and engravings are found in Palaeolithic art which depict animals in such detail that it is not at all difficult to identify them. On the other hand there are also very simpli-

521 Stone oil lamp. La Mouthe, France. Length 17 centimetres.

522 The underside of the same oil lamp with an ibex head engraved on it.

523 Oil lamp from Lascaux, France.

523

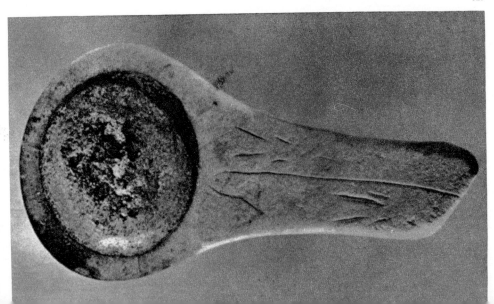

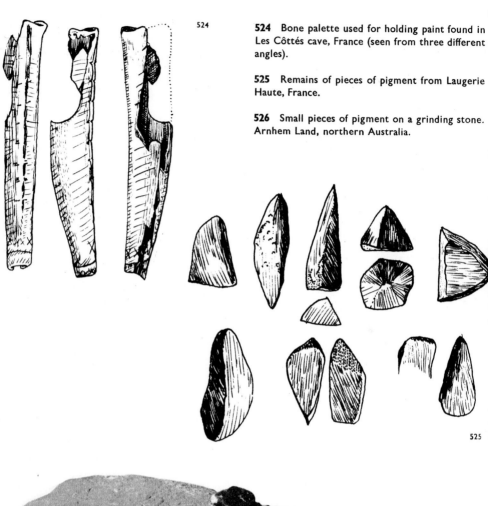

524 Bone palette used for holding paint found in Les Côttés cave, France (seen from three different angles).

525 Remains of pieces of pigment from Laugerie Haute, France.

526 Small pieces of pigment on a grinding stone. Arnhem Land, northern Australia.

525

526

Venus figurine from Avdieievo, Ukraine, USSR. Height 12.5 centimetres.

Female figurine carved from mammoth ivory. Avdieievo, Ukraine, USSR. Height 16 centimetres.

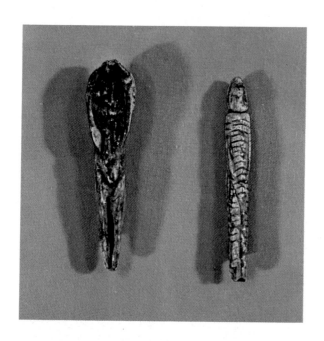

Two figurines carved from mammoth ivory. On one there are indications of clothes and a hood. Malta, Siberia, USSR. Height 5.8 centimetres.

Carved female figurine from the Upper Palaeolithic site at Malta, Siberia, USSR. Height 13.6 centimetres.

Head broken off from a human figurine (back view). The hairstyle is very distinctive. Malta, Siberia, USSR. Height 5 centimetres.

Stylized figurine of a pregnant woman carved from the bone of a mammoth phalange. Pavlovian culture, Předmostí, Moravia, Czechoslovakia. Height 14 centimetres.

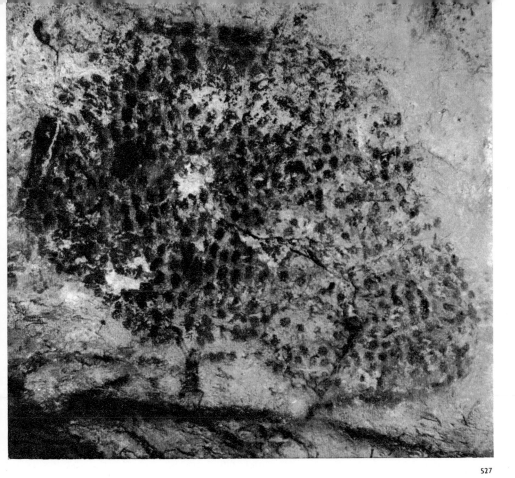

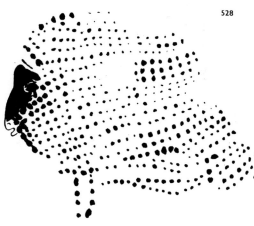

fied, almost abstract engravings or paintings which are very difficult to interpret. Uncompleted paintings are as frequent in the Palaeolithic as pictures which only show parts of the animal (the heads of stags or ibex at Lascaux).

Sculptures and small figurines were made from mammoth ivory, stone, bone, or clay. Mammoth ivory was preferred for making small sculptures throughout the period of Palaeolithic art in Europe and Asia. Other figures were made from clay mixed with bone flour. Figures like this have been found at Dolní Věstonice which had been fired. Implements made for hunting, such as spear-throwers (530 to 532) were made from antlers and often beautifully decorated. Decorated bones have been found only occasionally. Mammoth ivory and stone was mainly used for small sculptures in the areas stretching from central and eastern Europe to Siberia. Antler was the main material used in sites of the Magdalenian culture of western Europe.

527–528 Painting of a bison made up of dots and short lines, and a sketch of it. Marsoulas cave, France. Length 87 centimetres.

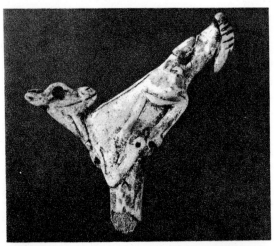

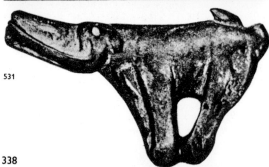

529 Hatched drawing of a horse from Niaux, France. Length 170 centimetres.

530 Young ibex; sculpture on a fragment of a spear-thrower. Bédeilhac cave, France. (Photograph by Romain Robert.) Length 8 centimetres.

531 Stylized sculpture of a mammoth; originally part of a spear-thrower. Bruniquel, France. Length 12.5 centimetres.

532 Two ibexes, sculpture on spear-thrower. Les Trois Frères, France. (Photograph by Musée de l'Homme, Paris.) Length 6 centimetres.

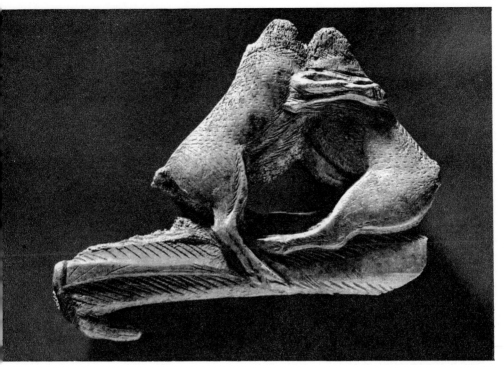

Themes in Palaeolithic art

Animals

Animals are often portrayed so realistically and so naturally that we can easily distinguish not only the type of animal depicted, but can also differentiate between species that look very alike. The mammoth was widely distributed in western Europe during the Palaeolithic period and we can assume that the majority of depicted proboscids belonged to the species of *Mammuthus primigenius*. The mammoth is characterized by its long coat, a hump on the back, and a round head. The gigantic tusks are swept outwards and then back. These characteristics differentiate the mammoth from the real elephant which, in the Palaeolithic it seems, did not have a long-haired coat nor a hump on its back, but straight tusks and a back which was not as arched as that of the mammoth (533 to 539).

There are numerous paintings and engravings from the Palaeolithic depicting horses. It is extremely difficult to distinguish between the different breeds of horse, although it has often been tried, and the characteristics are probably as much a manifestation of the artist's style as they are of the horse's breed (540 to 548).

There is at present only one certain picture of a donkey *(Equus hydruntinus)* which is to be found at Lascaux. This identification is justified by the long, pointed ears, and the long, thin tail as well as the proportions of the body and head of the animal. Bison are, however, the most popular animals of the Palaeolithic artist. In the Upper Palaeolithic period lived the species *Bison uriformis* (Holzheimer) (549 to 551) which is distinguished from the older kind of fossil bison *(Bison priscus)* by the shape and size of its horns. According to Zeuner, who believed that the paintings at Lascaux are very old and date back to the beginning of the Aurignacian period, the long horns of bison found in paintings in this cave are of the fossil bison *(Bison priscus)*. According to Laming,

533

533-534 A mammoth, and outline sketch, engraved on a piece of bone from La Madeleine, France (after Breuil). Length 24.5 centimetres.

535 Mammoth engraved on a piece of ivory. Malta, Siberia. Length 8 centimetres.

534

535

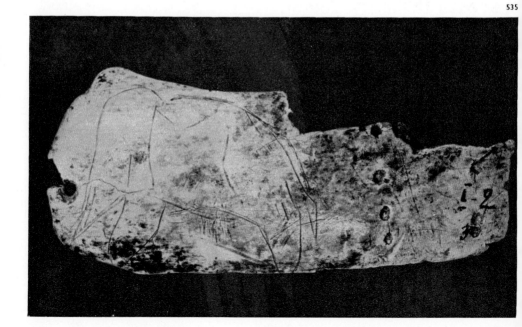

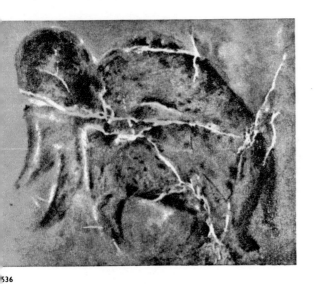

536 Painting of a mammoth from the Kapova cave, Urals, USSR, (after Bader).

537 A mammoth engraved on mammoth ivory. Klausen, Bavaria, Germany. Length 9 centimetres.

537

however, the length of the horns is a result of an individual artistic conception. The dating of the Lascaux cave, carried out by the radiocarbon method, agrees with Laming's findings and not Zeuner's.

The aurochs *(Bos primigenius)* is also a popular subject for Palaeolithic art (552 to 554). It is larger than most domestic cattle and has large, long horns. Another species of aurochs *(Bos brachyceros* or *Bos longifrons)* is known from the post-glacial period. It had short horns and was smaller. Aurochs with short horns are also depicted at Lascaux, although this is probably an indication of sex differences, and not a sign of a different species. The reindeer, surprisingly, is not depicted as often even though it was present in abundance during the cold periods of the Upper Palaeolithic in western Europe. It can be seen, however, on small art objects; either on stone engravings, reliefs, or small figurines. Paintings of stags, probably dating from the end of the Pleistocene period, were found at Lascaux where they are depicted with very wide shovel-like ends to their antlers. This is obviously not a realistic painting.

The Irish elk *(Megaloceros giganteus)* is only rarely found. It was as large as a horse, had a hump on its back and enormous antlers. The ibex *(Capra ibex)* was well established during the Upper Palaeolithic period and is often depicted in paintings, engravings, reliefs, and on small objects all across western Europe.

538 A mammoth sculptured in mammoth ivory. Pavlovian culture, Předmostí, Moravia, Czechoslovakia. Length 12.8 centimetres.

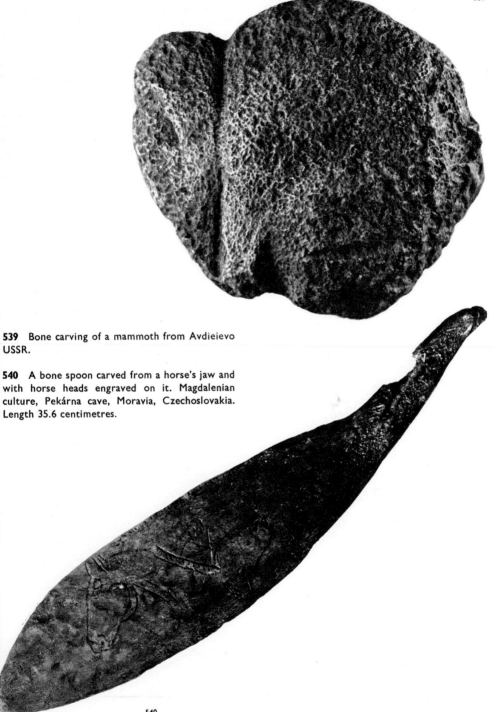

539 Bone carving of a mammoth from Avdieievo USSR.

540 A bone spoon carved from a horse's jaw and with horse heads engraved on it. Magdalenian culture, Pekárna cave, Moravia, Czechoslovakia. Length 35.6 centimetres.

540

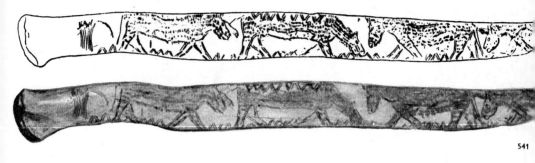

541

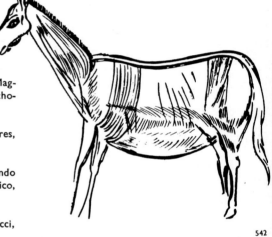

541 Bone engraving of four horses from the Magdalenian culture. Pekárna cave, Moravia, Czechoslovakia (after Klíma).

542 Engraving of a horse from Les Trois Frères, France (after Breuil).

543 Bone engraving of a horse from the El Pendo cave, Spain. (Photograph by Museo Prehistorico, Santander).

544 Painting of a horse from the Grotta Paglicci, Italy.

542

543

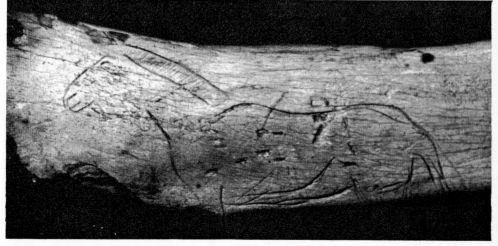

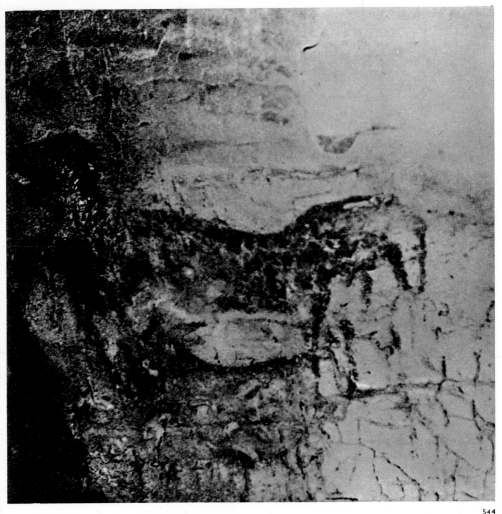

544

Pictures of ibex were also found in the southern Uzbekistan, Azerbaijan, Kirghizia, and Mongolia, and probably date back to the Mesolithic or later periods. Rarely, and only on small objects, do we find pictures of the chamois. The musk-ox is also only found rarely, but a stone head sculpture is known from Laugerie Haute (555 to 564).

Only a few pictures of beasts of prey exist. Engravings or small sculptures of cave lions (*Panthera spelaea*) are sometimes found, as well as European brown bears (*Ursus arctos*). The cave bear (*Ursus spelaeus*) was already extinct at the end of the Palaeolithic period in which

most of the engravings and sculptures were made (565 to 568).

The wild boar appeared during the warmer interstadial periods, and is known from the paintings at Altamira (570). More frequent are the paintings of rhinoceros, which are mainly found in western Europe. At this time it was probably the woolly rhinoceros (*Coelodonta antiquitatis*). Zeuner, according to his dating of the paintings at Lascaux which he thought were much older than they actually are, supposed that this painting was not of a woolly rhinoceros but the older *Rhinoceros merckii*. The rhinoceros is also known from

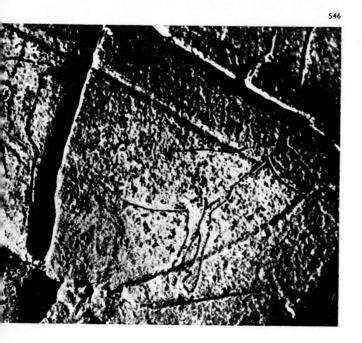

545 Dotted horses from Pech Merle, France. Length 340 centimetres.

546 Engraving of a horse from Levanzo, south Italy (after Graziosi).

547 Drawing of a horse in black from Niaux, France. Height 80 centimetres.

547

548 Painting of a mare with a foal from Altamira, Spain (after Breuil).

549 Bison lying down. Altamira, Spain (after Breuil). Length 150 centimetres.

550 Multicoloured painting of a bison at Altamira, Spain (after Breuil).

551 Painting of two bison from Niaux, France. Length 95 centimetres.

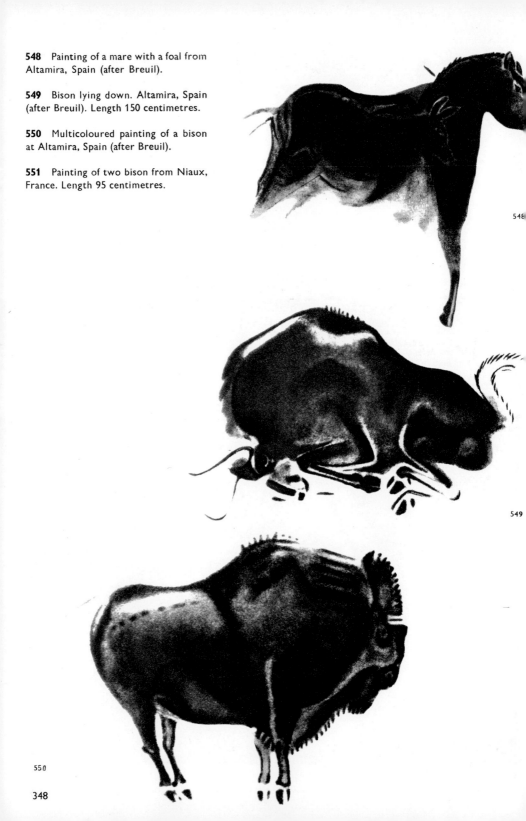

548

549

550

552

552–553 Stone engraving and sketch depicting an aurochs. Egadi Island, south Italy (after Graziosi). Length 17.5 centimetres.

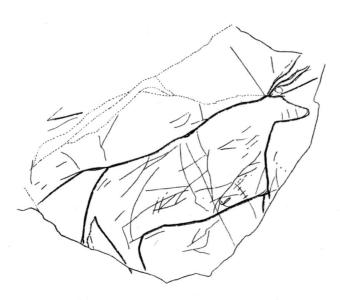

553

554

554 Aurochs engraved on a stone slab. Trou de Chaleux, Belgium. (Photograph by Institut Royal des Sciences Naturelles de Belgique.)

small objects; as can be seen from a small model of a rhinoceros head found at Dolní Věstonice in Czechoslovakia (571, 572).

There are very few pictures of fishes, snakes, birds, and insects, but a good example is an engraving of a grasshopper found on a bone fragment at Les Trois Frères. Sometimes we can find plants depicted, as in the Pekárna cave. The south Siberian carvings of birds are very interesting. These rare themes are usually depicted only on small objects carved of stone, bone or mammoth ivory, and found in occupation levels (569, and 573 to 576).

Fantastic animals and half-men

Figures of fantastic beings which do not belong to any known animal, are known from Palaeo-

lithic art. There are two types: either they are definitely animal, but quite different from all known animals, or they are fabulous creatures, half man, half beast. The first mentioned type often belongs to the category of mistaken identification which has come about through the criss-crossing of lines which are often wrongly connected. An example is the engraving called the 'Agnus Dei' from the Pair-non-Pair cave which depicts a combination of an ibex with a lowered head and a horse looking backwards (577, 578). The body of the ibex seems to merge with the head and neck of the horse, giving an impression of a fantastic animal.

Fantastic animal figures are known from Les Trois Frères (579). One of them has the body of a bear, while the head with its pointed ears looks more like that of a wolf. Others have bodies of bears, hairy paws, round heads, and

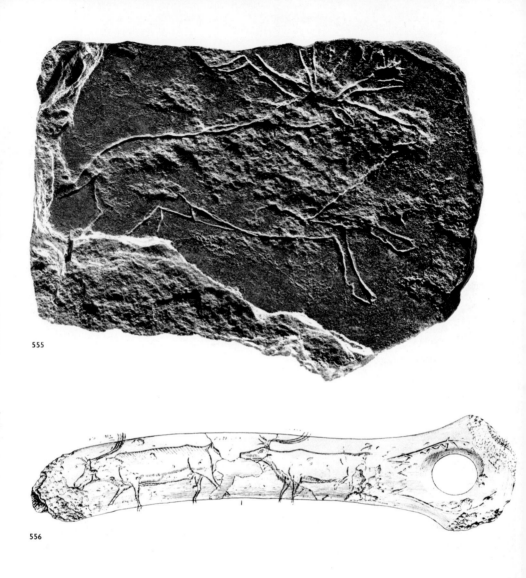

555

556

555 Stone engraving of a running reindeer from St Marcel, France. (Photograph by Musée des Antiquités Nationales, St Germain-en-Laye.)

556 A baton made of an antler engraved with two reindeer. Petersfels, Germany.

557 Stone engraving of a stag. La Madeleine, France. Length 65 centimetres.

558 Painting of a stag from Levanzo, south Italy (after Graziosi).

557

558

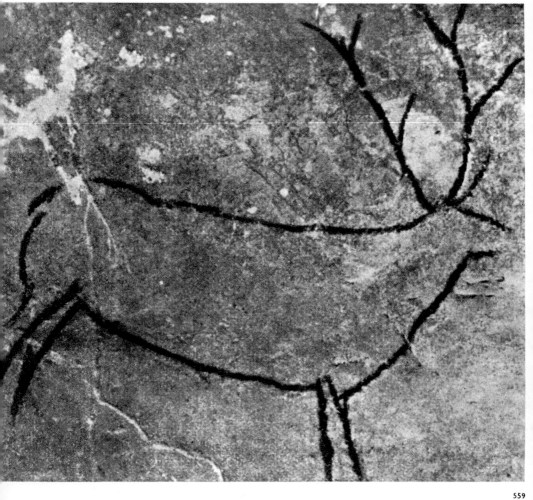

559

560

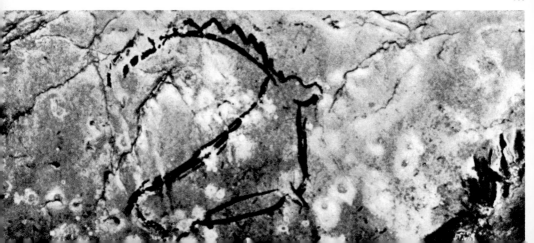

561

559 Outline painting of a stag from Las Chimeneas, Spain.

560 Drawing of an ibex from Niaux, France. Length 27 centimetres.

561 Painting of a stag with fantastic antlers. Lascaux, France. Length 140 centimetres.

562

562 Drawing of a stag from Niaux, France. Length 81 centimetres.

ears typical of a bear, but a flat nose and mouth and a mane running from the back of the neck to the tail. A bull can be seen depicted at Font de Gaume which is basically a correct and natural reproduction, except that its body is out of proportion (580). The body is crowned by a very long, large neck and a normal head of an aurochs. The most famous fabulous animal is an aurochs-like creature with two straight horns found at Lascaux. Leroi Gourhan believes that the two straight horns do not belong to the animal, but it is possible that they do, because they are shown to grow immediately from the animal's forehead. The body is similar to that of an aurochs, but the two straight horns, the tiny stump of a tail, and the short, broad head with a flattened mouth are not found in this species. The large oval-shaped patches on the animal are also unusual (581).

There are fantastic figures which are thought to be magicians possibly wearing masks (582). In the Tuc d'Audoubert is a curious engraving of an animal with a slightly bowed head, a

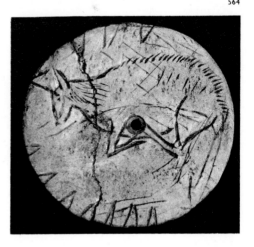

563 Sketch of engraved ibexes from Kamennaya Mogila, Sea of Azov, USSR.

564 Engraving of an ibex on a small disc. Mas d'Azil, France. (Photograph by R Gauthier, Musée du Perigord.) Diameter 3.2 centimetres.

565 Small sculpture in fired clay of the head of a lioness. A wound is visible above the ear. Pavlovian culture, Dolní Věstonice, Moravia, Czechoslovakia. Length 4.5 centimetres.

566 Flat ivory carving of a lioness. Pavlovian culture, Moravia, Czechoslovakia (after Klíma).

567 Small head of a lioness made from fired clay. Pavlovian culture, Dolní Věstonice, Moravia, Czechoslovakia. Length 6 centimetres.

568 Engraving of a cave lioness. Les Combarelles cave, France. Length 70 centimetres.

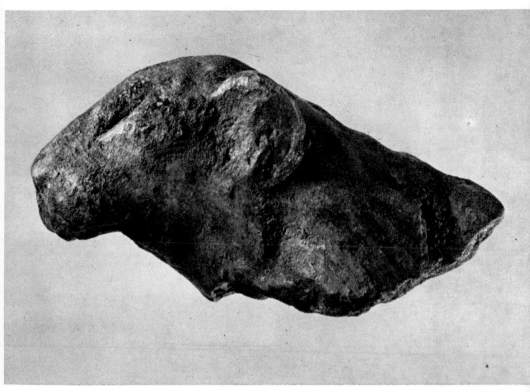

567

568

569

569 Carvings representing flying swans worn as pendants. Malta, Siberia. Length 12, 8.2, 6 centimetres.

570 Painting of a wild boar from Altamira, Spain (after Breuil).

570

A unique discovery of Palaeolithic art in the form of a face carved from mammoth ivory. Dolní Věstonice, Moravia, Czechoslovakia ($\times$ 2½).

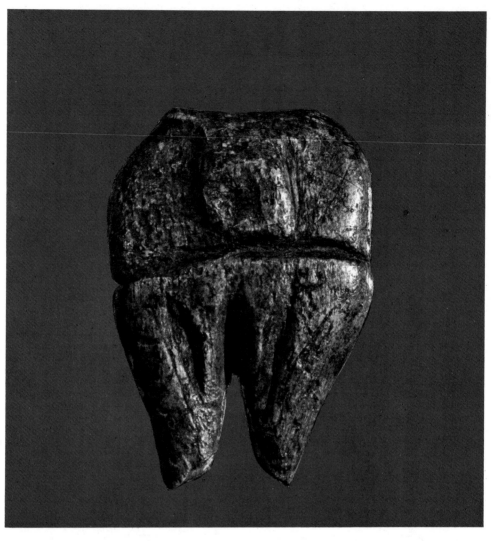

Lower part of a female body modelled in clay. Pavlovian culture, Dolní Věstonice, Moravia, Czechoslovakia.

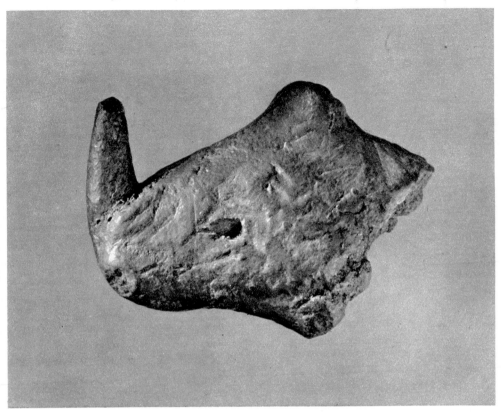

571

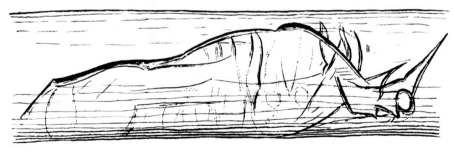

572

571 Head of a rhinoceros; small sculpture made of fired clay. Pavlovian culture, Dolní Věstonice, Moravia, Czechoslovakia. Length 4.2 centimetres.

572 Sketch of a rhinoceros engraved on an antler. Magdalenian culture, Le Placard, France.

573 Hare and horse. Engraving from Trou de Chaleux, Belgium. (Photograph by Institut Royal des Sciences Naturelles de Belgique.)

574 Engraving of birds and a grasshopper; above it a sketch of the latter. Les Trois Frères, France. Length 10 centimetres.

575 Carving of a flatfish from Lespugue, France. (Photograph by Musée des Antiquités Nationales, St Germain-en-Laye.) Length 4.5 centimetres.

576 Antler with engraved plant motif. Magdalenian culture, Pekárna cave, Moravia, Czechoslovakia.

broad mouth resembling an elk, broad ears
and short, slightly curved horns (583). A well-
known picture comes from Les Trois Frères
showing a figure in an upright position with
a long tail and human legs. The front limbs
are more like two paws, and the vaguely outlined sexual organ is not like that of man nor
like any known animal. Stag antlers crown
the head (584). According to the Abbé Breuil
the head has an *en face* expression and a long
beard; the eyes are round and the ears are
that of an aurochs. But it is this part of the
painting which is particularly difficult to distinguish, and the interpretation remains a per-
sonal one for the viewer. A similar picture of
a 'bison-man' at Les Trois Frères was discussed
earlier. Another upright figure in the same
cave shows the lower part of the body, including the sexual organs, of a man; the upper part
is that of a bison looking backwards.

We must include in this summary of fantastic drawings the engravings of little devils
from Teyjat. They are small figures with human legs with quite hairy bodies and chamois
heads (585).

An engraving was discovered at Los Casares,
described by the Abbé Breuil as a frog or a
fish. The large, round head pictured in profile
has a big eye and beak-shaped mouth; the
body is inflated like a ball and from below the
head two arm-like limbs appear (586). This
is certainly not a picture of a real animal.
A most unusual painting has been found at
Pech Merle; it is a complicated composition
of three fabulous creatures. They have enormous bodies but small limbs and very small

576

577–578 Photograph and sketch of the 'Agnus Dei' engraving. They are, in fact, two different engravings picturing a horse and an ibex. Pair-non--Pair cave, France. Length 63 centimetres.

579 Fantastic animals from Les Trois Frères, France; a bear with a long tail and a wolf without a tail but with bear's paws (after Breuil).

580 Bull with an unnaturally long neck. Font de Gaume, France (after Breuil). Length 65 centimetres.

578

heads (587, 588). This black drawing probably depicts a fantastic elk-like ungulate. The first head has a hump indicated by small vertical lines at the end of its neck, and looks like the Irish elk. There is no body because the second head appears immediately after the hump; the second animal is portrayed fully but without a hump. The lines of the first and second animals intermingle. The third one is complete but not as long as the others, and it gives the impression that it has a second hind part with two hind legs pushed backwards.

It is, of course, very difficult to explain paintings like this or make sense of them. Quite apart from the fantasy world of Palaeolithic man we would have to know more about his mythology and religious views to interpret a picture accurately. Primitive races have an understanding of the unity between man and animal, and it is only fair to assume that this is what the artists of the Upper Palaeolithic depicted.

579

580

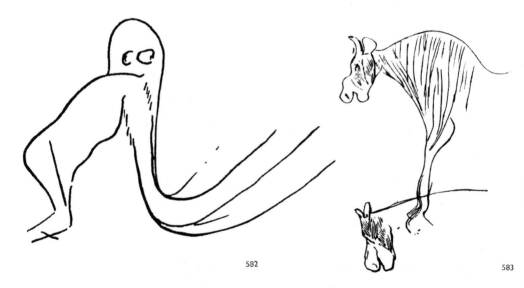

582

583

581 Fabulous animal with straight horns and a spotted body. Lascaux, France. Length 165 centimetres.

582 Sketch of an engraving depicting a fabulous creature from Les Combarelles (after Breuil).

583 Fantastic animal with bull's horns and an elk-like head. Tuc d'Audoubert, France. Length 42.5 centimetres.

584

584 Sketch of an engraving of a fabulous creature, the 'sorcerer', from Les Trois Frères, France (after Breuil). Length 75 centimetres.

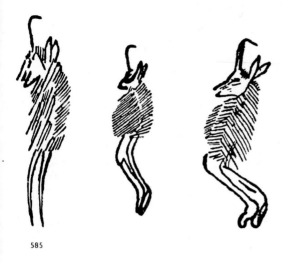

585

585 Engraving of small devils on a baton. Teyjat, France. Height 5 centimetres.

586 Fantastic creatures at Los Casares, Spain.

586

Human figures

Palaeolithic pictures of human beings can be divided into definable groups: women, men, faces, and human beings in relation to other objects. The representations of women fell into two groups divided by style and period. The realistic representations belong to the older period; these are the so-called 'Venus figurines' and reliefs. This group falls between the Aurignacian and Pavlovian to Solutrean periods (Angles-sur-l'Anglin to Magdalenian III; La Madeleine — Middle Magdalenian). The second and more recent group is basically part of the Magdalenian, particularly in its early phase. This group consists mostly of engravings of stylized figures bent slightly forward and presented in profile. These engravings are only occasionally found on small objects (589).

As well as the 'Venus figurines' of the first group, simple female sexual symbols are also known (590 to 592). From Kostienki I, a site in the Ukraine where several 'Venus figurines' have been found, came a number of small models made from soft stone. They are slightly rounded on one side and have an opening on the other, flat side which gives a clear indication that they are miniature models of a vulva. In accurately dated deposits at Abri Cellier (Aurignacian I), for example, and at La Ferrassie (Aurignacian II), stones have been found with drawings of vulvas on them.

Older figurines, reliefs, and engravings distinguish between the frontal and side view. The artist usually tried to avoid showing the face, and it is often just left flat — the Venus of Laussel is an example (593). Sometimes, the slightly forward bent head would leave the face in the 'shade' — flat and showing no features (594 to 596). Only in very rare cases can figurines with lifelike features be seen, such as the unique female head from Dolní Věstonice (597, 598). Figurines were also found in southern Siberian sites where the artist did not hesitate to add the features of the face (599, 600). These sites are, however, not part of the European Aurignacian-Pavlovian periods, but belong to another cultural horizon.

The second, more recent type of female figurine is also stylized. Characteristically, these figures have robust hips and buttocks, while the arms and legs are often reduced. Some artists portrayed the breasts as being large and hanging, as can be seen at Pech Merle, where these engravings on the ceiling are diffi-

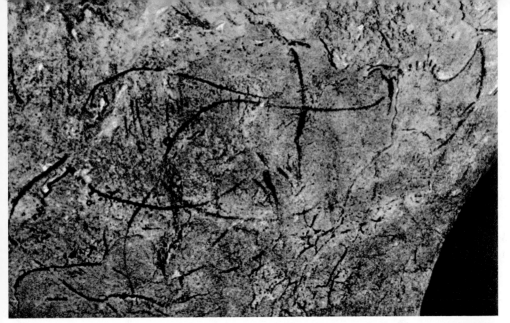

587

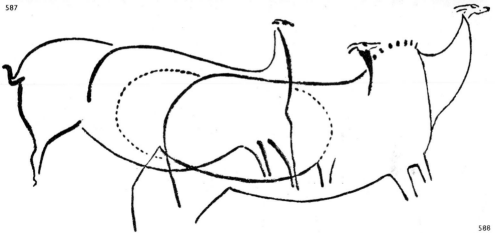

588

587–588 Three fantastic hoofed animals from Pech Merle, France, and a sketch of the painting.

cult to date. Some archaeologists, after careful study and comparison with the animal engravings close by, date them to the Upper Solutrean and the Lower Magdalenian period.

Typical stone engravings from the Magdalenian period come from La Roche Lalinde (601) where a group of figures has been engraved on a stone and the artist observed a very strict style. Every figure shows a line running across the lap for which there is no explanation. Red outlined engravings, like the

one just mentioned, are also found at Pech Merle. All these engravings seem to have one fundamental characteristic; they are close to the stylized outlines of animal bodies such as horses, bison, and mammoths, which is unlikely to have happened by chance (602). Some engravings belong only to the Upper Palaeolithic period, which means they are relatively recent. Female figures are rarely included. The older type of figurine is missing and the vulva engravings appear only in few places such as

589

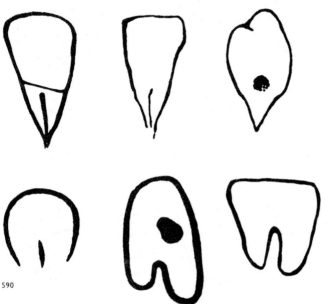

589 Reliefs of the lower parts of female bodies. Magdalenian culture, Angles-sur-l'Anglin, France. Height 160 centimetres.

590 Vulva symbols from La Ferrassie and Abri Cellier, France.

591 Two Venus figurines from Kostienki, USSR. Indications of clothes and jewellery being worn are seen on the front and back of the figures.

592 Symbolic carvings on stone of the vulva. Kostienki, USSR (after Yefimenko).

590

Les Combarelles, Arcy-sur-Cure, Pergonsset, Gargas, and Bédeilhac.

A relief of two naked women resting is known from La Madeleine, and although it is very 'modern' in conception, it appears to be made using the same technique as the other reliefs belonging to this period. Three figures are known from Angles-sur-l'Anglin showing the lower parts of the body only. The engravings from Arcy-sur-Cure, Les Combarelles, and Pergonsset belong to the same type but only show a frontal view of the pubic arch. The engraving of two figures from Laussel is often thought to show either coitus or birth (603). It should be noted that only one of these figures can be clearly distinguished showing the hands, head, breasts, and belly including the navel. The other figure remains indistinct. Therefore, it is difficult to give a clear interpretation of it. Two engraved figures were found at Les Combarelles by the Abbé Breuil. The larger of the two shows a figure with an erect penis; the smaller figure is seen to the right, half submerged into the lower part of the larger figure. Both figures are bent characteristically forward (604). This scene is often thought to represent coitus. Leroi Gourhan who studied this engrav-

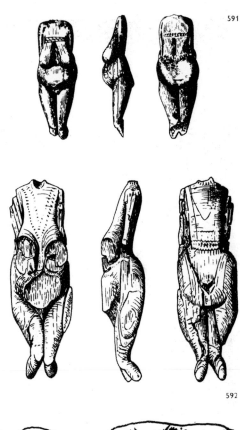

591

592

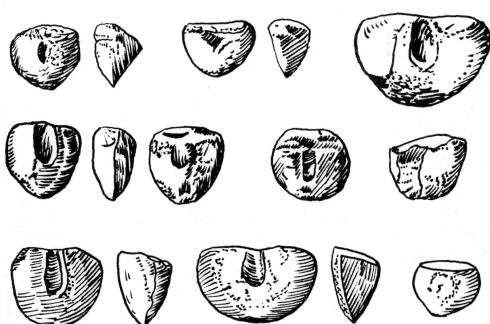

593

594

596

ing in detail came to the conclusion that the larger figure is formed by the back ends of two different animals which are covered by lines, and which in turn give the wrong impression of two human figures in coitus. This is one example of how difficult it can prove to explain or understand a complicated engraving such as this. The so-called steatopygous female figurines of the Aurignacian-Pavlovian period are often discussed by experts. According to recent discoveries and comparisons there are two types of figurine; one, a fat-bodied type resembling a spherical ellipsoid, the other a slim, more or less cylindrical type, which seems to be carved from a branch. The first type is found at Men-

593 Venus of Laussel, France. (Photograph by Musée d'Aquitaine, Bordeaux.) Height 4.3 centimetres.

594-596 The Venus of Willendorf. Aurignacian culture, Austria. (Photograph by Naturhistorisches Museum, Vienna.) Height 11 centimetres.

597 Unique realistic head carved from mammoth ivory. Pavlovian culture, Dolní Věstonice, Moravia, Czechoslovakia. Height 4.8 centimetres.

598 The same carving from Dolní Věstonice, seen in profile.

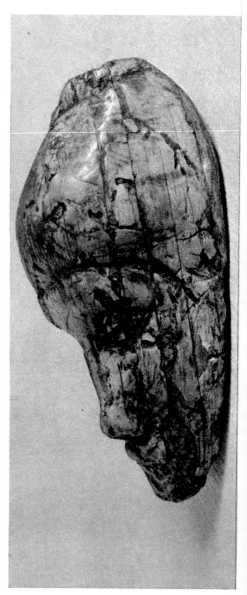

598

597

599–600 Two Venus figurines from Malta, Siberia. The second of them has a hole drilled through the lower part and could be worn as a pendant; first figure shows an attempt at facial expression. Height 8 and 9.7 centimetres.

599

600

601 Engraving on stone with female figures from La Roche Lalinde, France. (Photograph by J Guichard, Musée des Eyzies.)

602 Stylized female figures from Les Combarelles, France.

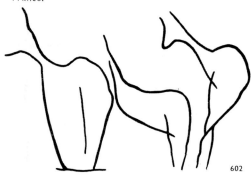

602

tone (605), Lespugue (606, 607), Savignano (608, 609), Grimaldi, Willendorf, Věstonice, Kostienki, and Gagarino. The other type is known from Laugerie Haute, Gagarino and Malta (610 to 612). Figurines of the obese type were also found at Malta, but they were flatter and none of these could be classified as truly steatopygous. They all had only full, obese figures which had further been exaggerated by the artist. It would, however, be wrong to assume that because these figures depicted fat females that this was the usual case in actual life. The living conditions of Palaeolithic people were hard and women of this period were unlikely to have had so much food as to be able to achieve the obese figures indicated by the carvings. These steatopygous figurines were obviously images with a sexual and economic implication (613).

The Venus of Dolní Věstonice; front and back view of this remarkable figurine in fired clay. Pavlovian culture, Dolní Věstonice, Moravia, Czechoslovakia. Height 11.5 centimetres.

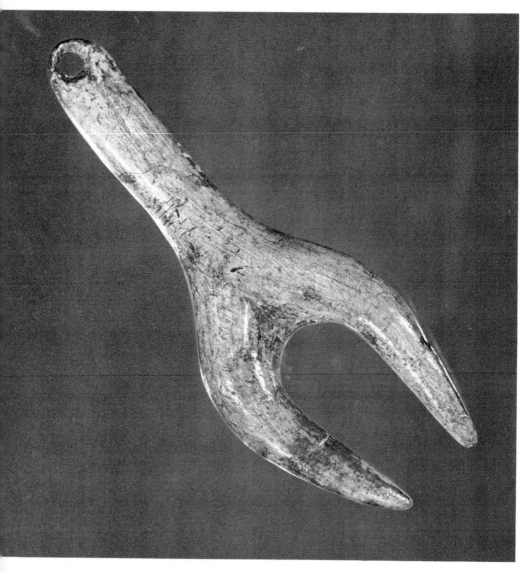

Stylized female figurine used as a pendant. Pavlovian culture, Dolní Věstonice, Moravia, Czechoslovakia. Height 8.6 centimetres.

The slim type of figurine typical of Siberian sites, appears together with obese types in some localities such as Gagarino and Avdieievo (Ukraine) (614); and at Brassempouy and Abri Pataud (western France). Women are usually depicted naked (615); only one Venus, that from Lespugue, has a small apron which can be seen on the back wrapped around the waist but unable to cover up her large exaggerated buttocks (607). Two Venus figures from Kostienki wear belts with a pattern, one of them also has a belt which can be seen above her breasts. It is interesting to note the incredible similarity between the Venus of Willendorf (594 to 596) and the small Venus figurine from Gagarino. Both show the same posture of the head and the same form of body. Both have hands crossed over their breasts, and a similar hairstyle.

The western European stylized figures of women from La Roche, Les Combarelles, and so on, are comparable to the central European Magdalenian figures from Pekárna (616) in Czechoslovakia and from Petersfels and Nebra in Germany. A comparison of characteristic stylization (617), which in western Europe is known as the claviform (club-shaped, or clavate) type is very interesting. One of the three stylized figures from Nebra (618 to 620) is a true claviform; breasts have been indicated on the other figures, which prove that the western European claviforms known from many Magdalenian cave paintings are really female symbols (621). A very interesting transition from a female figure to a phallic symbol comes from Belgium (622). Highly stylized female figures are also known from a Ukrainian site called Mezin. Z A Abramova thought that some of these figures were stylized birds and some phallic symbols (623 to 630). Experts on stylized figurines, symbolic models, and engravings, from western Europe were convinced, however, that they represent anthropomorphous figures. This is confirmed by the fact that the pubic arch and the protruding round posterior are indicated similar to many central European figurines. A highly stylized carving from Krasnyj Yar points to a connection between Siberian and central European figures. The view that this is definitely a female figure is further strengthened by a similar, though more elaborate female figure from Buret. It shows a similar profile, but the form is more realistic and worked out, showing the head and hands as well as the characteristic protrusion of the posterior. The clothes and hoods decorated with notches worn by the slim figures from Buret and Malta (631, 632) look like the anoraks worn by the Nordic people and the Eskimos (633, 634). A strange carving of a large female figure from Yeliseievitchi, a site in the Ukraine (635), is of great interest. The bust is well developed, but the upper part of the body is narrower and not as full as the lower part. Despite this the figure does not lose its proportions; the fullness of the body below the waist, particularly the thickness of the legs resembles Neolithic figurines from

603 Two figures. An engraving which could be interpreted as either coitus or birth. Laussel, France. (Photograph by H P Herdeg, Zurich.) Height 20 centimetres.

603

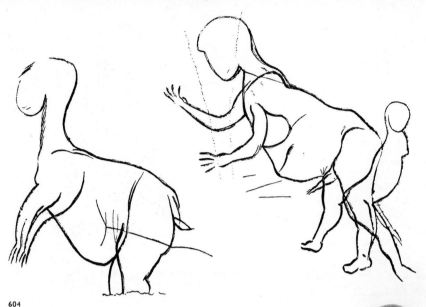

604

604 Sketch of an engraving from Les Combarelles, which was interpreted by the Abbé Breuil as showing coitus.

605 Venus from Mentone, Italy. (Photograph by Musée des Antiquités Nationales, St Germain-en--Laye.) Height 4.7 centimetres.

605

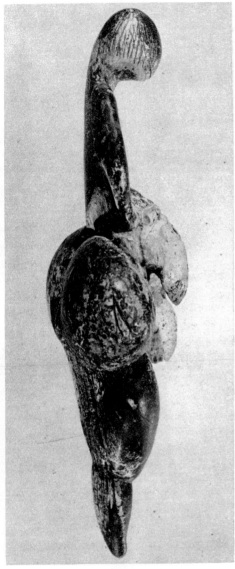

606 Side view of the Venus figurine from Lespugue, France. (Photograph by Musée de l'Homme, Paris.) Height 14.7 centimetres.

607 Venus figurine from Lespugue, the rear view showing her skirt or apron.

608

609

610–612 Venus figurines from Malta and Buret, Siberia, USSR. The long slim Venus figurine from Malta shows notches indicating clothing. Height 9.6, 12.1, 12.2 centimetres.

608–609 Venus from Savignano, Italy. Height 22 centimetres.

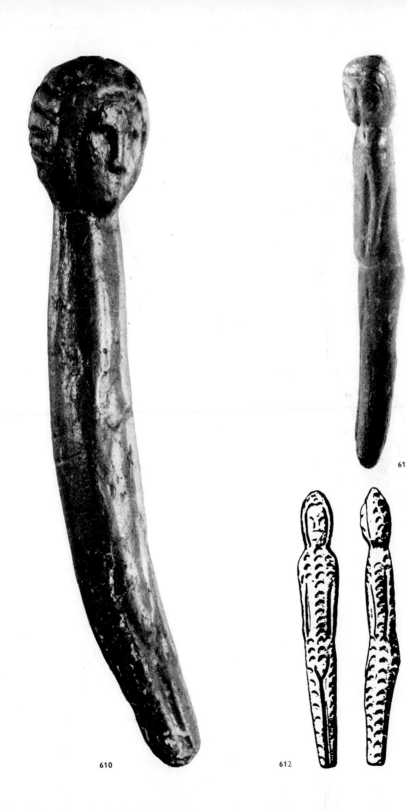

610

611

612

613

614 Venus from Avdieievo, Ukraine, USSR. Height 16 centimetres.

615 Venus from Sireuil, France. Height 9 centimetres.

613 Venus from Parabita, Italy.

614

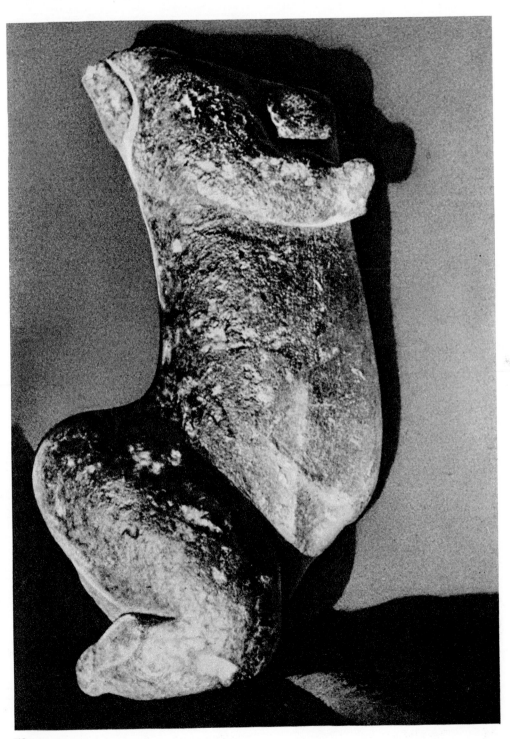

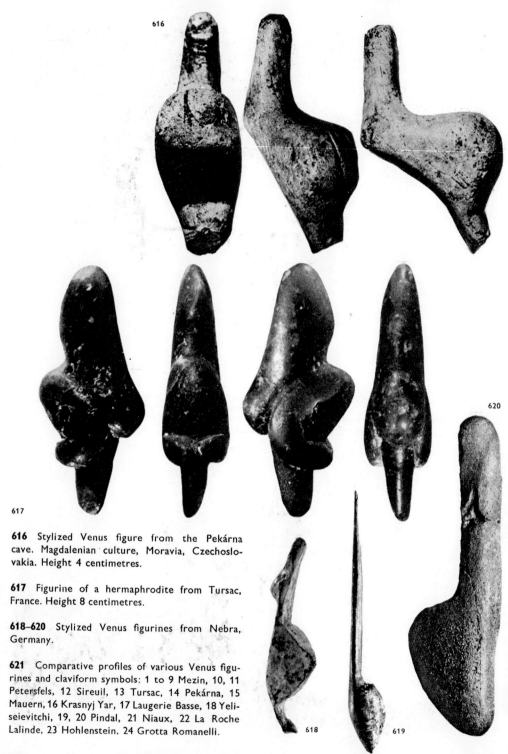

616 Stylized Venus figure from the Pekárna cave. Magdalenian culture, Moravia, Czechoslovakia. Height 4 centimetres.

617 Figurine of a hermaphrodite from Tursac, France. Height 8 centimetres.

618–620 Stylized Venus figurines from Nebra, Germany.

621 Comparative profiles of various Venus figurines and claviform symbols: 1 to 9 Mezin, 10, 11 Petersfels, 12 Sireuil, 13 Tursac, 14 Pekárna, 15 Mauern, 16 Krasnyj Yar, 17 Laugerie Basse, 18 Yeliseievitchi, 19, 20 Pindal, 21 Niaux, 22 La Roche Lalinde, 23 Hohlenstein, 24 Grotta Romanelli.

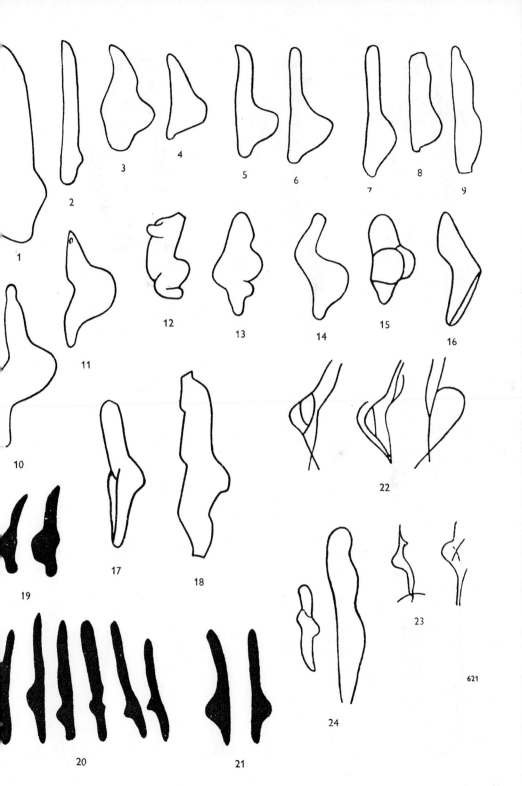

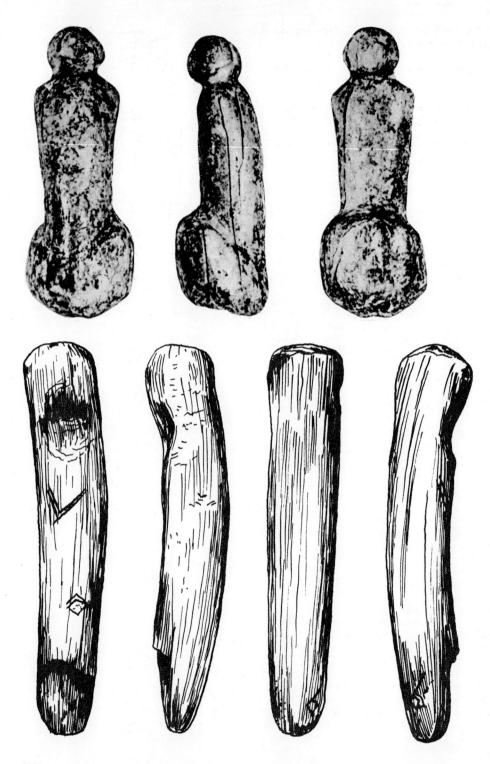

622 Stylized female figurine from Trou Magrite, Belgium (after Twiesselmann).

623 Stylized human figurine from Mezin, USSR (after Shovkoplias). Height 31 centimetres.

624 Stylized female figurine from Mezin, USSR. Height 12.5 centimetres.

625 Stylized female figurine from Mezin, USSR (after Shovkoplias).

Europe (636). In particular it resembles figures from the Tripolje culture (for example, the Moravian painted culture, the Venus from Hluboké Mašůvky (637), the Venus from Střelice, Czechoslovakia (638), and those from Cucuteni, Rumania).

Numerous caricatures of human heads and faces carved from stone are known from Kosienki I, where also several Venus figurines were found. These caricatures almost give the impression of being repetitions of engravings of human heads or faces from west European cave walls (639, 640).

Two interesting engravings are known from the Pavlovian culture at Předmostí: an ornamental stylized figurine of a woman, and five rudely carved female figures made from mammoth bones (641, 642). There is nothing similar to the first engraving in Palaeolithic art either in the east or west. The figure is in an upright position, and the body, head, arms, and legs are clearly marked. The breasts, navel, and posterior are also clearly indicated. The head is almost triangular with an indented hairparting and raised sides, while the nose and eyes are indicated by horizontal and vertical lines. The arms are indicated by three deep lines while the legs are shaped by six simple lines running parallel. Obviously the artist thought the breasts and posterior to be the most important parts of the body, and he indicated these by six circular lines. The navel was also shown by the same decorative methods.

The five female figures made of mammoth toe bone clearly show the various stages of their construction. The best figure has a well-developed head, and the arms, folded across a bulging body, indicate that this must be a pregnant woman. The most primitive of these figures has the head and body only vaguely indicated. These figures relate to two other

624

625

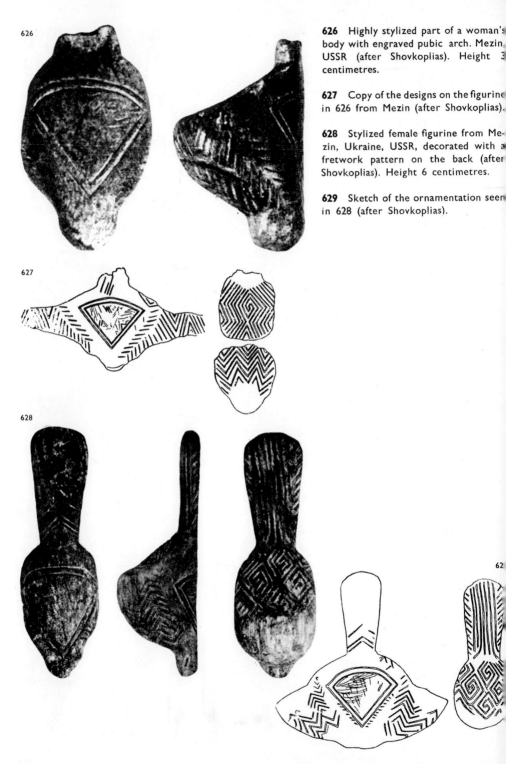

626 Highly stylized part of a woman's body with engraved pubic arch. Mezin, USSR (after Shovkoplias). Height 3 centimetres.

627 Copy of the designs on the figurine in 626 from Mezin (after Shovkoplias).

628 Stylized female figurine from Mezin, Ukraine, USSR, decorated with a fretwork pattern on the back (after Shovkoplias). Height 6 centimetres.

629 Sketch of the ornamentation seen in 628 (after Shovkoplias).

630 Stylized female figurine from Mezin, USSR (after Shovkoplias).

631 Venus from Malta, Siberia, USSR. Height 13.6 centimetres.

632 Venus from Malta, Siberia, USSR. Height 9.8 centimetres.

630

631

632

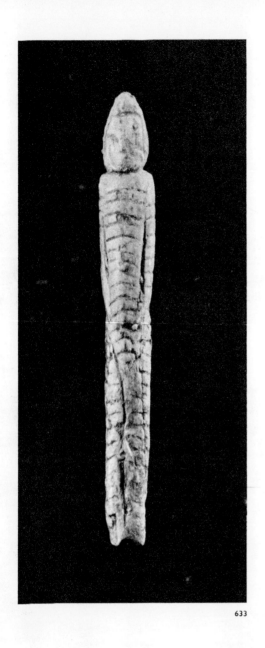

633

633 Human figurine with a face and clothing indicated. Malta, Siberia, USSR. Height 4.2 centimetres.

634 Venus from Avdieievo, Ukraine, USSR. Height 12.5 centimetres.

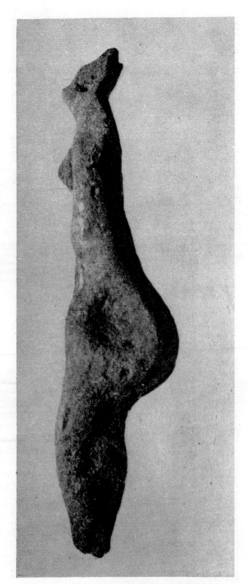

635 Venus from Yeliseievitchi, Ukraine, USSR. Height 15 centimetres.

636 Venus from Macomer. Neolithic, Sardinia, Italy.

carvings: one, a Palaeolithic, crudely carved figure made from a reindeer antler found at Avdieievo (643); and another carved from bone made in the 1800s. This latter figure was used by the Chuckchee as a magic object assisting at birth, and shaped rather like the figures found at Předmostí in Moravia (644).

The anthropomorphous figurines from the Pavlovian deposits found at Dolní Věstonice are interesting and important. As well as the realistic head already mentioned, another, almost complete Venus figurine was found there in addition to a number of fragments belonging to similar female figurines (645, 646). The obese Venus has shoulders forming a horizontal line, but no arms. Two deep lines run down on both sides of the spine indicating the fat cushions. The face is very simply carved; three lines form the eyes and nose. Along the hair-parting there are small holes into which feathers or plants might have been put (647 to 649). Highly stylized and standardized anthropomorphous figurines have also been found at Dolní Věstonice. One of them, a pendant, is carved from mammoth ivory and looks like a two pronged fork. It has a deep line, probably indicating the vulva, and for this reason it is thought to be a female figurine (650). Other small, highly stylized, feminine pendants are also known from Petersfels, Germany (651, 652).

The second pendant from Věstonice is shaped like a small stick and has geometric ornaments. The stick depicts the body, with breasts carved at the upper end (654). There are also several pairs of breasts made from ivory in various sizes from the middle of which thorn-like shapes protrude. The 'thorns' are pierced and it can be assumed that these models were part of a necklace (653).

Among the discoveries made in Moravia is a beautiful torso of a woman (655) made from haematite and belonging to the Pavlovian settlement at Ostrava-Petřkovice. It is similar to a piece of modern cubist sculpture. This is a remarkable piece of art which, together with the discoveries from Předmostí and Věstonice indicate the broad variability in style exercised

637 Venus from Hluboké Mašůvky. Neolithic Moravia, Czechoslovakia.

within one culture and in a small area such as Moravia. If the development and character of ancient art are to be understood, facts like these are of great importance.

Male figures were not as common in the Palaeolithic period as female figures. One of the male figures found in a grave at Brno is of particular interest (656). It was put together like a doll, with separate head, body, arms, and legs. This is a unique case in Palaeolithic art and is of particular interest because this discovery comes from the Middle Würm period (Würm II, Early Pavlovian)and is, therefore, roughly the same age as the Venus of Willendorf. The facial expression is impressive too. We can detect the rest of the broken-off nose, the deep-set eyes, and a longish, probably bearded, chin. The forehead is very low, and the head — as seen from above — is round. Three small points can be seen on the body. One of them indicates a nipple, the other the navel, and the third the penis. The urethra is indicated by a small vertical incised line. Other male figures come from Brassempouy and Laussel (657). No uniform style can be found among these figures even if they are compared to well-known figures from caves at Villars, Lascaux, Roc de Sers, La Colombière, Laugerie Basse, and others. The most interesting feature of these figures is that they almost all tend to depict dramatic moments (658). There is a man with outstretched arms awaiting an attacking bison; a man standing in front of a dead bison with the broken-off spear still in its wound; a man attacked by a bear; men pierced by several spears (Pech Merle and Cougnac). The bodies of male figures are usually not anatomically exact and the head has only faint facial expression (659, 660). This might possibly be a primary step towards drawings of 'masked magicians'; half man, half animal.

The engravings of fantastic faces from Les Combarelles, Marsoulas, and La Marche belong to a special group. These faces are obviously deliberately unrealistic, particularly because the animals around them, which presumably have been drawn by the same artists,

638 Venus from Střelice. Neolithic, Moravia, Czechoslovakia.

638

397

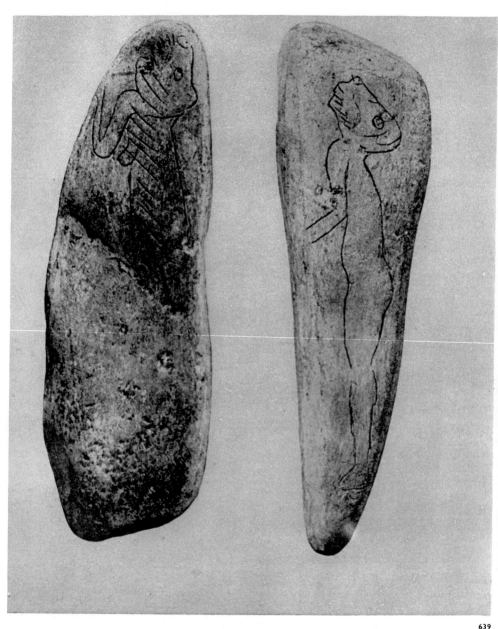

639

639 Caricature of a man and woman. Engraving on a pebble from La Madeleine, France. Height 9.3 centimetres. (Photograph by Musée des Antiquités Nationales, St Germain-en-Laye.)

640

640 Caricature of a male figure. Gourdan, France. Height 11.5 centimetres.

641

641 Ornamental stylized female figure. Engraving on a mammoth tusk. Pavlovian culture, Předmostí, Moravia, Czechoslovakia. Height 15.5 centimetres.

642 Four figures carved from mammoth phalanges representing pregnant women. Pavlovian culture, Předmostí, Moravia, Czechoslovakia.

are depicted in a most natural and true fashion. In contrast to some earlier sculptures there is not a single engraving known from the end of the Upper Palaeolithic which portrays human likeness accurately. It is, of course, very difficult, when looking at these extraordinary grimacing faces to distinguish whether they are male or female. They could be thought to represent sexually indeterminate beings (661, 662).

Our description would, of course, be lacking if we passed over the phallic designs which are known from small carvings and engravings. A double phallus carved from an antler is a good example of such work. It comes from the Gorge d'Enfer in the Dordogne, France (663). Another engraving on a bone is known from La Madeleine showing a bear's head, phallus, and vulva (664, 665).

643 Bone carved figure from Avdieievo, Ukraine, USSR. Height 10.5 centimetres.

Jewellery

Some works of art were used for decorative or ritual purposes; Palaeolithic man wore them next to the skin or put them on his clothes (666, 667). They consisted mostly of different pendants, ornaments for the hair, necklaces, bracelets, and bands worn around the forehead (668, 669). It is quite easy to distinguish them because they are usually small objects with holes with which they could be threaded or sewn on. Sometimes it is possible to see how they were worn by noting their location in burials. Jewellery made of shells is worn around the head, where it would either cover the head or decorate the hair. It was also worn around the neck, on the breasts, waist, wrists, knees and ankles. Shells and deer canines with holes drilled through them were often used like this. Necklaces were often made from teeth belonging to bears, arctic foxes, and other animals (670), which would have some ornament engraved here and there. Pebbles, small carvings made from mammoth ivory, bones, or clay,

644 A figurine carved from bone which was used as a magic object during birth by the Chuckchee people.

645–646 Parts of Venus figurines from Dolní Věstonice, Moravia, Czechoslovakia.

647-649 Venus figurine from Dolní Věstonice (front, rear, and side views). Height 11.5 centimetres. Note especially the heavy breasts and full buttocks, typical of these Pavlovian figurines.

647

648   649

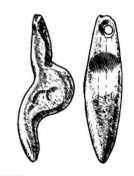

650 Pendant made from mammoth ivory in the shape of a stylized female figure. Dolní Věstonice, Moravia, Czechoslovakia. Height 8.6 centimetres.

651 Small stylized pendant, supposedly of a female figure. Petersfels, Germany. Height 4 centimetres.

652 Stylized figures used as pendants. Petersfels, Germany.

650

651

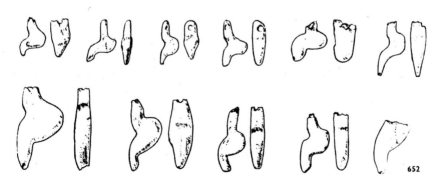

652

Fragment of a clasp (or belt end) made from mammoth ivory. Pavlovian culture, Pavlov, Moravia, Czechoslovakia.

Stylized female figurine with simple decoration made from mammoth ivory. Pavlovian culture, Dolni Věstonice, Moravia, Czechoslovakia. Height 8.7 centimetres.

Pendant made of mammoth ivory representing a woman's breasts. There is a perforation at the back of the pendant. Pavlovian culture, Dolní Věstonice, Moravia, Czechoslovakia. ($\times$ 2½).

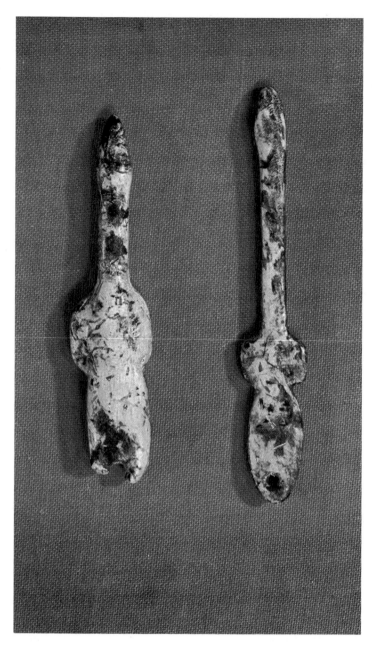

Pendant made from mammoth ivory representing flying swans. Malta, Siberia, USSR ($\times$ 2½).

653 Stylized female breasts made from ivory
which were worn as pendants. Pavlovian culture,
Dolní Věstonice, Moravia, Czechoslovakia.

654

654 Schematic female figurine. Pavlovian culture, Dolní Věstonice, Moravia, Czechoslovakia. Height 8.7 centimetres.

655 Venus figurine carved from haematite rock. Pavlovian culture, Ostrava-Petřkovice, Moravia, Czechoslovakia.

656 Statuette of a man from the burial Brno II. It was carved from ivory and had mobile limbs. The head is slightly coloured with ochre. Early Pavlovian culture, Moravia, Czechoslovakia. Height 13.3 centimetres.

655

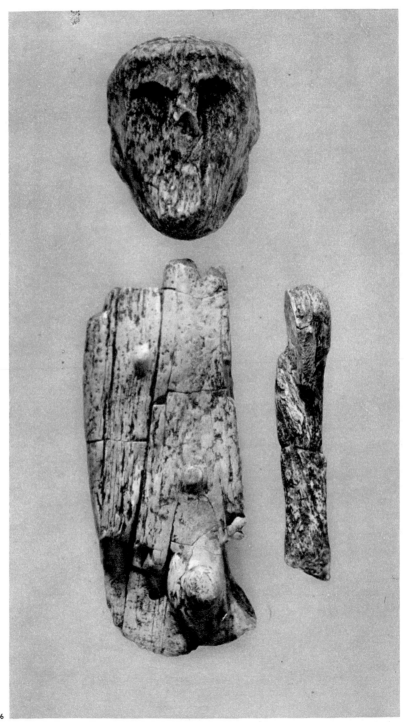

657 Relief of a male figure. Laussel, France. Height 50 centimetres. (Photograph by Musée d'Aquitaine, Bordeaux.)

658 Masked hunter hit by a spear. Valtorta, Spain.

657

658

and shells with holes drilled through are on rare occasions used as pendants, and sometimes, again rarely, human teeth might be worn (671 to 675).

A particular group of jewellery consists of discs with holes in the middle made from various materials and often covered with simple ornamentation (676, 677), although seldom decorated with engravings. From central and eastern Europe (Pavlov, Dolní Věstonice, Mezin) finely made and richly ornamented head- and neck-bands are known, all made from mammoth ivory (678, 679). Also known are decorated rings and discs of various sizes made from mammoth ivory (680 to 685). An interesting ring-like pendant was found at Pair-non-Pair (682).

Signs and symbols

Painted or sometimes engraved standardized signs and symbols are known from cave walls dating back to the end of the Upper Palaeolithic period. They are often discovered in narrow hidden passages as if they were meant not to be found (El Castillo, La Passiega), or sometimes they have been put next to animal pictures. Forms which are like feathered arrows are found placed above animal pictures, and are either painted or engraved (686 to 688). They are probably not arrows, because such long, barbed arrow or harpoon points only appeared towards the end of the Magdalenian culture (689 to 691).

What the connection between these symbols or signs and the animal pictures could be, seems impossible to find out today. The experts distinguish several types according to their shapes: claviform, square, bell-shaped and circular symbols. Well-known and often discussed are the so-called tectiform symbols found in caves like Font de Gaume, Les Combarelles, La Pileta, Bernifal, and so on. These give the impression of huts with central supporting pillars, low walls, and arched entrances. Similar signs from Font de Gaume (692 to 694) are like the round huts in the Ukraine known from the site at Mezhirich. One of these signs found painted across a picture of a mammoth at Bernifal led to the conjecture that these signs signified animal traps (695). Leroi Gourhan divided these symbols into male and female elements: the female symbols are the tectiform, rectangular, claviform, and bell shapes, while the arrow-type symbols are male.

659

659 An engraving of a male figure from Isturitz, France (after Breuil).

The dots, often connected and forming lines, from El Castillo (696) and Niaux are thought to be some kind of signpost. Above the water-level of a subterranean lake in the Niaux cave, dots have been found which give the impression of faint fingerprints. It might be that someone had made lines or dots with his finger to prove that he had swum to this dangerous and hidden place.

Engraved or painted squares, which often have further painted squares inside them are very interesting. Engraved squares are known from the Buxu cave; painted squares accompanied by animals from Lascaux (698). These could be symbols of animal traps, but it is thought that Leroi Gourhan was nearer the truth in suggesting that they signified female symbols. Longish, boat-like shapes exist as horizontal and vertical signs. Once they are even crossed (El Castillo, 697, 699) and remind us of the symbols found at La Passiega or

413

660

660 Engraving of a figure of a man threatened by a bear's paw. Mas d'Azil, France. Height 7.5 centimetres. (Photograph by Musée des Antiquités Nationales, St Germain-en-Laye.)

661 Fantastic mask on a rock at Altamira, Spain. (Photograph by A Weider, Zurich.)

Altamira. Other symbols from El Castillo are similar to simple signs from La Passiega and Altamira and could be defined as claviform. Other claviform signs are made from lines which give the impression that they are stylized female figures (700 to 703). Numerous signs like these can be found at Altamira, Niaux, Pindal, and Les Trois Frères.

The mysterious 'inscription' from La Passiega has proved to be quite a riddle (704). Two horizontal lines support several vertical lines and two double arches. A sign like a letter E is seen on the right, as well as two kinds of footprints. But, it is not clear what this drawing might signify. Various shield or bell-shaped signs are thought now to be female symbols (705).

Cultural layers revealed small objects and figures with strange signs and symbols on them (706), usually different from those found in cave paintings. Often they consist of slanting or broken lines, as on the horse's head at Arudy (707). Are they ornaments or true symbols? Rows of deep lines were always thought to indicate some method of calculation or calendar reckonings (708), a view which was recently confirmed by J Marshack.

Bone discs from Mas d'Azil and Laugerie Basse with chamois and aurochs on them were decorated around the edge with V-shaped symbols (709). A holed bone object made from an antler, found at Laugerie Basse, has zigzag lines engraved along it (710). Another such object comes from Le Placard and has an animal head together with some slanting lines engraved on it. Numerous objects like this were found in Pavlovian settlements in Moravia and the Ukraine. Bone objects found in Moravia are decorated with straight or broken lines, rarely with wavy lines (711 to 714; Předmostí, Dolní Věstonice). The above-mentioned jewellery could be said to be similar to the complicated, engraved meander or fretwork found at Mezin, Ukraine, which had a purely decorative function (715, 716).

When taking the decoration of these objects into account, it becomes clear that there are two main groups which are mixed up. On the one hand there are geometric-ornamental decorations; on the other there are symbols and stylized objects (717, 718). Small plaquettes made of mammoth ivory come from the Siberian site of Malta and are examples of the first group. The plaquettes are covered with simple decorative notches. Another example is a bracelet of mammoth ivory engraved with

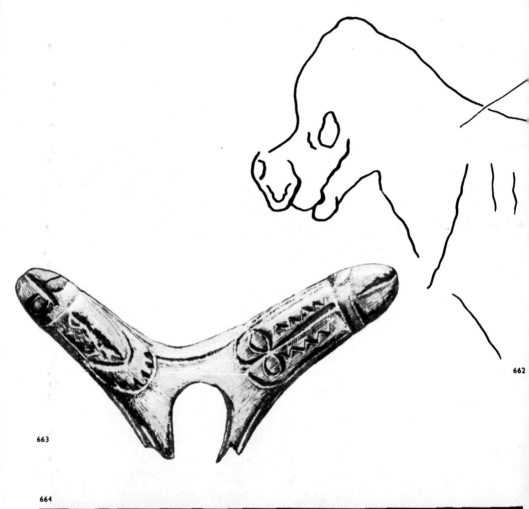

662

663

664

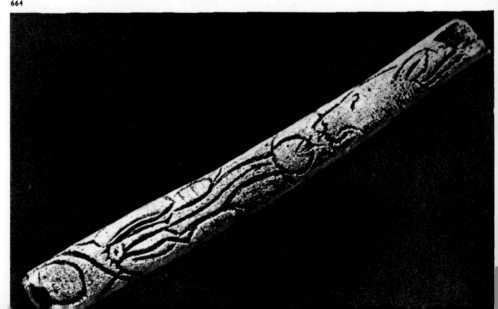

662 Human face. A caricature drawing from Les Combarelles, France.

663 Double phallus carved on an antler. Gorge d'Enfer, France. Length 9.5 centimetres.

664–665 An engraving on bone with a phallus and the head of a bear, and a sketch of it. La Madeleine, France. (Photograph by H P Herdeg, and A Weider, Zurich.)

666 Burial of a boy at Malta, Siberia. A necklace and curious pendant are visible in the region of the left shoulder.

665

666

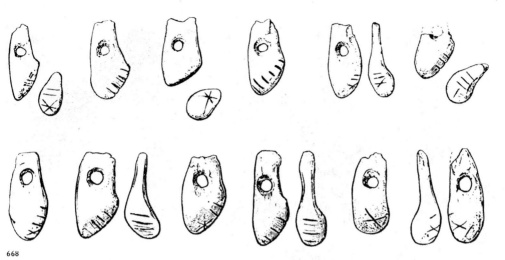

668 The canine teeth of stags with holes drilled through them and decorated with crude ornaments. Saint-Germain-La-Rivière near Libourne, France.

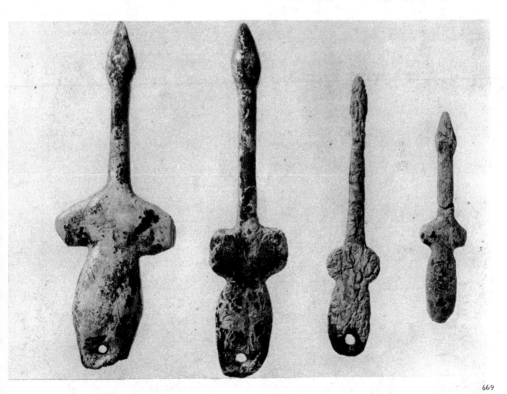

667 A burial at Sunghir, USSR. The head and chest were decorated with many ivory beads, originally sewn on cloth (after Gerassimov).

669 Four sculptures, interpreted as flying swans. Malta, Siberia, USSR. Height 10, 10, 8, 6.5 centimetres.

670

670 Examples of teeth from various animals with holes drilled through them which were made into a necklace. Pavlovian culture, Dolní Věstonice, Moravia, Czechoslovakia.

671 Necklace made from Tertiary shells and the teeth of the arctic fox. Pavlovian culture, Dolní Věstonice, Moravia, Czechoslovakia.

672 Necklace made from Tertiary shells. Pavlovian culture, Dolní Věstonice, Moravia, Czechoslovakia

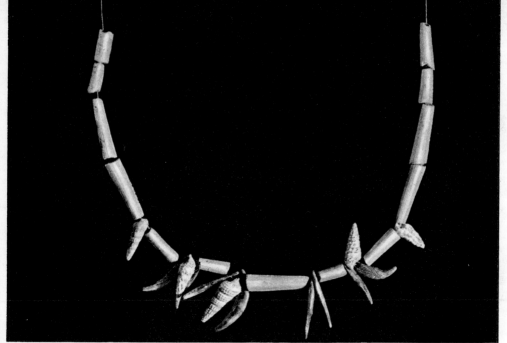

671

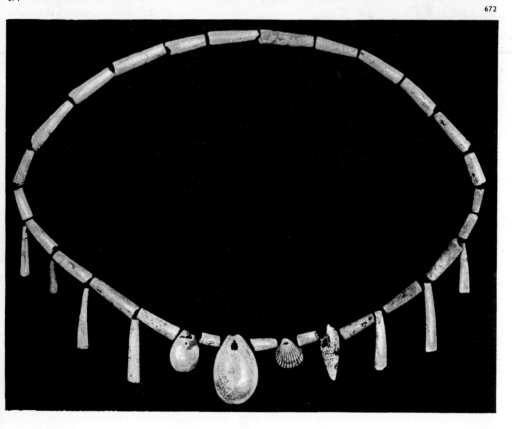

672

673

673 Necklace made from Tertiary shells and the teeth of the arctic fox. Pavlovian culture, Dolní Věstonice, Moravia, Czechoslovakia.

674 A pierced slate-like pebble and beads carved from bones, forming part of a necklace. Pavlovian culture, Předmostí, Moravia, Czechoslovakia.

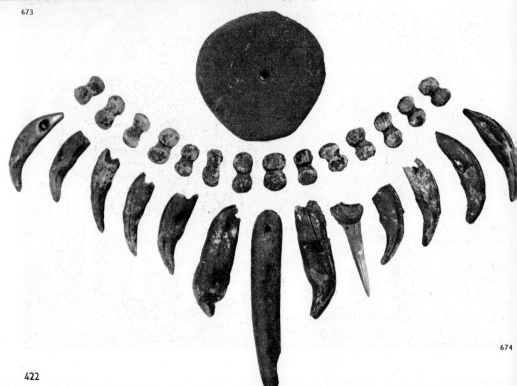

674

675 Two canine teeth joined together at the roots to form a pendant. Pavlovian culture, Předmostí, Moravia, Czechoslovakia.

675

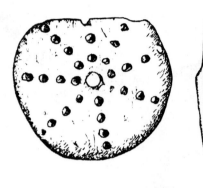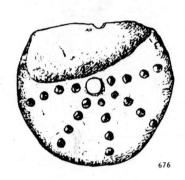

676

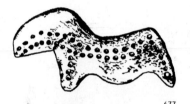

677

678

676 Pierced circular disc, shown from both sides and in profile. Sunghir, USSR.

677 Sketches of a decorated sculptured horse which was worn as a pendant. Sunghir, USSR. Length 5.5 centimetres.

678 Part of a decorated flat head-band carved from mammoth ivory. Pavlovian culture, Pavlov, Moravia, Czechoslovakia.

680

679 Necklace made of small mammoth ivory rings. Pavlovian culture, Dolní Věstonice, Moravia, Czechoslovakia.

680 Bone pendant in the shape of an owl. Pavlov, Moravia, Czechoslovakia.

broken lines and meander patterns found at Mezin, Ukraine. Two ribs from Předmostí, Czechoslovakia, with wavy lines and simple engravings in fishbone pattern also belong to this group.

Discoveries of bone objects in western Europe belonging to the Magdalenian culture, in particular from Isturitz, Arudy, Lespugue, and Lourdes, form a special group. It is not impossible that they were, at times at least, stylized objects with originally realistic motifs (plants, animal heads?) which, seen as a whole, looked like twisted spirals. A very interesting peg-like object with purely ornamental patterns was found at Brassempouy; from Saint Marcel comes a richly decorated object with simple geometric ornament, shaped almost like a chisel and made of bone; and from Lespugue a complicated geometric ornament on a bone is worth mentioning (719 to 722). These few examples give not only an insight into varying geometric ornaments, but also show that the discoveries from central and eastern Europe are richer in ornamental decoration (723 to 725) and in realistic Venus figures than western Europe. There is also no lack of realistic small

Swan carved in mammoth ivory. A perforation for suspension occurs by the legs. Malta, Siberia, USSR. Length 8 centimetres.

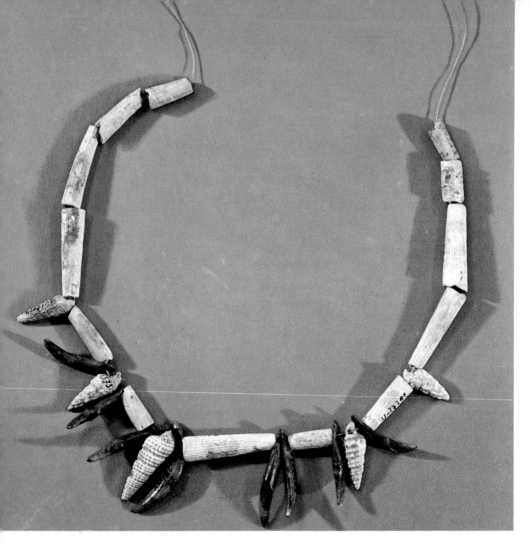

Necklace made of fossil shells and teeth of the arctic fox. Pavlovian culture, Dolní Věstonice, Moravia, Czechoslovakia.

Necklace made of teeth from arctic foxes. Pavlovian culture, Dolní Věstonice, Moravia, Czechoslovakia.

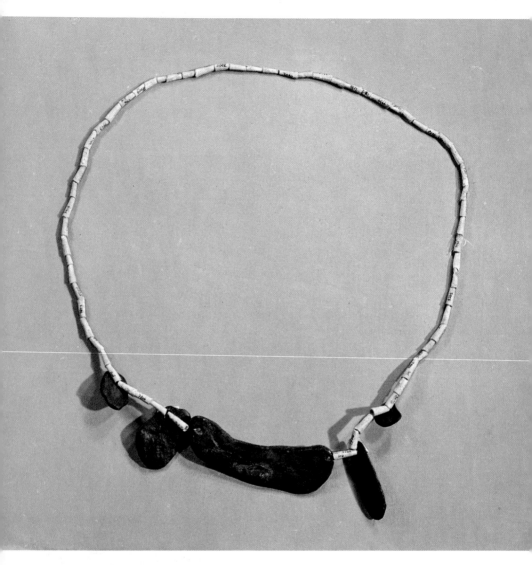

Necklace made of teeth and perforated pebbles. Magdalenian culture, Pekárna cave, Moravia, Czecho-slovakia.

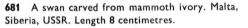

682

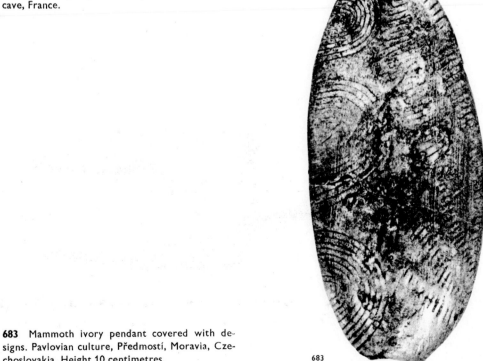

681 A swan carved from mammoth ivory. Malta, Siberia, USSR. Length 8 centimetres.

682 Ring-shaped pendant from the Pair-non-Pair cave, France.

683 Mammoth ivory pendant covered with designs. Pavlovian culture, Předmostí, Moravia, Czechoslovakia. Height 10 centimetres.

683

684 Unfinished jewellery made of mammoth ivory. Pavlovian culture, Předmostí, Moravia, Czechoslovakia.

685 A 'fork' carved from mammoth ivory which might have been used as a costume-fastener. Pavlovian culture, Předmostí, Moravia, Czechoslovakia.

684

685

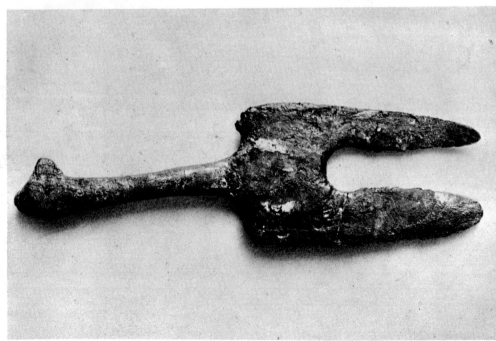

686 Bison with arrows, which are positioned near the heart. Niaux, France. Length 100 centimetres.

687 Bison with arrow-like symbols. Niaux, France. Length 150 centimetres.

688 Sketch of horses with arrow-like symbols. Lascaux, France.

432

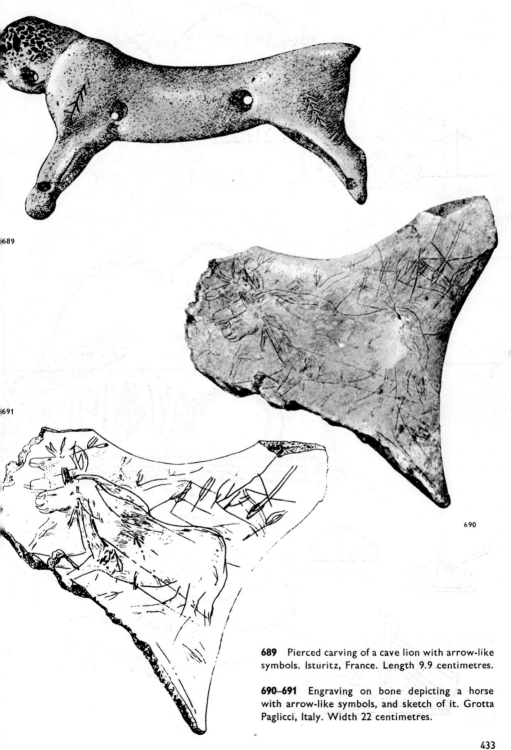

689 Pierced carving of a cave lion with arrow-like symbols. Isturitz, France. Length 9.9 centimetres.

690–691 Engraving on bone depicting a horse with arrow-like symbols, and sketch of it. Grotta Paglicci, Italy. Width 22 centimetres.

433

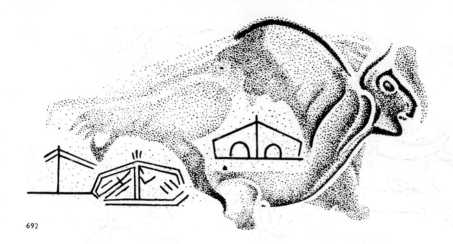

692

693

694

695

692 Painting of a bison with tectiform symbols. Font de Gaume, France.

693 Painting of a hut-like construction superimposed across a mammoth. Font de Gaume, France.

694 Drawings of hut-like symbols. Font de Gaume, France.

695 Engraved tectiform symbols over pictures of mammoths. Bernifal, France (after Graziosi).

objects (horse engravings from the Pekárna cave, Ukrainian and Siberian figures of men and animals) nor of stylized pictures which were originally of a realistic nature.

Palaeolithic art in western Europe has particularly beautiful carvings and engravings from the Magdalenian culture. Notable are the stylized pictures and engravings on bone, horn, and mammoth ivory, but there are also plenty of discoveries of artistic objects with ornamental elements. As examples of the tran-

sitional form which lies between the geometric pattern and a developed stylization we may mention a bone engraving of a plant design found at Laugerie Basse; the large pendant (known as a bull roarer) from Lalinde with geometric drawings; the pendant from Saint Marcel, notched around the edge with three engraved concentric circles; the small pierced disc from Petersfels which has concentric and small, slanting, wavy lines; the oval-shaped engraved objects which obviously originated from the pattern of a fish found at La Madeleine; the decorated rib from Novgorod-Seversk with its simple, incised lines; and the large plaque of mammoth ivory, decorated with zigzag lines, from Malta (726 to 733), symbolizing snakes.

Other examples of symbols in the Palaeolithic art come from Gvardshilasklde, in the Caucasus, where an engraving on a fragment of bone looks like the arrow-like symbols found in western Europe. Another example is a pebble from La Colombière with a rhinoceros and a reindeer (734, 735) engraved on it. The triangle on the figures found at Mezin clearly symbolizes the female genitals.

435

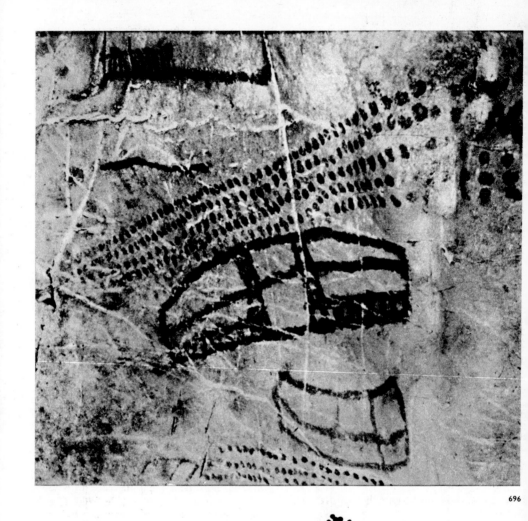

696

697

696 Painted squares and dots from the El Castillo cave, Spain. Width 63 centimetres.

697 Symbolic drawing made of dots. El Castillo, Spain.

698 Painted square and branch-like symbols associated with a horse. Lascaux, France. Length 140 centimetres.

699 Drawing of geometric symbols from the El Castillo cave, Spain.

698

699

700   Geometric symbols from Altamira, Spain.

701   Heart-shaped symbol from Le Portel, France.

702   Claviform and dotted symbols from Niaux, France.

703   Branch-like symbols and aurochs. Lascaux, France. Length 200 centimetres.

704   So-called 'inscription' from the La Passiega cave, Spain. It has not been possible to decipher these symbols.

705   Bell-shaped female symbols from El Castillo, Spain.

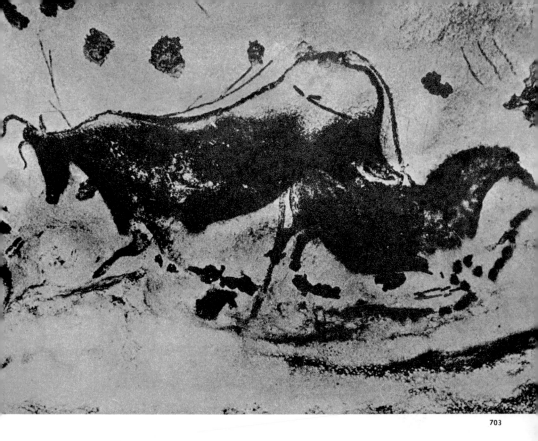

703

704

705

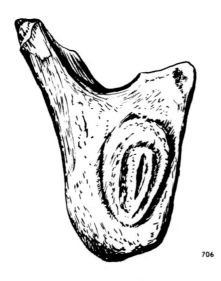

706 Symbolic vulva carved on a piece of antler. Pair-non-Pair, France.

707 Carved horse's head with decorative geometric designs. Arudy cave, France. Length 4.5 centimetres.

708 Radius bone of a wolf decorated with counting notches. One double notch divides the first thirty single notches. Magdalenian culture, Pekárna cave, Moravia, Czechoslovakia.

706

707

440

A fragment from Isturitz shows two engraved symbols of an arrow. Similar symbols are also known from a tooth with a drilled hole found at Duruthy (736) and a carving of a wild cat from Isturitz with arrows attached to the body. On some of the animal carvings found at Vogelherd (737) dimples, lines or nets can be seen.

Also well-known is the fragment with a realistic engraving of a bison's head, found at the La Vache cave in the Pyrenees, which has four slanting branches incised in front of it (738). On the antler found at Raymonden, a picture of a bird was incised, and underneath it is a zigzag line and a circular symbol (739). Very impressive is the stylization of ibexes engraved on fragments of bone found at El Pendo near Santander (740). The well-known engraving from Lorthet, Pyrenees, showing a stag looking back over its shoulder and several salmon also depicts two rhomboids with incised lines above the stag's back which have as yet not been explained (741). Also important is the engraving depicting an animal, probably a deer, from Parpalló in Spain (742). An engraving on a bone fragment, found at Les Eyzies, shows nine stylized human figures each with a slanting line across their shoulders and each with two pairs of hands (743). The realistic engraving of a bison's head on a bone found at Raymonden gives the impression that the head was pierced by a long barbed harpoon (744). On either side of the harpoon are shown three and four stylized figures facing each other. Highly stylized engravings of ibexes were discovered at Gourdan, and peculiar lines (like string) were engraved on flat stones found at Parpalló in Spain and in the Grotta di Romanelli (745). Their significance is not known. Discoveries of small objects with simple, often stylized engraved decorations are known from Czechoslovakia (746 to 750).

Hands

Hands are among the most frequent subjects in cave painting. Particularly rich in such paintings in western European Palaeolithic art are the caves at Gargas and El Castillo; in about twenty other caves painted hands also occur. There are negative pictures; which means that the artist placed his hand on the wall, covered the wall with paint, and so outlined the shape of the hand (751). Positive prints were made by covering the palm and

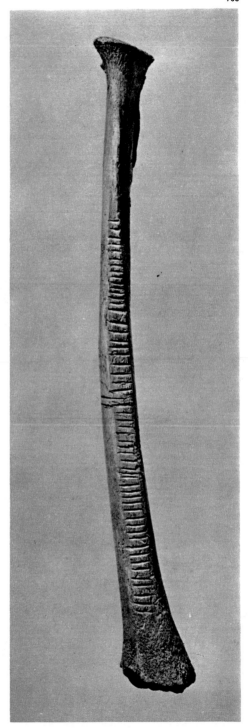

709

710

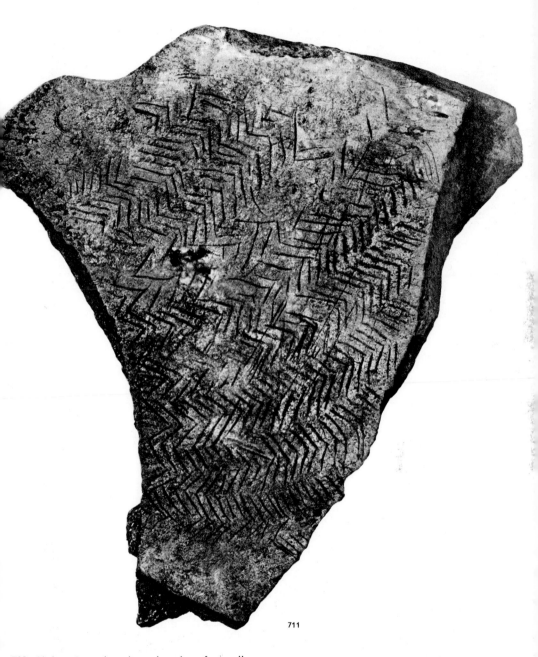

711

709 V-shaped notches along the edge of a small disc from Laugerie Basse, France (Musée Perigord). Diameter 3.2 centimetres.

710 Small disc with an engraving of an aurochs from Laugerie Basse, France. (Photograph by Musée des Antiquités Nationales, St Germain-en-Laye).

711 Geometric designs on the hip bone of a mammoth. Pavlovian culture, Předmostí, Moravia, Czechoslovakia.

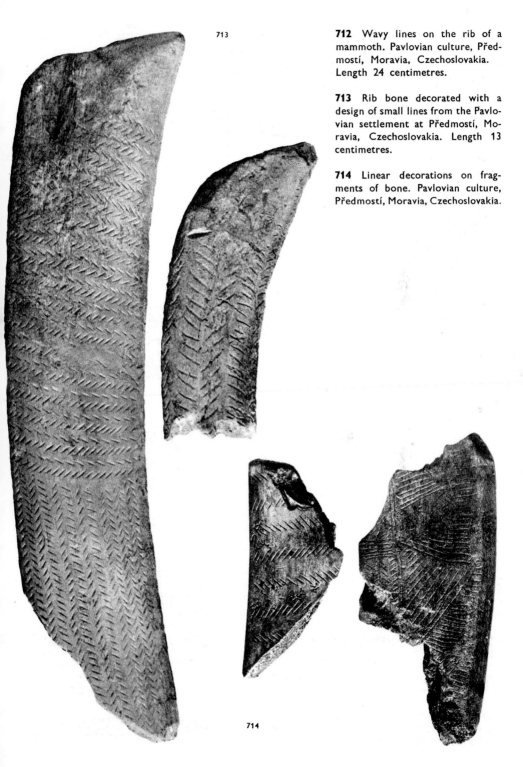

712 Wavy lines on the rib of a mammoth. Pavlovian culture, Předmostí, Moravia, Czechoslovakia. Length 24 centimetres.

713 Rib bone decorated with a design of small lines from the Pavlovian settlement at Předmostí, Moravia, Czechoslovakia. Length 13 centimetres.

714 Linear decorations on fragments of bone. Pavlovian culture, Předmostí, Moravia, Czechoslovakia.

713

714

715

715 Fretwork design on a bracelet made of mammoth ivory. Mezin, USSR (after Shovkoplias).

716 Patterned pendants from Malta, Siberia, USSR.

717–718 Shafts of implements made of mammoth ivory. Avdieievo, Ukraine, USSR.

719 Antler, decorated with horizontal and diagonal lines. Magdalenian culture, La Vache cave, France (after Nougier).

716

717

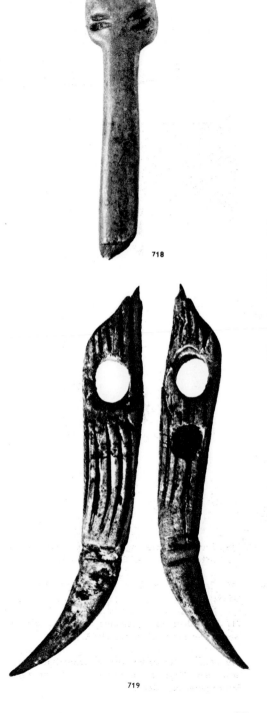

718

fingers with paint and then pressing them against the cave wall. The prints could be retouched, and sometimes they were even painted freehand without the initial prints. The negative print of the left hand is the most common, which is not really surprising because this was the passive hand resting against the wall while the right hand did the painting, mixing, and covering the hand, and so achieved the print. In the Cougnac cave only prints of the fingertips are found.

The paintings of hands are usually either red or black, sometimes yellow, and rarely white (Gargas). They are very small at times and obviously are the hands of children (Les Combarelles, Gargas, Le Portel, Altamira); even the hand of a baby can be seen at Lascaux. The small hand from Le Portel shows an unusually large and long thumb print, which might have been made because the hand slipped down the wall.

Lively discussions arose because of pictures of hands with missing fingers (752); the so-called 'mutilations' which are frequently depicted at Gargas. It is either a symbol (Leroi Gourhan, Saint-Yves, Luquet) or a picture of a voluntary mutilation; the sacrifice of several fingers (Breuil). This is a ritual known among several primitive races, particularly the Australian Aborigines. Mutilations occurring after

719

720

720 Decorated points. Epipalaeolithic period, north-west Germany (after Rust).

721 Bone implement decorated with simple diagonal lines. Saint-Marcel, France. Length 10.6 centimetres. (Photograph by Musée des Antiquités Nationales, St Germain-en-Laye.)

722 Bone or antler tools decorated with spiral patterns found at Isturitz, France. Length 19.8 centimetres.

723 Pierced slate pebbles used as pendants and decorated with simple notches. Magdalenian culture, Pekárna and Býčí skála caves, Moravia, Czechoslovakia.

721

723

722

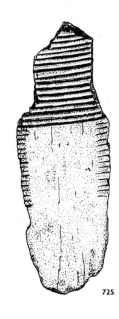

724 Rib decorated with diagonal lines. Aurignacian culture, Kůlna cave, Moravia, Czechoslovakia.

725 Bone decorated with diagonal lines. Aurignacian culture, Kůlna cave, Moravia, Czechoslovakia.

726 Small jewellery disc from Petersfels. Magdalenian culture, Germany. Diameter 8 centimetres.

727 Plant motif on a baton from Laugerie Basse, France.

724

725

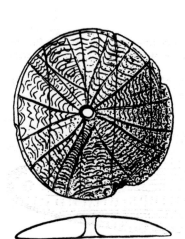

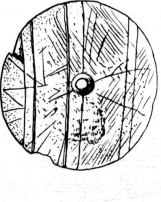

726

727

728

729

729 Pendant with circular motifs from Saint-Marcel, France. Length 5.5 centimetres. (Photograph by Musée des Antiquités Nationales, St Germain-en-Laye.)

728 Wavy and fish-scale ornament on a flat bone used as a piece of jewellery. Yeliseievitchi, USSR.

730 Sketch of a large pendant from Lalinde, France. Length 15.7 centimetres.

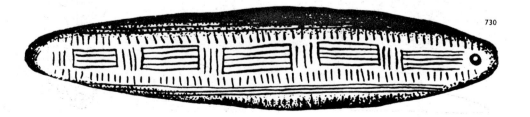

730

731

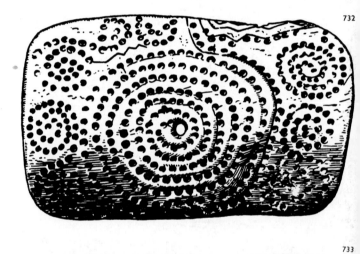

732

733

731 Sketch of a rib-bone decorated with diagonal lines. Whether this is purely ornamental or whether it is a counting stick is not known. Novgorod-Seversk, USSR.

732 Plaque with a punched spiral design. Malta, Siberia, USSR.

733 Large mammoth ivory plaque decorated with a zigzag line, probably representing a snake. Malta, Siberia, USSR. Length 14 centimetres

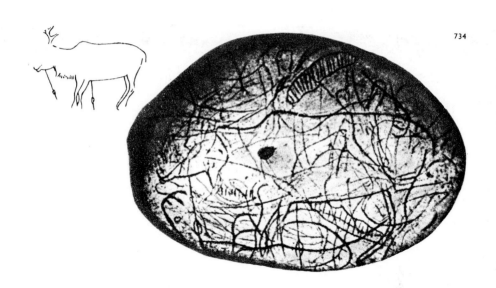

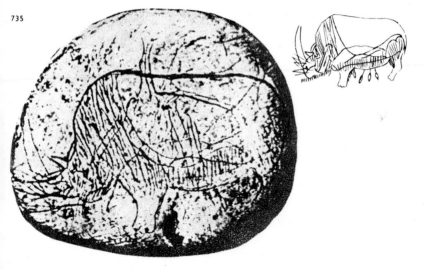

734 Engraved pebble from La Colombière, France. Width 9.5 centimetres.

735 Pebble engraved with animals and arrows. La Colombière, France. Width 8.3 centimetres.

736 A tooth with symbolic arrows. Duruthy, France.

737

737 Three animal carvings, two of them decorated with shallow notches and grooves. Vogelherd, Germany. Length 4.8, 6.9, 9 centimetres.

738

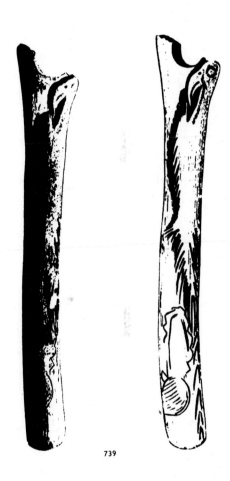

740

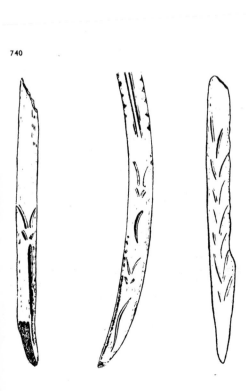

739

738 Bison's head and four branches on a bone. Magdalenian engraving from the La Vache cave, France. Length 12.5 centimetres.

739 Fragment of a shaft engraved with a bird from Raymonden, France. Length 16.5 centimetres.

740 Highly stylized heads of ibexes. Engraving from El Pendo, Spain.

741

742

741 Fish and stags with rhomboid symbols engraved above them. Lorthet, France.

742 Simple engraving on stone showing an animal. Parpalló cave, Spain.

743 Engraving with nine stylized human figures. Les Eyzies, Spain. Length 13 centimetres.

an illness (Reynolds' disease) have been discussed by Obermaier, Breuil, Dekeyser, and Sahly.

Engravings of hands are rarer than the paintings and only known from Barabahau (753) and Cap Blanc. The stylized drawings from the Santian cave (754, 755) are often thought to be hands or arms. They are long lines, which end in three or four claw-like fingers. Some lower arms are hairy but these drawings have not been fully explained.

Dating

The first proof of an existing art form comes from the early Upper Palaeolithic, which means it is about 30 000 years old. It appeared rather suddenly, but the technical and artistic skills shown were so perfected that these examples could not be mistaken for first attempts. We must also realize that only works of art made of lasting materials survive. Organic materials, such as wood, bark, leather, and so on, which must have played a large role in prehistoric life, are rarely preserved. The discoveries of large amounts of red paint found in cultural deposits of the Mousterian period are in some ways proof that Upper Palaeolithic art must have developed over a long period of time.

In order to understand the development of this art it is necessary to put all the discoveries into a chronological order. Art objects are more difficult to sort out chronologically than

stone tools, and it is advisable to use well-known cultures as 'measuring rods' for accurate dating.

Rare engravings and drawings found sealed under undisturbed deposits (as is the engraving of a reindeer at Isturitz), often represent the best guidelines for accurate dating. A discovery made under such circumstances could not be from a later period than the deposits immediately above it. Accurate dating can also be achieved if a cave has been covered up and inaccessible since the Palaeolithic period. Obviously in these cases the engravings and paintings inside the cave could not be more recent than the deposits sealing the entrance. On the other hand, wall paintings in a cave that has served as a settlement are not precisely dateable. The cave could have been inhabited long before the pictures were created or vice versa.

Occasionally, a part of a wall would collapse because of intense frost or other natural hazards, and the fragments of it, together with the pictures, would fall on to a later cultural deposit. In such cases the work of art would be older than the deposit and it would be difficult to date it accurately. This happened at Abri Labatut (756) where a painted stone fragment was discovered between two layers of the Upper Perigordian. This also happened in a cave nearby (Abri Blanchard) where a piece of a fallen rock, with remains of black and red paint, was found in deposits belonging to the Upper Perigordian period. At Grotte du Poisson in the Gorge d'Enfer flat fragments which

743

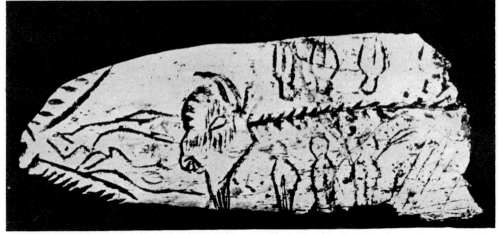

744

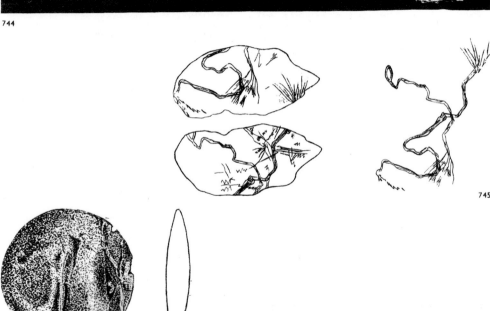

745

746

744 A bison's head impaled on a long harpoon-like point, and six human figures engraved on a bone fragment found at Raymonden, France. Length 8.7 centimetres.

745 Engravings with strange string-like designs on fragments of stone. Grotta di Romanelli, Italy (after A Blanc).

746 Small, round discs made of bone and mammoth molars, decorated with lines which might be symbolic vulvas. Early Pavlovian culture, Brno, Moravia, Czechoslovakia.

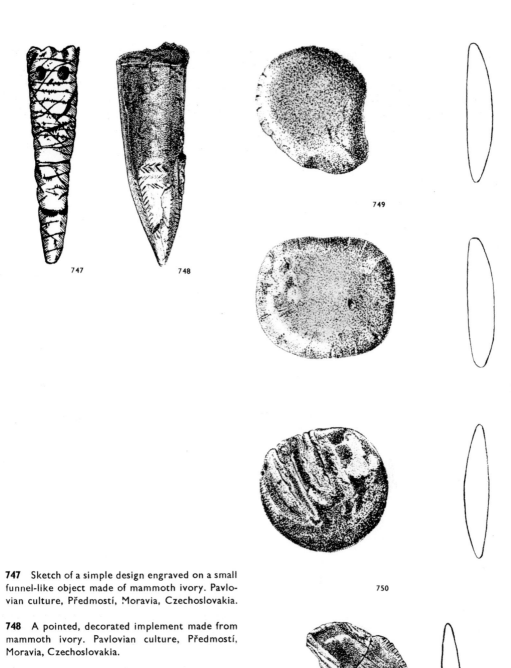

747

748

749

750

747 Sketch of a simple design engraved on a small funnel-like object made of mammoth ivory. Pavlovian culture, Předmostí, Moravia, Czechoslovakia.

748 A pointed, decorated implement made from mammoth ivory. Pavlovian culture, Předmostí, Moravia, Czechoslovakia.

749 Small discs carved from stone, decorated with fine lines. Early Pavlovian culture, Brno, Moravia, Czechoslovakia.

750 Small, round discs carved from mammoth tusks and molars; Early Pavlovian culture, Brno, Moravia, Czechoslovakia.

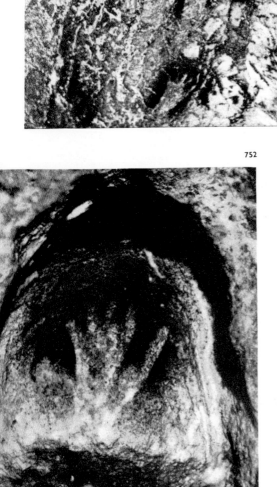

751

752

had fallen from the frost-damaged rock-wall were found. A relief of a fish which had not disintegrated through weather was found in the same cave, and it can be assumed that it was a later work than that found on fragments from the collapsed rock. The cultural deposits revealed weather-beaten, painted fragments of rock which were then covered by deposits from the Perigordian period, so that the fish relief on the wall in the same cave must also belong to the same period, because the cave entrance was totally blocked by Perigordian deposits.

Fairly accurate datings can be gained from reliefs on blocks of stone. They were almost always present in the cultural deposits of the period in which they were made. Therefore, it was possible to date other objects found in the

751 'Negative' pictures of hands in the Gargas cave, France.

752 'Negative' picture of a hand with fingers missing. Gargas, France.

Necklace made of small perforated and decorated cylinders of mammoth ivory. Pavlovian culture, Dolní Věstonice, Moravia, Czechoslovakia.

Implement with geometric designs made from a mammoth's rib. Pavlovian culture, Předmostí, Moravia, Czechoslovakia.

Large decorated spoon made from mammoth ivory. Pavlovian culture, Dolní Věstonice, Moravia, Czechoslovakia.

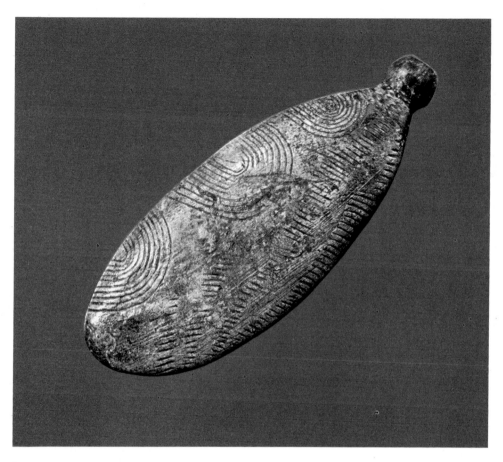

Pendant made of mammoth ivory with geometric designs.Pavlovian culture, Předmostí, Moravia, Czechoslovakia. Length 10 centimetres.

753

753 Engraving of a hand from the Barabahau cave, France.

754–755 Pictures of 'hands'. Santian cave, Spain.

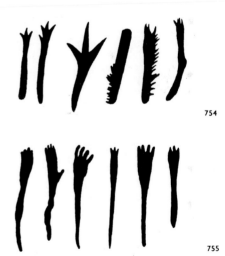

754

755

same deposits by the same method. Examples are the well-known reliefs from Le Roc de Sers (757 to 759) belonging to the Solutrean; the aurochs from Fourneau du Diable, also from the Solutrean; the human figures from Laussel (Lower Magdalenian culture); the figures from Angles-sur-l'Anglin (Magdalenian culture); and the crude engravings and paintings from La Ferrassie (760) from the Aurignacian period (the beginning of Palaeolithic art).

Some engravings or paintings are partly covered by stalagmite deposits. This calcareous layer has been thought to be quite accurate proof that the work of art belonged to the Palaeolithic period; but, we know today that the formation of such deposits in some caves will last thousands of years, whereas in other caves stalagmite layers can be produced under special circumstances within a few decades. Therefore, it is not to be taken as proof of authenticity regarding prehistoric discoveries. The theme of the picture is not accurate evidence either. It is known today that several

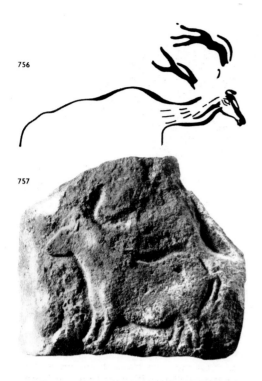

756

757

756 Painted stag from Abri Labatut. Perigordian culture, France.

757 Relief of a horse. Solutrean culture, Le Roc de Sers, Dordogne, France. Length 66 centimetres.

758 Rock face with reliefs of horses. Solutrean culture, Le Roc de Sers, Dordogne, France (after Martin).

759 Relief of a horse and a bison. Le Roc de Sers, Dordogne, France. Length 164 centimetres.

758

759

animals depicted were already extinct at the end of the Palaeolithic (mammoth, and so on) and this could be taken as a guideline for dating, but it is no guarantee that the painting is not a fake.

The dating of Palaeolithic works of art is assisted by the superimposition of paintings and engravings. These can be distinguished by the technique that was used to produce them. If a painting with strong colours was superimposed on a painting having fainter colours, the first impression could be misleading. The more recent, fainter paint is less expressive and usually difficult to see, which often gives the impression that this is the older painting, whereas it is actually the more recent one.

When dating a work of art it is not only necessary to consider the style and technique used, but also the probable use of tools, themes, composition, and type of presentation. Caves with paintings and engravings have rarely been found to contain small engraved objects in the same style. If they were of the same style, however, both works of art would obviously date from the same period. The similarity is at times so remarkable that they could seem to have been created by the same artist. Such a case is known from Altamira. A finely engraved hind on the cave wall and the engraving of a hind's head on a bone, found in Solutrean deposits at the entrance of the cave, show the same stylistic features (761). The fact that similar engravings of hinds' heads have also been found in the older Magdalenian layers at El Castillo is even more interesting. The date is either wrong, or this very distinct style was present over long periods. In Hornos de la Peña, Cantabria (in Spain) a picture of

a horse was discovered in Aurignacian deposits which is very similar to the ones found on the stalagmites near the entrance of the cave. This similarity made it not only possible to date the engravings on the stalagmites, but with comparative methods the others could also be dated.

The radiocarbon method of dating is today one of the most important techniques for absolute dating. Palaeolithic art from the Lascaux cave has been estimated by radiocarbon methods to be 15 515 ± 900 years old. The dating method has been tested on various objects so that it can be assumed to be trustworthy, although it does reduce the age of paintings in this cave considerably and places them in the Magdalenian period. The dating of the deposits from the Middle Magdalenian period at Angles-sur-l'Anglin resulted in an age of 14 050 years, which was also below the estimation originally given by experts. The well-known small figurines from the Pavlovian period found at Dolní Věstonice are, according to the radiocarbon method, 24 000 ± 150 years old.

Now let us turn to the deposits which, apart from the radiocarbon method, give us the most accurate chronological guidelines. No discoveries of works of art have been made belonging to the oldest Perigordian period and the somewhat crude art of the Aurignacian is not well-known either. Many works of art, previously thought to belong to the Aurignacian period, are today known to belong to the late Perigordian.

The simple, linear drawings in profile, of animals with only one foreleg and one hindleg, a single horn, one ear or only one antler, are typical of the Aurignacian period. Sometimes

760

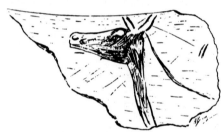

761

760 Crude engraving of animal legs and vulva symbols from La Ferrassie. Aurignacian culture, France. Length 67 centimetres. (Photograph by J Guichard, Musée des Eyzies.)

761 Engraving of a hind's head from Altamira. Solutrean culture, Spain.

762 Crudely engraved female figures from Abri Cellier. Upper Aurignacian culture, France. Length 20 centimetres. (Photograph by R Gauthier, Musée du Perigord.)

horns or hooves have been drawn in pairs on the animal's profile. There are also pictures with only half-drawn legs or some without hooves and they look rather stiff, not portraying much movement.

The earliest stones with engravings and paintings were found in deposits belonging to the older Aurignacian from the La Ferrassie cave. Engraved symbols from the Upper Aurignacian have also been found in this cave. Stones with similar, stylized engravings were discovered in the Aurignacian layers in Arcy-sur-Cure, Laussel, and Abri Cellier (762). At Pair-non-Pair (763) engravings were found on a wall covered by Perigordian layers, and it is thought that these engravings belong to the Aurignacian. Pebbles, stones, and slabs of stone with crude engravings come from the Perigordian period, and in the Parpalló cave more than a thousand slabs with engravings of varying artistic value have been found.

The small sculptures from the Middle and Upper Perigordian, the Pavlovian, and related cultures are a characteristic group. They are carved from stone and mammoth ivory or are modelled in clay. Most common among them are human figures, in particular those of women (Venus figurines), and only rarely those of animals (764 to 768). Most of these discoveries are from the Ukraine and central Europe, fewer were found in France and Italy. Some traces of paintings, belonging to these early periods, are also found on stones. There are probably not as many paintings as engravings because the weather and elements have destroyed the paintings.

Accurately dated reliefs with human figures are known from Laussel. A relief of a Venus figurine carved in stone was found together with numerous tools in deposits of the Upper Perigordian. But not all the figurines found at this site have been accurately dated. One of the men helping with the digging handed over an engraving of a woman with a horn in her right hand to an antique dealer, and consequently it was impossible to trace exactly how and where it was found (769). The engraving of two figures, either depicting coitus or birth, was thought by Lalanne, who carried out excavations here, to belong to the Solutrean period. It could be that the bifacial retouching typical for this culture, and found on the engraving,

763

764

763 Horses engraved at the Pair-non-Pair cave. Aurignacian culture, France. Length 75 centimetres.

764 Stylized rhinoceros carved from stone. Pavlovian culture, Kostienki, USSR (after Rogatchev). Length 2.8 centimetres.

765 Small stone figurine of a stylized animal. Pavlovian culture, Kostienki, USSR (after Rogatchev). Length 2.8 centimetres.

misled him. But this is also evident on some tools of the Perigordian period. In Lalanne's time, however, the Perigordian had not been divided from the Aurignacian, and because this 'Perigordian site' also contained Solutrean layers, the question of dating is problematic.

A simple, deep engraving from La Grèze shows a bison with one foreleg and one hindleg only but two horns (770). This engraving is thought to come from the Perigordian period because it was found beneath a Solutrean layer.

Only rarely do we find engravings from the Lower Solutrean; whereas they are more common in the Upper Solutrean. But, they are difficult to distinguish from engravings belonging to the Magdalenian period.

Several animal engravings do belong to the Solutrean, and probably include the deer at Altamira (771). A rock discovered in a Soluttrean deposit at Fourneau du Diable showed traces of red paint. The carefully made animal reliefs from Le Roc de Sers also belong to the Upper Solutrean, and it was possible to date them quite accurately because this layer revealed many other archaeological discoveries. The stratigraphic conditions became, however, much more difficult at Isturitz, because the reliefs and deep engravings were mostly covered by layers of the Middle Magdalenian period. Below one of these layers another layer of earth was found which had been deposited there by water and which contained a thin Solutrean layer, producing a few stone tools. The other parts of the water-deposited layer yielded Aurignacian and Perigordian finds. It could be assumed' that the engravings found are from the Solutrean period. According to the thinness of this layer which indicates only a short stay of Solutrean people it is more probable that the engravings come from the Middle Magdalenian, which did reveal many art objects with animal carvings. But it is also quite possible that the engravings should be attributed to the Aurignacian or Perigordian.

Most of the discoveries of small art objects come from the Magdalenian period. They usually consist of small sculptures carved in antler, mammoth ivory or bone depicting animals and sometimes also human beings. Carvings are often found decorating antlers, spear-throwers and batons which probably also had a ritual use (772, 773). Engravings are found on a wide variety of objects such as hunting weapons, bone and stone fragments, on the wide parts of the antlers, and so on. Engravings

765

on rock walls were found at Les Combarelles, especially in the long passage of this cave (774, 775). The shorter passage, which branches off from the entrance to the cave, revealed a settlement belonging to the Middle and Upper Magdalenian period, although no engravings were found. Breuil thought that this cave living site was not connected with the discoveries from the long passage, and that the engravings could belong to a later period, in which case they would be more recent than the well-known relief from Abri Cap Blanc (776). Intense research at Les Combarelles revealed, however, that they must be of the same age as the Cap Blanc relief just mentioned, and belong to the Middle to Upper Magdalenian period. Reliefs and engravings from Angles-sur-l'Anglin were partly covered by deposits from the Magdalenian period and were attributed, stratigraphically, to Magdalenian III (it was below this deposit that they were found).

Many remarkable scholars have taken part in the search for Palaeolithic works of art. The research began about the middle of the 1800s and one of the first names connected with it is

766

767

768

766 Small stylized mammoth carved from stone. Pavlovian culture, Kostienki, USSR (after Rogatchev). Length 2 centimetres.

767 Stylized small animal. Pavlovian culture, Kostienki, USSR (after Rogatchev). Length 2.8 centimetres.

768 Stylized small animal. Pavlovian culture, Kostienki, USSR (after Rogatchev). Length 2 centimetres.

769 Relief of a Venus figure holding a horn. Laussel, France. Height 36.5 centimetres.

Eduard Lartet. He believed that Palaeolithic art was an expression of man's natural creativity. The Frenchman Salomon Reinach, thought that they might have been an expression of magico-religious ideas. The Abbé Breuil made the most important contribution towards the understanding, interpretation, and chronology of the oldest art-forms. During his extensive studies he came to the conclusion that Palaeolithic art was divided into two groups. The first group belonged to the Aurignacian/Perigordian period; the second to the Soluttrean/Magdalenian period. His main error occurred, however, when he took the technically most primitive hand-prints and finger-drawings to be the oldest works of art (777). More recent studies have proved that primitive techniques like this were also used in later periods.

New information is constantly being gained by using modern dating methods and it becomes necessary to make several revisions. It is not always possible to find much accompanying archaeological material in the same layers which would be useful for dating art objects; sometimes they got lost or were badly damaged. These factors make dating difficult, while the radiocarbon method has, of course, made it possible to be far more accurate.

Further difficulties appear when studying superimposed paintings or engravings. It has been found that linear engravings under multicoloured paintings are not necessarily older. They are often paintings produced during the same period, and are a type of painting for which the artist first drew the approximate outlines and then covered them with paint. But even if two different paintings, one superimposed upon the other, are of different periods it is still difficult to date them. The time span could be a large one or may only be a short period. The paintings and engravings could also have been made by different artists, immediately after one another. It could mean, therefore, either that two different cultures were at work producing a work of art, or it could have been done within the same cultural period but in two different phases. The French archaeologist, Annette Laming-Emperaire, thought that superimposition was probably a normal Palaeolithic technique and was meant to indicate two pictures painted next to one another, the concept of which was shown at that period by overpainting. She further stressed the interesting parallels of classification suggested by Breuil and the difficult division between the reliefs of the Solutrean and Peri-

770

770 Bison. Perigordian culture, engraving from La Grèze, France. Length 60 centimetres.

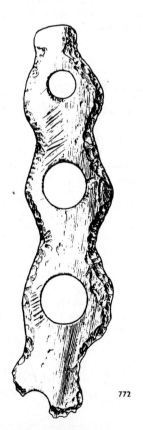

771

771 Deer. Solutrean culture, engraving from Altamira, Spain (after G Guinea). Length 62 centimetres.

772 Antler with four holes, one of which is broken away. Petersfels, Germany.

773 Antler with seven drilled holes and a simple engraved pattern. It is difficult to decide whether this represents a ritual object or a tool (for example, could the holes and lines represent vulva symbols?) La Madeleine, France. Length 30 centimetres.

772

gordian periods. She recommended that a 'three stage development' of Palaeolithic art be considered:

1 the archaic group of the Aurignacian and Perigordian periods with 'negative' hand prints, crudely outlined engravings of animals and, rarely, incomplete paintings;
2 a transitional period which embraces the latest phases of Breuil's Aurignacian and Perigordian periods, and the earliest phases of his Solutrean and Magdalenian periods. Painting can be characterized by the 'broken' or 'turned' perspective of horns and hooves;
3 the third group falls into the main Magdalenian period with its monumental multicoloured paintings. Here we meet with normal perspective of horns and hooves. These pictures are never overpainted, usually well preserved, and archaeologically datable.

Leroi Gourhan is also of the opinion that Palaeolithic art developed on a concept of the single line. His theory is not only based on the cave paintings and engravings but also on the small art objects found in cultural layers. He also admits that not all primitive paintings have necessarily to be oldest, and he shares the view with Laming that most paintings and engravings are part of underground sacred places. It would only be possible to explain these works of art if all the paintings belonging to one cave and painted at one period could be viewed and evaluated as a whole. Intensive studies made it clear to Leroi Gourhan that most of the pictures of animals and symbols represent male or female elements.

The weak point in the argument lies in the assumption that Palaeolithic art developed along the 'one line' method, whereas the extraordinary variety of these works of art is so remarkable and corresponds with the archaeological development of the Upper Palaeolithic cultures. The assumption of a uniform line of development which was supposed to show that works of art had developed from the primitive to the complicated, simply does not take into account the differences in tradition and technique, nor the high diversity of Palaeolithic art.

Therefore, we can assume that the speed of development was most irregular. If we take the small objects from the Magdalenian period as an example, we can see that the development in the Lower Magdalenian progressed very slowly only to flourish in the Middle Magdalenian and reach impressive heights of artistic and technical ability. A unification of style and technique followed in the Lower Magdalenian as well as a simplification of form, particularly in the direction of geometric signs and symbols. We can only say that the development of art proceeded much faster than that of the stone tool technology.

The surprising wealth and variety of Palaeolithic art is a good guideline for the study of human culture, the structure of prehistoric society, its development and changing position, but there are still many questions which remain unanswered.

Art at the end of the Old Stone Age

Eurasian art

A long time passed between the end of the Palaeolithic and the Neolithic period. The climate and living conditions of man had changed slowly, the population expanded and settled in new areas. In Europe, Asia, and

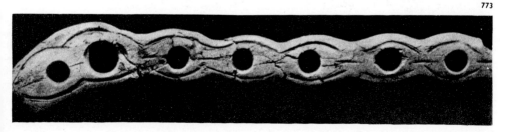

774

774 Horse with triangular drawings across its body. Magdalenian engraving from Les Combarelles, France.

775 Engraving depicting a cave lion. Magdalenian culture, Les Combarelles, France.

North America settlements tended to move further north, as the ice retreated.

Several artistic styles are known from the Mesolithic period. In northern Europe and Asia we saw the development of the 'nordic' or 'arctic' art of rock paintings and engravings, which came from the Middle and New Stone Age, the Bronze Age and Iron Age (778). The oldest engravings and paintings usually consist of simple outlines depicting animals; pictures of humans are rare. Many pictures are presented in a simple form of picture signs, and because of a general tendency to stylize it is relatively easy to distinguish the styles of particular geographical areas; for example, the Scandinavian, the north Russian, the south Siberian (779, 780) and those of the Chukotski Peninsula. The engravings from west and north Scandinavia are naturalistic and can be easily distinguished in their conception, theme, and technique from the well-known engravings of the Bronze Age. According to the themes they must have been made by hunters and fishermen, who were neither concerned with agriculture nor animal breeding. Similar engrav-

ings are known from the region around Lake Onega and the White Sea, USSR (781). As in the Upper Palaeolithic engravings and paintings the drawing of human figures or scenes is an exception. In most cases the picture would show a reindeer, elk, or whale; birds or fish are usually only rarely depicted and their stiff appearance points towards an archaic style (782, 783). Style and content of the picture can be compared with rock paintings of the Stone Age hunter. They are basically naturalistic but it is possible, in isolated cases, to find a tendency towards standardization or even symbolic drawings. The site of Bardal in Norway is of importance as far as chronological dating is concerned. Here, engravings of arctic style were found beneath other engravings which obviously belong to the Bronze Age. This site is evidence that 'arctic' art is not only more archaic in style but also older than the engravings of the Bronze Age (784, 785). It is almost certain that arctic art, which is bound to be discovered in still inaccessible places, is going to present us with many surprises.

Some scholars tried to find a connection between the Palaeolithic art in Europe and arctic art. But because northern Europe was still covered by glaciers towards the end of the Palaeolithic period and nearly totally uninhabited, this assumption is unlikely. If Norwegian art had its source in European art we would find traces of older and older engravings as we travelled south. In fact, it is exactly the other way round; the southern Scandinavian and Danish engravings are more recent than the engravings from northern Norway, and we must assume that the arctic art of Europe, particularly the Scandinavian, is of eastern origin (786). However, chronological and developmental data have as yet not been finalized.

The arctic art of Siberia and Chukotski Peninsula shows a number of archaic characteristics pointing towards the Epipalaeolithic as far as the early Neolithic period. The latest discoveries of Upper Palaeolithic cultures and settlements made in the central Chukotski Peninsula, Kamchatka and in the area around Yakutsk provide further evidence in that direction. The Upper Palaeolithic set-

777

776 Part of a relief of horses from Abri Cap Blanc. Magdalenian culture, France.

777 The head of an aurochs. A 'macaroni' drawing. Altamira, Spain. Width 100 centimetres.

tlements found at Lake Baikal, in the area of rock engravings along the upper reaches of the rivers Lena and Angara, are well-known and revealed rich finds of small art objects. The engravings probably date from between the Epipalaeolithic to the early Neolithic.

As well as the 'Franco-Cantabrian' style in Palaeolithic cave art found in Europe, paintings of so-called 'Levantine' art also exist (787 to 799), and have mainly been found in eastern Spain. They were painted on overhanging rock walls, and have been known since the beginning of the 1900s.

The first discovery was made in 1903 near Calapata not far away from Teruel, and in 1908 black and red paintings picturing dancing women were found near Cogul (791). In 1910 Alpera was discovered: this meant as much for 'Levantine' art as Altamira or Lascaux meant for 'Franco-Cantabrian' art. Further discoveries were made in 1917 in Val del

778 Rocks with engravings at Shishkino, on the
upper reaches of the river Lena, east Siberia,
USSR.

779 Engraving of an elk dating from between the Palaeolithic and Mesolithic period. Shishkino, east Siberia, USSR.

780 Engraving of a bull dating from between the Mesolithic and Neolithic period. Shishkino, east Siberia, USSR.

Geometric stylized female figurine engraved on a mammoth's tusk. Pavlovian culture, Předmostí, Moravia, Czechoslovakia.

Prehistoric rock painting of a fabulous animal. Shishkino, east Siberia, USSR.

Sefar, site of the Tassili cave paintings, Africa.

Rock painting of cattle. Tassili, Africa.

781 'Arctic' style engraving from Zalavruga, Karelia, USSR. Width 14.5 centimetres.

782 Human figure wearing a mask, and an elk. Engraving from Karelia, USSR.

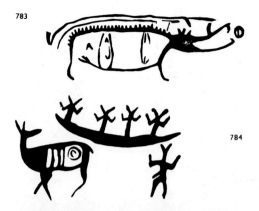

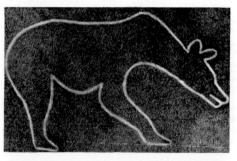

Charco del Agua Amarga (793) and near Minateda in the Valltorta gorge not far from the coast. Then followed discoveries from Cueva de la Araña (Valencia), Tormón, and in the early 1930s, the paintings in the Gasulla gorge, at Cueva Remigia, and others. It is quite clear to us today, that by no means all the works of art in this area have been found.

'Levantine' art usually consists of monochrome paintings, and engravings are very rare. Many different shades of black and red were used, and very occasionally even white. The paints were made of manganese, limonite, haematite, charcoal, or soot. The liquidized colours were sometimes applied with a small stick. They were mixed with water and probably with a binding agent. This is proved by the strange grey paint with which some paintings have been primed before the actual picture was painted, usually in red paint. The difference between the Palaeolithic art of the Cantabrian era and the 'Levantine' art is as follows. 'Levantine' paintings are usually done in one colour only; they are simple, and show no details on the inner surface of the objects painted; they are very small paintings (rarely larger than 300 millimetres) and they often depict human figures and scenes. The paintings of animals are usually naturalistic, while the human figures are highly stylized. Hunting scenes are common, but there are also 'fighting' scenes in which men with bows

783–784 Engraving of a fabulous animal trying to devour the sun. The second engraving represents a female deer and a boat with four men wearing strange head-gear or masks. Shishkino, east Siberia, USSR.

785 Engraving of the outlines of a bear. 'Arctic' style art, Valle near Lödingen, Norway. Width 226 centimetres.

786 Unusual picture in the 'arctic' style. The fret ornaments known already from the Palaeolithic period in the Ukraine are interesting. Honnhammer, Norway. Length 140 centimetres.

and arrows commonly appear. Scenes of every-day life can also be detected, as can scenes of religious significance, and sometimes even masked figures.

The pictures give evidence of many details regarding clothing and weapons of this period. The women are often seen wearing long skirts but naked from the waist up. Both men and women wear bangles around their wrists and arms which could have been made from leather or plants. The men are usually naked, but sometimes they wear knee-length trousers, and different kinds of belts. Much care is taken with the head-dress and hair-style, however. It is also possible at times to distinguish some kind of bag, perhaps made from leather, as well as quivers and arrows.

As far as the sense and purpose of these paintings are concerned, we can assume that they were either reporting news or showing the events of a hunt, fight, and so on. Sometimes they seem to have a ritual character.

Without any doubt, this art is that of hunting people from eastern Spain. The people who lived in a rocky area must have been cut off from the sea, as is clearly indicated by the location of sites and the themes of the paintings. Most of the archaeological discoveries in this area date back to the Epipalaeolithic or Neolithic period. It is possible to assess the age of these paintings at 8000 to 5000 years B.C. The question of chronological data has not been solved; nor have some questions of cultural

relations of these people and the North African culture of the Capsian, or their cultural and chronological relationship with the Palaeolithic 'Franco-Cantabrian' art.

North African art

The rock engravings and paintings of North Africa can be grouped on the basis of their location:

1　the area covering present-day Morocco, Algeria, and Tunisia, with a high concentration of engravings in the southern part of the High Atlas Mountains and south of Oran;
2　the Sahara with mountain sites in Hoggar, Tassili, Tibesti, Ennedi, Borku, and Fezzan;
3　the area of Libya and Egypt.

The 'Levantine' art of Spain and the engravings from southern Italy show a stylistic similarity with the North African works of art (800 to 802). Also these North African engravings and paintings are made on rock walls, or on huge rocks at the foot of high cliffs, and rarely on overhanging rocks.

The dating of works of art from North Africa is not an easy task. The sites situated deep in the deserts have not been accurately studied yet, and the evaluation of connections between archaeological culture and the various styles of art is very difficult. The most reliable guideline is still the theme of the pictures, particu-

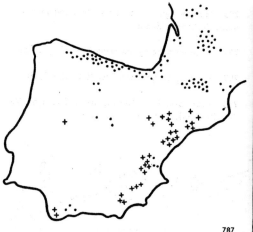

787

788

larly the animal world (803 to 805). Using present-day knowledge, however, it is possible to make some more general assessments. The engravings are thought to be the earliest art in the area. They usually portray extinct animals, like the *Homoioceros antiquus* — a buffalo with large horns — which are drawn in simple outlines and in the naturalistic style. The engravings found in the areas of Morocco, Algeria, and Tunisia are thought to belong to the Epipalaeolithic and the early Neolithic periods. During research carried out in the last few years scanty engravings of stone fragments belonging to the oldest style have been found in Capsian deposits of Algerian sites. These engravings are undoubtedly connected to others made in the same style and technique, portraying elephants, giraffes, rhinoceroses, and other animals. These animals too are extinct in these areas. The animals depicted always give a fairly accurate picture of the living conditions and climate which existed at the time when the picture was created. Engravings found in the Sahara desert indicate that rivers and marshlands existed and that the climate must have been similar to that existing in a present-day savannah. Engravings with dogs and other domestic animals (cows, sheep, and goats) are considerably more recent. This indicates that the original hunting people were replaced by pastoral (or nomadic) tribes. We have many multicoloured paintings from this period — for instance, at Tassili (806) — which are often discovered in the vicinity of Neolithic sites (807 to 809). But no archaeo-

787 Distribution map showing finds of 'Franco--Cantabrian' (.) and 'Levantine' (+) art in Spain.

788 Two different styles represented at El Prado del Torrero, Spain.

789 Walking woman. Drawing from Cueva Saltadora, Valltorta, Spain.

789

790 Human figure with bow, depicted in movement. Valltorta, Spain.

791 Women dancing. Painting from Cogul, Spain.

792 Hunting scene from Gasulla Gorge, Spain.

793 Warriors. Red painting from Cueva de Val del Charco del Agua Amarga, Spain.

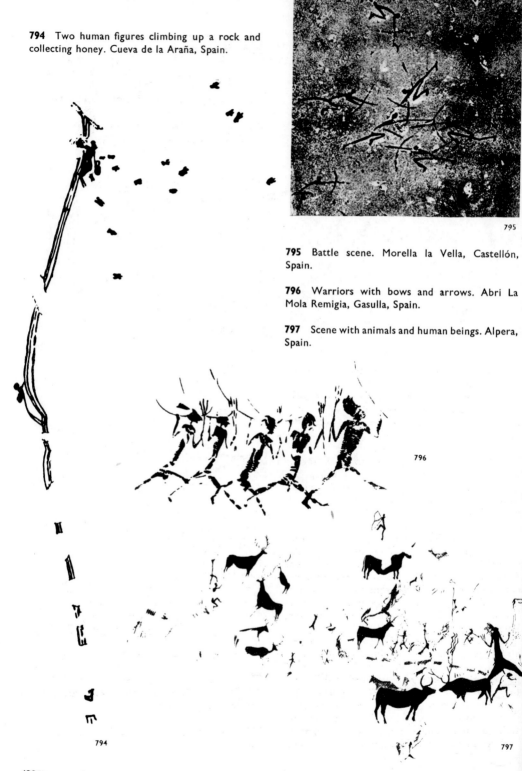

794 Two human figures climbing up a rock and collecting honey. Cueva de la Araña, Spain.

795 Battle scene. Morella la Vella, Castellón, Spain.

796 Warriors with bows and arrows. Abri La Mola Remigia, Gasulla, Spain.

797 Scene with animals and human beings. Alpera, Spain.

795

796

794

797

logical discoveries have been made near these sites belonging to older periods.

The engravings and paintings of horses are even more recent, and are as different in style from the above-mentioned pictures, as are the even later pictures of camels or Libyan Berber inscriptions from prehistoric and historic times. The Arabian inscriptions are the most recent together with several indistinct scribbles. But we are only interested in the oldest discoveries from the Capsian, or **early** Neolithic period, where there are engravings and paintings made by hunting peoples of the Stone Age.

Important information is gained from pictures of human beings. They **are** rare in the oldest drawings (810), and as well as drawings of *Homoioceros*, simple figures with a faint indication of steatopygia can sometimes be found. The oldest layers of the Neolithic culture at Tassili (811, 812), the actual site being Sefar, have revealed paintings which have recently been dated by the radiocarbon method to almost exactly 5000 years old. This means that they are really quite old and this holds true for the other paintings discovered at the same time too. The oldest paintings from Sefar were probably made by hunting peoples, because there is no evidence of any domestic animals. In Tassili too, isolated engravings showing just outlines in the 'archaic-naturalistic style' (for

798 Archer. Cueva del Civil, Valltorta, Spain. Length 24 centimetres.

799 Hind, stag, and wild goat. Cueva de la Araña, Spain.

800

800 Engraving depicting 'acrobats', from the Grotta dell'Addaura near Palermo, Sicily. Mesolithic period.

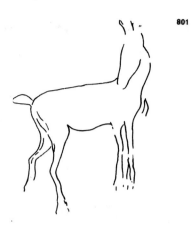

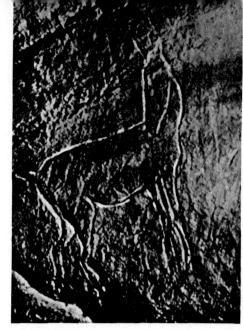

801–802 Sketch and view of a stag-like animal. Engraving from Levanzo, Sicily. Some south Italian and Sicilian engravings show a similarity in style to those found in North Africa (after Graziosi).

example, elephants) have been found, but no works of art in an archaeological context can be traced which could be compared with discoveries from Morocco, Algeria, and Tunisia.

Complicated scenes are not found in the oldest North African art. Isolated scenes of two animals fighting can be seen or, for instance, a female elephant protecting her young against a leopard. The designs are usually connected with hunting or some kind of ritual scene.

In Egypt and Libya engravings are far more common than paintings. They are found between Luxor and the Second Cataract in the Nile Valley, and in the Nubian and the Libyan deserts. The paintings seem to be more concentrated in sites of the Libyan desert. The technical approach of the Egyptian engravings is basically the same as that found in North Africa. The older engravings are quite deeply incised, and a cross-section reveals the cuts to be U-shaped, which means they were made with stone tools. The later engravings, made with metal tools, were V-shaped. The old engravings are often very patinated, the style is naturalistic, and they could be compared with the oldest engravings found in Morocco, Algeria, and Tunisia. Noticeable also are naturalistic scenes made in pecking technique. Sometimes both techniques are used on the same picture. The outline of the animal would be

engraved and the inner surface is either pecked or ground.

Pictures of various kinds of rafts or boats are found in the area of the Nile. Unfortunately it has not been possible to reach an accurate chronological order for these Egyptian engravings. Like those in the area of Morocco, Algeria, and Tunisia the oldest engravings in Egypt are created by hunting people.

A connection between Egyptian and Libyan engravings and paintings and the rest of North African art obviously exists. They use the same style and technique, and frequently the same motifs occur right across North Africa. This is quite understandable if we take into account that, during the periods of emergence of the oldest North African arts, this part of the continent including the Sahara desert was densely populated and regular contacts had been established.

South African art

The rock engravings and paintings in the southern part of the African continent, are found across present-day Rhodesia, South Africa and the south-western parts of Africa. They are further connected with the arts of Zambia and Tanzania as well as the arts developed in the region around the Equator. Many archaeo-

803

804

803 Giant bull and ostrich, engraving from North Africa (after Frobenius).

804 Two gigantic bulls *(Bubalus antiquus)* and a human figure. These simple outline North African engravings are usually thought to belong either to the Epipalaeolithic or Mesolithic period. Enfus, Algeria.

805 Giant bull, one of the oldest North African engravings dating back to the Capsian. This one comes from the Epipalaeolithic (after Balout).

806 The site at Sefar. Rock paintings in the Tassili-n'Ajjer Mountains in the Sahara desert.

logists are trying to date the discoveries and work out a chronological system, but this complicated task has as yet not been fully achieved.

The most recent paintings show European objects or sometimes even Europeans. They also depict scenes of fighting between small men, evidently bushmen, and large negroes. The advance of the Bantu tribes into the areas previously inhabited by the bushmen occurred between about A.D. 1300 and 1850. The engravings of a buffalo, which became extinct during the last Pluvial period, are undoubtedly old. Comparative ethnological studies prove that the creators of this art must have been the

805

806

807 Two human figures with a large bow, which might also represent a boat possibly a mythological event. Sefar, Tassili, Sahara desert.

808 Painting of a man with a large round head. Neolithic period, Sefar, Tassili, Sahara desert.

809 Overhanging rock with paintings. Tassili, Sahara desert.

807

80

mmediate ancestors of present-day bushmen,
or often even the bushmen themselves (813 to
818). This is particularly so in South Africa,
because the drawings discovered in Rhodesia
are different in style from the art of the bushmen. It is, of course, important for the studies
of South African paintings to take the ethnography of the present-day bushmen into account, which will help to clarify the function
and meaning of this art.

The sites of discovery in South Africa can
be divided into geological and geographical
areas:

1 granite caves which stretch from the north
of south-west Africa to Rhodesia and the
northern parts of the Transvaal;

2 sandstone-like rock galleries which make a
half-circle around South Africa;

3 the interior of South Africa with its smooth,
lava-like stones (mainly dolerite or basalt).
These surfaces are ideal for engravings.

The use of colours indicates that of the
pictures from the eastern parts of southern
Rhodesia (819), often covered with three or
four superseding layers, the single-coloured
ones — either black or yellow — are the
oldest. The multicoloured picture appears only
in the third layer. Characteristic pictures of
single-coloured, black silhouettes, often depicted together with human hands can be
found in the southern region. Scenes are more
typical of western areas. Two different areas
of style can be detected; the southern area
which includes Cape Province and the Transvaal and stretches right up to the Limpopo
river, which we also find in Botswana. This
style tends strongly towards multicoloured
paintings, and often covers whole flat areas
with colour. Many archaeologists compare this
style with the pecking technique of engraved
surfaces. The paintings depict far more complicated subjects than the engravings. They show,
for instance, hunting and festive scenes, or
meetings. The human figures sometimes have
animal heads, and previously it was thought
that they depicted hunting masks to trick the
animals. Intensive studies revealed another
reason; these masks were probably used on
a mythological level, because pictures of elephants with masks of other animals, or human

810

811

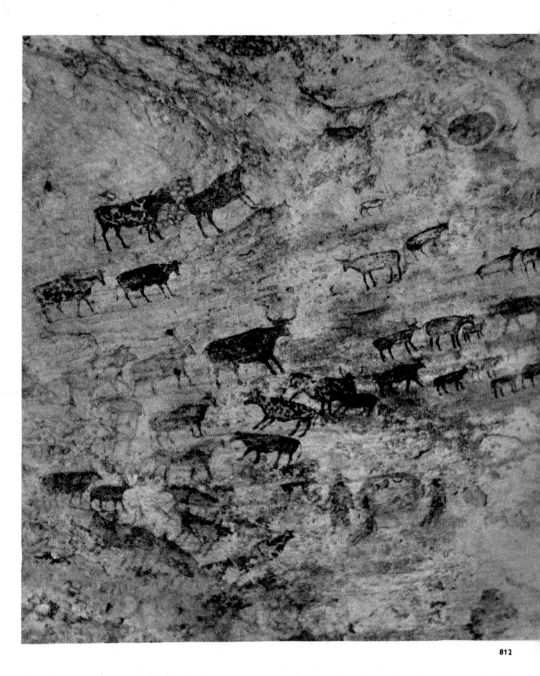

812

810 Engraving of an elephant. Tibesti, North Africa.

811 Simple painting of a bull. Sefar, Tassili. These and similar paintings from Sefar date back to between the Mesolithic and Neolithic period, during which time the Sahara desert was a savannah and inhabited by numerous animals that are extinct today in this area.

812 Herds of cattle of Neolithic shepherds. Painting from Sefar, Sahara desert.

499

figures with vultures' heads or goats' heads were found. The mythology of primitive peoples suggests an awareness of the transition from the human to the animal world, which is probably what these paintings are all about. They are of invaluable artistic worth (820 to 826).

The art of the bushmen shows remarkable powers of observation as well as talent. A large number of these works of art can be classed, without any doubt, among the most valuable treasures of prehistoric man.

No accurate dates have yet been established, but it seems that the engravings are older than the paintings, which are between 1000 to 3000 years old. It is most likely, however, that their beginning is closely linked with the Wiltonian culture and date back as far as 8000 years. They were created by a race of hunting people with a Stone Age culture (827 to 829).

813 Engraving on an ostrich egg made by present--day bushmen.

Australian art

Prehistoric art also occurs in Australia (830), where there are rock paintings and engravings. Small objects of art are found sometimes in cultural deposits in living sites or in burial places. They are mostly small pieces of jewellery, such as teeth with small holes in them, which were worn around the neck. The rock paintings together with modern bark-paintings and wooden sculptures made by the Aborigines represent the acme of artistic creation. The naturalistic style is found mainly in the north and north-west of Australia (831 to 833), and stretches across from Kimberley and Arnhem Land (834) to Queensland in the north-east and further to New South Wales and Victoria in the south. The second group includes paintings or engravings of a linear or geometric style. They come usually from areas in central or western parts of Australia (835) and in isolated cases from the east. The two different styles overlap both in western and south-eastern parts of Australia.

813

Rock painting of a female figure. Arnhem Land, northern Australia.

Human and animal painted figures from Arnhem Land, Australia.

Cult object *(murayian)*. Bark painting from inner Arnhem Land, northern Australia.

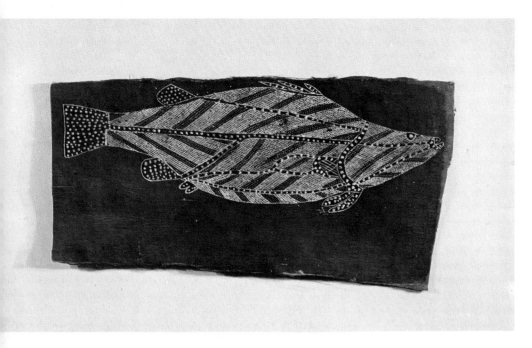

Bark painting of a fish in the 'X-ray' style, indicating the intestines of the fish. Inner Arnhem Land, northern Australia.

814

814–815 The so-called 'White Lady'. This mistakenly interpreted picture from Brandberg, South Africa, is more likely to represent an archer (after Breuil).

815

816 Antelopes. Engraving made by bushmen from Gestopftefontein, South Africa.

817 Ostrich and antelope. Engraving made by bushmen from Fauresmith, South Africa.

818 Engraving depicting an elephant with a calf. Pecked outline by the bushmen from Gestopftefontein, South Africa.

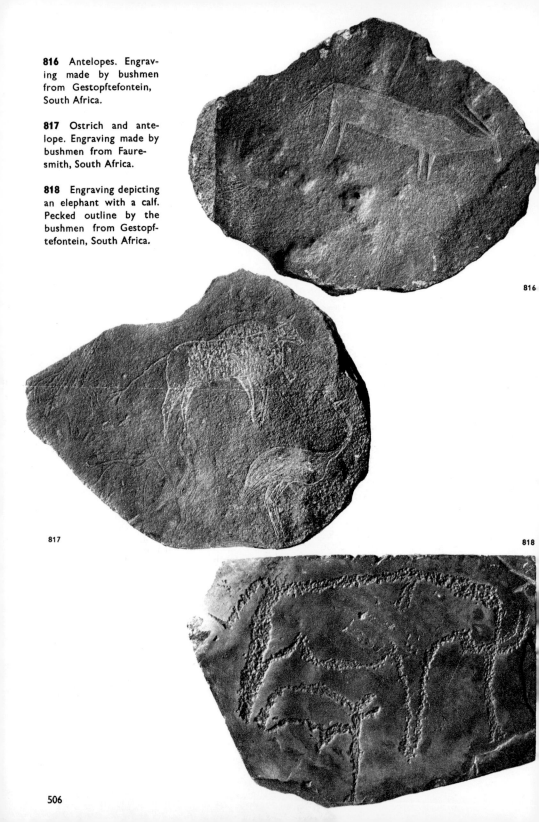

816

817

818

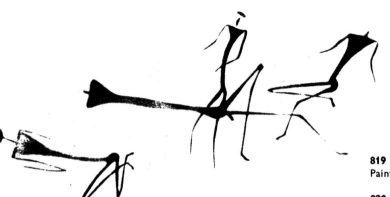

819 Human figures. Painting from Rhodesia.

820 Human figures painted across an older picture of an antelope. Drakensberg, Natal, South Africa.

821

823

821 Procession of bushmen musicians. Tsisab Gorge, South Africa.

822 A beautiful multicoloured painting of an antelope made by bushmen. Kamberg, Drakensberg, Natal, South Africa.

823 Engraving of an eland-antelope, South Africa.

824 Human figure. Rhodesia.

825 Scene, representing a royal burial. Rusape, South Africa.

824

825

The themes are usually of actual events and could be called 'picture reports'. Mythological events (836) are also depicted either in part or whole; and sometimes also legends or fables can be seen. The pictures often show symbols or geometric signs, or are placed inside such a sign. The inexperienced observer must often see them in an abstract way, although they are depicting reality and have a very particular significance (837 to 839).

In the south-west, east, and north of the continent, pictures of hands with spread out fingers are often found (840, 841). They are similar to the paintings of hands from the European Palaeolithic period, from North and South Africa and other regions. It is still pos-

sible today in Australia to follow the technique used to produce such pictures. The Aborigine chews the pigment first, mixes it with water, and then splashes it over his hand and the rock, so that when he removes his hand, the outline of the hand and fingers are clearly visible, making a 'negative-picture'. This method has also been adopted to produce pictures of whole arms in northern parts of Arnhem Land (842), which have later been cleverly decorated with multicoloured ornaments. These hand pictures are rare in the central desert of Australia, but instead, geometric patterns, spirals, circles, lines, and wavy lines can be seen. Here too, are sacred sites which are prohibited to women, and sometimes even to young men.

509

826 Wild elephant. Painting from about 1500 B.C. Philipp cave, South Africa.

827 Human figures. Painting made by bushmen, Tsisab Gorge, South Africa.

828

829

828 Countryside with hunting scene. Painting made by bushmen.

829 Painting on a rock made by bushmen near Salisbury, Rhodesia.

830

831

832

830 Map of the naturalistic and geometric styles of rock paintings found in Australia. The northern, south-eastern, and western areas are naturalistic, the central, southern, and south-western areas are geometric (after Lommel).

831 Wooden sculptures from north Australia. They were made under the influence of 'pearl hunters' from Makasan, who came, during the last 300 years to the north Australian coast.

832 Wooden sculptures from northern Australia.

According to Mountford one of these paintings depicts the journey of *Yarapis*, a legendary snake and its companions. It is over 30 metres long and totally expressed in symbols, which can only be interpreted by the Aborigines. This area has an awe-inspiring atmosphere; meetings take place here to ensure the reproduction of the snakes.

Wondjina pictures from northern Australia, which depict standing or lying persons, or often only the heads, are very significant. Arms and legs are usually only depicted on one side and footprints are sometimes there instead of legs. The faces have eyes and noses but no mouths. The heads are surrounded by arch-like lines looking like halos. Occasionally we can see an oval-shaped object on a chest which is supposed to be the heart or breast-bone. The oldest members of a tribe renew these pictures regularly even to this day (843). Other monumental paintings also belong to this group.

833

834

835

833 Realistic paintings depicting a snake and ghosts. Bokolo, Northern Territory, Australia.

834 Australian echidna – a realistic picture in red paint. Cadell River, northern Australia.

835 Churinga, a sacred stone from central Australia, with mythological engravings.

836 Realistic painting of a man, ostrich, and snake. Northern Australia.

837 Realistic scene, painted by a youth. Northern Australia.

838

838 Large painting of the mythical Burlung snake. The red dots on the body symbolize eggs. The artist, an Aborigine, sits below the picture. Arnhem Land, northern Australia.

839

840

839 Geometric painting. Ayers Rock, central Australia (after Lommel).

840 Negative print of a hand, a painted yam root, and fish. Northern Australia.

841 Negative prints of hands. Northern Australia.

842 Painted lower arm and a sailing boat. This painting is dated to the 1700s or 1800s because of the boat. Arnhem Land, northern Australia.

841

842

It seems that Australia gives us a last chance to see at first hand work which represents a large part of Palaeolithic art. Here we are able to observe the position of the artist among his people, his technique (844), and his understanding of the work. We are able to study the basic idea of his works (845 to 848). The sense and message which these pictures convey are closely connected with the religious ideas of these primitive people. And yet it is often difficult to understand what has been painted or drawn, even with the help of the Aborigines, because their own understanding today is often vague and fragmentary. Usually, only the oldest men are capable of giving any useful information.

Latest studies in Arnhem Land have revealed that the monochrome red, stylized human figures showing vigorous movements are part of the oldest drawings (849 to 851). These figures show a great resemblance to the 'Levantine' drawings of Spain or some South African paintings, but cannot in any way be

843 Wondjina picture. Maning Creek, northern Australia (after Crawford).

844 Palette and brushes made from bark, together with a lump of paint. Northern Australia.

844

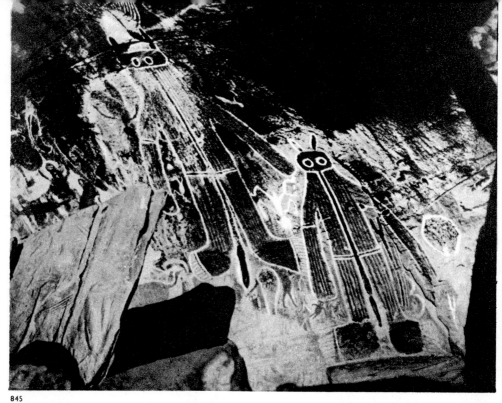

845

845 'Lightning Brothers'. Painting from Delamere, northern Australia.

846 Figures carrying spears, in the 'Mimi-style'. The figure at the top carries a modern axe in his hand, the figure in the middle carries it in his belt. Therefore, it is clear that the painting was made after first contacts with Europeans. Oenpelli, northern Australia.

847 Monumental painting of figures from El Sherano, northern Australia.

847

848

848 'Muli-Muligan', painting of a ghost. Arnhem Land, northern Australia.

849 Drawing of a moving human figure. Cadell River, northern Australia (detail from 851).

850 Drawing of a woman's figure in dancing movement. Cadell River, northern Australia.

851 Graceful human figure in rapid movement. Red ochre drawing from Cadell River, northern Australia.

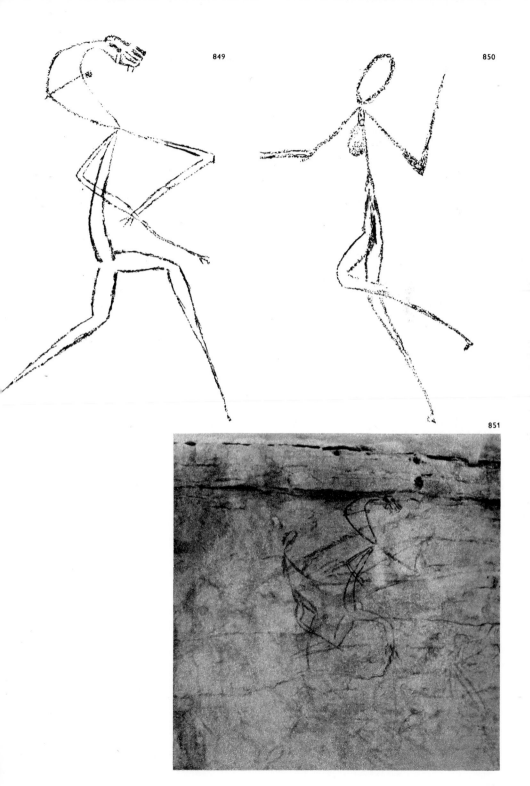

849

850

851

852

852 Gallery of rock paintings in 'X-ray' style. The paintings are on the cave ceiling. Oenpelli, in the north of Arnhem Land, northern Australia.

connected with them. According to archaeological discoveries made at the same sites of north Australia, they are connected with the Pirri culture, the age of which has been checked by the radiocarbon method and is thought to be around 3000 years. The monochrome drawings of the so-called Mimi-style are connected with the above mentioned culture (846) and are, according to the Aborigines, the work of rock ghosts. Some of these drawings are from recent times, as is proved by the depicted implements, such as an axe of European type. They are undoubtedly contemporary with the 'X-ray' pictures which show parts of the intestines and bone structures. Some parallels can be found in the bark paintings and sometimes among the most recent 'X-ray' pictures made about the beginning of the 1900s (852 to 860).

We can easily become fascinated watching the work of an Aborigine artist, whose society still exists on a similar cultural level to the ancient hunting societies. The archaeologist becomes aware of convincing parallels which make it easier to understand the sense and message of this, and prehistoric art.

853

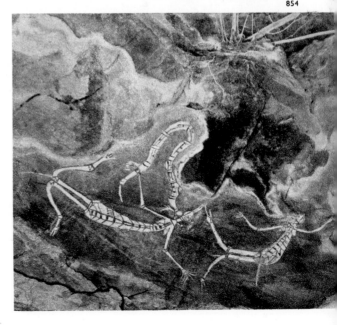

854

853 Fish painted in the 'X-ray' style. The intestines are clearly visible as well as the spine and muscles. Oenpelli, Arnhem Land, northern Australia.

854 Evil female ghosts. Arnhem Land, northern Australia.

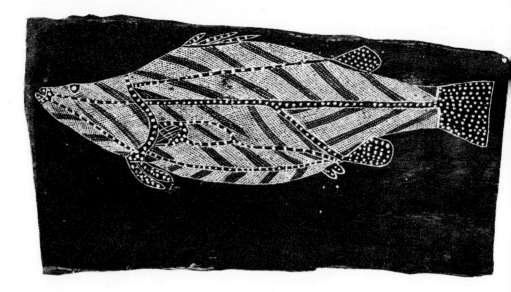

855

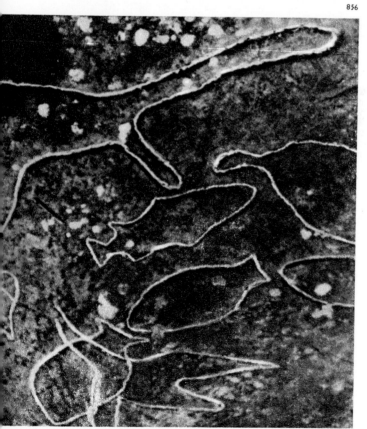

856

855 Fish painted in the 'X-ray' style on bark, central Arnhem Land.

856 Fish. Engraving made by Australian Aborigines.

857 An Australian Aborigine drawing the black contours of a fish on a red background. The colours are prepared on a flat stone. Northern Australia.

858 Aborigine collecting white earth for rock paintings from a crevice under water. Such find spots are often thought of as family property in Arnhem Land.

857

858

860

859 Aborigines from Arnhem Land painting on eucalyptus tree bark. The colours are prepared on flat stones. Northern Australia.

860 Simple Aboriginal painting on bark with mythological significance.

Conclusion

The period in which man, during his development, has lived as a hunter and collector was considerably longer than any of the other following developmental stages in which he started farming and animal breeding, and began to form tribal societies. The study of the earliest periods of man's existence gives us an insight into the basis of human development, and the material and intellectual roots from which it all sprang; as well as being able to explain and understand the oldest and most important discoveries made of man.

This study can make use of two authentic records: the anthropological and archaeological discoveries which illustrate the physical and cultural development of prehistoric hunting societies. On the other hand, recent primitive races, who today still live the life of hunters and collectors, or at least races which have done so until recently, are making it possible to make comparative observations.

In the past more discoveries have been made in Europe. This is understandable because it was here that the first and most frequent excavations and studies were carried out, and of course this is one of the reasons why so many discoveries were made in relatively small areas. This knowledge which grew up during further anthropological and archaeological studies changed ideas about the development of man. Many new and important discoveries from all over the world proved that the development of prehistoric man was not centred on Europe but also took place in other continents. This is why we have discussed in this book the newer discoveries made in eastern Europe, Africa, particularly in east Africa, in Siberia, and also in North and South America and Australia. These discoveries have changed our ideas about the beginnings of the cultural development of man. They have shown that continents like Australia and America had been inhabited long before anybody had previously thought, and also that regions like the mainland of the

Bering Sea, the Arctic circle, or the tropical regions have not only been temporarily inhabited by man, but consistently been lived in. This influenced also the old idea of large migrations and exchanges of whole populations which were considered to be a sufficient explanation of conspicuous physical and cultural changes in individual geographical regions. We know today that nomadic movements of whole populations played only a small part in the development and change of human biology and culture.

We are sometimes given to believe that the ancestor of man and that of present-day apes did not develop from the same basic stock. This might still be an echo of the passionate opposition which Darwin and Huxley experienced during the 1800s. You should only look briefly at the various attempts at an artistic reconstruction in which Neanderthal-man is often represented as a degenerate, inferior being. This assumption is unthinkable if we consider that he was forced to live under the most difficult circumstances during the last Ice Age; and was not only able to exist but also able to develop. Neanderthal discoveries have also revealed that he enjoyed a relatively highly developed mental and material culture with tools, hunting weapons, settlements, ritual burials, and so on. Or what about the hunters from the Upper Palaeolithic? Their highly developed and strongly distinctive culture left only sparse fragments behind, because objects made of wood or leather, of bark or plants, or even implements made of bone often did not survive. How much will there be left of the rich culture of present-day Eskimos after a thousand years in the ground? And what could the invaluable art of the Australian Aborigines offer us, if it was not documented in collections or reproduced? This mainly consists of bark or wood objects, or if the pictures are incised on clay they are often wiped off immediately after the ceremony has finished.

Recent research, carried out with the latest methods to hand, has brought us to the conclusion that neither the material nor the mental culture of the prehistoric hunters can be termed 'primitive'. The technology shown in working bones, as well as their artistic production, prove the high level of technical skill and artistic imagination that these people were capable of. It was absolutely correct to compare the artist who made the paintings at Altamira or Lascaux with Michelangelo; artistic genius is not confined to technical development of civilizations.

Another thought should be included in this stage; only one kind of man — *Homo sapiens* — lived on this planet for at least the last 100 000 years, maybe even 200 000 years. All prehistoric populations of the Middle and Upper Palaeolithic and the following period right up to the present-day, have been part of this *(Homo sapiens)* type of man. Cultural development did not take place everywhere at the same speed, and has also many different elements. But man everywhere has shown remarkable talent for adapting himself, which made it possible — quite apart from other factors — for man to assure himself a reasonable development on all continents. The contacts achieved today between the various countries and races, which might have been isolated, are of incredible variety. As part of an easily flowing exchange of information we can see the development of a united world-wide culture and civilization. When studying our past we are forced to admit that there has not been one race or population, however 'primitive', which has not been part of the progress achieved by man. And if this book has helped to convince the reader of the accuracy of the statements made here, it has fulfilled its purpose.

GLOSSARY

Abbevillian a Lower Palaeolithic stone tool culture of France characterized by crude oval or pear-shaped hand-axes

Acheulean a Lower Palaeolithic stone tool culture of France in which the tools are commonly pointed or almond-shaped hand-axes

Ahrensburgian Epipalaeolithic culture of northern Europe characterized by small points with bevelled edges

alveolus the socket within the jawbone in which the roots of a tooth are set

Anthropoidea the sub-order of the order *Primate* comprising the living higher primates

anthropology the scientific study of the origin and development of mankind

anthropomorphous resembling the human form

Anyathian Lower Palaeolithic stone tool culture of Burma characterized by primitive pebble tools and a poor flake industry

archaeology the scientific study of any previous culture, particularly a prehistoric one, by excavation

artefact any object made by man with a view to subsequent use

Aterian a stone tool culture characterized by tools which have clearly defined areas for holding, found in the Middle Palaeolithic of Africa and Upper Palaeolithic in Europe

Aurignacian an Upper Palaeolithic culture marking the beginning of the working of bone pins and spear-points

aurochs a European wild ox which is now extinct

Australopithecinae sub-family of the family *Hominidae* including the genus *Australopithecus*

basalt dark, dense rock of volcanic origin, composed essentially of plagioclase feldspar and pyroxene

brachiation a form of locomotion used by early Hominoids by securing handholds in trees with the forelimbs overhead, and moving forward by swinging with one arm then the other

burin a tool used for engraving on bone or stone

calvaria the dome of the skull

canine tooth one of the four pointed teeth particularly prominent in dogs

Capsian a stone tool culture following the Aterian in the Epipalaeolithic of Maghreb in North Africa

Catarrhini a sub-order of the order *Primate* including the Old World monkeys, the apes, and man

Ceboidea a super-family of the order *Primate*; The New World monkeys

Cenozoic the most recent geological era occupying the last 70 million years of Earth's history

Cercopithecoidea a super-family of the order *Primate*; The Old World monkeys

Charentian Mousterian culture of the so-called La Quina type which is confined to the Charente area in France

Chatelperonian the earliest known Upper Palaeolithic culture characterized by a flint blade with a blunt back

Chellean a Lower Palaeolithic stone tool culture following the Abbevillian

chignon a large rolled arrangement of the hair, worn at the back of the head by women

cingulum a belt, zone or girdle-like part

Clactonian a culture from the Middle Pleistocene of Europe consisting of tools struck from flint cores by making use of an anvil stone

claviform club-shaped

Cretaceous the youngest system of the Mesozoic era

cusp an elevation, as on the crown of a tooth

diastema a space between the canine and incisor teeth as found, for example, in members of the *Pongidae*

diorite a granular igneous rock consisting essentially of the minerals plagioclase feldspar and hornblende

dolerite a medium-grained dyke rock with the composition of basalt

dolichocephalic having a skull shape which is narrow as compared with its length from front to back

Dryopithecinae sub-family of the family *Pongidae*

Dryopithecus-pattern an arrangement of five cusps on the occlusal surface of the molar teeth such that the pattern resembles that of the Miocene ape *Dryopithecus*

Eocene a period in the Tertiary system from 60 to 40 million years ago

eolith a crude flint implement shaped by, rather than for, use

Epipalaeolithic a cultural period intermediate in character between that of the Palaeolithic and the Neolithic

epiphyses parts of a bone which are separated from the main body of the bone by a layer of cartilage and which became united with it by ossification

ethnography the scientific description and classification of the various cultural and racial groups of man

ethnology the study of the distinctive subdivisions of mankind

eucalyptus any member of the genus of trees which includes the blue gum native in Australia at the present time

fibula the outer and thinner of the two bones of the lower leg

fossil any remains or trace of an animal or plant of a former geological age

fresco a method of painting on a wall or ceiling before the plaster has dried so that the colours become incorporated in it

frieze a decorative band or feature, as on a wall

Glacial Ice Age

granite a granular igneous rock composed essentially of the minerals quartz and orthoclase feldspar

graver any of the various tools used for chasing or engraving

Gravettian Upper Palaeolithic culture characterized by backed blades found in France, Spain, Belgium, and Italy

Günz Glacial first major Ice Age in the Pleistocene period. *See* Geologic Time Scale

haematite an iron oxide commonly occurring as a red earthy mass

half-life the time required for one half of a sample of a radioactive substance to undergo decay

Hamburgian Upper Palaeolithic culture of northern Germany

hermaphrodite an animal having normally both the male and the female sexual organs

Holocene the most recent geological period about the last 11 000 years

Hominidae a family of the super-family *Hominoidea* comprising the man-like beings

Hominoidea a super-family of the order *Primate* comprising the apes and man

Homo sapiens the single surviving species of the genus *Homo*. Modern man

hornstone a variety of quartz resembling flint

humerus the single long-bone in the arm which extends from the shoulder to the elbow

Hylobatidae a family of the super-family *Hominoidea* including the modern gibbons

Ibero-maurusian a stone tool culture following the Aterian in the Epipaleolithic of Maghreb in North Africa

incisor a tooth in the anterior part of the jaw adapted for cutting

interglacial between two glacials

ironstone any ore of iron — commonly a carbonate — with clayey impurities

kaolin a fine white clay

Levalloisian a Middle Palaeolithic technique of producing flint flakes from a prepared core

limonite a hydrated iron oxide varying in colour from dark brown to yellow

loess a loamy deposit of wind-blown origin, usually yellowish and calcareous, common in Europe and Asia

Lupembian stone tool culture of the Lower Palaeolithic of Africa characterized by tools which seem to be appropriate for rough woodwork

macaroni style a style of cave decoration found at Pech Merle in France and also in Spain in the Mesolithic and Neolithic in which figures are represented schematically by lines looking like pieces of macaroni

Magdalenian Upper Palaeolithic bone and stone tool culture consisting of blades and burins

mammoth a large extinct species of elephant

Mesolithic the period of the Stone Age following the Palaeolithic

metatarsus the part of the foot between the tarsus and the toes

microlith small flint implement generally set in some form of haft for use, such as in a sickle, and noted especially from the Pavlovian and Upper Palaeolithic cultures

Mimi style a style of art associated with the Pirri culture of Arnhem Land in which plain red stylized human figures showing vigorous movement are depicted. The paintings are thought to be about 3000 years old

Mindel Glacial second major Ice Age in the Pleistocene period. *See* Geologic Time Scale

Miocene a period of the Tertiary system from about 25 to 12 million years ago

molar tooth a tooth adapted for grinding with a broad biting surface. There are twelve molar teeth in man

Mousterian a Middle Palaeolithic stone tool culture of scrapers, cores, and points represented in Europe, Asia, and North Africa

Neanderthal-man species of ancient man who lived in Europe in the Palaeolithic period. Named after its type area Neanderthal, a valley near Düsseldorf in Germany

Neogene the upper division of the Tertiary system including the Miocene and Pliocene periods

Neolithic the more recent or New Stone Age characterized by polished stone tools

obsidian volcanic glass which breaks with a conchoidal fracture

occlusal surface the chewing surface of a tooth

Oldowan a Lower Palaeolithic culture consisting of simple stone tools that have been flaked in one or two directions

Oligocene a period in the Tertiary system from 40 to 25 million years ago

osteodontokeratic pertaining to bone, tooth, and horn

Palaeocene the oldest period of the

Tertiary system, beginning about 70 million years ago, and lasting 10 million years

Palaeogene the lower division of the Tertiary system including the Palaeocene, Eocene, and Oligocene periods

Palaeolithic the earliest part of the Stone Age. The Old Stone Age, characterized by chipped stone tools

palaeontology the scientific study of the forms of life which existed in former geologic periods, as represented by their fossil remains

pandanus any member of a family of trees and shrubs having a palm-like or branched stem and long, narrow, rigid leaves

Paranthropus a genus of the family *Hominidae* found in Swartkrans, South Africa

patina a surface calcification, especially of implements

Patjitanian Middle Pleistocene stone tool culture from Java characterized by coarse flakes in the shape of cleavers

Pavlovian eastern Gravettian. Upper Palaeolithic culture found in central and eastern Europe

periglacial regions immediately beyond the ice-front during a glaciation

Perigordian a stone and bone culture of the Upper Palaeolithic

phalange any of the bones of the fingers or toes

Pirri culture northern Australian prehistoric stone tool culture of about 3000 years ago characterized by Pirri points which are 3 to 7 centimetres long with one side flat

Pleistocene the oldest division of the Quaternary system (the Glacial epoch or Ice Age) from 2 or 3 million to about 11 000 years ago

Pliocene the most recent period in the Tertiary system from about 12 to 2 or 3 million years ago

pluvial a rainy season

Pongidae a family of the super-family *Hominoidea* which includes the great apes such as the modern orang-utan

potassium/argon dating a method of dating rocks by determination of the ratio of potassium-40 to radiogenic argon-40 contained in them

premolars the permanent teeth in mammals in front of the molar teeth

Primate the order of mammals which includes man, the apes, monkeys, lemurs, and so on

Prosimii a sub-order of the order *Primate*

pseudo-artefact an object which appears to be a man-made tool, but actually has been moulded by natural forces

Quaternary the most recent geological system occupying the last 2 or 3 million years

radiocarbon dating the method of estimating the age of an object of plant or animal origin by determining the proportion of radioactive carbon (C 14) contained in it

Riss Glacial the third major Ice Age in the Pleistocene period. *See* Geologic Time Scale

sacrum a bone resulting from the adhesion of two or more vertebrae in the spine

Sangoan stone tool culture of the Lower Palaeolithic of Africa characterized by tools which seem to be appropriate for rough woodwork

savannah a plain characterized by coarse grasses and scattered trees especially on the margins of the tropics where the rainfall is seasonal

simian shelf a strengthening of the lower jaw characteristic of all recent and fossil apes

Soan Middle Pleistocene stone tool culture from India characterized by coarse flakes shaped to form cleavers

Solutrean an Upper Palaeolithic culture

characterized by finely made laurel-leaf blades using the pressure flaking technique

stalactite a deposit of calcium carbonate shaped like an icicle hanging from the roof of a cave formed by the dripping of percolating calcareous water

stalagmite a deposit of calcium carbonate in the form of a column from the floor of a cave formed by the dripping of calcareous water

steatopygous having huge accumulations of fat about the buttocks

steppe an extensive plain, especially one without trees

stratigraphy classification, correlation, and study of stratified rocks

supra-orbital torus a protuberant part situated above the eye-socket of an animal

Szeletian The Lower Palaeolithic stone tool culture of central Europe

tang a long, slender prong forming part of an object, often serving as a means of attachment for a handle

tectonic pertaining to building or construction, or to earth movements

terra rossa a reddish clay soil characteristic of limestone regions

Tertiary the geological system occupying a period in time from about 2 to about 70 million years ago

tibia the shinbone

tortoise-core a nodule of flint prepared

to form a core resembling a tortoise, from which flakes are struck. Characteristic of the Levalloisian culture

travertine a form of limestone deposited by springs

Triassic the geological system which constitutes the first division of the Mesozoic era, and is characterized by terrestrial deposits

tschum a seasonal dwelling used by hunting people

ulna that one of the two bones of the forearm which is on the side opposite to the thumb

urethra the membranous tube which extends from the bladder to the exterior

Villafranchian an assemblage of new mammals which suddenly appeared in the Lower Pleistocene period

viscera the soft internal organs of the body

vulva the external female genitalia

Wiltonian Upper Palaeolithic stone tool culture of South Africa

Würm Glacial final major Ice Age in the Pleistocene period. *See* Geologic Time Scale

X-ray painting a style of art used by primitive man and modern aborigines in which internal structures as well as external features of the animal are depicted

BIBLIOGRAPHY

General Reading

Buettner-Janusch, J *Origins of Man : Physical Anthropology*. Wiley, Chichester, 1966.

Butzer, Karl *Environment and Archaeology*. Methuen, London, 1965.

Clark, W E Le Gros *The Antecedents of Man*. 2nd ed. University of Edinburgh Press, Edinburgh, 1962.

Clark, W E Le Gros *Fossil Evidence for Human Evolution*. Chicago University Press, 1964.

Clark, W E Le Gros *History of the Primates*. British Museum (Natural History), 1970.

Colbert, E H *Evolution of the Vertebrates*. John Wiley & Sons, New York, 1955.

Cole, Sonia *Early Man in East Africa*. Macmillan, London, 1958.

Cole, Sonia *Races of Man*. British Museum (Natural History), 1963.

Darwin, C *On the Origin of Species by Means of Natural Selection*. John Murray, London, 1859.

Day, M H *Guide to Fossil Man*. Cassell, London, 1965.

Flint, R F *Glacial and Quaternary Geology*. Wiley, Chichester, 1971.

Laming, A *Lascaux and Engravings*. Penguin, Harmondsworth, 1959.

McBurney, C B M *The Stone Age of northern Africa*. Penguin, Harmondsworth, 1960.

Oakley, K P *Man the Tool Maker*. British Museum (Natural History), 1963.

Oakley, K P *Framework for Dating Fossil Man*. Weidenfeld and Nicolson, London, 1964.

Romer, A S *Man and the Vertebrates*. Penguin, Harmondsworth, 1970.

Rosenfeld, A *Inorganic Raw Materials of Antiquity*. Weidenfeld and Nicolson, London, 1965.

Zeuner, F E *The Pleistocene Period:* Hutchinson, London, 1959.

Other Selected References

Allchin, B *The Indian Stone Age Sequence*. J.R.A.I.G.B. 93, 210—234, 1964.

Baldwin, C *Biochemistry and Evolution*. In Symposia of the Society for Experimental Biology 7, 1953.

Black, D *On a lower molar hominid tooth from Chou-kou-tien deposit*. Pal. Sinica, Ser. D, 7, No. 1, Peking, 1927.

Black, D *On an adolescent skull of Sinanthropus pekinensis*. Pal. Sinica Ser. D, 7, No. 2, Peking, 1931.

Black, D R, Chardin, T de, Young, C C, Pei, W C *Fossil Man in China, The Chou-kou-tien Cave Deposits, with a Synopsis of our Present Knowledge*. Mem. Geol. Surv. China, Ser. A. No. 11, 1933.

Brace, C L *The fate of the 'classic' Neanderthals*. Current Anthrop. 4, 3—19, 1963.

Broom, R, Robinson, J T *Swartkrans Ape-Man, Paranthropus crassidens*. Transvaal Mus. Mem. No. 6, Pretoria, 1952.

Broom, R, Robinson J T, Schepers, G W H *Sterkfontein Ape-Man, Plesianthropus*. Transvaal Mus. Mem. No. 4, 1950.

Broom, R, Schepers, H *The South African Fossil Ape-Man, the Australopithecinae*. Transvaal Mus. Mem. No. 2, Pretoria, 1946.

Campbell, B G *Quantitative taxonomy and human evolution*. In S L Washburn (ed) Classification and Human Evolution. 50—74 Viking Fund Publs. Anthrop. No. 37, Chicago, Aldine Publishing Co., 1963.

Carpenter, C R *A Field Study in Siam of the Behavior and Social Relations of the gibbon*. Comp. Psychol. Monogr., No. 16, 5, 1940.

Clark, J G D *The mesolithic settlements of northern Europe, a study of the food gathering peoples of northern Europe during the early post-glacial period*. Cambridge, 1935.

Clark, W E le Gros *New palaeontological evidence bearing on the evolution of the Hominoidea*. Quart. J. Geol. Soc. London, 105, 225—64, 1950.

Clark, W E le Gros, Leakey, L S B *The Miocene Hominoidea of East Africa*. British Museum (Natural History), London, 1951.

Colbert, E H *Siwalik mammals in the American Museum of Natural History*. Trans. Amer. Phil. Soc. n.s. 26, 1935.

Colbert, E H *Fossil mammals from Burma in the American Museum of Natural History*. Bull. Amer. Mus. Nat. Hist. New York 74, 1935.

Cole, S *The Prehistory of East Africa*. New York, 1963.

Dart, R A *Australopithecus africanus: The Man-Ape of South Africa*. Nature, London, 1925.

Dart, R A *The predatory implemental technique of Australopithecus* Am. J. Phys. Anthrop. 7, 1949.

Dart, R A *The adolescent mandible of Australopithecus prometheus*. Transvaal Mus. Mem. No. 10, Pretoria, 1957.

Dart, R A *The osteodontokeratic culture of Australopithecus prometheus*. Transvaal Mus. Mem. No. 10, Pretoria, 1957.

Dart, R A *Substitution of stone tools for bone tools at Makapansgat*. Nature, vol. 196, No. 4852, 315—316, 1962.

DeVore, I *A comparison of the ecology and behaviour of monkeys and apes*. In S L Washburn (ed) *Classification and Human Evolution*, 301—19 Viking Fund Publs. Anthrop. No. 37, Chicago, Aldine Publishing Co., 1963.

Dobzhansky, T *Genetics and the Origin of Species*. Columbia University Press, New York, 1940.

Dobzhansky, T *Mankind Evolving*. New Haven, Conn., and London, Yale University Press, 1962.

Dobzhansky, T *Cultural direction of human evolution: a summation*. Hum. Biol. 35, 311—16, 1963.

Dobzhansky, T and Montagu, M F A *Natural selection and the mental capacity of mankind*. Science, 105, 587—90, 1947.

DuBrul, E L, Sicher, H *The Adaptive Chin*. Springfield III, Charles C Thomas, 1954.

Erickson, G E *Brachiation in New World monkeys and in anthropoid apes*. Symp. Zool. Soc. London 10, 1935—164, 1963.

Evernden, J F, Curtis, G H *The potassium-argon dating of late Cenozoic rocks in East Africa and Italy*. Curr. Anthrop. 6, 343—85, 1965.

Ewer, R F *The fossil carnivora of the Transvaal Caves: two new viverrids, together with some General Considerations*. Proc. Zool. Soc., London, 126, 1956.

Freedman, L Z, Roe, A *Evolution and human behavior*. In A Roe and G G Simpson (eds) Behavior and Evolution 455—79, New Haven, Conn., Yale University Press, 1958.

Garn, S M *Human Races*. Springfield, III. Charles C Thomas, 1961.

Garrod, D, Bate, D M A *Stone age of Mount Carmel*. Oxford, 2 vol., 1937—1939.

Garrod, D A E, Buxton, L H D, Smith, G E, Bate, D M A *The excavation of a Mousterian rock-shelter at the Devil's Tower, Gibraltar*. J.R.A.I.G.B. 58, 1928.

Gimbutas, M *The prehistory of Eastern Europe*. Cambridge, Mass., 1956.

Goodall, J *Chimpanzees of the Gombe Stream Reserve.* In I DeVore (ed) Primate Behavior. 425—73, New York, Halt, Rinehart, and Winston, 1965.

Gregory, W K *Origin and evolution of the human dentition.* Baltimore, 1922.

Gregory, W K *Evolution emerging.* New York, 1951.

Gregory, W K, Hellman, M *The dentition of Dryopithecus and the origin of Man.* Anthrop. Papers Amer. Museum Nat. Hist., 28, New York, 1926.

Gregory, W K, Hellman, M, Lewis, G E *Fossil anthropoids of the Yale-Cambridge India Expedition of 1935.* Carnegie Inst. Washington, Publ. No. 495, 1937.

Hall, K R L *Tool-using performances as indicators of behavioral adaptability.* Curr. Anthrop., 4, 479—94, 1963a.

Hallowell, A I *Culture, personality, and society.* In A L Kroeber (ed), Anthropology Today, 597—620, Chicago, University of Chicago Press, 1953.

Hallström, G *Monumental Art of northern Europe from the Stone Age.* (The Norwegian localities). Stockholm, 1938.

Hallström, G *Monumental Art of northern Sweden from the Stone Age.* (Nörmforsen and other localities). Stockholm, 1960.

Heekeren, H R van *The Stone Age of Indonesia.* The Hague, 1957.

Hooijer, D A *Prehistoric teeth of Man and the Orang-utan from central Sumatra, with notes on the fossil orang-utan from Java and southern China.* Zool. Mededeel. 29, Leiden, 1948.

Howell, F C *Pleistocene glacial ecology and the evolution of 'classic Neanderthal' Man.* Southw. J. of Anthropology 8, Albuqurque, 1952.

Howell, F C *Upper Pleistocene Man of southwest Asian Moustérian.* Neanderthal Centennary Wenner-Gren Foundation, 1958.

Howell, F C *Early Man.* Life Natural Library, 1965.

Howell, F C, Bourlière, F *African Ecology and Human Evolution.* 666 p. Aldine Publishing Company, Chicago, 1963.

Jacob, T *The sixth skullcap of Pithecanthropus erectus.* Am. J. Phys. Anthrop. 25, 243—260, 1966.

Jarvik, E *The oldest tetrapods and their fore-runners.* Scient. Monthly 80, 141—154, 1955.

Kawai, M *Japanese monkeys and the origin of culture.* Animals 5, 450—455, 1965.

Keith, A *The Antiquity of Man.* London, 1925.

King, W *The reputed fossil Man of the Neanderthal.* Quart. J. Science 1, London, 1864.

Koenigswald, G H R von *Fossil Hominids from the Lower Pleistocene of Java.* Proc. Int. Geol. Cong. Gt. Britain, 1948, 9 London, 1950.

Kohler, W *The Mentality of Apes.* Kegan Paul, New York and London, 1925.

Kretzoi, M, Vertes, L *Upper Biharian (Inter-mindel pebble-industry occupation site in western Hungary).* Current Anthrop. 6, 74—87, 1965.

Krishnaswamy, V D *Stone Age India.* Ancient India, 3, 11—57, 1947.

Leakey, L S B *Was Kenya the centre of human evolution?* III. London News Nr. 5601, 1946.

Leakey, L S B *The bolas in Africa.* Man. London, 1948.

Leakey, L S B, Leakey, M D *Recent hominids in Tanganyika: at Olduvai and near Lake Natron.* Nature 202, 3—5, 1964.

Leakey, L S B, Tobias, P V, Napier, J R *A new species of Homo from Olduvai Gorge.* Nature 202, 5—7, 1964.

Levy-Bruhl, L *Primitive Mentality.* London, 1923.

Lewis, G E *Preliminary notice of new man-like apes from India.* Am. J. of Science 37, 1934.

Mathew, W D, Granger, W *New Fossil mammals from the Pliocene of Sze-Chuan,*

China. Bull. Amer. Mas. Nat. Hist. 48, New York, 1923.

Mayr, E *Animal Species and Evolution*. Cambridge, Mass. Harvard Univ. Press, 1963.

McCarthy, F D *Report on Australia and Melanesia*. Asian Persp. 5, No. 2, 141—155, 1961.

Meggers, B J, Evan, C *Aboriginal cultural development in Latin America: an interpretative review*. Washington, (Smithsonian miscellaneous collections.)

Montagu, M F Ashley *Time, morphology, and neotony in the evolution of man*. In M F Ashley Montagu (ed) Culture and the Evolution of Man. 324—42, New York, Oxford Univ. Pres, 1962.

Movius, H L *Early man and Pleistocene stratigraphy in southern and eastern Asia*. Cambridge, Mass. Papers of the Peabody Museum of American Archeology and Ethnology, 19, No. 3, 1944.

Movius, H L *The Monsterian cave of Teshik-Tash*. Cambridge, Mass., American School of Prehistoric Research, 17, 11—71, 1953.

Movius, H L Jr. *Bas-relief Carving of a Female Figure Recently Discovered in the Final Perigordian Horizon at the Abri Pataud*. Les Eyzies (Dordogne) Festschrift für Lothan Zotz, Bonn, 1960.

Movius, H L Jr., Judson, S *The Rock Shelter of La Colombière*. American School of Prehistoric Research (Cambridge, Mass.) Bull 19, 1956.

Mulvaney, D J *The Stone Age of Australia*. Proc. of the Preh. Soc. n.s. 27, 56—107, 1961.

Napier, J R *The evolution of the hand*. Scient. Amer. 207, 56—62, 1962.

Napier, J R *The evolution of bipedal walking in the hominids*. Arch. Biol. (Liège), 75 (suppl.), 673—708, 1964.

Napier, J R, Davis, P R *The Forelimb Skeleton and Associated Remains of Proconsul africanus*. London, British Museum (Natural History), 1959.

Napier, J R, Napier, P H *Handbook of living Primates*. London and New York, Academic Press, 1966.

Noback, C R, Moskowitz, N *The primate nervous system: functional and structural aspects in phylogeny*. In J Buettner-Janusch (ed), Evolutionary and Genetic Dictionary of Primates 1: 131—177, New York Academic Press, 1963.

Nougier, L R, Robert, R *The Cave of Rouffignac*. London, 1958.

Oakley, K P *The fluorine dating method*. Yb. Phys. Anthrop. (Viking Fund, New York), 5, 1949.

Oakley, K P, Campbell, B G *Catalogue of Fossil Hominids*. London, British Museum (Natural History), 1966.

Obermaier, H *Fossil Man in Spain*. New Haven, 1924.

Okladnikov, A P *Ancient population of Siberia and its cultures*. Cambridge, Mass., 1959.

Oppenheimer, O *Tool use and crowded teeth in Australopithecinae*. Curr. Anthr., 5, 19—21, 1964.

Osborn, H F *New fossil mammals from the Fayum Oligocene Egypt*. Bull. Amer. Mus. Nat. Hist., New York, 24, 1908.

Patterson, B, Howells, W W *Hominid humeral fragment from Early Pleistocene of north-western Kenya*. Science, 156, 64—66, 1967.

Pei, W C *New fossil materials and artifacts collected from Chou-kou-tien during the years 1937 to 1939*. Bull. Geol. Soc. China, 19, 207—234, 1939.

Pei, W C, Li, J H *Discovery of a third mandible of Gigantopithecus in Liu-Cheng Kwangsi, south China*. Vertebrata Palasiatica 2, Peking, 1959.

Pilgrim, G *New Siwalik Primates and their bearing on the question of the evolution of Man and the Anthropoidea*. Rec. Geol. Survey India, 45, 1915.

Pilgrim, G E *A Sivapithecus palate and other primate fossils from India*. n.s. 14, Calcutta, 1927.

Pirie, N W *Some aspects of the origin of life considered in the light of the Moscow International Symposium.* ICSV, Review 1, 40—48, 1959.

Raphael, M *Prehistoric Cave Paintings.* (Bollingen Series IV), New York, 1945.

Robinson, J T *Meganthropus, Australopithecines, and hominids.* Am. J. Phys. Anthrop. n.s., 11, 1—38, 1953.

Robinson, J T *The genera and species of the Australopithecines.* Amer. J. Phys. Anthrop., 12, 1954.

Robinson, J T *The dentition of Australopithecinae.* Transvaal Mus. Mem. No. 9, Pretoria, 1956.

Robinson J T *Occurrence of stone artefacts with Australopithecus at Sterkfontein.* Nature 180, London, 1957.

Robinson, J T *Australopithecines: culture and phylogeny.* Amer. J. Phys. Anthrop. 21, 595—605, 1963.

Robinson, J T *Homo 'habilis' and the Australopithecines.* Nature, 205, 121—124, 1965.

Schultz, A H *Characters common to higher primates and characters specific for man.* Quart. Rev. Biol. II, 259—283, 425—455, 1936.

Schultz, A H *Man and the catarrhine primates.* Cold Spring Harbour Symp. Quart. Biol. 15, 35—53, 1953.

Schultz, A H *Past and present views of Man's specialisations.* Irish J. Medical Sci., 1957.

Schuster, C *Some Geometric Designs of Upper Paleolithic Art.* Fifth International Congress of Pre- and Protohistory, Hamburg, 1958.

Simons, E L *The phylogenetic position of Ramapithecus.* Postilla, Yale Peabody Museum, 64, 1—12, 1962.

Simons, E L *Two new Primate species from the African Oligocene.* Postilla, Yale Peabody Museum, 64, 1—12, 1962.

Simons, E L *On the mandible of Ramapithecus.* Proc. Nat. Acad. Sci. USA, 51, 528—536, 1964.

Simons, E L, Pilbeam, D R *Preliminary revision of the Dryopithecinae (Pongidae, Anthropoidea).* Folia primat., 3, 81—152, 1965.

Simpson, G G *The principles of classification and a classification of mammals.* Bull. Amer. Mus. Nat. Hist., 85, New York, 1945.

Simpson, G G *The Meaning of Evolution.* New Haven, Conn., Yale University Press, 1949.

Simpson, G G *Evolution and Geography.* Oregon, 1962.

Singer, R *The Saldanha skull from Hopefield, South Africa.* Amer. J. Phys. Anthrop. 12, 1954.

Solecki, R S *Shanidar Cave.* Sci. American 197, 58—64, 1957.

Spencer, B *Native Tribes of the Northern Territory of Australia.* London, 1914.

Stewart, J H *Handbook of South American Indians.* Washington, 5 vol. Bureau of American Ethnology, 143, 1946—1950.

Stewart, T D *The restored Shanidar I skull.* Smithsonian Rep. 473—480, 1958.

Stirton, R A *Observations on evolutionary rates in hypsodonty.* Evolution 1, 32—41, 1947.

Strauss, W L *The riddle of man's ancestry.* Quart. Rev. Biol. 24, 200—223, 1949.

Tobias, P V *Cranial capacity of Zinjanthropus and other Australopithecines.* Nature, 197, 743—746, 1963.

Tobias, P V *The distinctiveness of Homo habilis.* Nature, 209, 953—957, 1966.

Tobias, P V *Olduvai Gorge: The cranium of Australopithecus (Zinjanthropus) boisei.* Camb. Univ. Pres., 1—252, 1967.

Tobias, P V, Koenigswald, G H R von *Comparison between the Olduvai hominines and those of Java and some implications for hominid phylogeny.* Nature, 204, 515—518, 1964.

Tobias, P V, et al *New discoveries in Tanganyika: their bearing on hominid evolution.* Curr. Anthrop. 6, 391—411, 1965.

Tylor, E B *Primitive Culture.* London, 1871.

Vallois, H V *The Fontéchevade fossil Man.* Am. J. Phys. Anthrop. 7, 1948.

Vallois, H V *The pre-moustérien human mandible from Montmaurin.* Am. J. Phys. Anthrop. 14, 1956.

Van Valen, L, Sloan, R E *The earliest primates.* Science, 150, 743—745, 1965.

Washburn, S L *Behaviour and human evolution.* In S L Washburn (ed) Classification and Human Evolution, 190—203, Viking Fund Publs. Anthrop. No. 37, Chicago, 1963.

Washburn, S L *The analysis of primate evolution with particular reference to the origin of man.* Cold Spring Harbour Symp. Quant. Biol. 15, 57—78, 1950.

Washburn, S L, DeVore, I *Social Behavior of baboons and early man.* In S L Washburn (ed) Social Life of Early Man, 19—105, Viking Fund Publs. Anthrop. No. 31, Chicago, 1961.

Weidenreich, F *The dentition of Sinanthropus pekinensis.* Pal. Suiica No. 101, 1937.

Weidenreich, F *The extremity bones of Sinanthropus pekinensis.* Pal. Sinica No. 116, Peking, 1941.

Weidenreich, F *The skull of Sinanthropus pekinensis.* Pal. Sinica. No. 127, 1943.

Weidenreich, F *Giant Early Man from Java and south China.* Anthrop. Pap. Amer. Mus. Nat. Hist., New York, 40, 1945.

Weidenreich, F *Morphology of Solo Man.* Anthrop. Pap. Amer. Mus. Nat. Hist., New York, 43, 1951.

Weiner, I Q *The Piltdown Forgery.* London, 1955.

White, L A *The concept of culture.* Amer. Anthrop. 61, 227—251, 1959.

Woo, J K *Preliminary report on a skull of Sinanthropus lantianensis of Lantian.* Shensi. Scientia. sinica. 14, 1032—1036, 1965.

Wormington, H M *Ancient Man in North America.* Denver Museum of Natural History. Popular Series No. 4, 1957.

Zdansky, O *Preliminary notice on two teeth of a hominid from a cave in Chili (China).* Bull. Geol. Soc. China 5, Peking, 1927.

PICTURE ACKNOWLEDGEMENTS

(The figures refer to the numbers of the illustrations)

Archeologický ústav ČSAV, Brno 326, 678, 680
British Museum 531
Burian, Z 104, 108
Dania, E 355, 421, 487, 538, 540, 565, 567, 571, 576, 595, 596, 616, 618—620, 646—650, 653—655
Ermitage 644, 666
Gabus, J 427—430
Gauthier, R Musée du Périgord 564, 762
Guichard, J Musée National de Préhistoire, Les Eyzies 601, 760
Herdeg, H P 603
Herdeg, H P and Weider, A 509, 664
Hofer, M 27, 33, 35, 39—41, 45, 46, 49, 62, 64, 66, 68—70, 72, 85—89, 91—98, 100, 101, 111, 121, 127, 134, 138, 144, 146, 148, 150, 151, 153—157, 173, 174, 182—185, 204, 209, 214, 216, 218, 220, 221, 228—231, 233, 234, 239, 240, 257—261, 267—269, 271, 273, 276, 278, 279, 281, 283, 285, 290—294, 296—307, 309—317, 320, 321, 327, 527, 528, 539, 569, 597—600, 608—611, 614, 615, 617, 624, 631—635, 637, 638, 641—643, 645, 656, 669—676, 679, 681, 683—685, 708, 711—714, 717, 718, 723, 737, 746, 786
Holub, E 816—818, 823
Institut Royal des Sciences Naturelles de Belgique 554, 576
Istoričeskij Muzej, Moscow 325
Jelínek, J 23, 34, 84, 109, 112—115, 117, 118, 128, 132, 161, 175—180, 186—203, 205—208, 226, 232, 235—238, 241, 243, 244, 246—249, 251—253, 255, 256, 263, 264, 266, 272, 274, 275, 277, 280, 282, 284, 286—289, 291, 295, 308, 322—324, 329, 361, 425, 426, 434—438, 451, 455, 468, 470—472, 482, 483, 504, 526, 747—750, 778—780, 806—809, 811, 812, 831—838, 840—842, 844, 846—855, 857—860

Mazák, V 1—3, 17, 50
Musée d'Aquitaine, Bordeaux 593, 657
Musée de l'Homme, Paris 606
Musée des Antiquités Nationales, St Germain-en-Laye 492, 555, 575, 605, 660
Musée du Périgord 709
Museo Prehistorico, Santander 543
Naturhistorisches Museum, Vienna 594
Robert, R 530
Rogatchev, A N 164
Staněk, V J 4—9
Vertés, L 110
Weider, A 661
Illustrations 509, 543, 603, 661, 664 are reproduced by permission of the Princeton University Press from the following source: S Giedion, 'The Beginnings of Art' (Volume 1 of *The Eternal Present*), The A W Mellon Lectures on the Fine Arts, 1957; Bolligen Series XXXV, 6, 10, New York: Bolligen Foundation, 1962, Copyright © 1962 by the Trustees of the National Gallery of Art, Washington, D C

COLOUR PLATES

(The figures refer to the page numbers)

Burian, Z 41, 43, 44, 69, 70, 87, 88, 216
Jelínek, J 482—484, 501—504
Marco, J 98, 99 below, 197 above, 259, 260, 285, 303, 304, 314—316, 333—336, 361, 362, 380, 405—408, 425—428, 461—464, 481
Moravské muzeum, Brno 42, 97, 99, 100, 133—136, 153—156, 197, 198, 215, 257, 258, 286, 313

OTHER AUTHORITIES

(The figures refer to the numbers of the illustrations)

Allchin 432, 433; Almagro 791; Arambourg 116; Bader 449; Balout 223—

225, 227; Bánesz 366; Beltran 789, 790; Benitez 795; Blanc 745; Bordes 213, 335—338, 473, 474; Boule 130, 131, 135, 137, 165; Bouyssonie 769; Breuil 442, 443, 446, 460, 461, 465, 466, 479, 485, 489, 497, 506, 513, 520, 533, 534, 542, 548—550, 570, 579, 580, 582, 583—585, 639, 659, 773, 796, 814, 815, 821; Broom 59—61, 63, 69, 72, 74, 77; Cabré 793, 799; Capitan 639; Carthailac 663; Crawford 843; Dart 73, 79, 80; David 577; Davis 28, 32; Delvert 581; Eppel 133; Formosov 563; Gabus 427—430; Gaudry 38; Gerassimov 270, 401, 402, 404—419, 667; Gieseler 159; Graziosi 505, 546, 552, 553, 557, 558, 686, 687, 695, 743, 744, 753; Guinea 440, 441, 771; Hauser 318; Heberer 170; Hürzeler 22, 24, 48, 50; Kälin 15; Keith 140; Klíma 354, 356—360, 362—365, 541, 566; Lalanne 769; Leakey 20, 26, 29, 119; Le Gros Clark 18—21, 29, 31, 71; Lemozi 456—459, 493, 587, 588; Leroi-Gourhan 353, 519; Leuzinger 813; Lhote 810; Lommel 830; Lumley 169, 330, 332—334; McCown 140; McGregor 149; Malvesin-Fabre 577; Martin 758; Movius 735; Napier 28, 32, 90; Nougier 547, 562, 719; Obermaier 796; Octobon 171, 172; Osborn 11; Pacheco 794; Packenberg 120; Peters 556, 726, 772; Peyrony D 339, 495, 639; Peyrony E 495; Pidoplitchko 392, 398, 453; Piette 524, 707, 741; Pilgrim 37; Porcar 792, 796; Potapov-Levin 423, 424; Prošek 367; Radmili 613; Ravdonikas 781, 782; van Riet Lowe 67; Robert 547, 560, 562, 738; Robinson 59—61, 63, 69, 72, 74, 77; Rogatchev 370, 379—381, 764—768; Rust 340—343, 345—352, 720; Saint-Périer 659; Saller 160; Scheppers 72; Schlosser 10, 12, 14; Schoetensack 105; Schultz 147; Semenov 168, 245, 254, 265, 319; Sergi 126; Shovkoplias 384—390, 393—397, 623, 630, 715; Simons 12, 47, 53; Solecki 142, 143; Tchernysh 368, 369; Thomas 18, 19, 21; Tobias 65, 76; Twieselmann 622; Verneau 162; Virchow 125; Weidenreich 98, 145; Wilcox 822; Windels 561; Wrangel 422; Yefimenko 372—378; Zapfe 24, 25; Zorzi 690, 691

GENERAL ACKNOWLEDGEMENT

For much of his anthropological work, and material in related branches of knowledge, the author is indebted to his friends and colleagues for their advice. He wishes to express his thanks particularly to Professors M M Gerassimov, J Gabus, C P Groves, I G Shovkoplias, and A N Rogatchev for lending photographs, to Dr V Mazák for the sketches and reconstructions of fossil Hominoids, and to all his colleagues at the Moravian Museum, Brno for their help in creating this book.

INDEX

Abbeville 100, 137
Abbevillian 82, 100, 121, 137, 149
  -Acheulean 84
  (Chellean) 85, 132
Abramova, Z A 381
Abri Blanchard 457
Abri Cap Blanc 283, 289, 321, 457
  471, 478
Abri Cellier 370, 372, 469
Abri Labatut 457, 466
Abri La Mola Remigia 490
Abri Montastruc 307, 310
Abri Pataud 381
Abri du Poisson 139, 293, 300
Absolon, K 227, 264
Abstraction 317ff
Acheulean 89, 90, 122, 132, 133, 137,
  138, 144, 149, 150, 213, 214, 216,
  264
'Advanced *Australopithecus*' see
  Australopithecus habilis
Aegyptopithecus 21, 23, 24, 29
Afalou-bou-Rhummel 110
Africanthropus njarasensis 85
'Agnus Dei' 351, 366
Ahrensburgian culture 220, 222
Ait Tsenker cave 282, 283
Alexandrovka (Kostienki IV) 238
Alpera 478, 490
Altamira cave 276, 277, 278, 279,
  283, 291, 308, 312, 321, 323, 329,
  331, 345, 348, 360, 414, 415, 438,
  447, 467, 468, 471, 474, 478, 479
Ambrosievka 113
Amphipithecus 21, 22
Anderson, J G 77
Andrews 47
Angles-sur-l'Anglin 323, 370, 372,
  373, 465, 467, 471
Anthropoidea 10, 11, 17, 40
Anthropozoic 8
Anyathian culture 149
Apidium 21, 22, 39, 45
Arago cave 90, 92, 93
Arambourg, C 55, 56, 84, 89
Arcy-sur-Cure 92, 331, 373, 469
Art, Animals in 339
  'arctic' 283, 476, 485, 486
  Australian 500ff

Cantabrian 486
Franco-Cantabrian 282, 283, 478,
  487, 488
'Levantine' 478, 486, 487, 488
'nordic' 301, 476
North African 487ff
South African 493ff
Stone Age 275ff
Arudy 424, 440
Aterian culture 147, 151, 152
Atlanthropus mauritanicus 84
Aurignacian period 139, 146, 147,
  167, 207, 233, 235, 264, 289, 290,
  307, 308, 313, 339, 370, 375, 450,
  465, 467, 468, 469, 470, 471, 473,
  475
  I 370
  II 370
  -Pavlovian 375
Australopithecinae 43, 58
Australopithecus 11, 13, 16, 44, 49, 50,
  52, 54, 55, 56, 57, 58, 59, 60, 61,
  63, 65, 66, 67, 68, 77
  africanus 50, 51, 54, 55, 56
  habilis 68
  prometheus 56
  transvaalensis 54, 55
Avdieievo 213, 247, 259, 265, 268,
  333, 342, 381, 386, 396, 400, 447
Ayers Rock 517
Azerbaijan 318

Bader 281, 282, 341
Baikal, Lake 159, 478
Balaton, Lake 129
Balout 152, 157, 158, 160
Bánesz 235
Bañolas 92
Barabahau 457, 465
Bardal 477
Baume Latronne, La 319, 320, 322
Bédeilhac cave 283, 293, 338, 373
Beiuk-Dash 318
Berckhemer, F 89, 90, 91
Bernifal 281, 413, 435
'Bison-man' 365
Bison priscus 339
  uriformis 339
Black, D 77

Blade industry 131
Blanc, A 458
'Block-on-block' technique 168
Bohlin, B 77
Bone, The working of 185ff
Bone-tooth-antler culture *see*
    Osteodontokeratic culture
Bordes 146, 218, 219, 298
Borneck 219, 220, 221, 222
Bos brachyceros 342
    longifrons 342
    primigenius 342
Boule, P M 96, 102, 103, 115
Brachiation 20, 29
Brain, Development of 19, 20
Bramapithecus 46
Brassempouy 381, 397, 424
Breuil, Abbé H 278, 279, 280, 290,
    291, 292, 300, 306, 308, 309, 322,
    326, 330, 340, 344, 348, 365, 367,
    369, 373, 382, 447, 457, 473, 475,
    505
Brézilon, M 227
Brno 85, 86, 123, 208, 397, 458, 459
    II 115, 206, 208, 411
Broken Hill 107, 108, 110
Broom, R 48, 49, 50, 51, 52, 53, 54,
    55, 56, 58, 59, 60, 84
Bruniquel 338
Bubalus antiquus 494
Buret 263, 265, 266, 381, 385
Burian, Z 41, 43, 70, 77, 80, 88, 216
Býčí skála cave 449

Cadell River 320, 514, 522
Calapata 478
'Cannibal cave' 102
Capitan 279
Capra ibex 342
Capsian 147, 157, 158, 487, 488, 491,
    495
Carmel, Mount 104, 105
Carthailac, E 279, 281
Casares, Los 365, 370
Castillo, El 281, 283, 323, 377, 413,
    414, 436, 437, 439, 441, 467
Catarrhini 17
Catlin, G 179
Cave of Hearths 144
Cave paintings 277ff
Ceboidea 10, 11, 17, 18, 20
Cenozoic 8
Cercopithecoidea 10, 11, 17, 18, 19, 20,
    21
Chabot cave 279
Chaffaud cave 276, 277

Chapelle-aux-Saints, La 92, 96, 102,
    103
Charente cave 283
Charentian 137
Chatelperonian blade 146
Chellean-Acheulean 144
Chen-chia-wo 81
Chesowanja 56
Chimeneas, Las 354
Chiron 279
Chopra 35
Chou-kou-tien 73, 76, 79, 81, 82, 84,
    85, 149, 159
Chuckchee 180, 264, 265, 266, 267,
    269, 270, 396, 401
Clactonian culture 132, 139, 140
Clacton-on-Sea 139
Clark, W E Le Gros 25, 26, 29, 31,
    32, 46, 57
Clovis point 161
Coelodonta antiquitatis 345
Cogul 478, 489
Colbert, E H 29
Colombière, La 397, 435, 453
Combarelles, Les 281, 283, 359, 368,
    373, 381, 382, 413, 416, 447, 471,
    476
Combe Capelle 110
Coppens, Y 55, 56
Corbiac 218
Core industry 131, 132
Côttés, Les 329, 332
Cougnac 293, 298, 299, 397, 447
Covalanas, Las 258, 281, 307, 310
Cretaceous 17
Cro-Magnon 110
Cro-Magnon-man 109, 110
Cucuteni 318
Cueva de la Araña 486, 490, 491
Cueva del Civil 491
Cueva Remigia 486
Cueva Saltadora 488
Cueva de Val del Charco del Agua
    Amarga 489

Dart, R A 48, 49, 51, 54, 55, 58, 60,
    62, 63, 122
Darwin, C 68, 277
Davis 31, 32
Dekeyser 457
Delamere 520
Del Romito 281
Dental formula 19, 20
Děravá cave 235
Děvínská Nová Ves 27, 29, 34, 35
Dikov 284

Djebel Irhoud 102
Djebel-Kafzeh 104
Djetis layer 72, 73, 77, 81, 84, 85
'Djetis-man' 77, 84
Dobranitchevka 244, 245, 246, 251, 261, 265
Dolní Věstonice 99, 110, 111, 113, 115, 117, 118, 127, 153, 154, 176, 183, 186, 187, 188, 189, 191, 193, 200, 203, 213, 227, 229, 230, 231, 232, 259, 260, 263, 264, 265, 266, 269, 270, 272, 303, 304, 314, 337, 351, 358—9, 361, 362, 363, 370, 376, 378, 379, 396, 401, 402, 403, 404, 405, 406, 409, 410, 413, 414, 420, 421, 422, 424, 425, 426, 428, 462, 467
II 230
Domicá cave 283
'Dragon teeth' 33
Dryopithecinae 33, 35, 37
Dryopithecus 20, 23, 29, 32, 33, 34, 35, 36, 46, 48
  indicus 37
  -pattern 18, 20, 23, 29, 39, 58
  punjabicus 46
Dubois, E 68, 71, 73, 75, 77, 86
Duruthy 441, 453
Dzeravá Skála 234

Ebbou cave 289, 307
Egadi Island 350
Ehringsdorf 92, 93
Elora 156
el Ubedyia 149
Enfus 494
Eocene 8, 9, 17
Eoliths 121, 124
Epipalaeolithic 139, 141, 147, 207
Eppel 101
Equus hydruntinus 339
Eyasi, Lake 85
Eyzies, Les 441, 457

Fayum 21, 22, 29, 39
Fejfar, O 84
Fell cave 162
Ferrassie, La 92, 97, 102, 115, 372, 465, 468, 469
Fire, Use of 82
Flake industry 131, 132, 140, 142, 164ff
Flint, Lieutenant 86
'Folsom-point' 162
Font de Gaume 280, 281, 282, 291,

292, 295, 306, 307, 329, 330, 331, 357, 367, 413, 434, 435
Font-Robert point 146
Fort Ternan 48
Fourneau du Diable 219, 220, 465, 471
Fuhlrott, C 86, 90

Gabilou cave 283
Gagarino 213, 264, 316, 378, 381
Gamblian 143
Gánovce 92, 94
Gare de Couze 293, 298
Gargas cave 139, 281, 283, 322, 373, 441, 447, 460
Garusi 56
Gasulla gorge 486, 489
Gaudry 36
Gerassimov, M M 182, 252, 253, 254, 255, 256, 261, 262, 263, 264, 265
Gervais, P 37
Gieseler 114
Giganthropus blacki 33
Gigantopithecus 35—9, 73, 79
  bilaspurensis 37, 39
  blacki 33, 35, 36, 37, 39
Gillen 129
Glacial *see* Ice Age
Glaessner 35
Gorge d'Enfer 401, 416, 457
Gorilla gorilla 19, 33
Gourdan 399, 441
Gourhan, L 227, 228, 320, 357, 373, 413, 447, 475
Gravettian, eastern *see* Pavlovian
Graziosi 321, 346, 350, 352, 435, 492
Gregory, W K 20, 29
Grèze, La 281, 471, 474
Grimaldi cave 284, 378
Grotta dell'Addaura 492
  Paglicci 345, 433
  di Romanelli 388, 441, 458
Grotte du Cavillon 115
  des enfants 116
  du Lazaret 122, 213, 214, 216
  du Poisson 457
Groves, C P 21
Guattari cave 92
Guinea, G 276, 277, 474
Günz 8, 9, 16
  -Mindel 8, 9
Gvardshilasklde 435

Haeckel, E 68, 73
Hamburgian culture 219, 220, 221, 223

Harlé, E 279
Haua Fteah 102
Hauser 206
Heberer, G 85, 121
'Heidelberg lower jaw' 82
Heidelberg-man 82, 84
Hohlenstein 318, 388
Holocene 8, 9, 10
Holzheimer 339
Hominidae 10, 11, 21, 39, 47, 56, 58
Hominoidea 10, 11, 17, 18, 19, 20, 23, 39, 40
Homo 55, 63, 75
  erectus 11, 12, 13, 68, 69, 70, 71, 75, 77, 79, 81, 82, 84, 85, 86, 90, 93, 104, 107, 109, 110, 132
    capensis 16, 85, 110
    erectus 16, 70, 72, 77, 80—2, 86, 109
    heidelbergensis 16, 78—80, 86, 90
    lantianensis 82, 85
    leakeyi 16, 85, 86, 90, 110
    mauritanicus 16, 85, 86, 89
    modjokertensis 16, 69, 72, 77, 79, 80, 81, 82, 85
    officinalis 16, 75, 81
    palaeohungaricus 16, 84, 85, 86
    pekinensis 16, 73, 76, 79—82, 86, 90, 109, 161
  habilis 16, 63, 65, 66, 67, 68, 85, 122, 143, 213
  heidelbergensis 82
Homoioceros antiquus 488, 490
Homo leakeyi 85
  modjokertensis 75
  sapiens 12, 17, 68, 85, 91, 92, 96, 107, 110
    neanderthalensis 12, 16, 92, 110, 138
    rhodesiensis 110
    sapiens 11, 12, 16, 96, 104, 109, 110, 161
    soloensis 109, 110
    steinheimensis 16, 90, 93
Honcy 261, 265
Hopwood, A 25
Hornos de la Peña 281, 283, 467
Hortus cave 98
Howells, W W 29, 85, 90
Howitt, A W 129
Hungaropithecus 29
Hürzeler, J 27, 28, 37, 39, 45
Huxley, T H 86
Hylobates lar 21
Hylobatidae 21

Ibero-maurusian 147, 155, 159, 160
Ice Age 8, 13, 73
In Amenas 125
Isturitz 424, 441, 457, 471

Java-man 73, 77, 79, 80, 81, 82, 84, 109
Jaw, Development of 19, 20
Jelínek, J 114
Jochelson 271

Kačák cave 192
Kagerian 143, 144
Kalambo Falls 144
Kamasian 143, 144
Kamennaya Mogila 351
Kanapoi 56
Kapova cave 281, 282, 283, 341
Karelia 485
Kedung Brubus 75
Keilor 159
Keith 105
Kenyapithecus 48
  wickeri 48
Kiik Koba cave 105, 115
Kimberley (Australia) 129, 130, 168
King 92
Klausen 341
Klíma, B 116, 227, 229, 230, 231, 232, 233, 234, 235, 264, 344, 358
Koenigswald, G H R von 33, 36, 54, 55, 56, 73, 75, 77, 80, 81, 110
Koobi Fora 55, 56
Kostienki 117, 237, 253, 265, 268, 373, 378, 381, 470, 471, 472, 473
  I (Polyakovo) 213, 238, 239, 240, 242, 245, 247, 248, 370, 391
  IV 237, 238
  -Anosovskaya 241, 247
Krapina 88, 102, 104, 115
Krasnyj Yar 381, 388
Kromdraai 54, 55, 56
Kůlna cave 105, 134, 135, 235, 450
Kung-wang-ling 81

Lalanne, J G 469, 471
Laming-Emperaire, A 339, 342, 473, 475
Lan-tian 75, 81, 85
  -man 81, 84
Lartet, E 277, 471
Lascaux 216, 281, 282, 283, 289, 291, 292, 295, 306, 307, 308, 323, 328, 331, 337, 339, 342, 345, 355, 357, 368, 397, 414, 432, 437, 439, 467, 478

Laugerie Basse 388, 397, 414, 435, 442, 450
Laugerie Haute 308, 311, 331, 332, 345
Laussel 323, 373, 381, 397, 412, 465, 472
Leakey, J 61
Leakey, L S B 25, 26, 29, 30, 33, 48, 54, 55, 56, 61, 65, 85, 90, 122, 143, 213, 265
  M 25, 143
  R 63
Lei-yaun 48
Lemozi, Abbé 288, 307, 310, 312
Lespugue 365, 378, 381, 383, 424
Levallois 141
Levalloisian 137, 140, 142, 143, 147, 149
Levanzo 346, 353, 492
Levickij, I F 261
Lewis, G E 46, 47
'Lightning Brothers' 520
Limnopithecus 23, 26
Lindenmeir 161
Linnaeus 96
Lin-tscheng 33
Lorthet 307, 441, 456
Lothagam 56
Lourdes 322, 424
Love, J R B 129
Lowe, van Riet 54, 130
'Lower jaw from Mauer' see 'Heidelberg lower jaw'
Luka-Vrubleckaya 178
Lumley, H de 92, 121, 212, 213, 214, 216
Lupembian 149

'Macaroni' style 307
MacGregor, D E 109
Madeleine, La 277, 289, 290, 291, 307, 340, 353, 370, 373, 398, 401, 416, 435, 475
Magdalenian culture 98, 113, 115, 126, 136, 139, 141, 163, 164, 181, 182, 184, 185, 188, 193, 194, 195, 199, 201, 202, 203, 205, 206, 208, 210, 219, 220, 224, 227, 228, 233, 235, 257, 267, 288, 290, 291, 295, 307, 308, 310, 312, 314, 317, 321, 337, 343, 344, 363, 365, 370, 371, 372, 381, 388, 413, 424, 427, 435, 441, 449, 450, 465, 467, 471, 473, 475, 476, 478
  III 370, 471
Mainz 225

Makapansgat 54, 55, 56, 57, 60, 62
Malta 182, 183, 209, 215, 253−6, 261−4, 265, 315, 334, 335, 340, 360, 377, 378, 381, 385, 393, 394, 407, 408, 414, 417, 419, 429, 435, 446, 452
Mammuthus primigenius 339
Mapa 107
Marche, La 397
Marshack, J 414
Marsoulas cave 279, 283, 331, 337, 397
Martin, H 102
Mas d'Azil 308, 311, 357, 414
Mauer 78, 82, 84, 85, 90
Mauern 388
Mazálek, M 233, 234
McCown 105
'Mea Culpa d'un Sceptique' 281
Megaloceros giganteus 342
Meganthropus see Paranthropus palaeojavanicus
  africanus 56
  palaeojavanicus 54
Menindee 159
Mentone 375, 382
Mesolithic 10, 13, 39, 267
Mesozoic 17
Metharnis de Gramar I 219
Method of Making Stone Arrow Points, The 168
Mezhiritch 248, 256, 265, 284, 287, 413
Mezin 248, 256, 265, 287, 381, 388, 390, 391, 392, 393, 413, 414, 424, 446
Microlith 139, 149, 156, 175, 181, 183
Micromousterian 138
'Mimi-style' 520, 524
Minateda 486
Mindel 8, 9, 16
Mindel-Riss 8, 9
Miocene 9, 16, 29
Mladeč 113
Mlazice 137
Modjokerto 74, 75
Molodova 115, 236, 237, 264
Monte Bamboli 37
Monte Circeo 114, 115
Montespan 330
Montmaurin 89, 90, 92, 93
Moravian culture 391
Morella la Vella 490
Mountford 513
Mousterian 93, 101, 134, 135, 137,

138, 139, 141, 143, 144, 147, 150, 159, 174, 192, 236, 264, 329, 457
, La Ferrassie type 137
, La Quina type 137
Moustier, Le 92, 101, 115, 144
Mouthe cave, La 279, 307, 331
Mugharet es-Skhul 104
Mugharet es-Tabun 104, 105
Mungo, Lake 159

Napier, J 20, 30, 32, 65, 67, 68
Naulette, La 92
Neanderthal 86, 92
'Neanderthal, classic' 92, 93, 96, 102, 103, 104, 105
'Neanderthal, early' see 'Preneanderthal'
'Neanderthal, extreme' see 'Neanderthal, classic'
Neanderthal-man 86, 87, 88, 90, 92, 93, 94, 98, 101, 102, 104, 105, 106, 107, 110, 114, 115
, 'tropical' 110
Nebra 381, 388
Neeb, E 225
Neogene 8, 9
Neolithic 10, 183
Ngandong 107, 110
Niah cave 161
Niaux cave 281, 283, 288, 294, 323, 327, 328, 331, 338, 347, 349, 354, 356, 388, 413, 414, 431, 432, 438
Nová Drátenická cave 200, 202, 203
Novgorod-Seversk 435, 452

Oberkassel 110
Obermaier, H 457
Octobon 122
Oenpelli 159, 183, 520, 524, 525
Ofnet cave 114, 115
Okladnikov, A P 263, 284
Oldowan-Industry 61, 64, 144
Olduvai Gorge 54, 55, 56, 61, 64, 67, 68, 85, 90, 143, 144, 213, 264
Oligocene 8, 9, 17, 19
Oligopithecus 21, 22
Omo 55, 56
Ondratice 128
Oppenorth, W F 109
Ořechov 167
Oreopithecidae 10, 11, 39, 40
Oreopithecus 37, 39, 40, 45
  bambolii 37, 45
Osborn 22
Osteodontokeratic culture 62, 121, 122

Ostrava-Petřkovice 233, 235, 397, 410

Packenberg 90
Pair-non-Pair cave 139, 279, 351, 366, 413, 429, 440, 469, 470
Palaeogene 8, 9
Palaeolithic 10, 13
  cultures 130ff
Palli Aike cave 162
Pan paniscus 33
  troglodytes 21, 33
Panthera spelaea 345
Parabita 386
Paranthropus 16, 43, 53, 55, 56, 59, 60, 61, 144
  boisei 54, 55, 56, 60, 61, 68
  crassidens 56
  palaeojavanicus 54, 55, 56, 58
  robustus 52, 54, 55, 56, 61
Parapithecus 21, 22, 24
Paraustralopithecus aethiopicus 55, 56
Parpalló 441, 456, 469
Passiega, La 281, 283, 413, 414, 439
Patjitanian 149
Patterson, B 54
Pavlov 206, 209, 232, 234, 303, 380, 413, 423, 424
Pavlovian culture 99, 111, 112, 115, 117, 127, 141, 146, 150, 153, 154, 163, 176, 177, 178, 181, 184, 186, 187, 188, 189, 190, 191, 193, 197, 200, 203, 206, 208, 209, 213, 227, 229, 232, 234, 235, 260, 264, 265, 267, 285, 304, 314, 336, 342, 358, 359, 362, 363, 370, 376, 379, 380, 391, 396, 397, 399, 400, 402, 403, 405, 406, 409, 410, 411, 414, 420, 421, 422, 423, 424, 425, 426, 428, 429, 430, 443, 444, 445, 458, 459, 461, 462, 463, 464, 469, 470, 471, 472, 473, 481
'Pebble' culture 149
Pech Merle 288, 289, 290, 293, 299, 307, 308, 310, 312, 317, 318, 319, 346, 365, 370, 371, 397
Pei, Wen-Chung 33, 35, 77
Pekárna cave 98, 163, 181, 182, 183, 184, 185, 194, 195, 199, 201, 202, 205, 208, 209, 285, 295, 307, 314, 317, 318, 343, 344, 351, 365, 381, 388, 427, 435, 441, 449
Peking-man 79, 80, 81, 82, 85, 90
Peninj 54, 55, 56
Pergonsset 373
Perigordian 139, 146, 218, 291, 457,

460, 466, 467, 469, 471, 473, 474, 475
-Aurignacian 138
Petersfels 318, 352, 381, 388, 396, 404, 435, 450, 474
Peyrony 220
Philip cave 510
Pidoplitchko, J G 248, 251, 256, 284
Pikarna hill 234
Pileta, La 413
Pilgrim 35, 46
Pincevin 227, 228, 268
Pindal cave 283, 293, 300, 388, 414
Pinneberg 223, 225, 226, 269
Pirri culture 524
Pithecanthropus 68, 70, 73, 75, 77, 79, 82
  A 75
  B 75
  I 75, 77
  II 72, 75, 77
  III 75
  IV 72, 75, 77
  alalus 73
  erectus 73, 75
  modjokertensis 75
  robustus 75
Placard, Le 118, 363, 414
Plateau Parain 218, 219
Pleistocene 8, 9, 10, 16
Plesianthropus 50, 51
  transvaalensis 54, 55
Pliocene 9, 16
Pliopithecidae 10, 11, 24, 39
Pliopithecus 23, 24, 26, 27, 28, 29
Poggenwisch 220, 222, 223, 224
Polykarpovitch, K M 246
Pongidae 10, 11, 19, 21, 35, 39, 47
Pongo pygmaeus 20, 23
Portel, Le 281, 283, 291, 293, 307, 309, 331, 438, 447
Potapov-Levin 266, 267
Prado del Torrero, El 488
Prebrachiator 20
Předmostí 109, 110, 112, 113, 115, 163, 177, 178, 183, 186, 187, 189, 190, 191, 197, 285, 336, 342, 391, 396, 399, 400, 414, 422, 423, 424, 429, 430, 443, 444, 445, 459. 461, 463, 464, 481
'Preneanderthal' 92, 93, 94
Pre-soan 149
'*Prezinjanthropus*' see *Homo habilis*
Přezletice 84
Primate 7, 10, 17, 19, 21
Proconsul 23, 25, 29, 32, 33, 48

africanus 25, 30, 31, 42
major 25, 41
nyanzae 25, 32
Propliopithecus 21, 23, 24, 26
Prošek, F 234, 235
Prosimii 11, 17, 40
Pseudo-artefacts 189
Purgatorius 17
Pushkari 243, 248
Putim 233

Quaternary period 8, 9, 12, 16
Quina, La 92, 102, 143

Račice 233
Radiocarbon dating 8ff
Ramapithecus 11, 46, 47, 48
  brevirostris 46
  punjabicus 46, 47, 48
  wickeri 48
Raymonden 441, 455, 458
Redding, B B 179
Reinach, S 473
Rhinoceros merckii 345
Rhodesia-man 118
Riss 8, 9, 16, 218
Riss-Würm 8, 9
Rivière, E 279
Robinson, J T 50, 51, 52, 53, 55, 56, 58, 59, 84
Roche Lalinde, La 317, 318, 371, 378, 381, 388, 435, 451
Roc, Le 320, 323, 325
Roc de Sers, Le 397, 465, 466, 467, 471
Rogatchev, A N 237, 238, 241, 242, 245, 246, 247, 471, 472
Romer, A S 21, 29
Roufignac cave 281, 329
Rust, A 82, 219, 220, 221, 223, 224, 225, 226, 448

Saccopastore 92, 93
Sahly, A 457
Saint-Acheul 133, 138
Saint Gaudens 33, 35
Saint-Germain-La-Rivière 419
Saint Marcel 424, 435, 448, 451
Sala 105
Saldanha Bay 108, 110
Saller 114
Salon Noir 257, 329
Sandia cave 161
  point 161
Sangiran 54, 72, 75
Sangoan 149

Santander cave 277, 279, 441
Santian cave 457, 465
Sautuola, Marcelino de 276, 277, 279
Savignano 378, 384
Sbaika 89, 133, 134
Scheppers 58
Schlosser, M 21—3
Schoetensack, O 78, 82
Schultz 108
Sefar 491, 495, 496, 498, 499
Semenov 120, 170, 174, 180, 206
Sergi 93
Shanidar cave 104, 106
Sherano, El 521
Shishkino 480, 482
Shovkoplias 244, 245, 246, 249, 250,
    251, 253, 256, 261, 390—3, 446
Simons, E 21—3, 29, 35, 39, 45, 47
Sinanthropus 79, 80, 81, 115, 161
    officinalis 81
    pekinensis 79
Šipka cave 105
Sireuil 387, 388
Sivapithecus 29, 33, 35, 48
    africanus 48
    giganteus 37
    indicus 35
Siwalik Hills 29, 35, 46, 48, 149
Snyder 168
Soan 149
Solecki 106
Solo 107
Solo-man 107, 109, 110
Solutré 113
Solutrean 139, 141, 148, 321, 370,
    371, 465, 466, 467, 468, 469, 471,
    473, 474, 475
Speech, Development of 82
Spencer, B 129
Spy sur L'Orneau 92
Steinheim 89, 90, 91, 92, 93, 114
Steinheim-man 90, 113
Stellenbosh culture 144
Stereoscopic vision, Development of
    19, 20
Sterkfontein 50, 51, 52, 55, 57, 58
St Marcel 352
Stone tools 119ff
Stránská skála 84, 85, 86, 123, 129,
    198
Subalyak 105
Sunda-Archipelago 73
Sunghir 287, 418, 423
Švédův stůl 105, 123
Swanscombe 89, 90, 91, 92, 93
Swanscombe-man 90

Swartkrans 52, 53, 55, 56, 60, 84, 85
Szalay, A 17
Szeletian 141, 166, 167

Talgai 161
Tassili cave 483, 484, 488, 491, 496,
    497, 498
Taung 49, 51, 54, 56
    -baby 49
Tautavel 92
Tchernysh 236
Telanthropus capensis 85
Telmanskaya 237
Temara 102
Ternifine 84, 89
Terra Amata 212, 213
Tertiary period 8, 9, 16, 17
Teshik-Tash 105, 107, 115
Teyjat 281, 283, 289, 290, 295, 307,
    320, 365, 370
Thoma, A 84
Thomas 25, 26
Tibava 233, 235
Tibesti 498
Tobias, P V 54, 60, 65
Toggles 189
Torman 486
Tortoise-cores 137, 140, 142
Triassic period 17
Trinil 71, 72, 73, 75
    layer 75, 77, 81, 84, 85
    -man 77
Tripolje culture 391
Trois Frères, Les 281, 283, 295, 308,
    321, 326, 344, 351, 364, 365, 367,
    369, 414
Trou de Chaleaux 351, 364
Trou Magrite 390
Tschum 251, 266, 267
Tsisab Gorge 510
Tuc d'Audoubert 281, 283, 321, 322,
    323, 324, 351, 368
Tursac 388

Udabno 29
Udabnopithecus 29
Ursus arctos 345
    spelaeus 345
Ushtata 155

Vache, La 441, 447, 455
Val del Charco del Agua Amarga
    478
Vallonet cave 121
Valtorta 412, 486, 488, 489
Venus figurine 139, 284, 333, 370ff

Venus from Avdieievo 394
  Cucuteni 391
  Dolní Věstonice 379, 396, 401, 402
  Hluboké Mašůvky 391, 396
  Laussel 370, 374
  Macomer 395
  Střelice 391, 397
  Willendorf 375, 381, 397
  Yeliseievitchi 395
Verneau 116
Vertés, L 82
Vertésszöllös 81, 82, 83, 84, 85
Vienne cave 283
Vilanova, J 277
Villafranchian 8, 9, 16, 121, 122, 149
Villars 397
Virchow, R von 86
Vogelherd 313, 317, 441, 454
Vojevodski, M 247
Vrangel 266

Walker 47
Weidenreich, F 33, 72, 75, 77, 107
Weinert, H 56, 85
'White Lady' 505

Willendorf 378
  II 148
Wilson, D 129
Wiltonian culture 500
Woo 81
Woodward, J 110
Würm 8, 9, 16

X-ray style 295, 301, 302, 305, 504, 524, 525, 526

Yarapis 513
Yashtush 132
Yefimenko, P P 237, 238, 239, 240, 242, 245, 247, 248, 373
Yeliseievitchi 206, 381, 388, 451
Yenisei 159
Yudinovo 247, 253

Zamjatnin, S N 213
Zapfe 28, 29
Zdansky, O 77
Zeuner, F 339, 342, 345
Zinjanthropus see *Paranthropus boisei*
'*Zinjanthropus boisei*' 56, 143
Žitný cave 126, 136